Studies in Eighteenth-Century Culture

VOLUME 6

Studies in Eighteenth-Century Culture VOLUME 6

EDITED BY *Ronald C. Rosbottom*
Ohio State University

PUBLISHED for the
AMERICAN SOCIETY FOR EIGHTEENTH-CENTURY STUDIES
by THE UNIVERSITY OF WISCONSIN PRESS

Published 1977
The University of Wisconsin Press
Box 1379, Madison, Wisconsin 53701

The University of Wisconsin Press, Ltd.
70 Great Russell St., London

First printing

Printed in the United States of America

LC 74-25572
ISBN 0-299-07130-8

Contents

Preface

Discovering an a posteriori order in a varied collection of essays is an artificial enterprise. Yet, such artificiality fascinated the thinkers and writers of the eighteenth century in Europe. The readers of this volume will take, I trust, subtle esthetic pleasure in the realization that, through no fault of the editor, these essays as a group treat, with varying emphasis, one of the universal problems that confronted the writers of the Enlightenment. In fact, had a title been required for this collection, I would have provided something like "Seeing is Believing: Essays on Cultural Perception in the Eighteenth Century." For the majority of the essays in volume six of *Studies in Eighteenth-Century Culture* treat perceptual activities as specific as reading or as general as recognizing the presence of an Other: the self, another, or other societies. The analysis of the act of perception and how it leads to cognition and how the resultant knowledge is turned into action does provide the artificial order referred to above.

This is a strongly literary volume, with a good number of essays on the verbal arts (though one, that of Professor Carroll, deals effectively with how one French composer "perceived" Horace and brought him into the musical context of the eighteenth century). Among the dominant figures in this collection are Johnson, Lessing, Rousseau, Franklin, Prévost, Swift, and Wollstonecraft. However, such a bias is to be expected, since literature was, more than any other artifact, at the interface of the self and society. It dealt then, even more than now, in a consistently efficacious and insinuating way, with perception and the processes of cognition. In one of the most influential essays written in the eighteenth century, we read,

> The fact of our existence is the first thing taught us by our sensations and, indeed, is inseparable from them. From this it follows that our first reflective ideas must be concerned with ourselves, that is to say, must concern that thinking principle which constitutes our nature and which is in no way distinct from ourselves. The second thing taught us by our sensations is the existence of external objects, among which we must include our own bodies, since they are, so to speak, external to us even before we have defined the nature of the thinking principle within us.

This passage, written and published at mid-century, comes from D'Alembert's "Preliminary Discourse" to the *Encyclopédie.* It is the formalization of two of the most significant ethical and esthetic preoccupations of the eighteenth century, namely, how civilized man perceives others, himself, and his cultures, and how he defines the relationships among these activities.

There are several essays in this volume which examine in depth such concerns as cultural definition and perception. Pierre Aubéry's essay subtly delineates the complex way in which the French saw the English in America, as well as how the European French perceived the American French. He shows how stereotypical images became concretized and discusses the political significance of their maintenance. There are also several papers (forming one of the ISECS workshops) which deal effectively with the perception of women and of woman's "place" in the context of eighteenth-century society. Besides Professor Myers' somewhat revisionist view of Mary Wollstonecraft, Professors Cynthia Matlack, Irene Dash, and Roseann Runte all discuss the relationship between cultural values and esthetic considerations in terms of the depiction of women in literature and on the stage. Dash's paper especially shows to what lengths writers went to define and propagate a feminine image consonant with the dominant perception of the social function of woman. Specifically, she discusses how Shakespeare's *A Winter's Tale* was bowdlerized so that "the weaker sex" syndrome could be emphasized. Christine Sjogren's essay analyzes the role that Lessing played in the defense of feminism. English Showalter's study of the novelist Madame de Graffigny reveals the precarious social and financial status of female artists in eighteenth-century France. And Kay Wilkins details how the French image of womanhood changed over several decades (from the 1720s to the 1780s) as seen in the pages of two influential journals of the period, *Le Journal encyclopédique* and *Le Mercure de France*. The fascinating concept of cultural maintenance and its relationship to the arts is integral to this collection of essays on "woman perceived and perceiver."

One of the activities which had more to do than any other with how the Enlightenment advertised itself was publishing. Concomitantly, an increasingly sophisticated reading public, and the awareness of the function of reading by artists as disparate as Sterne and Rousseau, had a definite impact on the cognitive processes of the eighteenth century. In the ASECS Prize Article for 1975, "The *Encyclopédie* Wars of Prerevolutionary France," Robert Darnton, through the careful and meticulous culling of archives, continues to inform us about the fate and possible influence of the Enlightenment's most audacious publishing venture. More such research is needed if we are to understand the impact of publishing on the opinions of eighteenth-century French readers. The Editor's essay is a theoretical piece on how the need to invent a readership for the "modern novel" affected France's best narrative writers as they worked to define the limits of fiction. Professors Mylne and Martin also analyze how fiction was increasingly seen as the meeting place for all types of experiments in the re-creation of "real" experience. The former essay examines the problematics of reproducing conversation in the form of dialogue in a novel, and the social implications of doing so. The Martin essay shows definitely that fiction was seen as an efficacious vehicle for the transmission of moral and cultural precepts. Finally, Professor Keener's essay on *Rasselas* raises important queries about generic ambiguity, and about the coincidence of reading and the creation of fictions. The eighteenth century was fascinated with the awesome power that the reader and the spectator had in the creative process. These essays all address themselves, in varying degrees, to this phenomenon.

The eighteenth century was also probably the last epoch in history which could examine itself with little or no feeling of guilt or alienation. In his recent study *The Life of the Novel,* David Goldknopf states: "Subconscious resonance, which we insist on discovering today in almost every human art and act, was barely felt [in the eighteenth-century novel]. . . . It is this confidence and sufficiency of the ego that makes the outlook of the time look shallow, . . . [but] there *was* less subconscious at that time." And further on, in his analysis of Defoe's use of first-person narrative, Goldknopf concludes that "however strange it may seem, 'alienation', today regarded as the root of a pervasive if not indeed universal malaise, was in Defoe's time the liberative fulfillment of a new dream, 'to be on one's own'." The preponderance of first-person narrative made unavoidable the discussion of the concepts of authenticity and sincerity and the relationship between how we see ourselves and are perceived in turn. There is a liberating quality which escapes from the first-person narratives of this period (fictional as well as nonfictional). This quality is translated into self-awareness, yet without the overbearing self-consciousness that distinguished Romantic and post-Romantic first-person narrative from their pre-Romantic predecessors (see Professor Francis' adumbrations on Prévost for an elaboration of this theory). Self-consideration and self-identity became increasingly important activities as the move toward the secularization of moral values gained strength in the eighteenth century. Yet despite the apparently liberating and therapeutic preoccupation with the self, there were those who were not so unfettered. In a fascinating analysis of deism, Robert Luehrs shows how such thinkers had to exercise a sort of self-deception in order to effect a compromise between religious and secular strains of thought. The need to satisfy the self became a key component in a deist's sentimental education. And in Hopewell Selby's article on Swift, we find a thematic and structural study of this writer's preoccupation with the dangers of solipsism. His metaphors of enclosure, often leading to claustrophobic images, show a pre-Rousseauian fascination with the dark cave of the mind.

In this same vein, there are four papers in this collection that deal specifically with autobiography. Frank Ryder's piece on Lessing can be read as a general introduction to the problematics of autobiographical criticism. He tries to isolate the "deep structures" of a writer's mind, the "hidden" urge to write autobiographically. How much does a writer reveal or conceal? This is an excellent essay on one of the most intractable areas in literary history. The other three papers deal with different authors and genres: Parke with Johnson's tale *Rasselas* and "fictional" autobiography in general; Lustig with Boswell and the problematics of biography; and Perkins with the surprising parallels, ironic and otherwise, between the autobiographies of Franklin and Rousseau. As Parke explains, different autobiographical stances create distinct types of autobiography, and these works are sustained by different ways of knowing and teaching, of transmitting cultural patterns. For various reasons, the eighteenth century saw the development of a powerful autobiographical impulse. Autobiography has remained a dominant genre, and has changed less than any other literary genre that developed in the eighteenth century, so its study is less subject to the vagaries of tradition and influence, and the pertinence of these four essays is thereby enhanced.

And after one knows how and what to read, after one learns about the importance of self-knowledge, how is this new knowledge applied? Do we just dream about better worlds or do we make them? The utopian dream and the utopian mania are impossible to avoid in the study of this period. From the Glorious Revolution of 1688 to its antithetical successor of 1789, utopias dazzled and bemused most of the important writers. We are fortunate to have complete in this volume of *Studies in Eighteenth-Century Culture* the workshop on utopia which was presented at the ISECS Congress, and whose participants examined many of the manifestations of the topos of utopia. Oscar Haac gives a courageous introduction to this group of papers by attempting to broaden the definition and description of utopias. He shows how thinkers of the period vacillated between two poles of interpretation: one which led to refuge and the other which heralded reform. The ideological stance of each writer determined whether he or she saw the utopian dream as an escape from commitment or as a chance for action. Roger Clark continues Haac's theoretical introduction in his essay. He sees the utopian topos as a combination of myth, ideology, and ontology which brings reality and dream into the same framework. Isabel Knight suggests convincingly that the attraction that many had for the utopia was a result of a displacement of the anxiety felt over the increasing disintegration of the value system of the Ancien Régime *before* 1789. And Jean Garagnon and Iris Zavala reveal the failure of the utopian myth: the former through an analysis of the works of Prévost and the latter in a study of the "enlightenment" of late eighteenth-century Spain. All these papers point out the dilemma of those torn between dream and action. How does one reconcile the ideal and the practical? Again, Voltaire's not-so-cryptic answer, in *Candide*, seems the best way out of the labyrinth: make your dream grow, but keep it within limits; don't lower your standards, but do lower your expectations. Dreams are models, and not goals.

As I observed at the beginning of this preface, most of the essays in this volume study with varying emphasis the relationship between cognition and action in the Age of Enlightenment. John McCarthy's paper on enthusiasm offers as well an interesting analysis of how creative enthusiasm could be harnessed so as not to affect a work's authenticity or validity, underlining the fact that "enthusiasm" did indeed affect the perceptual process and eventually the cognitive functions of both writer and reader. The desire to know and to control knowledge, the wish to refine the techniques of perception and expression are, as I pointed out in the preface to volume five of this series, integral to the world view of that community of scholars, writers, and artists that promulgated the myths and hopes of the period known as the Enlightenment. Increasingly, we must, as critics and students of the Enlightenment, turn our attention to the formulating principles and patterns of the eighteenth century if we would understand and accept its diversity. I believe that the papers in this rich collection give impetus to that endeavor.

The interdisciplinarity of these essays, despite their literary bias, is indicative, again, of our Society's wide range of interests. At a time when "interdisciplinary" or "transdisciplinary" studies are under increasing attack from both within and without the academy, it is appropriate that such volumes appear regularly. This volume also, more than any previous one, shows the vitality not only of the national society but of the regional and international societies as well. The growth of societies for eighteenth-century studies throughout the world during the past decade has been impressive. As many readers of these pages know, the Fourth (quadrennial) Congress of the International Society for Eighteenth-Century Studies was held at Yale University during the week of 13–20 July 1975. Thanks largely to the universally acclaimed organizational skills and diplomacy of its Executive Secretary, Georges May (who was also the outgoing President of the American Society), as well as to the guidance of the President of ISECS, Lester Crocker, the Congress was an unqualified success.

We are fortunate to be able to include here three of the more than forty workshops held during the Yale Congress. The President of the American Society, in consultation with the Executive Secretary and the Editor, chose three workshops which, it was felt, best defined the international scope and interdisciplinary nature of the Congress. These workshops were chosen and accepted on the basis of abstracts submitted to the Editorial Board of *Studies in Eighteenth-Century Culture,* and are reproduced here in much the same state as they were presented at Yale. Every effort was made to ensure that all the papers in each workshop would appear together, thereby maintaining the coherence of the seminar. The Editorial Board concluded that, for this special year, it was advantageous to open the pages of this publication to scholars from abroad who are not members of the American Society. As the table of contents will verify, we have a good selection of international scholars.

The present volume also contains four essays from four different regional conferences: Luehrs, 1974 Midwest ASECS Meeting in Dekalb, Illinois (for editorial reasons this paper was not included in volume five of the *Studies*); Myers, 1975 Southwest ASECS Meeting in Los Angeles; Carroll, 1975 Southeast ASECS Meeting in Knoxville; and Park, 1975 Central Region Johnson Society Meeting in Minneapolis. The quality of these four essays substantiates what many of us had already intuited, namely, that the regional societies continue to grow and to prosper.

Finally, there are five essays in this collection which were presented at two of the ASECS Sections during the Annual Meeting held concurrently with the International Congress. They are those of Keener and McCarthy (Sections C1 and C2: Language, Rhetoric, Style, and Comparative Literature) and those of Lustig, Perkins, and Ryder (Section H: Ancillary Disciplines). Two more of the papers were given by members of ASECS (Selby and Aubéry) in two of the ISECS workshops, number 11 ("The Prison in Literature and Art") and number 37 ("France-America"), respectively. The reader can see from this list that volume six of *Studies in Eighteenth-Century Culture* is indeed representative of the scholarly activities of our Society and its wide membership during the academic year 1974-1975.

Editing such a publication as *Studies in Eighteenth-Century Culture* is of necessity a cooperative enterprise. As I pass on the responsibility for future volumes to my successors, I want to thank, once again, those who have helped and sustained me during the past two and a half years. Paul Korshin and Georges May have provided the moral support necessary in such an undertaking.

Their counsel has been most beneficial. My task would have been much more difficult if the Administration here at Ohio State University had been less understanding. Robert Cottrell, Chairman of the Department of Romance Languages and Literatures, and Arthur Adams, Dean of the College of Humanities, have both been generous in the provision of amenities as well as patient about my requests. The three organizers of the workshops that are included in this volume—Cynthia Matlack, Richard Frautschi, and Oscar Haac—were very generous with their time, acting as co-editors as they collected and collated the essays of their colleagues. The quality of this volume is due in large part to Eric Rothstein's generous and perceptive advice. Others who helped me in various ways and to whom I extend my appreciation are: Paul Alkon, Wallace Anderson, Richard Beeman, Renée Kingcaid, Albert Kuhn, Rainer Nägele, John C. Rule, Henry Schmidt, Charles Williams, and Franklin Zimmerman. I would like especially to thank Mary Maraniss, Wisconsin's editor for volumes five and six, who has been both patient and understanding during our association. Finally, my wife, Betty, whose support is essential to any task I perform, was again unselfish in providing it.

RONALD C. ROSBOTTOM

Columbus, Ohio
March 1976

Studies in Eighteenth-Century Culture

VOLUME 6

The Encyclopédie *Wars of Prerevolutionary France*

ROBERT DARNTON

The publication of the *Encyclopédie* has long been recognized as a turning point of the Enlightenment. In permitting Diderot's text to appear in print, the state, however reluctantly and imperfectly, gave the philosophes an opportunity to try their wares in the market place of ideas. But what was the result of this break-through in the traditional restraints on the printed word in France? By concentrating on the duel between the *encyclopédistes* and the French authorities, scholars have told only half the story. The other half concerns some basic questions in the social history of ideas: how did publishers plan and execute editions in the eighteenth century? How well did works like the *Encyclopédie* sell? And who bought them? This essay is addressed to those questions. By recounting the life cycle of one book, it is intended to suggest some of the possibilities in the history of publishing, a field that has lain fallow too long despite its attractive location at the crossroads of intellectual, social, economic, and political history.[1]

Reprinted from the *American Historical Review*, 78 (1973): 1331-52.

When Diderot and his publishers brought out the last volume of the *Encyclopédie* in 1772, they had won more than a moral victory over the system for controlling French publishing. The first edition probably produced about 2,500,000 livres in gross profits. But the government refused to let the book sell openly, and most of the 4,225 sets went to customers outside France.[2] The second edition also seems to have been primarily a non-French affair. It was a folio reprint of the original text, produced in Geneva by a consortium of publishers allied with Charles Joseph Panckoucke of Paris. Its sales records have not survived, but its publishers originally hoped to market half of their 2,200 sets in France; and they had sold 1,330 sets throughout Europe when they settled their accounts in June 1775.[3] So by that date only 3,000 copies of the first two editions, at the very most, existed in France. The country had not been inundated with *Encyclopédie*s, despite the semilegal status granted to the book.

But the publishing of the next editions—the three quarto and the two octavo printings of the original text—is a very different story; and unlike the publishing history of the first two editions, it can be told in detail, thanks to the papers of the Société typographique de Neuchâtel in Neuchâtel, Switzerland. The story begins with Panckoucke, the extraordinary entrepreneur known as "the Atlas of the book trade,"[4] and his system of alliances and alignments within the world of publishing and politics.

In December 1768 Panckoucke bought from the original publishers the plates of the *Encyclopédie* and the rights to future editions of it. Precisely what these rights were is difficult to say. Panckoucke used the terms "droits" and "privilège" throughout his correspondence, but the government had revoked the formal privilege of the *Encyclopédie* in 1759, and the registers of privileges in the Bibliothèque nationale give no indication that it was ever restored. They do reveal that Panckoucke received a twelve-year *privilège général* on March 29, 1776, for a "Recueil des planches sur les sciences, arts et métiers," which may have been enough to substantiate his claim to possess a kind of copyright.[5] In any case, he asserted that claim in the most absolute manner, citing not only the contract by which he bought out the original publishers but also the sanction of the French government; and he sold portions of his "privilege" to a whole series of partners, periodically buying them back and reselling them again to new associates for new editions.

Panckoucke's first *Encyclopédie* was the second edition, the folio reprint of 1771-76. Those were hard years in the book trade, owing to the repressive measures of the "triumvirate" ministry of Maupeou, Terray, and d'Aiguillon, so Panckoucke had the edition printed in Geneva by his partners, who included Voltaire's publisher, "the angel Gabriel" Cramer. It was a stormy affair, involving quarrels among the associates, conflict with a rival, a "Protestant" *Encyclopédie* being produced by Barthélemy de Félice in Yverdon, and a losing battle with the French government, which had confiscated 6,000 volumes that Panckoucke had originally printed in Paris. Whether Panckoucke ever had much success in cracking the French market with this edition cannot be known, but his difficulties did not discourage him. By the accession of Louis XVI he remained convinced that there was still a fortune to be made in *Encyclopédie*s, and the liberal character of the new ministry swelled his hopes. He found doors opening for him everywhere within the government. His coach carried him into Versailles "like an official with a portfolio."[6] And his letters burgeoned with assurances of "protections" from lieutenants of police, directors of the book trade, and ministers.

On July 3, 1776, Panckoucke sold an interest of fifty per cent in his newly consolidated "rights and privileges" in the *Encyclopédie* for 143,000 livres to the Société typographique de Neuchâtel, one of the most important publishers of French books during the twenty years before the Revolution. After toying with a plan to publish another folio reprint, this new association decided to produce a completely revised edition. The text was to be rewritten by a whole stable of philosophes—including Marmontel, Morellet, La Harpe, D'Arnaud, St. Lambert, and Thomas—under the direction of Suard, with D'Alembert and Condorcet as associates. Panckoucke did not enlist Diderot, "*une mauvaise tête,* who demanded 100,000 écus and would have driven us to despair."[7] But he counted heavily on D'Alembert, who was to solicit the protection of Frederick II and perhaps even to persuade him to accept the dedication of the new work. D'Alembert also considered writing a history of the *Encyclopédie* for the new edition, but that essay died stillborn, like other potential classics of the Enlightenment—a history of French Protestantism by Raynal, a history of Turgot's ministry by Voltaire—that never got beyond the stage of projects knocked about in negotiations between authors and publishers. In the end this new *Encyclopédie* itself miscarried, despite the grandiose plans of its backers, because it was undercut by a quarto edition of the original text, which was launched in 1776 by Joseph Duplain of Lyons, the antihero of this story and one of the most intrepid buccaneers in the era of "booty capitalism."

Like many provincial bookdealers Duplain built his business on the demand for cheap, pirated works, often of a racy or philosophical character, which were produced in the printing houses flourishing beyond the fringes of France's borders, thanks to the system of privileges and thought control that stifled innovative publishing within the kingdom. Duplain smelled a fortune in cut-rate *Encyclopédies*. He announced the opening of a subscription for a cheap quarto edition, which would incorporate the five-volume supplement in the original text. He protected himself by attributing the edition to Jean Léonard Pellet, a Genevan printer who received 3,000 livres for acting as straw man. And when the flow of subscriptions proved strong enough, Duplain contracted the printing to several Genevan shops, keeping the financial and administrative work to himself. He counted on getting the books into France either by smuggling—he had great influence in the booksellers' gild of Lyons, although he had powerful enemies in the Parisian gild—or by winning the benevolent neutrality of the French authorities. But he had not reckoned with Panckoucke.

Panckoucke could choose either to beat Duplain or to join him. The first alternative appealed to Panckoucke because he was convinced that he could use his protections effectively enough to block the channels of the underground book trade. But the success of the subscription created a greater temptation. Panckoucke knew "every step that Duplain takes,"[8] thanks to secret reports from an allied Lyonnais bookseller called Gabriel Regnault. Regnault learned that the subscription was selling spectacularly, and corroborative information "from everywhere"[9] made it look as though the quarto *Encyclopédie* could turn into the most profitable publication of the century. So Panckoucke shelved the project for the revised edition and entered into negotiations, bartering his monopoly on legality against a cut of the subscriptions. On January 14, 1777, he and Duplain signed what later became known as the "Treaty of Dijon." Each took a half interest in the quarto enterprise, which they subsequently divided among their own associates (the Société typographique de Neuchâtel eventually came to own five twenty-fourths of the entire enterprise). Duplain committed himself to administer the production, distribution, and financing of the edition according to conditions specified in great detail by the contract. And Panckoucke promised to supply half the capital, the three volumes of plates, and the covering protection of his privilege. The last item was no small advantage. In August 1777 Panckoucke wrote that Le Camus de Néville, the director of the Librarie, "will protect our great affair" and had even given permission for Panckoucke to import the books directly to his warehouses in Paris, bypassing the customs, the booksellers' gild, and the censorship.[10] At the same time, writing as if he were himself a minister, Panckoucke directed the inspector of books in Lyons to give clear passage to the crates being shipped from Switzerland.[11] In fact Panckoucke pulled strings so effectively that the Swiss printers began to stuff their shipments of *Encyclopédies* with prohibited books. Far from drawing the fire of the established authorities, as it had done in the 1750s, the *Encyclopédie* circulated under the protective covering of their patronage; and that protection served as camouflage for the diffusion of works that the state wanted to suppress.

Panckoucke and Duplain had no idea that a small smuggling operation had grafted itself onto their enterprise. They gave all their attention to the maximization of profits, and the quarto proved to be extraordinarily profitable: orders poured in from everywhere, traveling salesmen reaped unheard-of harvests, and booksellers marveled at a hunger for the *Encyclopédie* that had remained dormant among clients who had not been able to buy the folio editions. "There is no other work so universally widespread," wrote Dufour of Maestricht. "Our streets are paved with it," said Resplandy of Toulouse, echoing exactly the observation of a Lyonnais salesman: "Our town is paved with it." And Panckoucke exulted, "The success of this quarto edition passes all belief."[12] In opening the subscription Duplain had set his sights high: he hoped to sell 4,000 copies. The subscription filled to overflowing with astonishing speed; so Duplain opened another, for 2,000 more copies. It, too, filled rapidly, and Duplain opened a third, making a total of 8,000 sets of 39 quarto volumes each—an extraordinary amount for an era when printings of single-volume works normally ran to 1,000 copies or so.

This succession of subscriptions explains the mystery of the missing second quarto edition, which has plagued bibliographers who have been able to locate only the first, or "Pellet," edition and the third, or "Neuchâtel," edition of the quarto *Encyclopédie.*[13] Duplain committed himself to print the second subscription when the printers had reached sheet T of volume 6, working at a press run of 4,000 copies. He directed them to reprint 2,000 copies of everything they had completed and then to continue at a run of 6,000. So there was no distinct second edition. The third subscription coincided with a separate "third edition," because each sheet was reset and run off at 2,000 copies, and the title page of each volume proclaimed it to be "troisième édition, à Neuchâtel, chez la Société typographique." In fact this imprint was a ruse devised by Duplain to inveigle subscriptions from persons who had been put off by the slipshod quality of the Pellet editions. The Société typographique actually printed only one volume of "its" edition and four of the volumes that appeared under Pellet's name. In every case Duplain subcontracted the printing and remained hidden behind his typographical false fronts.

Duplain used printers in Neuchâtel, Geneva, Lyons, Trévoux, and Grenoble, putting more than forty presses to work to turn out about 300,000 volumes. To produce and distribute books on such a scale required assembling one of the largest operations in premodern printing, and strained resources throughout the publishing industry. For two and a half years the *Encyclopédie* dominated printing in the region around Lyons. "Except for a few liturgical works, nothing else is being printed here, in all the shops, only the *Encyclopédie*," an agent reported in 1778.[14] The Société typographique took five months, using about half the capacity of its twelve presses and its work force of about thirty-five men, to print a press run of 6,000 copies of one of the huge, double-column tomes. Financing 8,000 copies of thirty-six such volumes required so much capital that Panckoucke and Duplain fell back on consortia of French and Swiss bankers, and the same agent in Lyons observed, "Whoever had a little money to put into books every month or every year has placed it on the *Encyclopédie* quarto."[15] The *Encyclopédie* consumed so much paper that in December 1777 a buyer for the Société typographique could not find a single sheet of the requisite kind in Lyons. The Société managed to continue printing only by sending paper scouts throughout France and western Switzerland in search of every last ream of *fin*, twenty-pound (Lyonnais measure) *carré* or *raisin.* Founders could not supply type rapidly enough to satisfy the demand (the quarto was printed, appropriately, in a type called "Philosophie"), and so some Genevan printers failed to begin work on schedule in 1777. The Neuchâtelois had to suspend printing at a crucial moment because they received a barrel of bad ink, and the inkmaker, a Parisian called Langlois who had a stranglehold on the quality-ink trade, kept inching up his prices, while lamenting about his own increased costs, which he attributed to poor olive harvests in the Midi. Wagoners also took advantage of increased orders to force up their rates. And the *Encyclopédie* produced chaos in the labor market of printing. Not only did the printers have to send hundreds of miles for workers, but the supply was so scarce that they took to raiding each other's shops through the use of industrial spies like

Louis Marcinhes, a down-and-out watchmaker in Geneva, who wrote to the Société typographique in July 1777,

> Pellet and Bassompierre have by inflated promises seduced many workers and drained off the printing shops of the surrounding area. But they only want to pay them 15 florins 9 sols of our money per sheet. So a good number want to leave, because they are asking for 17 florins per sheet. The man leaving this week [for Neuchâtel] is one of those. He is called Caisle. Two pressmen, who have promised to come talk with me, also should leave. . . . I won't lose sight of any occasion to send to you the discontented from the shops of Pellet, Bassompierre, and Nouffer.[16]

In short, the quarto *Encyclopédie* sent repercussions into the remotest sectors of the economy. For it to come into being a whole world had to be set in motion: ragpickers, olive growers, financiers, and philosophers collaborated to create a work whose corporeal existence corresponded to its intellectual message. As a physical object and as a vehicle of thought, the *Encyclopédie* synthesized a thousand sciences, arts, and crafts; it represented the Enlightenment, body and soul.

Its publishers probably spent too much time calculating costs and profits to entertain such lofty thoughts. The Société typographique estimated the total revenue of the enterprise at 2,454,092 livres, the total cost at 1,117,354 livres, and the gross profit at 1,336,738 livres: a return of one hundred twenty per cent on expenditures. No wonder they considered this affair "the most beautiful ever to be done in publishing,"[17] or that it touched off a series of fierce commercial wars.

Duplain, who had originally floated the quarto as a privateering venture, had no way, once he turned legitimate, of burying his treasure. Other pirates got wind of it and raced to the attack. First came announcements of rival counterfeit editions from Geneva and Avignon. Panckoucke read them as bluffs and counseled his associates to ride them out, since "I have arranged everything here in such a manner that none of those editions can enter France, and without France no success."[18] He was right: the announcements were a way of holding the quarto publishers up for ransom by threatening to undersell them unless they paid a certain sum of protection money. The danger in this game was that one could not distinguish between a fake and a real attack until he saw the whites of his assailant's eyes. After the quartos of Geneva and Avignon had disappeared over the horizon, J. S. Grabit and J. M. Barret of Lyons announced plans to publish another quarto *Encyclopédie*, and they proved that they meant business by actually printing a few volumes. In this case Duplain and Panckoucke agreed that it would be wiser to capitulate. They bought out Grabit and Barret for 27,000 livres—the rough equivalent of a lifetime's wages for one of their printers—and received in return only a legalized promise to abstain from further counterfeiting. Then they learned that a consortium of publishers in Lausanne and Bern planned to produce an even smaller, even cheaper *Encyclopédie,* an octavo edition that would sell for approximately 200 livres. This time Duplain and Panckoucke decided to stand and fight.

At first the quarto publishers hoped that the octavo venture would simply collapse. They joked that the small type of "cette miniature" would blind its readers, and Panckoucke proclaimed "that octavo edition may cause some alarm, but it won't hurt us. . . . It is folly to print the *Encyclopédie* in such a small text. Moreover, we will be defended here. I am waiting for the magistrate [Le Camus de Néville] to return so that I can reveal everything to him. I promise you firmly that that *Encyclopédie* will never enter France." The Société typographique replied, "You hold the keys to the kingdom."[19] But reports from provincial booksellers indicated that the octavo subscriptions were selling as spectacularly as the quarto had done. So the quarto group began pourparlers—not with any serious intention of making peace but rather to delay the execution of the octavo until the quarto could be completed and the new, revised edition announced, thereby stealing the octavo market. The publishers of Lausanne and Bern, who were veterans of pirate publishing, detected this strategy after a few rounds of negotiation and resolved to proceed with their printing. Duplain then attempted to overwhelm them with a frontal assault: he published an announcement that the quarto group would produce its own octavo edition at an even cheaper price than the octavo of Lausanne and Bern. On November 1, 1777, Lausanne and Bern retaliated with an ultimatum: withdraw your announcement within fifteen days, or we will drop the price of our octavo to the level of yours, and we will undermine your quarto by producing a still cheaper quarto of our own.

> You will have to give in to us or lower your own price. In this way we will cut each other's throats, but you have set the example and are forcing this necessity upon us. And don't think that this is an idle threat. The prospectuses are ready, and we have the same type, the necessary presses etc. at our disposition in Yverdon.[20]

This maneuver forced Duplain to retreat, but it also resulted in open war; for although negotiations continued intermittently—the usual style in eighteenth-century warfare—each side campaigned fiercely, attempting to destroy the other's market.

The octavo group relied on a strategy of smuggling. They filled their subscription and counted on reaching their clients through the underground circuits of the clandestine book trade. The quarto group calculated on blocking those circuits. Panckoucke promised his partners, "I guarantee that they will not penetrate France. The magistrate promised me so. . . . You understand, Messieurs, that being armed with a privilege, you should not concede your rights any more than I. Because of our contracts, our privilege, Duplain had to come make terms with us. The Lausannois will have to do the same."[21] The system of privilege and protection that had nearly destroyed the first edition of the *Encyclopédie* was being used as the main line of defense in the effort to save its successor. So much had conditions changed from the reign of Louis XV to that of Louis XVI that the government treated *encyclopédisme* more as a commercial than as an ideological matter. This new attitude suggests that enlightened ideas permeated the government itself, but it does not necessarily imply weakness; in fact the contest between the strategy of smuggling and the strategy of policing provides a test case of the government's ability to control the printed word.

In mid-1778 the Société typographique de Neuchâtel sent an agent, Jean-François Favarger, on a tour of southern and central

France. Favarger's first assignment was to check the society's supply lines along the French-Swiss border. In Saint Sulpice, the last town on the Swiss side of the border, he learned that the smuggling outfit of Meuron Frères had recently taken care of five 500-pound crates containing volume 1 of the octavo *Encyclopédie*. The Meuron brothers told him so themselves, with more than a hint of professional pride, because they handled the society's own smuggling, but only as occasional substitutes for Pion of Pontarlier, the society's first-string smuggler, whom they wanted to replace. On the other side of the border, in Pontarlier, Pion told Favarger that he had seen five *acquits à caution*—a customs permit used by the French state to control imports of foreign books—that had been fraudulently discharged by Capel, syndic of the booksellers' gild in Dijon. Since Capel was officially required to confiscate the books that he forwarded, Dijon now promised to surpass Besançon as the main entrepôt of the underground route, as Favarger announced triumphantly in notifying his employers that the ocatavo had passed from Bern to Saint Sulpice to Dijon and was now headed toward Paris. The Société typographique hid Capel's name in the hope that "for money he will provide us with the same service"[22] and relayed the rest of the information to Panckoucke, who alerted the French authorities, who eventually captured the crates. The authorities engineered other confiscations on their own—in Toulouse, for example, where a big bust inflicted huge casualties on the octavo group. By August Favarger's field reports showed that subscribers were deserting the octavo in droves throughout the Midi. And in early 1779 the octavo publishers sued for peace.

The negotiations dragged on for a year, while the quarto group finished a mopping-up operation in France and the octavo group tried to repair its losses through sales in Central and Eastern Europe. Finally in February 1780 Panckoucke sold the entry into France to the Lausanne-Bern consortium for 24,000 livres. That was a steep price—roughly eight per cent of the octavo's current manufacturing cost—and it shows how strong the demand for *Encyclopédies* remained, at least in the calculations of publishers who had discovered a new, undernourished public. Thinking they were safe at last, the octavo group increased their printing to 6,000 copies—hence the explanation of another "missing" edition[23] —and promptly fell into another of Panckoucke's traps. Because they had not been able to pay off Panckoucke in cash, they had persuaded him to accept his ransom in kind—that is, in 24,000-livres' worth of octavo *Encyclopédies*. Panckoucke dumped his octavos on the French market at a reduced price and then compounded the damage to the octavo group's future sales by spreading the word that he would soon produce an *Encyclopédie* to end all *Encyclopédies*—not the revised edition that he had originally planned with the Société typographique de Neuchâtel, but the *Encyclopédie méthodique*, which he was then organizing with the support of a consortium from Liège. That was not the last low blow in this battle, because four years later the old members of the octavo group, joined by none other than Panckoucke's former ally, the Société typographique, announced a plan to pirate the *Encyclopédie méthodique*.[24] It did not get far beyond the drawing board, however; so the quarto-octavo war may be said to have ended in the defeat of Lausanne and Bern.

The publishing wars did not cut off the supply of relatively inexpensive *Encyclopédies* to France. On the contrary they show how fiercely publishers struggled to satisfy the French market and how important that market must have been. They also illustrate the aggressive, entrepreneurial character of Enlightenment publishing in contrast to the conservative publishing industry that was dominated by the gild structure within France.[25] And finally they expose the inadequacy of the common view that the Enlightenment and the regime were locked in a fight to the death; for the quarto group captured the market by enlisting the state on its side—a strategy of protection and privilege that typifies the ways of the Old Regime and that also suggests a shift in the tone of government in the mid-1770s. The book that had barely survived persecution under Louis XV became a best seller under Louis XVI—with the blessing of the government.

The last episode in the *Encyclopédie* wars was purely domestic, a civil war between Duplain and his associates. In February 1779 they met in Lyons to assess their affairs. Contrary to all expectations, Duplain gave a pessimistic account of the sales. The first two subscriptions had done splendidly, he explained, but that very success had tempted the associates to overextend themselves, and the third edition now looked like a disaster. They might rescue it, however, if they divided up 1,000 unsold sets so that each associate could market them in areas where his sales were normally strongest. Panckoucke accepted this proposal, because the Parisian territory was reserved for him and, anyway, he would allot almost half of his 500 sets to the Société typographique. Six months later, in a still gloomier report, Duplain warned that this maneuver had not sufficed to save the third edition. Hundreds of volumes would rot in their warehouses unless they took drastic measures. Fortunately Duplain had found a merchant, a certain Perrin, who had caught the *Encyclopédie* fever, and they could dump their unsold copies on him. To be sure, Perrin demanded extraordinary terms—a fifty-per-cent reduction—but they would be lucky to get rid of their excess stock at any price, and Perrin would take a huge number: 422 sets, as well as 160 from Panckoucke's share of the thousand that had been split between him and Duplain in February. Panckoucke accepted the proposal, but soon after signing the Perrin contract he began to harbor suspicions. He learned that Duplain had tried to involve a mutual friend in a secret conspiracy to raid his reserved quarto market in Paris, and he found that Duplain's letters sounded disturbingly vague about Perrin, whom they described as "a commercial agent in Strasbourg, who has a business in Lyons, or rather, I believe, in Paris, anyhow an extremely rich man for whom I can reply."[26] By September 1779 Panckoucke confided to the Société typographique, "I am quite persuaded that this Perrin is only an imaginary being or, at most, a straw man. Duplain is avaricious and makes no pretense about being delicate."[27] He had become convinced that Duplain was "a vile soul," "a voracious man, who loves money with a fury"; "his rapacity has no limits."[28] And he advised the Société typographique to slip a spy into Duplain's shop. They needed no prompting, for they had done so long ago. In fact all the associates spied on each other. Panckoucke had his own man watching Duplain; the Neuchâtelois received secret reports on Panckoucke; they kept an agent in Geneva; and their man in Lyons spun such a web of industrial espionage that they finally trapped Duplain in February 1780.

The Lyonnais network managed to track down the elusive Perrin, who indeed turned out to be a straw man in Duplain's pay, and then it made an even bigger catch: it got hold of a copy of a secret subscription list, Duplain's record of the actual number of *Encyclopédie* sales. The list made no reference to the Perrin sale; instead it contained 978 more subscriptions than Duplain was later to report at the final settling of accounts in February 1780. The Société typographique suspected the fraud before this meeting and verified it, once Duplain made his report, by writing to the booksellers whose subscriptions had been falsified, according to a comparison of the reported subscriptions and the secret list. So it discovered that the flow of orders never had dried up, as Duplain had claimed. On the contrary, the entire third edition had been sold at the normal price, except for the 500 sets that Duplain had dumped on Panckoucke. Duplain had hidden the sales in order to collect the full amount from them, while paying nothing for 500 of the *Encyclopédie*s that he sold and paying for the rest at half price through the phony intermediary of Perrin.

Instead of contenting himself with this spectacular double swindle, a matter of more than 200,000 livres, Duplain piled fraud on fraud in combinations too complex to be fully explained here. His role as general administrator of the enterprise offered enormous opportunity for peculation, because the quarto association allotted him set amounts for all his expenses. He therefore contracted the printing to the lowest bidder, pocketing the difference between what he was allotted and what he paid. He also cheated on the costs of paper and transport and even collaborated in a technique of fraudulent spacing and paragraphing worked out by a

Genevan printer—an item that might have seemed trivial to a lesser embezzler but that expanded volume 19 by 96 unnecessary pages, worth 744 livres. Panckoucke and the Société typographique calculated that Duplain's kickbacks and rake-offs came to 127,000 livres, but that was only an estimate, one that probably did not do justice to his genius. His intentionally unintelligible accounts could have concealed far more peculation, because they scrambled more than three million livres of expenses and revenues, and Duplain seems to have cheated at every possible point. For example, he attributed 494 subscriptions to the Lyons firm of Audambron and Jossinet at the usual reduced price for booksellers of 294 livres plus one free set for every twelve subscribed, which brought their total up to 535 subscriptions. The anti-Duplain network discovered that Audambron and Jossinet operated as a false front to hide the fact that Duplain had sold all 535 sets at the full subscription price of 384 livres, thereby robbing the association of 60,204 livres.

Since the quarto enterprise had been conducted like a conspiracy from the beginning, it exploded in the end like the denouement of a *drame bourgeois*—or an "English cockfight," as the Société typographique put it.[29] The anti-Duplain forces had concealed their suspicions while they accumulated enough ammunition to destroy Duplain at the final meeting for the settling of accounts at Lyons in February 1780. This strategy of counterdissimulation had not been easy, as the Société typographique confessed to Panckoucke: "You have wisely counseled us to dissimulate with him until the very end and not to reveal our just discontent, but by devil it gets more and more difficult every day."[30] When the showdown came, therefore, Duplain's associates surprised him with a barrage of accusations that they had been preparing for almost a year. They produced a correct version of the accounts, exposing a spectacular string of embezzlements. They unveiled the Perrin affair; they stripped the camouflage from Audambron and Jossinet; and they produced the secret subscription list with letters from booksellers testifying to the enormity of the swindles in sales. Even then Duplain refused to break down and confess. So they raided his office with a police commissioner, an attorney, and a bailiff, demanding confiscation of his papers; and they turned his family and friends against him, threatening to ruin the family's name by revealing the entire affair to the public. Finally Duplain surrendered. He agreed to compensate his partners with 200,000 livres, if they would sweep everything under the rug, where it has remained until today.

What sort of a man was this Duplain? The question has a certain fascination, both for economic history and for the history of the human soul. Duplain was a robber baron of the book trade, a gambler who played off high risks against high profits and who made a business of Enlightenment. He decided to stake everything on the quarto *Encyclopédie*. He sold his shop, his stock of books, his house, and his furniture and moved into a furnished room in order to concentrate exclusively on the great affair. Then he hit the jackpot; for this supreme gamble made him a rich man, even after the settlement of 200,000 livres. And once he knew he was wealthy, Duplain began to buy. First he acquired a wife, a beautiful young Lyonnaise who dazzled Panckoucke; then an estate in the provinces; finally the office of *maître d'hôtel du Roi*—that is, nobility. He began signing his letters "de St. Albine." He served the king for the requisite time in Versailles and lived with his bride in offensive luxury in Paris before carrying her off to his château.

What is the moral of this story? It is a Balzacian drama: the tale of a bourgeois entrepreneur who clawed his way to the top and then consumed his fortune conspicuously, in aristrocratic abandon. It is a saga of fortunes made and *illusions perdues* in publishing. In a way it is the story of French capitalism. And its supreme irony is that the vehicle for Duplain's rise into France's archaic hierarchy, only a few years away from destruction, was Diderot's *Encyclopédie*. Perhaps Duplain's story may also serve as a warning against placing too much confidence in sociological analysis of the sort that follows; for even if you can put a man perfectly in some socioeconomic category, his heart may be elsewhere. Duplain, the perfect bourgeois capitalist, turns out to be a pseudonoble—or was pseudonobility the essence of the French bourgeoisie?

The inside story of the warfare among the men who produced the *Encyclopédie* may reveal something of the spirit of entrepreneurial capitalism in early modern France, but it does not answer the larger question of what the battles were all about. Of course "booty capitalism" was waged for booty. Panckoucke and the pirates, Duplain and the Swiss, and their supporting cast of financiers, smugglers, and traveling salesmen all realized that they could make a fortune by satisfying the vast market in France for a "popular" edition of the supreme work of the Enlightenment. The ferocity of the competition to supply that demand suggests that the interest in enlightened ideas had spread very widely throughout France—to a *grand public* if not a mass audience. But what was the character of that public? That question, like so many problems in the sociology of literature, is difficult to resolve, but one can measure the outside boundaries of the readership of the *Encyclopédie*. First it is necessary to review the basic facts about all the editions of Diderot's text; then it should be possible to calculate the economic limits to their different consumption patterns; and finally one can attempt to chart the geographical and social distribution of the quarto editions, which were by far the most numerous in prerevolutionary France.

Aside from the Italian editions published (in French) in Lucca and Leghorn, the expurgated Protestant *Encyclopédie* published in Yverdon by Barthélemy de Félice, and the *Encyclopédie méthodique*—a completely reorganized work that ran to 202 volumes and was not completed until 1832—Diderot's text went through four main metamorphoses.[31]

1. The first edition (1751-52): this was a folio edition consisting of 17 volumes of text and 11 plates, followed by a 5-volume *Supplément* and a 2-volume *Table Analytique.* There were 4,225 sets printed, but only half, or perhaps merely a quarter, of them were sold in France. The subscription price was 980

livres, and the market price in the 1770s varied from 1,200 to 1,500 livres.

2. The Genevan reprint (1771-76): it had the same number of folio volumes in a printing of 2,200 sets. The subscription price was 794 livres, but by June 1777 it was selling at 700 livres, owing to competition from the quarto editions.
3. The three quarto "editions" (1771-81): these correspond to Duplain's three subscriptions and appeared under the names of Pellet and the Société typographique de Neuchâtel, as explained above. The quartos contained 36 volumes of text and 3 volumes of plates. They included 8,011 sets in all and were almost entirely sold out at the subscription price of 384 livres—the price paid by individual subscribers; booksellers subscribed at a reduced price of 294 livres and received one free copy for every dozen they ordered.
4. The two octavo "editions" (1778-82): these were really one expanded edition representing two subscriptions, published at Lausanne and Bern. The octavos consisted of 36 volumes of text and 3 of plates. They included 6,000 sets in all, and each sold at a subscription price of 231 livres.

This enumeration of facts and figures suggests a surprising conclusion: there were far more *Encyclopédie*s in prerevolutionary France than anyone—except eighteenth-century publishers—has ever suspected. Although the subscription figures in the publishers' papers make it difficult to calculate precisely how many copies remained in the kingdom, they permit a safe estimate: between 14,000 and 16,000 *Encyclopédie*s existed in France before 1789, and half of them can be traced. So without pretending to know how many of these *Encyclopédies* were read, or in what way the readers responded to them, it seems legitimate to hypothesize that *encyclopédisme* could have spread far more widely through French society than is generally believed.

As the *Encyclopédie* progressed from edition to edition its format decreased in size, it contained fewer plates, its paper declined in quality, and its price went down. And as the publishing consortia succeeded one another, they cast their nets more and more widely, reaching out with each new edition toward remoter sections of the reading public. The price differential set some rough limits to this ever-broadening sales pattern: the quarto edition cost a little more than one-fourth and the octavo edition about one-fifth of the market price of the first folio in the 1770s. But what were the social boundaries of *Encyclopédie* "consumption"? The question may seem impertinent, since economics offers no explanation of what it is to "consume" a book and since book buying and book reading are quite different activities. Nonetheless, the purchase of a book is a significant act when considered culturally as well as economically. It provides some indication of the diffusion of ideas beyond the intellectual milieu within which cultural history is usually circumscribed. And as there has never been a study of the sales of any eighteenth-century book, a sales analysis of the most important work of the Enlightenment ought to be worthwhile.

One can estimate how closely the *Encyclopédie* came into contact with the lower classes by translating its price into bread, the key commodity of the Old Regime and the basic element in the diet of most Frenchmen.[32] A first folio *Encyclopédie* was worth about 3,500 loaves of bread and a quarto 960 loaves, the standard of measurement being the "normal" price of 8 sous for a four-pound loaf of rye bread in prerevolutionary Paris. An unskilled laborer with a wife and three children would have to buy at least 18 loaves a week to keep his family alive. In good times he would spend half his income on bread. A "cheap" quarto *Encyclopédie* therefore represented more than a year of his family's precarious nutriment. It would have been as inconceivable for him to buy it—even if he could read it—as for him to purchase a palace. Skilled laborers—locksmiths, carpenters, and printers—made 15 livres in a good week. The first folio would have cost them ninety-three weeks' wages, the quarto twenty-six weeks' wages, and the octavo fifteen and a half weeks' wages. So even the upper strata of the working classes, artisans like the men who printed the book, could never have afforded to buy it.

But the men who wrote it, the "Gens de Lettres" invoked on its title page, could have purchased the cheaper editions. Diderot himself made an average of 2,600 livres a year for his thirty years of labor on the *Encyclopédie*.[33] A quarto would have cost him seven and a half weeks of his wages and an octavo four and a half–not an extravagant sum, considering that he had other sources of income. Many writers were wealthier than Diderot, thanks to patrons and pensions. B. J. Saurin, a typical figure from the upper ranks of the Republic of Letters, now deservedly forgotten, made 8,600 livres a year in pensions and "gratifications."[34] He could have treated himself to a quarto, the equivalent of two and a third weeks' income. The octavo was for hack writers like Durey de Morsan, a literary adventurer who lived off the crumbs from Voltaire's table and who wrote as one of the octavo's "zealous subscribers" to the Société typographique de Neuchâtel:

> The number of poor literary men far surpasses that of rich readers. I myself am delighted that this work, too expensive until now, does not exceed the means of the semi-indigent such as myself. I would like the door of the sciences, of the arts, and of useful truths to be open, day and night, to every human who can read.[35]

It is impossible to produce typical figures for the wide variety of incomes among the middling classes of the provinces, but the following calculations should give some idea of the expensiveness of the *Encyclopédie* for persons located well below the great noblemen and financiers and well above the common people. Although curés received only 500 livres as the *portion congrue* after 1768, their annual income often amounted to 1,000–2,000 livres.[36] So a quarto *Encyclopédie* represented ten weeks' income for a prosperous curé. Magistrates of the baillage courts stood at the top of the legal profession among provincial bourgeois and often earned 2,000-3,000 livres a year: a quarto *Encyclopédie* was worth six or seven weeks of their income. To live "noblement" a bourgeois had to count on at least 3,000–4,000 livres a year in *rentes*: the purchase of a quarto *Encyclopédie* would have taken five weeks of his revenue.[37]

In strictly economic terms, therefore, the first two editions were so expensive that they cannot have penetrated far beyond the restricted circle of courtiers, salon lions, and progressive *parlementaires* who made up the cultural avant-garde. The cheaper editions were luxury items, but with some squeezing they could have been made to fit into many middle-class budgets, rather as encyclopedias do today. The cost, like the content, of the quarto and octavo *Encyclopédie*s appealed to a wide variety of small-town notables and country gentlemen but not to anyone below the bourgeoisie. As the publishers remarked—and they knew their clientele—"The in-folio format will be for grands seigneurs and libraries, while the in-quarto will be within the reach of men of letters and interested readers [*amateurs*] whose fortune is less considerable."[38] The *Encyclopédie* entrepreneurs realized that they could widen their profit margin as they broadened their market. They had discovered a gold mine of untapped literary demand, and their scramble to exploit it shows how advanced culture reached the general reading public. But where were those readers located, and who were they?

The accompanying map, drawn up from Duplain's secret subscription list, shows the geographical distribution of almost all the quarto copies, that is, approximately half the *Encyclopédie*s that existed in prerevolutionary France. It demonstrates that the *Encyclopédie* reached every corner of the country and that its distribution coincided fairly well, as far as one can tell, with the distribution of population. Subscriptions in the Parisian area and the northwest were few, perhaps because those markets were sated by other editions. Beyond Rennes, Brittany looks like an intellectual desert, which might have been the case, but a surprising fertile crescent of *Encyclopédie*s curves through the Midi, from Lyons to Nîmes, Montpellier, Toulouse, and Bordeaux. Even the Massif Central shows a fairly high density of subscriptions. So there is little evidence here for the hypothesis that France was divided into

Subscriptions to the Quarto *Encyclopédie* in France

Town	Subscriptions
Abbéville	26
Aire	8
Aix	6
Alençon	34
Amiens	59
Angers	109
Argentin	3
Arras	26
Auch	65
Aurillac	13
Autun	39
Auxerre	10
Auxonne	1
Avignon	55
Bayonne	16
Beaune	26
Beauvais	8
Bergerac	13
Bergues	1
Besançon	338
Billom	2
Bordeaux	356
Boulogne-sur-Mer	34
Bourg	91
Bourg-Saint-Andéol	4
Bourges	20
Brest	20
Caen .	221
Cambray	57
Carpentras	2
Castelnaudary	27
Castres	28
Chalon-sur-Saône	67
Châlons-sur-Marne	1
Champagne	2
Cartres	75
Chatillon	39
Clermont	13
Colmar	1
Dijon	152
Dôle	52
Douai	14
Embrun	3
Evreux	65
Falaise	45
Grenoble	80
Gueret	19
La Fère	15
Langres	26
Laon	17
La Rochelle	56
Le Havre	52
Le Mans	40
Le Puy	39
Lille	28
Limoges	3
Lisieux	27
Lunéville	1
Laigle	3
Lyons	1078
Macon	17
Mantes	8
Marseilles	228
Meaux	30
Metz	22
Montargis	26
Montauban	105
Millau	8
Montbrisson	6
Montpellier	169
Morlaix	1
Mortagne	22
Moulins	52
Nancy	120
Nantes	38
Nîmes	212
Niort	58
Noyon	26
Orléans	52
Paris	487
Perigueux	36
Peronne	15
Perpignan	52
Poitiers	65
Reims	24
Rennes	218
Riom	46
Roanne	26
Rochefort	27
Rethel	40
Roquemaure	7
Rouen	125
St. Chamond	2
St. Didier	1
St. Etienne	13
St. Flour	24
St. Lô	7
St. Omer	5
St. Quentin	16
Saintes	26
Saumur	1
Sedan	2
Sète	13
Soissons	52
Strasbourg	2
Tarbes	52
Thiers	39
Toulouse	451
Tours	65
Troyes	53
Tulle	4
Valence	65
Valenciennes	13
Verdun	12
Versailles	4
Vichy	2
Villefranche	37

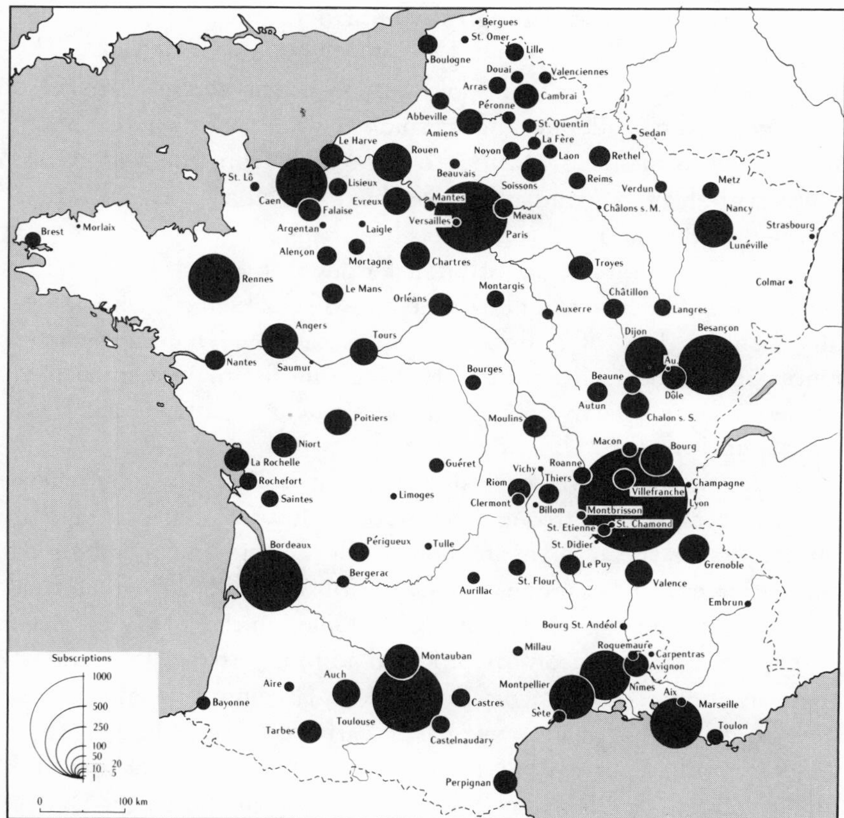

Distribution of quarto copies of the *Encyclopédie* in prerevolutionary France. The map is drawn up from Duplain's secret subscription list, MS 1220 in the Bibliothèque de la Ville de Neuchâtel. This list covers all but one of the 8,011 sets printed. Of these, 828 were foreign and so do not figure on the map. The map also excludes 76 sets that were sold to unidentified individuals and 25 sets that were given away—either as compensation for empoyees and associates or to procure protections; at least 10 of these went to Lyons, and Panckoucke dispensed 4 in Paris. The unidentified sales all involved single sets, except in four cases, which appear on the list simply as "Ollier 6," "Vasselier 4," "La Flèche 39," and "Berage 8." "La Flèche" could have been a person but probably represents La Flèche, Maine, where there was a famous school, originally founded for the Jesuits by Henry IV. The large number of copies sold in Lyons as compared with Paris resulted in part from the way the business was handled: Duplain directed the marketing operations from Lyons, while Panckoucke's many affairs kept him too busy to be much of a salesman in Paris. Also, the Parisian market was probably pretty well supplied by earlier editions. This map therefore should not be taken to prove that the capital of the Enlightenment absorbed relatively few *Encyclopédie*s. What it provides is a fairly accurate picture of *Encyclopédie* diffusion in the provinces.

a backward south and a progressive north by the "Maggiolo line" of literacy, running from Mont-St.-Michel to Geneva.[39] The *Encyclopédie*s seem to have sold best in towns where there were parlements and academies, but it sold very well everywhere: that is probably the main conclusion to be drawn from the map. Once reincarnated in a comparatively cheap edition, Diderot's text traveled farther and wider than has been appreciated.

Duplain's secret subscription list does not identify all of the subscribers; it contains only the names of booksellers, who generally boughts lots of a dozen or more sets, which they retailed among their local clients. But there is one list of individual purchasers of the quarto edition in the Franche Comté. It has been translated into the following bar graph, which covers Besançon, a judicial, administrative, ecclesiastical, and military center, where sales were unusually strong. The graph shows a high percentage of purchasers in the legal profession, both lawyers and members of the parlement of Besançon. The *Encyclopédie* sold well in the first two estates, and especially among noblemen in the army, as might be expected in a garrison town. Royal administrators, almost all of them nonnoble, also bought the book in large number, and so did bourgeois professional men, particularly doctors, though to a lesser extent. Fourteen of the 137 sets went to merchants and manufacturers—a large proportion in comparison with Daniel Roche's statistics on provincial academicians and Jacques Proust's analysis of the contributors to the *Encyclopédie*.[40] Approximately one-half of one percent of the people in Besançon bought the quarto *Encyclopédie*—a high percentage, but one that seems credible, given the above economic analysis of cost and clientele. The town's two main booksellers, Lépagnez and Charmet, had not expected to sell more than a dozen or so sets and were astounded at the book's success, especially as their trade had fallen into a slump since 1777. "Please don't believe that I enjoy any great consumption of books here," Lépagnez wrote to the Société typographique. "I swear to you that after *L'Histoire universelle*, *L'Histoire ecclésiastique*, that of the Gallican Church, the Bible of

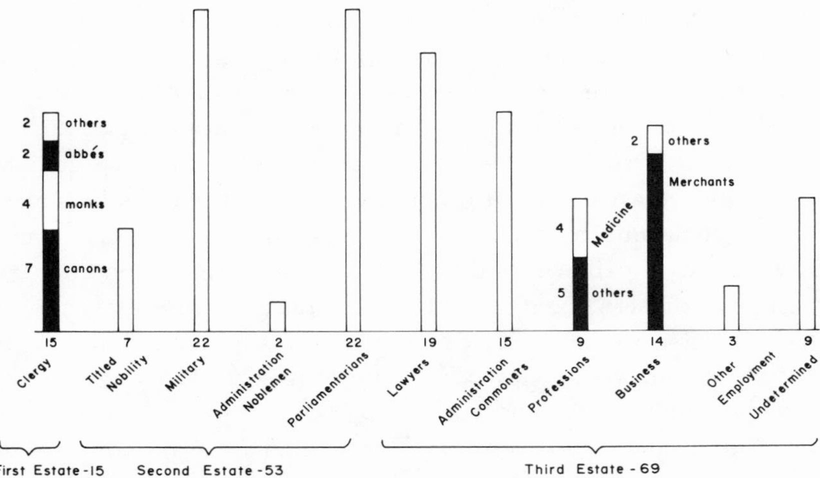

Subscribers to the quarto *Encyclopédie* in Besançon. The bar graph is drawn from the list of individual purchasers of the quarto edition in Lough, *Essays on the Encyclopédie,* 466-73. It contains the names and *qualités* of 253 subscribers from the Franche Comté, of whom 137 were from Besançon. Duplain's secret list shows there were 390 subscriptions sold in the province, a figure that is confirmed by letters from the two booksellers who collected them. Therefore the representativeness of the Comtois list, which was drawn up according to the order in which the subscriptions arrived, is far from being complete—it amounts to two-thirds of the subscriptions sold. But the last third of the subscribers probably tended to come from outlying areas of the large, mountainous province, and so the bar graph probably gives a fairly accurate picture of the subscription pattern within Besançon. The military category seems to have been made up entirely of noblemen—most had titles but are not entered under "titled nobility"—but the "parlementaires" probably included an undetermined number of commoners, so that the second estate appears somewhat larger on the graph than it was in reality. The same may be true of the third estate, because some of the "undetermined" category could have been noblemen. The three men represented by "other employment" were identified on the list as "intendant du Prince de Bauffremont," "Conseil de Mgr. le Duc du Châtelet," and "gardemagasin," presumably an army position.

Vance, the *Encyclopédie*, and the Rousseau, everything else has given me no business at all for the last two years."[41]

The sales pattern of Besançon may not have been typical of France as a whole, but nonstatistical information shows a similar enthusiasm for the *Encyclopédie* in other provincial centers. In Toulouse, at the other extremity of the kingdom, a bookbinder called Gastón sold 182 quartos in three weeks and expected to place 400 octavos. And in general, when French booksellers mentioned their quarto clients in their correspondence they named lawyers, royal officials, and local noblemen—unlike their counterparts in Northern, Central, and Eastern Europe, who referred only to courtiers. So all the evidence points in the same direction: in prerevolutionary France the *Encyclopédie* worked its way into the world of the provincial notables who assumed the leadership of the revolution and who continued to dominate the countryside throughout the nineteenth century.

No one can pretend to know what message "took" in the minds of those readers. Many of them must have bought the *Encyclopédie* for what it claimed to be: a compendium of all knowledge, rather than philosophic propaganda. As Panckoucke put it, "The *Encyclopédie* will always be the first book of any library or cabinet"[42]—but it could have been a book to display on shelves, not to read. In fact Panckoucke reported that some subscribers in Lyons could not read at all. But it is difficult to believe that a high proportion of its owners never got through even its Preliminary Discourse, which is a manifesto of the Enlightenment. And far more people must have read the *Encyclopédie* than owned it, as would be common in an era when books were liberally loaned and when *cabinets littéraires* were booming. It therefore seems legitimate to conclude that the biography of this book—the protection accorded it by French authorities, the struggle to exploit it among bookdealers, and its diffusion among a clientele of middle-range notables everywhere in the country—that this extraordinary success story reveals an Enlightenment that had spread far beyond the elite of court and capital and had penetrated throughout the upper echelons of the Old Regime. As the Société typographique wrote to a customer in August 1779:

> Never has an enterprise of this kind and this scope had a greater success, nor has one been conducted with such speed. In less than two and a half years, and after having renewed the subscription twice, we have printed 8,000 copies of this *Encyclopédie*, of which we have only a small number yet to sell. The public seems to have waited impatiently to be served by publishers less rapacious than the producers of the first edition [a dubious statement]. We and our associates pride ourselves in having satisfied it in this respect; and you will observe, Sir, that if Enlightenment [*lumières philosophiques*] lacks in this best of all possible worlds, it will not be our fault.[43]

NOTES

1 This essay, which is intended as a preliminary sketch for a full-length study of the quarto editions of the *Encyclopédie,* is based almost entirely on the papers of the Société typographique de Neuchâtel (hereafter STN) in the Bibliothèque de la Ville de Neuchâtel, Switzerland. All citations are to those manuscripts unless specified otherwise. Any researcher concerned with the later editions of the *Encyclopédie* is bound to feel indebted to the painstaking scholarship of two men: George B. Watts and John Lough. See especially Watts's articles, "Forgotten Folio Editions of the *Encyclopédie,*" *French Review,* 27 (1953-54), 22-29, 243-44; "The Swiss Editions of the *Encyclopédie,*" *Harvard Library Bulletin,* 9 (1955), 213-35; and "The Genevan Folio Reprinting of the *Encyclopédie,*" *Proceedings of the American Philosophical Society,* 105 (1961), 361-67; and see Lough's book, *Essays on the* Encyclopédie *of Diderot and D'Alembert* (London: Oxford University Press, 1968). As far as the circulation of books within France is concerned the first edition of the *Encyclopédie* was relatively unimportant, but it has attracted most of the attention of scholars because its publication became the crucial episode in the liberalization of the Direction de la librairie and in the battles between the philosophes and their opponents during the 1750s. A decree of the King's Council suppressed the first two volumes of the *Encyclopédie* in 1752; and the Council revoked the privilege for the book in 1759, when it had come under attack by the Pope, the Jesuits, the

Jansenists, the Parlement of Paris, and other enemies of the philosophes. But C. G. de Lamoignon de Malesherbes, the enlightened director of the Librairie, unofficially permitted the last ten volumes of text to appear in 1765. The last two volumes of plates were published in 1772. For an excellent synthesis of the scholarship on this aspect of the history of the *Encyclopédie,* see Arthur M. Wilson, *Diderot* (New York: Oxford University Press, 1957, 1972), and Jacques Proust, *Diderot et l'Encyclopédie* (Paris: A. Colin, 1967).

2 On the economic aspects of the first edition, see, in addition to the works cited above, Norman L. Torrey, "L'*Encyclopédie* de Diderot, une grande aventure dans le domaine de d'édition," *Revue d'histoire littéraire de la France,* 51 (1951), 306-17; John Lough, "Luneau de Boisjermain v. the Publishers of the *Encyclopédie,*" *Studies on Voltaire and the Eighteenth Century,* 23 (1963), 115-73; and Ralph H. Bowen, "The *Encyclopédie* as a Business Venure," in Charles K. Warner, ed., *From the Ancien Régime to the Popular Front: Essays in the History of Modern France in Honor of Shepard B. Clough* (New York: Columbia University Press, 1969), pp. 1-22. What little is known about the sales of the first edition comes from the papers of Luneau de Boisjermain, which are too polemical to be trustworthy and which justify estimates of the foreign sales ranging from somewhat more than one-half to three-quarters of the edition.

3 Lough, *Essays on the* Encyclopédie, p. 103.

4 George B. Watts, "Charles Joseph Panckoucke, 'l'Atlas de la librairie française'," *Studies on Voltaire and the Eighteenth Century,* 68 (1969), 67-205.

5 *Privilège* no. 613, Mar. 29, 1776, Bibliothèque nationale, fonds français, MS 21967. On February 10, 1776, Panckoucke had received a twelve-year *privilège général* (*privilège* no. 365, ibid.) for "un ouvrage qui a pour titre *Nouveau dictionnaire des arts et des sciences etc.,*" but nothing proves that this work was the *Encyclopédie* or had any connection with it. None of the other registers of *privilèges* or *permissions tacites* contain any references to the *Encyclopédie* for the period 1768-88; see MSS 21964-67, 21983, 21984, 21989, 22000-02, 22013, and 22073. On September 8, 1759, after the revocation of the original privilege of the *Encyclopédie,* its first publishers received a privilege to produce a collection of its plates, which they probably construed as a "copyright" for the entire work and sold to Panckoucke.

6 D.-J. Garat, *Mémoires historiques sur la vie de M. Suard, sur ses écrits et sur le XVIIIe siècle* (Paris: Philippe, 1820), I, 274. For more details about the second edition, see Lough, *Essays on the* Encyclopédie, 52-111.

7 Panckoucke to STN, Aug. 4, 1776. In this letter Panckoucke explained that he was referring to an interview with Diderot that had occurred eight

years earlier. For Diderot's version of the famous encounter, see Wilson, *Diderot*, pp. 578-79.

8 Panckoucke to STN, Dec. 26, 1776.

9 Panckoucke to STN, May 13, 1777.

10 Panckoucke to STN, Aug. 5, 1777.

11 "Je vous serai obligé de donner vos ordres pour que ces volumes passent sans difficulté et d'accorder toute votre protection à cet ouvrage. M. de Néville est prévenue de tout ce que j'ai fait à ce sujet." Panckoucke to La Tourette, July 18, 1777, Bibliothèque publique et universitaire de Genève, MS supp. 148.

12 Dufour to STN, Aug. 2, 1780; Resplandy to STN, Jan. 2, 1778; D'Arnal to STN, Nov. 12, 1779; Panckoucke to STN, Sept. 9, 1777.

13 George B. Watts made a good guess as to the explanation of the "second" edition, but he mistakenly believed that Pellet directed the whole affair; see "Swiss Editions of the *Encyclopédie*," p. 228. Lough agrees with Watts's version of this bibliographical imbroglio; *Essays on the* Encyclopédie, pp. 36-38.

14 Jean-François Favarger to STN, July 21, 1778.

15 Ibid.

16 Louis Marcinhes to STN, July 11, 1777.

17 STN to Panckoucke, Aug. 20, 1778. Because the accounts became extremely embroiled, it is impossible to know the exact costs and profit of the enterprise.

18 Panckoucke to STN, Sept. 9, 1777.

19 STN to Panckoucke, Dec. 18, 1777; Panckoucke to STN, Nov. 19, 1777; STN to Panckoucke, Dec. 7, 1777.

20 Société typographique de Lausanne to Pellet of Geneva, Nov. 1, 1777, copy included in a letter from the Société typographique de Lausanne to STN, Nov. 20, 1777.

21 Panckoucke to STN, Dec. 22, 1777.

22 Favarger to STN, July 8, 1778; STN to Favarger, July 11, 1778.

23 In the case of this second bibliographical mystery, Watts ("Swiss Editions of the *Encyclopédie*," pp. 230-32) and Lough (*Essays on the* Encyclopédie, pp. 40-41) differ slightly, but each did a good job at guessing at the solution, considering that they did not know who was behind the quarto enterprise or how it came into conflict with the octavo edition.

24 By this time the quarto association had been dissolved and the STN had split with Panckoucke and had formed the Confédération helvétique with the Sociétés typographiques of Bern and Lausanne. The plan of the Confédération helvétique was to reprint all the articles of the *Encyclopédie méthodique* that had not appeared in the earlier editions, to arrange them in alphabetical order—rather than according to subject, as they

appeared in the *Encyclopédie méthodique*—and then to sell them, in all three formats, as supplements to the early editions. In this way the owners of the first sets could acquire all the new material of the *Encyclopédie méthodique* by purchasing only a few volumes of supplements, and the Swiss printers could badly damage Panckoucke's potential market.

25 For further information on these contrasting types of publishing, see Robert Darnton, "Reading, Writing and Publishing in Eighteenth-Century France: A Case Study in the Sociology of Literature," *Daedalus* (Winter 1971), 214-56.

26 Panckoucke to STN, Sept. 10, 1779, citing a letter he had received from Duplain.

27 Panckoucke to STN, Sept. 27, 1779.

28 Panckoucke to STN, Nov. 6, 1778, Mar. 7 and 18, 1779.

29 F.-S Ostervald and Abram Bosset DeLuze, codirectors of the STN, writing to the STN from Lyons, Jan. 29, 1780.

30 STN to Panckoucke, Mar. 14, 1779.

31 The following information comes from the sources cited above (*nn* 1,2), except for the figures on market prices and on the sizes of the quarto and octavo printings, which come from the papers of the STN. The extraordinary richness of those papers makes it possible for the first time to estimate accurately the total volume and cost of the *Encyclopédie* trade in prerevolutionary France. The octavo publishers originally announced that their edition, which followed the quarto page by page, would sell at a subscription price of 195 livres—6 livres down, 5 livres for each volume of text, and 15 livres for each volume of plates. When they learned that the quarto would run to 36 volumes of text instead of 29, as was originally planned, they had to follow suit and therefore charged 231 livres for their subscriptions—contrary to what has been affirmed by Watts ("Swiss Editions of the *Encyclopédie*," p. 231) and by Lough (*Essays on the* Encyclopédie, p. 40). On the subscription prices of the octavo, see also the *Gazette de Berne*, Nov. 19, 1777, and Apr. 8, 1780.

32 The following information on artisans' "budgets" and the price of bread comes from the work of Ernest Labrousse, George Rudé, and Albert Soboul. For a convenient summary of their findings, see Rudé, *The Crowd in the French Revolution* (Oxford: Clarendon Press, 1959). The "Banques des ouvriers" in the STN papers contain full information on the wages of the printers of the Société typographique. Oddly enough, they corresponded exactly to the wages of skilled workmen in Paris, where the cost of living was higher.

33 Proust, *Diderot et l'*Encyclopédie, p. 59; for a detailed study of Diderot's income, see pp. 81-116.

34 Robert Darnton, "The High Enlightenment and the Low Life of Literature in Prerevolutionary France," *Past and Present*, no. 51 (1971), p. 87.

35 Durey de Morsan to F.-S. Ostervald of the STN, Apr. 17, 1778.

36 Marcel Marion, *Dictionnaire des institutions de la France aux XVIIe et XVIIIe siècles* (Paris, 1923), p. 446; Henri Sée, *La France économique et sociale au XVIIIe siècle* (Paris, 1933), pp. 64-66. The *portion congrue* allotted to every curé from the revenue of the *dîme* (tithe) was increased in 1786 to 700 livres.

37 Philip Dawson, *Provincial Magistrates and Revolutionary Politics in France, 1789-1795* (Cambridge: Harvard University Press, 1972), ch. 3; Sée, *La France économique et sociale*, p. 162.

38 STN to Rudiger of Moscow, May 31, 1777.

39 Michel Fleury and Pierre Valmary, "Les Progrès de l'instruction élémentaire de Louis XIV à Napoléon III," *Population*, no. 1 (1957), 71-92. Of course there is no reason to expect that the diffusion of the *Encyclopédie* should coincide with the primitive level of literacy indicated by Fleury and Valmary.

40 Daniel Roche, "Milieux académiques provinciaux et société des lumières," in François Furet, et al., *Livre et société dans la France du XVIIIe siècle* (Paris: 1965), pp. 93-185; Proust, *Diderot et l'Encyclopédie*, ch. 1.

41 Lépagnez to STN, Aug. 30, 1780.

42 Panckoucke to STN, Aug. 4, 1776.

43 STN to J. G. Bruere of Homburg, Aug. 19, 1779.

Des Stéréotypes ethniques dans l'Amérique du dix-huitième siècle

PIERRE AUBÉRY

Dans sa préface à l'édition originale de 1803 de son *Tableau du climat et du sol des Etats-Unis d'Amérique,*[1] Constantin François Chassebeuf dit Volney, comte et pair de France, membre de l'Académie française, honoraire de la Société asiatique, séante à Calcutta, nous explique sans ambages comment, en son temps, on se faisait un nom dans les Lettres. Une certaine fortune personnelle, modeste mais suffisante, qu'accroît un héritage de six mille écus, lui permet dès 1782 d'entreprendre un voyage d'étude en Egypte et en Syrie qui durera un peu plus de deux ans. Il y apprendra l'arabe et en ramènera un livre, son *Voyage en Egypte et en Syrie* qui fera rapidement de lui une autorité écoutée sur la question d'Orient.

Bien des années plus tard, célèbre auteur des *Ruines* mais fort éprouvé par les vicissitudes de la Révolution, il s'embarque à nouveau pour l'étranger. Cette fois, nous sommes en 1795, c'est vers les Etats-Unis qu'il fera voile pour un séjour d'étude qui se prolongera près de trois ans et aurait fort bien pu durer plus longtemps si de très précises menaces politico-diplomatiques ne lui avaient soudainement mis un terme.

Il a fallu trente-cinq mois à Volney, du 12 juillet 1795 au 5 juillet 1798 pour recueillir les informations et les documents qui lui serviront à la préparation de son ouvrage sur l'Amérique. Il y parcourut plus de 900 lieues, le plus souvent à pied, rendant visite aux plus célèbres personnages du pays, les Jefferson, Madison, Washington, mais aussi à des notables de moindre envergure. Il se trouve également par la force des choses en rapport avec le cercle disparate des émigrés français à Philadelphie ainsi qu'avec une extraordinaire variété de personnages de toutes races et de toutes nationalités sans exclure ni les noirs ni les indiens. C'est en 1803 que paraîtra le *Tableau* dont la rédaction aura beaucoup occupé Volney depuis la fin de son séjour à Philadelphie!

On peut donc dire, sans la moindre exagération, que notre auteur consacra intégralement cinq années de sa vie à de lointains voyages et un nombre presque égal à la rédaction de leur relation. Pendant tout ce temps Volney semble avoir vécu principalement de ses propres ressources, héritages, ventes de biens fonciers pour 43,400 francs et autres revenus, sans être astreint à un travail régulier ni à une résidence fixe. Il faut dire que Volney ne voyageait pas d'une manière fastueuse comme le feront certains de ses successeurs. Il s'ouvrait même à l'un de ses correspondants de ses soucis financiers comme nous l'apprend sa lettre datée de Philadelphie le 14 janvier 1797 à Laréveillère-Lépeaux, membre du Directoire, dans laquelle il écrit notamment: "Vous savez mieux que personne que le gouvernement n'a rien fait pour moi; je suis venu ici avec mes seules ressources, et elles ne peuvent tarder à s'épuiser."[2]

Quoiqu'il en soit on ne peut manquer d'être frappé par le considérable investissement de temps et d'argent sur lequel repose l'ouvrage dont nous voudrions discuter quelques aspects. Le contraste entre les conditions de travail de Volney et celles de la plupart d'entre nous contraints de rogner sur nos heures de sommeil pour griffonner hâtivement, entre préparations de cours et rapports administratifs, nos minces critiques, est fort révélateur des contraintes matérielles qui limitent notre quête du savoir et excusera peut-être le caractère cursif de nos remarques. D'ailleurs nous les limiterons à la présentation et à la discussion de l'image que Volney nous propose des Français vivant en Amérique dans les dernières années du dix-huitième siècle. Cette image nous la trouvons dans le *Tableau* mais aussi dans sa *Correspondance* et les fragments d'une "Relation manuscrite" conservée dans les archives de Baudinière dont l'édition nous a été procurée par Jean Gaulmier[3] que nous comparerons avec les témoignages et les récits d'auteurs plus anciens tels l'intendant de la Nouvelle France Hocquart, l'abbé Raynal et Crèvecoeur.

Assez paradoxalement, la justification théorique de notre démarche et de notre méthode d'élaboration de ce portrait composite du Français d'Amérique nous est fournie par Michel Foucault dont nous dénoncions naguère les procédés rhétoriques. Au cours d'un entretien avec un collaborateur du *Monde des Livres*[4] il déclarait:

> Je crois qu'il y a aujourd'hui un tel prestige des démarches de type freudien que très souvent les analyses de textes historiques se donnent pour but de chercher le "non-dit" du discours, le "refoulé", l'"inconscient" du Système. Il est bon d'abandonner cette attitude et d'être à la fois plus modeste et plus fureteur. Car quand on regarde les documents, on est frappé de voir avec quel cynisme la bourgeoisie du dix-neuvième siècle disait très exactement ce qu'elle faisait et pourquoi. Pour elle, détentrice du pouvoir, le cynisme était une forme d'orgueil. . . . Retrouver ce discours explicite, cela implique évidemment de quitter le matériel universitaire et scolaire des "grands textes". Ce n'est ni chez Hegel, Nietzche, Auguste Comte, que la bourgeoisie parle de façon directe. A côté de ces textes sacralisés, une stratégie absolument consciente, organisée, réfléchie, se lit en clair dans une masse de documents inconnus qui constituent le discours effectif d'une action politique.

Tel est précisément le cas de l'oeuvre de Volney peu connue et peu lue de nos jours mais qui parle comme devaient le faire les grands bourgeois de l'époque arrivés aux affaires grâce à la Révolution et à l'Empire.

Volney précisait dans son *Voyage en Egypte et en Syrie* "que le genre des voyages appartenait à l'histoire et non aux romans." Aussi n'y a-t-il guère de récits d'aventures plus ou moins imaginaires dans ses relations et son plus grand mérite reste sans doute son refus de céder à la facilité de peindre d'attrayants tableaux d'imagination comme tant de voyageurs d'autrefois. Il note d'ailleurs: "Je n'ai point représenté les pays plus beaux qu'ils ne m'ont paru: Je n'ai point peint les hommes meilleurs ou plus méchants que je ne les ai vus; et j'ai peut-être été propre à les voir tels qu'ils sont, puisque je n'ai reçu d'eux ni bienfaits ni outrages."[5] Il exposera effectivement dans son *Tableau du climat et du sol des Etats-Unis* l'accueil et les conditions d'existence que des Français pourraient s'attendre à trouver en Amérique. Il conclut que le pays ne leur offrirait guère de facilités s'ils y venaient avec des ambitions politiques ou l'espoir de s'y enrichir. Nous verrons plus loin comment et pourquoi, à l'occasion de la description par Volney des grandes lignes du stéréotype du Français tel qu'il était alors répandu en Amérique, stéréotype qui se dégage d'une observation personnelle et méthodique, soigneusement étayée par une étude parallèle de témoignages écrits et oraux de colons de l'époque appartenant eux-mêmes à plusieurs groupes ethniques tant européens qu'Amérindiens. Nous montrerons aussi la transformation profonde mais graduelle que subit ce stéréotype lorsque le Français d'Amérique cesse d'être craint comme un concurrent redoutable sur les plans politiques et militaires, imbu d'idées féodales et chevaleresques justifiant la domination d'une soi-disant "aristocratie," pour devenir successivement et simultanément: un libre penseur soupçonné d'athéisme, un révolutionnaire indiscipliné, un agriculteur négligent et instable, plus attiré par la vie aventureuse du coureur des bois et du trappeur, qui s'indianise volontiers par ses amours et par ses moeurs.

Volney, très proche de la classe politique dirigeante du Directoire puis de celle du Consulat et de l'Empire, était un de ces idéologues bourgeois éclairés dotés d'une parfaite bonne conscience qui n'hésitaient pas à formuler sans inutiles circonlocutions les objectifs des enquêtes minutieuses auxquelles ils se livraient avant d'investir leurs capitaux. De la bourgeoisie ascendante Volney avait les qualités, la clarté d'esprit, la puissance de travail, l'art de se faire d'utiles relations et de défendre, avec une vigilance jamais en défaut, ses intérêts personnels. Mais il en avait aussi les défauts, que souligne son ami et correspondant Laréveillère-Lépeaux, dont cette immense vanité susceptible parfois de les aveugler et d'en faire les dupes des plus vulgaires escrocs. "Vaniteux, susceptible, capricieux et enthousiaste, il s'engoue facilement et se dégoûte aussi vite. Ainsi, avec la louange, on lui fera faire soit des concessions, soit des confidences . . . avec la contradiction et la hauteur, on excitera sa bile, et dans ses accès d'humeur, sa morgue blessée laissera échapper son secret."[6] En Amérique Volney n'exerce aucune fonction officielle et il y est accueilli, tant par les autorités du pays que par les milieux cultivés, comme le célèbre auteur des *Ruines* dont Jefferson lui-même entreprendra une traduction. Plus tard il sera au centre de polémiques religieuses et politiques qui hâtèrent son départ. Mais, venu en candidat à l'immigration permanente, il ne se laissera jamais aller à aucun mouvement d'humeur contre le peuple ni contre le gouvernement des Etats-Unis. Son témoignage critique n'en a que plus de poids.

Voyageur consciencieux, soucieux d'apprendre la langue du pays, Volney ne recherche pas particulièrement la compagnie de ses compatriotes. Mais lors de son arrivée à Philadelphie c'est auprès d'eux qu'il trouve le plus cordial accueil. Là se côtoient des représentants de plusieurs vagues successives d'émigration dont Gilbert Chinard brossait un vivant portrait dan son ouvrage cité plus haut.[7]

Mais c'est surtout un petit groupe qui avait fait son quartier général de la boutique de librairie de Moreau de Saint-Méry, ancien vice-président de la Commune de Paris, que Volney fréquenta. Il y rencontra Talleyrand—alors citoyen américain—Baumetz, Talon, Blacon, Noailles, Demeunier, Boislandry, Payen de Boisneuf. Ce n'est d'ailleurs ni de leurs espoirs ni de leurs intrigues que nous entretiendra Volney. Ces Français, liés aux classes dirigeantes, rentreront pour la plupart en France dès que la situation politique le leur permettra. Ceux qui intéressaient vraiment Volney, comme ils nous intéressent, ce sont ceux qui s'étaient établis en Amérique avec la ferme intention d'y demeurer et d'y faire souche. Volney s'intéressait à eux parce que, fatigué des convulsions politiques de l'Europe, il envisageait, au départ, de suivre leur exemple, mais aussi peut-être parce qu'il aurait été chargé secrètement d'étudier la possibilité—à laquelle il semble n'avoir jamais cru personnellement—de reprendre pied en Louisiane au nom de la France et d'y implanter des colonies françaises, enfin parce que l'observation de leur mode de vie et de leur acclimatation allait lui permettre de critiquer quelques-uns des mythes mis à la mode par Saint John de Crèvecoeur sur les vertus de la vie rustique dans le soi-disant "nouveau" monde, dans un état proche de celui de la nature.

Dans son livre *Lettres d'un cultivateur américain* (1787) Crèvecoeur avait longuement fait l'éloge de l'Amérique et des Américains ces hommes nouveaux qui "avec joie quittèrent le nom d'Anglais, d'Irlandais, d'Allemands, de Suédois, de Français." Et en quels termes n'avait-il pas chanté leurs bonheurs!

> Leur industrie, protégée et libre, produisit bientôt des richesses; ces richesses leur acquirent un poids et une importance nouvelle, comme le sol qu'ils cultivaient leur avait déjà procuré un nouveau rang. D'êtres errants, sans demeure et sans asyle, de soldats fanatiques, persécuteurs ou persécutés, ils devinrent des citoyens. Ce fut alors que parurent des périodes de bonheur et de simplicité, d'industrie et de paix, qui vraiment ressemblent aux rêves de l'âge d'or;—l'union, la frugalité, l'abondance, la liberté, l'heureux établissement de leurs enfants, et la santé, devinrent le partage de ces nouveaux colons. . . . Ils n'étaient sujets qu'à peu de maladies; de ce côté-là ils ressemblaient aux Sauvages qui souvent étaient mêlés avec eux; leurs provisions étaient saines et simples, l'eau leur servait de boisson.—Leurs passions et leurs désirs étaient heureusement retenus par la nécessité du travail, la religion, simple comme les hommes qu'elle instruisait, n'exigeait d'eux qu'un culte de reconnaissance . . . l'hospitalité générale tenait lieu d'Hôpitaux et d'Auberges.—Ils étaient nourris, protégés et conduits par la nature elle-même, par la tempérance et l'industrie.[8]

Et plus loin Crèvecoeur précisait encore: leurs "travaux sont fondés sur la grande base de la nature même, l'intérêt personnel, qui, sans [qu'ils y] songent, s'accorde avec celui des autres."[9] "La culture de la terre purifie les moeurs, conduit à la tempérance, à la paucité des besoins, à la simplicité, elle adoucit la férocité naturelle aux hommes; car c'est à la campagne qu'on a souvent besoin des secours des autres." [10]

La stabilité, l'égalité dans l'aisance, la santé et la vertu, venaient récompenser les efforts de ces hommes lavés des péchés d'Europe par l'émigration et régénérés par le travail. Comment n'aurait-on pas voulu jouir de toutes ces prospérités! Aussi rien d'étonnant à ce que vers 1790 "plus de cent vingt familles" françaises furent convaincues, par les tableaux idylliques dont le livre de Crèvecoeur était rempli, les voyages de Brissot et une adroite publicité d'une compagnie dite du *Sioto,* à émigrer vers de si plaisants rivages.

On leur promettait "un climat délicieux et *sain*; à peine de gelées en hiver;—une rivière, nommée par excellence *la belle Rivière* [Ohio], riche en poissons excellents et monstrueux; des forêts superbes, d'un arbre qui distille le sucre [l'érable à sucre] et d'un arbuste qui donne de la chandelle [myrica cerifa]." Certes, ainsi que le rappelle Volney dans son article sur Gallipolis, [11] "les distributeurs de tant de bienfaits ne disaient pas que ces belles forêts étaient un obstacle préliminaire à tout genre de culture; qu'il fallait abattre les arbres un à un, les brûler, nettoyer le terrain avec des peines et des frais considérable; que pendant au moins une année il fallait tirer de loin toute espèce de vivres; que la chasse et la pêche, qui sont un plaisir quand on a bien déjeuné, sont des très dures corvées dans un pays désert et sauvage." [12]

Les promoteurs de cette magnifique spéculation n'indiquaient pas non plus que ces terres qu'ils offraient au prix de "dix livres l'acre" ne valaient guère sur le marché local que "six à sept sous." Mais tout cela était si loin, si tentant, vu de Paris, où la terre coûtait cent fois plus cher, qu'effectivement en 1791 un certain nombre d'individus et de familles appartenant aux classes moyennes s'embarquèrent pour l'Ohio qui au Havre, qui à Bordeaux, qui à Nantes, qui à La Rochelle.

En juillet 1796 Volney retrouva à Gallipolis, sur l'Ohio, ce qui restait des "cinq cents colons, tous artistes ou artisans ou bourgeois aisés" arrivés au pays entre 1791 et 1792. Nous n'entrerons pas ici dans le détail des déboires, déceptions et litiges divers qui devaient leś accabler dès leur débarquement. Sans organisation ni direction, délestés du plus clair de leur argent par les promoteurs et les transporteurs, ils virent bientôt leurs titres de propriété contestés, faillirent être définitivement dépouillés par de peu scrupuleux compatriotes des terres qui finalement leur furent allouées. Mais déjà la plupart des colons s'étaient dispersés et ceux qui étaient restés—84 au plus—végétaient assez misérablement lorsque Volney leur rendit visite. Ces aspirants spéculateurs espérant une fortune rapide en bon gogos qu'ils étaient, s'étaient bientôt retrouvés dupes. Quelques jours plus tard, en août 1796, Volney parvient à un autre établissement fondé par des Français sur la rivière Wabash qui porte le nom de *Poste-Vincennes*. Là les Français n'étaient guère plus prospères bien que souvent anciens militaires, venus du Canada, ils fussent fixés dans le pays depuis environ soixante ans. Alors que l'aspect même des colons anglo-saxons, arrivés depuis quatre à six ans "les cheveux blond ou châtains, le teint fleuri, la figure pleine, et le corps d'un embonpoint qui annonçait la santé et l'aisance" frappe Volney, il note que les Français avaient "le visage très maigre, la peau hâve et *tannée*, et tout le corps comme exténué de jeûne, sans parler des vêtements qui annonçaient la pauvreté." [13]

Sainte-Beuve, dans sa causerie du lundi 21 février 1853, nous dit qu'il ne citera pas ce qu'écrit Volney sur la différence non plus seulement d'aspect mais aussi de caractère du Colon américain et du Colon français "parce que la comparaison est trop à notre désavantage." [14] Nous n'aurons pas de tels scrupules. Nous ne reprocherons pas non plus à Volney, comme le fait Sainte-Beuve, de s'être interdit tout ornement, tout tableau d'imagination, toute impression personnelle, au point d'affecter plutôt l'aridité. Car aujourd'hui la sécheresse volontaire de son rapport nous semble infiniment plus pertinente et plus convaincante que "le débordement de couleur . . . et le déluge des impressions personnelles"[15] de ses plus illustres contemporains et successeurs. Volney nous indique modestement, au passage, qu'il a cru s'apercevoir, dans ses voyages aux Etats-Unis, "que les Français n'ont pas la même aptitude à y former des établissements agricoles, que les immigrants d'Angleterre, d'Irlande et d'Allemagne."[16] Il nous suffira de suivre Volney pas à pas pour découvrir avec lui les causes immédiates et lointaines de cet état de fait.

Les colons français que Volney rencontra n'étaient pour ainsi dire jamais des hommes de la terre, "gens élevés dans la vie aisée de Paris," anciens soldats habitués à l'oisiveté des garnisons, trafiquants et colporteurs, le dur travail du défricheur de forêts les rebutait. N'ayant pas d'ouvriers à leur disposition ils s'acquittaient négligemment, et plutôt mal, des mille travaux quotidiens sur lesquels se fonde la prospérité d'un établissement agricole. Très peu nombreux [la population de la Haute Louisiane n'aurait jamais compté plus de 2500 têtes françaises] leurs villages, tels Gallipolis ou Poste-Vincennes, ne comptaient guère que quelques dizaines d'habitants, ils étaient souvent tentés d'entreprendre de longs voyages de plusieurs centaines de milles pour aller "causer en ville," c'est-à-dire à La Nouvelle-Orléans. Volney réfute incidemment un préjugé, qui a la vie dure et subsiste encore de nos jours, selon lequel les Français d'Amérique parleraient une sorte de dialecte peu compréhensible sans grand rapport avec la langue de l'Académie. Il note justement que "Le langage de ces Français n'est pas un patois comme on me l'avait dit, mais un français passable, mêlé de beaucoup de termes et de locutions de soldat. Cela devait être ainsi, tous ces postes ayant été primitivement fondés ou habités en majeure partie par des troupes."[17]

Certes ces colons français sont peu lettrés n'ayant que de rares missionnaires parmi eux qui puissent pourvoir à leur instruction. Mais ils sont, dans l'ensemble, en bonne santé et ils supportent mieux les rigueurs du climat, résistent mieux aux fatigues que les Anglo-Saxons. Les officiers et les médecins de l'armée Rochambeau s'en étaient convaincus à l'expérience. Et Volney ajoute "Il paraît que notre fibre a plus d'élasticité et de *vie* que la leur; et la balance penche encore en notre faveur par le vice de leur régime diététique . . . et par l'abus des spiritueux auxquels ils sont presque aussi adonnés que les sauvages."[18] Les causes du dépérissement des rares colonies françaises dans ce qu'on appelait alors la Haute Louisiane et la Louisiane, ne sauraient donc être trouvées dans l'analyse des conditions matérielles de ces établissements, la nature du sol, le climat, l'étendue et le mode de régime des propriétés. Elles doivent plutôt être recherchées dans les particularités des habitudes des colons et celles de leur caractère qui influençaient leur manière d'établir leur emploi du temps et de travailler. Alors que les colons d'origine anglo-saxonne travaillent lentement, assidûment, silencieusement à la réalisation d'un projet longuement mûri, le Français se lance avec fougue dans des entreprises mal conçues et mal préparées dont il ne tarde plus à se dégoûter et que finalement il abandonne subissant ainsi de lourdes pertes. Le Français se lève tôt, souvent par gloriole, mais il se laisse facilement distraire par ses querelles avec sa femme, par ses causeries avec ses voisins, une partie de chasse, un voyage vite entrepris. Volney insiste longuement sur ce goût du bavardage où se dissipent les énergies du Français. Il y perd peu à peu sa puissance de concentration et de réflexion sur des objets précis et pratiques. Volney s'empresse d'ajouter que les caractéristiques nationales qu'il s'est efforcé de dégager, par l'observation de très minces échantillons, ne découlent d'aucun déterminisme matérialiste, lié à la race ou au sexe: "le climat et le tempérament, alors même qu'ils sont une cause physique primordiale du *caractère* d'un peuple, sont soumis à une cause postérieure et secondaire encore plus énergique, l'action des gouvernements et des lois qui ont la faculté de violenter ses actions, de créer des habitudes nouvelles et contraires aux anciennes, et par là de changer le caractère des nations. . . . Les Français de Louis XIV et de Louis XV, avec leurs idées féodales et chevaleresques, étaient de beaucoup inférieurs en industrie, en idée de police, à la génération qui, depuis 1771, a reçu l'impression de tant d'idées libérales en organisation sociale."[19]

Ces Français de Louis XIV et de Louis XV, aux idées féodales et chevaleresques, dont l'idéologie était en contradiction avec les conditions réelles de leur existence dans les postes frontières et les petites colonies agricoles qui s'étaient développées à l'ouest, n'étaient certes pas les boutiquiers parisiens, spéculateurs avides et maladroits, dupes de la compagnie du Sioto. Ce n'étaient pas non plus les quelques villageois misérables grelottant de fièvres, perdus au milieu des marécages de la Louisiane, obligés par leur dénûment de tout attendre de l'officier commandant de poste "qui donne, vend, ôte à son gré les privilèges d'entrée, de sortie, d'achat et d'accaparement de denrées; en sorte qu'il n'existe aucune liberté, ni de commerce, ni de propriété,"[20] mais c'étaient, bien plus vraisemblablement, ceux que les Américains appelaient les *Canadiens* qui s'étaient trouvés abandonnés, isolés, après la cession du Canada à l'Angleterre en 1763, sans guère de liaison avec le monde extérieur, dans une vaste région qui demeura presque totalement dépourvue de gouvernement pendant la période de paix qui se prolongea jusqu'aux années 1780. Tant que les autorités absentes, apathiques et corrompues s'étaient abstenues de gouverner les *Canadiens* "avaient joui . . . d'un degré et d'un genre singulier de bien être. Presque abandonnés à eux-mêmes au sein des déserts, éloignés de soixante lieues du plus prochain poste sur le Mississipi, sans charge d'impôts, en paix avec les sauvages, ils passaient leur vie à chasser, à pêcher, à faire la traite des pelleteries, à cultiver quelques grains et quelques légumes pour le besoin de leurs familles."[21]

Volney trouva là une première illustration de la théorie, qu'il défendra plus tard, selon laquelle ce qui se fait de bon et d'utile, ce qu'il existe de liberté civile, de sûreté des personnes et des propriétés dépend plutôt des habitudes populaires et individuelles, de la nécessité du travail, du haut prix de toute main-d'oeuvre, que d'aucune habile mesure, d'aucune sage politique du gouvernement. En bref que l'absence de gouvernement est la condition première de la prospérité.

Mais qui étaient donc ces *Canadiens* qui avaient su s'acclimater si heureusement dans la solitude des confins de ce qui restait de la

Nouvelle France? Dès le début du dix-huitième siècle Gilles Hocquart, intendant de la Nouvelle France de 1729 à 1748, avait fixé les traits saillants du type canadien, qui s'était peu à peu dégagé et affirmé en un siècle, dans un mémoire conservé aux Archives publiques du Canada.

> Les Canadiens sont naturellement grands, bien faits, d'un tempérament vigoureux. . . . La nécessité les a rendus industrieux de génération en génération, les habitants des campagnes manient tous adroitement la hache; ils font eux-mêmes la plupart des outils et ustensiles de labourage; bâtissent leurs maisons, leurs granges, plusieurs sont tisserands.
>
> Ils aiment les distinctions et les caresses, se piquent de bravoure, sont extrêmement sensibles au mépris et aux moindres punitions. Ils sont intéressés, vindicatifs, sont sujets à l'ivrognerie, font un grand usage de l'eau de vie, passent pour n'être point véridiques. Ce portrait convient au grand nombre, particulièrement aux gens de la campagne; ceux des villes sont moins vicieux, tous sont attachés à la religion: on voit peu de scélérats; ils sont volages; ont trop bonne opinion d'eux-mêmes: ce qui les empêche de réussir, comme ils pourraient le faire, dans les arts, l'agriculture et le commerce. Joignons à cela l'oisiveté à laquelle la longueur et la rigueur de l'hiver donne occasion. Ils aiment la chasse, la navigation, les voyages, et n'ont point l'air grossier et rustique de nos paysans de France. Ils sont communément assez souples lorsqu'on les pique d'honneur, et qu'on les gouverne avec justice, mais ils sont naturellement indociles.[22]

Sans trop s'arrêter aux contradictions qu'on pourrait relever entre ce portrait et les observations de Volney, on remarquera que l'habilité manuelle, l'indépendance de caractère ainsi qu'une certaine instabilité indocile apparaissent dès 1737 commes les caractéristiques dominantes du Canadien. Les Français qui s'étaient expatriés étaient souvent des cadets de familles nombreuses ayant une "tête chaude et imaginative, d'un natural indépendant et révolté d'avance, bref un réfractaire . . . qui . . . ne voulait pas ou ne pouvait pas se ranger" comme l'écrira plus tard Taine dans *Les Origines de la France contemporaine* . On les retrouvait "au Canada, à la Louisiane, chirurgiens, maîtres d'escrime ou d'équitation, officiers et ingénieurs, aventuriers surtout et même flibustiers, trappeurs et coureurs de bois, les plus souples, les plus sympathiques, les plus téméraires des colons."[23] C'est donc un certain type d'homme, doté d'un caractère bien tranché qui va fournir le fond de l'émigration française en Amérique, tantôt expatrié volontaire, tantôt contraint par l'état militaire et les hasards du racolage de tenter sa chance en terre lointaine.

Raynal brosse vers 1780, dans son *Histoire philosophique* un tableau moins optimiste, plus nuancé, des moeurs des Canadiens avant la conquête anglaise, colons et militaires par force mais éminemment sociables par inclination et vocation.[24]

> Le froid excessif des hivers qui suspendait le cours des fleuves, enchaînait toute l'activité des hommes. L'habitude du repos, qui, durant huit mois, était comme la suite d'une saison si rigoreuse, rendait le travail insupportable, même dans les beaux jours. Les fêtes nombreuses d'une religion qui s'est étendue par les fêtes mêmes, empêchaient la naissance, interrompait le cours de l'industrie. Il est si facile d'être dévôt, quand c'est pour ne rien faire! Enfin, la passion des armes qu'on avait excitée à dessein parmi ces hommes courageux et fiers, achevait de les dégoûter des travaux champêtres. Uniquement épris de la gloire militaire, ils n'aimaient rien tant que la guerre, quoiqu'ils la fissent sans paie.
>
> Les habitants des villes, surtout de la capitale, passaient l'hiver comme l'été, dans une dissipation générale et continuelle. On ne leur trouvait aucune sensibilité pour le spectacle de la nature, ni pour les plaisirs de l'imagination; nul goût pour les sciences, pour les arts, pour la lecture, pour l'instruction. L'amusement était l'unique passion; et la danse faisait dans les assemblées, les délices de tous âges. Ce genre de vie donnait le plus grand empire aux femmes qui avaient tous les appas, excepté ces douces émotions de l'âme, qui seules font le prix et le charme de la beauté. Vives, gaies, coquettes et galantes, elles étaient plus heureuses d'inspirer une passion, que de la sentir.
>
> On remarquait dans les deux sexes plus de dévotion que de vertu, plus de religion que de probité, plus d'honneur que de véritable honnêteté. La superstition y affaiblissait le sens moral, comme il arrive partout où l'on se persuade que les cérémonies tiennent lieu de bonnes oeuvres, et que les crimes s'effacent par des prières.[25]

Chez eux, on retrouve comme trait dominant le goût du loisir, de la vie de société, des intrigues amoureuses, goût qu'encourageait l'inaction imposée par les longs hivers et la militarisation de la population masculine de la Nouvelle France. Raynal montre très clairement comment la situation précaire des quelque 80,000 habitants du Canada, luttant sans cesse contre une nature hostile, contre les Anglais et les sauvages, fit d'eux des militaires, avec tout ce que cet état entraîne de détérioration des qualités domestiques et morales des individus qui de gré ou de force s'y consacrent, perdant l'habitude du travail régulier et de la sobriété indispensables à la discipline de l'économie quotidienne. Plus encore que toute inclination naturelle

> La nécessité rendit soldats tous les Canadiens. Une éducation mâle et toute militaire les endurcissait de bonne heure à la fatigue, il les familiarisait avec le danger. A peine sortis de l'enfance, on les voyait parcourir un continent immense, l'été en canot, l'hiver à pied, au travers des neiges et des glaces. Comme ils n'avaient qu'un fusil pour moyen de subsistance, ils étaient continuellement exposés à mourir de faim: mais rien ne les effrayait, pas même le danger de tomber entre les mains des sauvages, qui avaient épuisé tout leur génie à imaginer, pour leurs ennemis, des supplices dont le plus doux était la mort. . . . Les arts sédentaires de la paix, les travaux suivis de l'agriculture, ne pouvaient pas avoir d'attrait pour des hommes accoutumés à une vie active, mais errante.[26]

Bien des années plus tard Volney observa sur place les conséquences néfastes de la militarisation de la population. "Soldats dans le principe, ou contraints de le devenir par leurs guerres avec leurs voisins, ces colons ont été conduits par la nature des choses à préférer une vie tour à tour agitée et dissipée, indolente et oiseuse, comme celle des sauvages, à la vie sédentaire, active et patiente des laboureurs Anglo-Américains." [27]

Raynal donne ailleurs une description sans doute quelque peu optimiste de la population française de la Louisiane Septentrionale dont Volney devait observer, une trentaine d'années plus tard, les misérables vestiges. Raynal suppose d'ailleurs que les anciens militaires canadiens, tels les légionnaires romains sur les marches de l'Empire, avaient volontiers renoncé à vivre en hommes de proie, pour subsister de leurs travaux. Il introduit lui-même quelques correctifs à son tableau en nous montrant les Canadiens saisis par la passion de courir les bois, pour y trafiquer avec les Indiens, activité plus variée, plus lucrative et moins pénible que le défrichement et la culture.

> Ils ont formé peu-a-peu une population de deux mille trois cents quatre vingts personnes libres, et de huit cents esclaves, distribués dans dix bourgades, dont cinq sont situées sur le bord oriental du fleuve. Malheureusement, la plupart d'entre eux ont eu la passion de courir les bois, pour y acheter des pelleteries, ou d'attendre dans leurs magasins que les sauvages leur apportassent le produit de leur chasse. . . . Cette faible population [de 7 à 9,000] était dispersée sur les bords du Mississipi, dans un espace de cinq cents lieues, et soutenue par quelques mauvais forts, situés à une distance immense l'un de l'autre. Cependant elle n'était point engendrée de cette écume de l'Europe, que la France avait comme vomie dans le nouveau-monde, au temps du système Law. Tous ces misérables avaient péri, sans se reproduire. Les colons étaient des hommes forts et robustes, sortis du Canada, ou des soldats congédiés, qui avaient su préférer les travaux de l'agriculture à la fainéantise où le préjugé les laissait orgueilleusement croupir. Les uns et les autres recevaient du gouvernement un terrain convenable, et de quoi l'ensemencer, un fusil, une hache, une pioche, une vache et son veau, un coq et six poules, avec une nourriture saine et abondante, durant trois ans. Quelques officiers, quelques hommes riches avaient formé des plantations assez considérables, qui occupaient huit mille esclaves.[28]

En réalité en 1796 lorsque Volney parcourut ces régions mêmes très peu de chose demeurait de cette prospérité toute temporaire alléguée par Raynal. Les Anglo-Saxons avaient su acquérir les meilleures terres et ils s'employaient avec bonne conscience à discréditer leurs malheureux prédécesseurs dans ces lieux. Lors de son passage au Poste-Vincennes, Volney n'avait manqué de noter la réputation que les Américains donnaient aux Français de gâcher leur temps "en amourettes de *sauvagesses*, espèces de filles aussi coquettes et bien plus gaspilleuses que les blanches."[29] L'abbé Raynal avait d'ailleurs avancé une intéressante théorie pour expliquer l'attrait mutuel de nos Français-Canadiens et des "Sauvagesses." C'est, écrivait-il, que les sauvages "aiment moins les femmes que ne font les peuples policés"; "seule félicité," selon les termes mêmes du bon abbé, "qui manquait aux Américains," c'était "le bonheur d'aimer passionnément les femmes. En vain ont-elles reçu de la nature une taille avantageuse, de beaux yeux, des traits agréables, des cheveux noirs, longs et bien placés. Tous ces agréments ne sont comptés que durant le temps de leur indépendance. A peine ont-elles subi le joug de l'hymen que l'époux même qu'elles chérissent uniquement devient insensible à des charmes qu'elles prodiguaient avant le mariage."[30]

A ce régime on comprend que les "filles de sauvages" se laissaient volontiers séduire et épouser par des colons français et que ces alliances avaient créé des liens très forts entre eux et les tribus indigènes. Malheureusement l'idylle ne dura pas longtemps et la reprise de la guerre entre les Indiens et les Américains, vers 1788, plaça les colons français-canadiens dans une position très difficile entre leurs plus anciens alliés dont ils étaient devenus les fils et les frères, et les Anglo-Saxons. Mais ces derniers possédaient le savoir, les techniques et les ressources avec lesquelles il était déjà évident qu'ils ne tarderaient pas à éliminer les "sauvages" qui ne pouvaient subsister que s'ils gardaient à leur disposition leurs immenses terrains de chasse convoités par tous les gens sans terre d'Amérique et d'Europe.

Volney n'idéalisa jamais l'état de nature, ni les "sauvages" dont le mode de vie précaire et brutal lui semblait une survivance d'un état antérieur et inférieur de civilisation. Il n'a jamais cru aux "vertus" des hommes de la nature, qui lui semblaient posséder tous les défauts des civilisés avec quelques autres en plus.[31] Il est vrais que Volney, lorsqu'il a observé les Indiens d'Amérique les a vus déjà bien déchus–véritablement clochardisés–par l'influence corruptrice des Européens qui avaient déjà gravement compromis les bases mêmes de leur organisation sociale, notamment par l'intermédiaire des commerçants en fourrures, trafiquants d'armes et marchands d'alcool par surcroît.

Mais sur le plan des rapports personnels et intimes entre français et femmes indiennes il a peu à dire. Il note cependant dans ses "observations générales sur les Indiens ou sauvages de l'Amérique-Nord" publiées en appendice à son *Tableau*: "Je ne dis rien de leurs femmes, parce que leurs traits ne m'ont point paru différents. Je ne m'oppose point d'ailleurs à ce qu'il y en ait de jolies, comme le prétendent quelques voyageurs. En voyage l'appétit donne souvent du goût à des mets qui l'on trouverait insipides ailleurs."[32]

Peut-être que la chasteté professionnelle de l'abbé Raynal, plus encore que des documents avérés, lui avait dicté sa voluptueuse description des jeunes femmes indiennes. M. Wels, un Américain, enlevé par les Indiens à l'âge de treize ans et adopté par eux, confirma à Volney que "Les Anglo-Américains répugnent à mêler leur sang avec les *Sauvagesses,* tandis que pour les Canadiens c'est une friandise de libertinage." Ceux-ci, toujours selon M. Wels "sont en général de mauvais sujets, libertins, paresseux, de tempérament violent ou de peu d'intelligence. L'espèce de crédit qu'ils acquièrent chez les sauvages, flatte leur amour-propre, en même temps qu'une vie licencieuse avec les *squaws* ou *sauvagesses* séduit la passion dominante de leur fougueuse jeunesse; mais lorsqu'ils vieillissent, réduits à l'extrême misère, ils ne manquent presque jamais de se rapatrier, déplorant trop tard leur écarts."[33] On remarquera dans ce passage le vif contraste entre l'image du Canadien telle qu'elle était perçue et reflétée par des Français et celle que projetaient les Anglo-Américains.

Là où les premiers voient preuve de vitalité, d'esprit d'entreprise et d'aventure ainsi qu'absence louable de préjugés raciaux, les seconds discernent surtout les comportements d'esprits bornés, violents, salaces, cédant sans réflexion à l'attrait de la facilité et de la nouveauté pour s'en repentir après une jeunesse gâchée. Ces jugements des comportements individuels reflètent d'ailleurs des systèmes de valeur, des structures socioéconomiques et culturelles bien antérieures aux personnes qui en subissent l'influence ou les critiquent. Il semble en effet que l'Eglise catholique, dès les débuts de la colonisation, ait encouragé les unions entre Français et Indiennes à la fois par souci d'une évangélisation et d'une implantation durable de la religion dans ces territoires ainsi que dans l'intention de fixer et de moraliser une population où l'élément mâle l'emportait de très loin. A la fin du dix-huitième siècle, à l'époque où Volney parcourait l'ouest, il est certain que cette politique de l'Eglise portait ses fruits même si les "sauvages" ne s'étaient d'abord soumis aux pratiques extérieures, à l'assistance aux offices, à la récitation du chapelet qu'afin de recevoir le verre d'eau-de-vie et le pain que les Jésuites leur distribuaient sans croire à des dogmes incompréhensibles pour eux.

Sans vraiment se laisser prendre aux illusions dont Raynal se faisait l'écho, selon lesquelles "les peuples sauvages avaient toujours la prédilection la plus marquée pour la France"[34] ou à la naïve assurance de Taine que les Français avaient été "seuls capables de s'assimiler les indigènes en s'assimilant à eux, en adoptant leurs moeurs et en épousant leurs femmes."[35] Volney pensait que les mariages assez nombreux de Français avec des Indiennes avaient créé entre eux une amitié qui, même déçue et irritée par la guerre, ne laissait pas de subsister et il ne doute pas que sa qualité de Français ait diminué la méfiance et le soupçon du chef de guerre des Miâmis Petite-Tortue qui fut son principal informateur sur la situation des Indiens à cette époque et sur leurs perspectives d'avenir.

Il se montre par là moins réaliste que l'intendant Hocquart, dont nous avons déjà cité le mémoire de 1737, qui s'exprimait fort clairement sur ce point: "On ne craint point de dire que les sauvages, si on en excepte quelques-uns, n'aiment ni les Français ni les Anglais; ils savent que les uns et les autres ont besoin d'eux, et il est naturel qu'ils pensent que c'est l'intérêt seul du commerce qui nous les fait rechercher; les démarches que nous faisons incessamment pour nous les attirer ne doivent pas leur laisser de doutes là-dessus, mais comme les Anglais tiennent à leur égard la même conduite, et que même ils nous surpassent dans les caresses et les présents qu'ils leur font, il est à craindre que ces sauvages ne se détachent absolument de nous.''[36]

Même Crèvecoeur ne se faisait pas d'illusion sur le jugement que les Indiens portaient sur les blancs: "Nous avons beau les mépriser, ils nous méprisent encore bien plus souverainement," écrivait-il dans les *Lettres d'un cultivateur américain*,

> et ils ont peut-être raison: nous nous appelons des hommes vertueux, habiles, savants, etc. Hélas! quelle idée peuvent-ils avoir de nos sublimes lois, de nos Facultés supérieures? Dans presque toutes les Provinces, nous n'avons droit d'y être connus que comme des *bandits,* sans foi et sans loi. Partout on les a trompés, partout nous nous sommes montrés, en fait d'honnêteté, bien inférieurs à eux; on a voulu leur prêcher une Religion, sainte à la vérité, mais que nous démentons à chaque moment pour la plus petite cause. Ils ne voyent parmi nous que dissensions et procès, quand ils nous observent individuellement. Quand ils nous examinent nationalement, ils nous appellent des méchants et des voleurs.[37]

Il nous serait difficile, dans les limites de ce bref article d'évaluer la part de vérité objective qui entre dans les relations de Volney. Fussent-elles parfaitement fidèles à ses observations, elles n'en constituent pas moins nécessairement le reflet des témoignages qu'un homme seul peut recueillir dans un temps limité, au contact de quelques individus, sans doute bien informés, mais nullement universels, marqués par leurs préjugés et leurs préférences. Mais le discours qu'il nous tient nous paraît valoir surtout par le fait qu'il renforce et prolonge un ensemble de considérations et de jugements, toute une vision cohérente de l'Amérique et des Français d'Amérique déjà dite, déjà verbalisée et articulée—non sans quelques contradictions de détail certes—par d'autres voyageurs résistant comme lui aux comportements de la passion partisane et aux délires de l'imagination exotique qui transformaient si facilement les récits de voyages en rêveries romancées.

L'effacement progressif de la présence française en Amérique du Nord était un processus déjà en cours. Volney ne pouvait que constater cette dissolution-assimilation dans les régions qu'il avait visitées. Mais il ne semblait pas vraiment soupçonner l'extraordinaire vitalité dont la souche française au Canada ferait preuve au cours des deux siècles à venir. Impressionné par les qualités d'administration et de bonne gestion de leurs intérêts personnels des Anglo-Saxons, par leur flegme taciturne, leur judicieuse économie domestique, la docilité de leurs femmes, Volney tend à accorder trop de crédit aux jugements–qui ne sont finalement que l'expression d'impressions subjectives et partiales, souvent dictées par de très anciens préjugés–qu'ils portent sur leurs voisins français. On ne peut cependant pas manquer, en relisant aujourd'hui tous ces textes vieux de deux siècles et plus, d'être frappé par la permanence des caractéristiques nationales attribuées aux Français, en Amérique, légéreté, indiscrétion, babil, instabilité. L'existence même et les composantes des caractères nationaux ont donné lieu, et continuent à servir d'aliment, à d'interminables et indécises controverses. Volney se demandait déjà s'il ne faudrait pas analyser plus soigneusement "ce qu'on entend par *nation*; voir si chaque classe, chaque profession n'a pas un caractère moral propre, et si le caractère général politique est autre chose que celui de la classe ou des individus qui gouvernent."[38] Il n'en demeure pas moins certain qu'il existe des stéréotypes nationaux et que ceux-ci s'avèrent d'une étonnante stabilité. Ce qu'écrit Volney de la perception par les Américains d'origine anglo-saxonne des Français de l'ouest et du Canada en est un exemple particulièrement révélateur. Il y a peu de traits qu'on prêtait en 1796 aux Français d'Amérique que l'ethnologie populaire ne leur attribue encore de nos jours.

Les Français d'Amérique, à l'époque où Volney les observa dans l'ouest, n'étaient qu'un petit reste, que les vestiges d'une vaste tentative de colonisation remontant au seizième siècle. Jusqu'en 1763 la France avait pu se maintenir sur ce continent en tant de puissance colonisatrice. Sa défaite devant les Anglais, la guerre d'indépendance américaine, avaient mis un terme définitif à ses entreprises militaires et politiques sur le continent américain. Volney en était convaincu et il s'employa à le faire comprendre à ses amis politiques du Directoire parfois tentés, comme le sera plus tard Bonaparte, de chercher outremer un terrain où mettre en échec la puissance de l'Angleterre.

Les immigrants français qui avaient fait souche en Amérique, fussent-ils devenus Canadiens ou même à demi indiens, n'en restaient pas moins des Français aux yeux des colons d'autres origines nationales. Car, contrairement aux déclarations de Crèvecoeur, l'Américain d'alors n'était nullement un homme nouveau mais bel et bien un Anglais, un Hollandais ou un Allemand qui avait apporté avec lui ses préjugés nationaux et ses préventions à l'égard des Français perçus tantôt, au gré de la conjoncture comme papistes imbus d'idées féodales ou comme paresseux, athées, révolutionnaires! Volney a très bien vu

> qu'autant ce pays offre de facilités aux Anglais, aux Ecossais, aux Allemands, même aux Hollandais, par l'analogie du système civil et moral de ces peuples, autant il oppose d'obstacles aux Français par la différence du langage, des lois, des usages, des manières et même des inclinations; je le dirai avec regret: mes recherches ne m'ont pas conduit à trouver dans les Anglo-Américains ces dispositions fraternelles et bienveillantes dont nous ont flatté quelques écrivains [Crèvecoeur] j'ai cru au contraire m'apercevoir qu'ils conservent envers nous une forte teinte des préjugés nationaux de leur métropole originelle: préjugés fomentés par les guerres du Canada; faiblement altérés par notre alliance dans *l'insurrection*; très fortement ravivés dans ces derniers temps par les déclarations au Congrès, par les adresses des villes et corporations du président John Adams, à l'occasion des pillages de nos corsaires; enfin encouragés jusque dans les collèges par des prix d'amplification et de thèses diffamatoires contre les Français (Voyez la notice des prix de Princeton, en 1797 et 1798).[39]

Certes ces considérations, liées à la situation politique de l'époque et aux contrastes des moeurs, ont leur valeur. Mais Volney supposait un peu trop rapidement, qu'au stéréotype du Français tel qu'il existait dans l'esprit des Anglo-Saxons, correspondait un type réel de Français. En réalité, comme nous avons essayé de l'indiquer tout au long de ces remarques, c'est un genre bien particulier de Français, le plus souvent peu représentatif de la majorité ou même de la moyenne de la population métropolitaine, qu'on rencontrait en Amérique, même s'il n'est pas à l'origine du stéréotype. En France il aurait souvent été un inadapté, un marginal voire un délinquant. Son goût de l'aventure de la variété, du gain rapide pouvait trouver quelque satisfaction dans l'état militaire, ses prévarications et ses gaspillages, ou bien dans le trafic—souvent ni scrupuleux ni honnête—avec les "sauvages." Les réfugiés politiques, débris de l'aristocratie d'ancien régime ou d'éphémères gouvernements dictatoriaux n'ètaient guère plus recommandables en dépit de leurs prétentions à la bonne éducation et à la culture. Le peuple de France, le paysan, le laboureur n'envoyaient guère de représentants en Amérique. Il faudra plusieurs générations pour que ces douteuses origines soient oubliées et que, dans l'adversité et le malheur, se forge une nouvelle mentalité, donnant toute sa place aux vertus positives, au courage, à l'indépendance et au travail. Pour y parvenir il faudra que presque toute la population francophone d'Amérique, là où elle s'est maintenue, passe par le creuset de la condition prolétarienne qui au dix-neuvième siècle et au vingtième siècle sera celle de l'immense majorité au Canada, pour qu'émerge un nouveau type d'homme profondément lié à terre d'Amérique, à son immensité, à son climat, par deux siècles de labeur et aussi, peut-être, par le goût malicieux de quelque lointain ancêtre pour les belles sauvagesses aux yeux noirs et aux cheveux lustrés.

NOTES

1 Toutes nos références aux textes publiés par Volney lui-même sont tirées des *Oeuvres de C. F. Volney*, 2ème éd. (Paris: Parmantier et Fromont, 1826).

2 Gilbert Chinard, *Volney et l'Amérique*, Studies in Romance Literature and Language (Baltimore: The Johns Hopkins Press, 1923), p. 64.

3 Jean Gaulmier, *Un Grand Témoin de la Révolution et de l'Empire: Volney* (Paris: Hachette, 1959).
4 Roger-Pol Droit, "Entretien avec Michel Foucault: Des supplices aux cellules," *Le Monde,* 21 février 1975, p. 16, col. 3.
5 Cité par C.-A. Sainte-Beuve dans *Causeries du lundi* (Paris: Garnier Frères, s.d.), VII, 395.
6 Laréveillère-Lépeaux, *Mémoires,* II, 438.
7 Chinard, pp. 28-29.
8 Saint John de Crèvecoeur, *Lettres d'un cultivateur américain* (Paris: Cuchet, 1787), I, 22-23.
9 Ibid., p. 287.
10 Ibid., p. 290.
11 Volney, "Eclaircissements," *Oeuvres,* IV, 336.
12 Ibid., p. 336.
13 Ibid., pp. 348-49.
14 Sainte-Beuve, VII, p. 425.
15 Ibid., p. 395.
16 Volney, "Eclaircissements," *Oeuvres,* p. 345.
17 Ibid., p. 352.
18 Ibid., p. 362.
19 Ibid., pp. 367-70.
20 Ibid., p. 355.
21 Ibid., pp. 349-50.
22 Cité par Michel Brunet, Guy Frégault, et Marcel Trudel dans *Histoire du Canada par les textes* (Montréal: Fides, 1963), p. 79.
23 Hippolyte Taine, *Les Origines de la France contemporaine: Extraits présentés par Georges Pompidou* (Paris: Hachette, 1947), p. 81.
24 Guillaume-Thomas Raynal, *Histoire philosophique et politique des établissements et du commerce des Européens dans les deux Indes* (Genève: Jean-Lenard Pellet Imprimeur, 1780), VIII, 222. "Ceux que les travaux champêtres fixaient à la campagne ne donnaient, durant l'hiver, que des moments au soin de leurs troupeaux, et à quelques autres occupations indispensables. Le reste du temps était consumé dans l'inaction, au cabaret ou à courir sur la neige avec des traîneaux, comme les citoyens les plus distingués. Quand le printemps les appelait au travail indispensable des terres, ils labouraient superficiellement sans engrais, ensemençaient sans soin, et rentraient dans leur profond loisir, en attendant la saison de la maturité. Dans un pays où les habitants étaient trop glorieux ou trop indolents pour s'engager à la journée, chaque famille était réduite à faire elle-même sa récolte."
25 Ibid., Livre XVI, 223-24.
26 Ibid., pp. 244-45.

27 Volney, IV, 355.
28 Raynal, Livre XVI, 181-82.
29 Volney, IV, 353.
30 Raynal, Livre XV, 32-36.
31 Sur ce point voir Volney, IV, 413 et ss. où il critique explicitement ce qu'il perçoit comme les paradoxes de Rousseau qui ignorait tout des *faits* de la vie "sauvage."
32 Volney, IV, 388.
33 Ibid., p. 395.
34 Raynal, Livre XVI, 261.
35 Taine, p. 81.
36 Brunet, Frégault, et Trudel, p. 79.
37 Crèvecoeur, p. 345.
38 Volney, IV, 370.
39 Volney, Préface du *Tableau,* pp. xiii-xiv.

The Problematical Compromise: The Early Deism of Anthony Collins

ROBERT B. LUEHRS

No doubt English deism was, to use Peter Gay's felicitous description,[1] the last compromise with religion which reasonable men, those who fully participated in the critical spirit of the Enlightenment, were prepared to make. It was a compromise well suited to the temper of the age. Intelligent men were intrigued by John Locke's "historical plain method" of arriving at that clear knowledge which lay within human competency. They were also susceptible to a popularized Newtonianism, which pictured the universe as a vast, logically consistent machine, designed by the rational mind of God according to immutable physical laws and thus comprehensible to the rational mind of man. Sensible individuals had wearied of the social turmoil caused by excessive religious zeal and were ready for a measure of orderly toleration as well as dispassionate Latitudinarianism, a cerebral sort of Christianity which, as Locke had proposed, had reduced its tenets to a handful of readily understandable precepts.

Deism helped to shape this intellectual environment; it retained the basic humanitarian ethical standards of Christianity while purging the religion of disquieting miracles, revelation, and other supernatural trappings. Yet, although the deist compromise seemed appropriate for the last few years of the seventeenth century and the first two or three decades of the eighteenth, the inherent stability of this compromise must be questioned. It was a difficult, serious matter to be a complete advocate of the rights of reason in a civilization whose character was still determined by the requirements of faith, and the deists were the first conscious pioneers of this position. The age may have been spiritually lax or generous in its eclecticism, but it was hardly religiously indifferent.

Deism was the product of a time which took religious questions in earnest, and one should not be misled by the deist penchant for irony and satire.[2] Despite the disappearance of the Licensing Act in 1694, which opened the way to freedom of expression in even theological issues, limited only by libel laws, the deists had more to fear than being answered by country clergy trying to make names for themselves. John Toland's *Christianity Not Mysterious,* that great deist tract against revealed religion, was attacked in the Lower House of Church Convocation in 1700 as atheistic, condemned by the Grand Jury in Middlesex, and ordered burned by the hangman in Ireland.[3] The wildly eccentric Cambridge fellow Thomas Woolston so offended public taste with his discourses against Christ's miracles that he was placed under confinement, where he died unable to pay the fine and unwilling to promise the silence which would have accomplished his release. Another deist martyr was Peter Annet, who in 1761, when he was seventy, was condemned for blasphemy, pilloried twice, and compelled to serve a month in prison before being paroled. To participate in the creation of the deist school of thought took intellectual courage.[4]

The early deists commonly claimed to be Christians merely trying to return the faith to its first principles; their opponents commonly accused them of atheism. In reality, neither was the case. The deist campaign against transcendence and their mortal assaults on the very foundations of Christianity certainly precluded their membership in that community. Still, they did not want to be unbelievers either, although they often discovered relentless criticism to be an acid which tended to dissolve not only revealed religion but all religion and opened the door to agnosticism. They struggled with their own skepticism, but not always with the greatest success. Their insistence upon their own Christianity can be seen not as hypocrisy or a cynical shield or malicious humor but as a necessary self-deception, an identity required because the loss of it would open too many undesirable possibilities.

These two faces of the deist compromise can be readily discerned in the literary career of Anthony Collins, one of the more illustrious of the spokesmen for deism and thus of the eighteenth-century Enlightenment itself. His efforts to accommodate religion with reason in an honest fashion produced a problematic legacy which both Voltaire and Baron d'Holbach could later legitimately draw on directly for their different purposes.[5]

Standing as a discerning critic within Christian civilization and yet beyond it also, Collins acted as a notable catalyst for the transformation of the religious consciousness of western man. Subtly, he promoted a demystified view of the world and argued that unfettered reason alone will permit man to discover the truth. He was a major architect of the sort of antichristian scholarship appreciated by the deists, and diligently exposed the incoherent superstitions of the ancient Jews, the machinations of power-hungry priests, and the ignorance of the faithful. His demolition of the idea that Old Testament prophecies were a proof of the veracity of Christianity was so masterfully conceived that no deist ever improved on it.

It has become almost axiomatic to point out the lack of profundity in the deists,[6] but Collins was perhaps the exception. He was Locke's close friend during the last eighteen months of the latter's life, and in their epistolary discussions Locke showed keen appreciation of Collins' intellectual prowess.[7] Locke especially praised his young colleague for having an uncommon comprehension of the basic arguments of *An Essay concerning Human Understanding.*[8] Collins possessed an enormous library, one of the largest in England; the catalog of its contents drawn up for auction after his death had 5,673 entries, a number of them containing several titles.[9] He had few scientific treatises, preferring Locke's friend Robert Boyle to Newton, but a remarkable collection of works dealing with history, religion, and literature. Perhaps one-third of the total were editions of the Greek and Roman classics. His several essays in behalf of determinism and materialism were testimonies to a sophisticated mind.

Stylistically, Collins' writings were much more palatable than those of any deist except the Third Earl of Shaftesbury. He wrote without rancor or overt blasphemy, carefully measuring his words and lavishly supplementing them with documentation. He favored the citation of religious authorities, particularly when they contradicted one another, and, like Pierre Bayle, preferred to argue by indirection, suggesting conclusions rather than stating them, thereby leaving his own position ambiguous. He was adept in the use of wit and controlled ridicule against his more stodgy opponents; it was Collins who remarked of Samuel Clarke's rationalistic theology that nobody doubted the existence of God until Dr. Clarke undertook to prove it.[10]

Most deists, despite the bohemian John Toland and the chandler Thomas Chubb, were gentlemen, and despite Viscount Bolingbroke, most were Whigs. Collins was the son of a squire, was educated at Eton and Cambridge for a legal career he never pursued, and was married to a banker's daughter. He was solidly Whiggish and, after 1717, active in the local government of Essex as a justice of the peace and as Treasurer. More to the point, Collins was a life-long communicant member of the Anglican Church. To be certain, such membership was a necessity for participation in political life, but he always resented the charges of hypocrisy and cynicism and insisted on the authenticity of his Christianity in private as well as in public. Despite his published strictures against the Church, his letters displayed none of the religious estrangement visible later in David Hume's correspondence. Ardently anticlerical, he maintained good relations with certain Anglican divines as well as the Established Church.[11]

Collins personified the problematical compromise that was deism. In May 1703 Locke wrote Collins: "I consider you as a philosopher and a Christian."[12] Four years later, the appearance of Collins' first treatise, *An Essay concerning the Use of Reason in Propositions, the Evidence whereof depends on Human Testimony,* suggested Locke had erred on the second characteristic. The *Essay concerning the Use of Reason* is of significance not only as the earliest expression of Collins' thought, but as the initial definition of those fundamental ideas from which he subsequently operated and as the embryo for every religious and philosophic theme he eventually explored. It was the point of departure in particular for his three major deistic compositions, *A Discourse of Free-Thinking* (1713), *A Discourse of the Grounds and Reasons of the Christian Religion* (1724), and *The Scheme of Literal Prophecy Considered* (1726).

These later compositions were much more influential, formative powers within deism, the *Discourse of Free-Thinking* as a detailed consideration of how unfettered reason can root humbug out of religion and the two essays on prophecies as a carefully executed assault on the intelligibility of supposed Old Testament predictions of the coming of Christ. Thus all three words have quite properly been given close examination in studies of English deism. Yet this first, rather unsophisticated publication, an anonymous entry into religious dispute by a thirty-one-year-old squire, must be considered the seminal work for his views. Collins' argument subsequently did not seem to evolve so much as to elaborate upon the positions taken in the *Essay concerning the Use of Reason.* His thought displayed remarkable consistency throughout his literary career, and the maturation process was more a question of refining his original concepts than discarding them. This first work, therefore, would merit some attention, as would his second publication, *Priestcraft in Perfection* (1710), in which Collins' skepticism about both the clergy and the people was quite manifest. The rather obscure theological debate with Samuel Clarke over the question of the material nature of the soul, which fell between these two essays, as well as the more developed publications which came afterward, must be left to the side in this discussion.

The *Essay concerning the Use of Reason,* as the title suggested, derived a greater portion of its patrimony from Locke's *An Essay concerning Human Understanding.* Collins borrowed most of his definitions and basic assumptions concerning reasoning and its relationship to perception from Locke, although he went far beyond Locke in his conclusions. Collins' derogatory references to Christian mysteries and to power-hungry priests who talk unintelligibly to control men's minds[13] might well have been inspired by Toland's *Christianity Not Mysterious,* as might his insistence that nothing can be above reason or contradictory to it and still be acceptable.[14] Collins appropriated a passage from one of Pierre Bayle's works to argue against the idea that Divine reason might be of a different order from human reason.[15] He also seemed influenced by Baruch Spinoza.[16] Typically, he mentioned none of these sources by name and employed only acceptable Christian works as his illustration and foils. He cited Archbishop John Tillotson and Boyle with approval; introduced a passage from William Carroll, a critic of Locke and Toland, simply to use the passage's quotation from *An Essay concerning Human Understanding;* and quarrelled with another critic of Locke's, Bishop Edward Stillingfleet, over the latter's insistence that the external existence of God cannot be comprehended except through paradox. Collins devoted one section of his essay to exposing the illogic and formlessness of the attempt by Francis Gastrell, preacher at Lincoln's Inn and future Bishop of Chester, to explain the doctrine of the Trinity in a book aimed at Toland.[17] Confusion among theologians as to the character of the Trinity, the fundamental doctrine of Christianity, amused Collins greatly, and he devoted a particularly devastating section of his *Discourse of Free-Thinking* to listing the disagreements concerning this question.[18]

Still, it was Locke who supplied Collins with his concepts and direction. Collins opened his essay with a Lockean definition of reason as "that faculty of the Mind whereby it perceives the

Truth, Falsehood, Probability or Improbability of Propositions," and of propositions as "whatever consist of Terms or Words which stand for Ideas concerning which some agreement or disagreement is affirmed or deny'd. . . ."[19] He nowhere discussed what he meant by ideas beyond suggesting they were mental constructs corresponding to sense data, which was one of the ways Locke used the word; the ambiguity was quite common in philosophy since Descartes.[20]

The definition of reason in this essay was indistinguishable from the definition of freethinking which Collins gave in his *Discourse of Free-Thinking*: "The use of the Understanding, in endeavoring to find out the Meaning of any Proposition whatever, in considering the nature of the Evidence for or against it, and in judging of it according to the seeming Force or Weakness of the Evidence."[21] Inquiry carried on with no restraints and no limits into any field of knowledge was the absolute prerequisite for securing truth. Critics who have chided Collins for doing no more in his description of freethought than to define reason itself have missed the point.[22] To Collins they were identical. It was self-evident to him that a man could not reason clearly except by thinking freely; the opposite of free thought was superstition, ignorance, the lack of thought.[23]

The activities of the mind, according to Collins, fell into four categories: intuitive recognition of the validity of a given proposition, proof of the truth or falsehood of a proposition by logic (these two categories taken together constituted science), proof of the probability or improbability of a proposition by logic (which Collins designated as "opinion"), and acceptance of the probability or improbability of a proposition on the basis of testimony from an outside witness rather than the workings of our mental processes ("faith").[24] Collins was particularly interested in the question of how to judge the legitimacy of the last category, that of faith. Locke listed six criteria in judging the testimony of others: "1. The number. 2. The integrity. 3. The skill of the witnesses. 4. The design of the author, where it is a testimony out of a book cited. 5. The consistency of the parts, and circumstances of the revelation. 6. Contrary testimonies."[25] He also proposed that, in the last analysis, the listener would judge such testimony according to his own experiences. Collins reduced Locke's specifications to two: the credibility of the persons giving testimony and the intelligibility of what they related. Both Locke and Collins agreed that, in the last analysis, the listener must judge what he is told is true by his own experiences. We cannot be called upon to accept the veracity of that which is inconsistent within itself or with the self-evident truths of the perceived world.

Perception, then, had to be our ultimate criterion of truth. Whatever lay beyond our faculties of perception or could not be reflected in an idea we were capable of forming could not be known. Whatever contradicted perception, even if it was alleged to be a revelation from God, had to be rejected as false.[26] Collins specifically mentioned the doctrine of transubstantiation as falling into this category, thereby making manifest what Locke had only hinted at when he argued that God would never violate the principles of clear and distinct knowledge to the point of causing the same body to be in two places at the same time.[27] On the other hand, Collins argued, "let a Proposition be ever so improbable, if it amounts not to a repugnancy to another Proposition in the Historical Relation, or to one which is self-evident, or whose Ideas I perceive necessarily to agree by the intervention of an intermediate Idea, it may be perceived as a Truth from a credible Author."[28] It was improbable but still perfectly conceivable that an acorn should grow into an oak tree in an hour, for this was simply a matter of increasing the tempo of the natural growth process.[29] On the other hand, it was not credible that there might exist a nation where men lived forever.[30]

Collins stoutly denied the convenient theological assumption that besides propositions agreeable to reason and propositions contrary to reason there might exist a body of propositions above reason. Even Locke had permitted this third category, although he encountered considerable difficulty in reconciling it with his insistence that "reason must be our last judge and guide in everything."[31] Collins championed the unvarnished primacy of human reason and could find no definition for "propositions above reason" which was acceptable. The phrase "above reason" might refer simply to information secured from another person. However, Collins pointed out, we always evaluate such testimony by reason before we accept it; obviously, then, what is told us is not beyond the test of reason at all.[32] Perhaps "above reason" was a phrase applied to things only imperfectly understood. With great candor, Collins admitted that most if not all of our ideas were based on probabilities rather than certainties. Still, to the extent we did understand a thing, we judged its reasonableness. What lay beyond our understanding could not be an object of thought.[33] Likewise, there was no escape from the difficulties involved in classifying certain concepts as "above reason" when recourse was had to the argument that such concepts, being unintelligible, had to be accepted by faith alone. Collins considered this demand an impossible one. No proposition could be given assent if it involved logical absurdities, paradoxes, and contradictions.[34] At best we could note that the evidence for such a proposition was balanced by the incomprehensible elements within it and so suspend all judgment.[35]

Finally, Collins also thought it senseless to argue that what was above reason was in fact contrary to human reason but not to Divine reason. Unless God's reason was of the same order as ours, we had no understanding of what was acceptable to it and if Divine reason was equivalent to human reason, no distinctions between the two could be drawn.[36] Needless to say, this sort of approach tended to cause the evaporation of revelation as an identifiable entity. The whole concept of revelation thus ceased to have a useful purpose for Collins.

The Bible, too, had to pass the test of reason. Unfortunately its authors were more concerned with the impact of their moral message on an unsophisticated audience than they were in philosophical logic and precise use of language. Thus, for example, God was described as an invisible spirit in some sections of the Old Testament and in other sections as an entity endowed with human form and passions. The only solution must be to read the biblical texts allegorically. Here Collins laid the groundwork for his later *A Discourse of the Grounds and Reasons of the Christian Religion* and *The Scheme of Literal Prophecy Considered* in which he cast serious doubt on the value of the Old Testament prophecies for proving the truth of Christianity, since most of the prophecies were too difficult and obscure to be interpreted in any way but allegorically and allegory could twist any biblical passage to mean anything. This was certainly not the clear reasoning Collins demanded. Not only was it necessary to go beyond the literal meaning of the Scriptures to comprehend them, but the numerous spurious passages which had crept into the text over the centuries had to be weeded out. Collins specifically cited the notorious example of Moses discussing events which occurred after his death.[37] Yet, once it was admitted that the Bible was both vague and flawed and in need of editing, the book would have to be considered a most infirm foundation for religious truth.

Alongside this disturbing analysis of the Scriptures Collins' assertion that he found the resurrection of Christ a reasonable belief, a comment which he inserted briefly in a section attacking transubstantiation and for which he neglected to offer evidence, seemed an extremely weak concession to Christianity.[38] Collins gave no hint as to how he supposed the Resurrection to differ from transubstantiation in terms of credibility.

Indeed, Collins gave the figure of Jesus wide berth in most of his writings beyond scattered references to "Our Savior." Perhaps, in view of Locke's assertions that all a Christian had to believe was that Jesus was the Messiah,[39] Collins found it more comfortable to avoid examining the whole issue. Yet in his last major work, *The Scheme of Literal Prophecy Considered*, some reckoning had to be made. Here he had to admit that Jesus brought neither temporal victory to the Jews nor peace on earth for the Christians; Christian civilization had been twisted by violence, malice, hatred, fury, and madness for most of its history.[40] Had Jesus come as a man sent by God to reveal a new religion to humanity, then his miracles would have been sufficient proof of the legitimacy of his mission, assuming the miracles were consistent with reason, with one another, with God's honor, and with the good of humanity. Instead, he presented himself as the Messiah foretold in the Old Testament, making miracles a secondary consideration. Unfortunately, the Old Testament prophecies which were patently not composed after the events they were supposed to predict were either too obscure to be understood or so general as not to be prophecies at all.[41] In the end, Collins had to deny Jesus was the Messiah, although he shrank from actually stating it. Here was one concept not really presented in the *Essay concerning the Use of Reason,* but surely it was a logical extension of this pamphlet's suppositions.

Locke, in his discussion of eternity, excused himself from considering the "incomprehensibly infinite" character of God.[42] But Collins ended his seminal work not only attempting to prove Divine infinity quite comprehensible but also building Locke's concept of volition into an argument against free will. Locke treated this concept of infinite duration, which he admitted no man could clearly understand, to indicate that even this idea derived ultimately from sensation and reflection.[43] He considered volition as an adjunct to his theories on morality and argued that judgment can guide or override the will to satisfy a desire.[44] Collins, on the other hand, dealt with these two questions partly to illustrate the confusion introduced into intellectual life by the clerical "Men of Mystery" and partly to rescue reason itself from the charge that paradoxes and contradictions can flow from clearly demonstrated propositions. This he stoutly denied and, in the process, raised some troublesome religious problems.

In his discussion of eternity, Collins embodied his observations in a reply to Stillingfleet's insistence on the mystery of God's attributes. Collins defined eternity simply as "Duration, to which it is repugnant to assign a Beginning or End," and saw no need to indulge in speculations, as Stillingfleet did, over whether God was the author of His own being. Such a concept was both empty and redundant. However, with respect to Stillingfleet's question about how God could co-exist with all time periods and intervene in history without undergoing a "Succession" Himself, Collins proved ready to introduce God into history, otherwise all distinctions of past, present, and future would evaporate. For God too the future was yet to come. He did not actually exist simultaneously at the Creation, at the birth of Christ, and at the Last Judgment.[45] Needless to say, Collins' position was hardly orthodox and placed him closer to a Hegelian view of divinity than to a Christian one.

Collins' brief discussion of the idea of liberty was an attempt to bring clarity to Locke's muddled and extensive consideration of the same topic.[46] Although Locke had hesitations about determinism, Collins patently espoused it, insisting that all effects were necessary results of particular causes. Liberty, in the sense of being a power to override all reason, passion, appetite, and sensation so that choices might be made with pure arbitrariness, simply did not exist for man. Nor did chance, which was no more than ignorance of the cause of an action. Collins argued that will determined whether or not a given action was to be performed, the ultimate success of this performance being determined by the magnitude of any external impediments. The will, in its turn, was determined by considerations of the pain or pleasure likely to be the outcome of the action, and these considerations were the product of other causes.

> For suppose the Color and Flavor of a Peach makes me will it, while it appears thus agreeable, I must will it. The Peach must appear thus agreeable, while my Appetite and Organs are dispos'd as they are; and innumerable Causes have preceded to make the Peach appear in the manner it does, such as the Care of the Gardiner, *etc*. Now my Action of taking or forebearing this Peach is as certain, as is the Color and Flavor which makes it agreeable or disagreeable, or as is the Determination of my Will, according to its appearing agreeableness or disagreeableness. . . . for while I prefer or will taking the Peach to letting it alone, I cannot help acting, that Preference being the immediate, necessary, impelling Cause; tho I could as plainly, and must necessarily have left it alone, had my Mind given a different Determination. So that stop where you will in this Train of Causes you will not, nor cannot have the Idea of any Thing, but what has certain and necessary Causes, and consequently what must certainly and necessarily be.[47]

It was an ironclad statement of determinism, but the concept of an infinite number of causes, each the result of its predecessor, was uncomfortably close to the argument used by Sextus Empiricus to advance skepticism, for in the end we cannot really know the cause of anything.

Even God was limited by this system, for His will could overcome all obstacles, but presumably did not cause itself any more than God created Himself. What was implicit in this essay became explicit in Collins' 1717 *A Philosophical Inquiry concerning Human Liberty,* which spun out the implications of these few comments on free will and proved to be his most sophisticated philosophical statement. Here Collins noted that God was necessarily determined by what was best and the ultimate designs He had for the cosmos. God, then, could not do everything, only what was in harmony with His infinite wisdom and goodness.[48]

Collins closed his *Essay concerning the Use of Reason* with a freethinker's profession of principle:

> Thus I have drawn up my Thoughts on a nice Subject, in as little compass and as clear a light as I was able, without the mixture of any Art or popular Expressions to affect the Passions of the Reader, and hinder him from discerning the want of Connexion in any part of my Discourse, and shall be heartily glad if by this my *Essay* I shall provoke any one, that sees thro my Mistakes, to set me right in a matter of so great consequence as the Subject of it; or, if it be thought that I have truly and justly stated the matter, one more able to do justice to the Argument than I am, to handle it in a more extensive manner.[49]

In practice, Collins paid little attention to his critics, considering them close-minded, prejudiced, and incapable of questioning their beliefs. He insisted that he wrote for those already convinced of the value of freethinking and not to win converts.[50] His debate with Clarke was an exception. When his *Discourse of Free-Thinking* was roundly assaulted by a number of rationalistic Christians including William Whiston, George Berkeley, Bishop Benjamin Hoadly, and the eminent classical scholar Richard

Bentley, master of Trinity College, Collins was quite slow to correct in subsequent editions any of the flaws of scholarship and translation his critics found.

All in all, the *Essay concerning the Use of Reason* was a remarkably imaginative and stimulating work for a first publication. It not only set out the themes Collins could continue to work with and the viewpoint he would continue to hold, it was an excellent indication of the problematic character of Collins' entire intellectual enterprise. A brief examination of Collins' next pamphlet will bring out a further point of significance.

The anticlericalism evident in the *Essay concerning the Use of Reason* reached an early blossoming in Collins' ironically titled pamphlet of 1710, *Priestcraft in Perfection,* an attempt to prove that Article Twenty of the Anglican Thirty-Nine Articles contained a fraudulent clause never accepted by Convocation or Parliament and inserted by priestly treachery with the design of delivering the power to make doctrine into clerical hands. Such a fraud was easy to perpetrate:

> The Stupidity of Mankind, even in the times of the greatest Liberty and Freedom of Thinking, was always security enough for some Impositions. For who at this day among the Laity dare give themselves the trouble to examine into the Authority of the Articles of the Church (when meddling with such Sacred Things exposes a Man to the Imputation of Atheism) or who are able to tell what the Articles of their own Church are? The Laity are ever ready to fight the Priests Battles, and contend eagerly for what they determine in their Synods and Convocations, without ever troubling themselves to understand what it is they fight and contend for . . . . Nothing therefore can possibly hinder Frauds of this kind, but the Honesty and Integrity of the Clergy, or their fear of being discover'd: But neither of these can be thought a sufficient Security to any one who has look'd into the History of other Countries or even of his own. . . .[51]

Collins, in short, had no illusions about the intellectual capacity of the majority of the populace. The battle for reason would indeed be a difficult and lonely one, waged as much against the ignorance of the masses as against the treachery of the priests.

As far as religion went, he felt one should naturally assume that the priests had altered all the religious literature which passed through their hands and thus those writings were unsound authorities. Collins concluded his brief excursion into church history with the observation that since Councils, Church Fathers, and ecclesiastical tradition itself display only dispute and contradiction, the Protestants have found salvation through the Bible alone.[52] And yet, what justification did we have to assume that the Bible, that document which the priests have concerned themselves with more diligently than any other, had miraculously escaped corruption? On this point Collins was silent, although in his *Discourse of Free-Thinking* he did point out the immense range of knowledge necessary for understanding the Bible and propose that without freethinking, which has yet to be permitted on any scale, such knowledge could never be secured.[53] In short, Collins' arguments almost inescapably lead to the conviction that even if the Bible has survived without taint, no one has yet been in a position to comprehend its message.

At the conclusion of *Priestcraft in Perfection* Collins stated the alternative to revelation: "Let Religion (which signifys Man's duty to God) stand on those Reasons which must of course occur to everybody, without the assistance of Forgery from the Priests, and Persecution from Magistrates at their instigation . . . ."[54] Still, as Collins must have sensed from the beginning, the truths of religion were not so self-evident to the reasonable mind and did not survive well under close scrutiny. Collins' freethinking was a process which had no acceptable conclusion; it required total open-mindedness, candid willingness to change opinions as new information was secured. It promised no answers, only, ultimately, an intellectual life of ambiguity. Later in the century David Hume could accept this ambiguity with good-natured placidity; Collins, one of the first to feel this attitude, had a great deal more difficulty surviving in such a chilled atmosphere.

NOTES

1 Peter Gay, *The Enlightenment: An Interpretation,* vol. 1, *The Rise of Modern Paganism* (New York City: Vintage Books, 1968), pp. 148-49.

2 In the first decade of the eighteenth century, Parliament heatedly debated Occasional Conformity bills designed to exclude Dissenters from office. Such an act was actually passed in 1712 and was narrowly repealed six years later. The elections of 1710 were a resounding Whig defeat, partially because of the religious passions stirred up by "The Sacheverell Affair." In 1709 Henry Sacheverell, a High Church zealot, preached a Guy Fawkes Day sermon in St. Paul's attacking the Whig policy of religious toleration on the grounds that Dissenters were seditious and immoral. He also denounced the contract theory of government and argued that social tranquility could be maintained only if the people unconditionally obeyed the government. Sacheverell's warning that the Church was in danger because of maladministration by the government struck a responsive chord among the Tories and large sectors of the populace. Impeached by Commons, Sacheverell was narrowly convicted by Lords and merely forbidden to preach for three years, an insultingly light sentence. (On Sacheverell see Abbie Turner Scudi, *The Sacheverell Affair* [New York: Columbia University Press, 1939].) In 1710 William Whiston was expelled from his position as Newton's successor at Trinity College, Cambridge, for espousing Arianism. Even prominent theologians such as the rationalist Samuel Clarke and the Whiggish latitudinarian Benjamin Hoadley, Bishop of Bangor, risked censure by their colleagues for straying too far from orthodoxy.

3 Thomas Lathbury, *A History of the Convocation of the Church of England from the Earliest Period to the Year 1742* (London: J. Leslie, 1853), pp. 348-62; *An Historical Account of the Life and Writings of the late Eminently Famous Mr. John Toland . . . By one of his most intimate Friends* (London, 1722), pp. 49-75. Toland attempted to reply to the charges made against him in *Vindicius Liberius or M. Toland's Defense of himself Against the late Lower House of Convocation and Others* (London, 1702).

4 The best general survey of deism remains Leslie Stephen, *History of English Thought in the Eighteenth Century* (1876; rpt. New York: Harbinger Books, 1962), I, 62-234. Stephen's work established the categories by which deism is still usually analyzed. Other useful surveys of the deist movement are Roland N. Stromberg, *Religious Liberalism in Eighteenth Century England* (London: Oxford University Press, 1954), pp. 52-87; Frank E. Manuel, *The Eighteenth Century Confronts the Gods*

(New York: Atheneum, 1967), pp. 57-81; Norman L. Torrey, *Voltaire and the English Deists* (New Haven: Yale University Press, 1930); Franklin L. Baumer, *Religion and the Rise of Skepticism* (New York: Harbinger Books, 1960), pp. 35-77; and Peter Gay, *Deism: An Anthology* (Princeton: D. Van Nostrand Company, 1968), which contains both perceptive analysis of individual deists and excerpts from their writings. John Orr, *English Deism: Its Roots and Fruits* (Grand Rapids: William B. Eerdmans Publishing Company, 1934), is too polemical to be of much value. Orr, a professor of the Bible at Westminster College in Pennsylvania, was more interested in defending Christianity than comprehending deism.

5 James O'Higgins, S.J., *Anthony Collins: The Man and His Works* (The Hague: Martinus Nijhoff, 1970), pp. 219-21. Norman L. Torrey, *Voltaire and the English Deists* (New Haven: Yale University Press, 1930), pp. 23-58.

6 For example: Gay, *Deism*, pp. 3, 10; Stromberg, *Religious Liberalism*, pp. 52-53; Stephen, *English Thought*, I, 73; G. R. Cragg, *The Church and the Age of Reason, 1648-1789* (Middlesex: Penguin Books, 1966), pp. 161-61; Ernst Cassirer, *The Philosophy of the Enlightenment*, trans. Fritz C. A. Koelln and James P. Pettegrove (Boston: Beacon Press, 1955), p. 174.

7 For Locke's thirty-two letters to Collins during the period from May 1703 to October 1704, see *The Works of John Locke* (London: Thomas Davison, 1823), X, 261-98. Collins' twenty-nine letters to Locke are in the Bodleian Library, Oxford.

8 Locke to Collins, March 1703-4. Ibid., p. 285.

9 Thomas Ballard, *Bibliotheca Antonij Collins, Arm. Or, A Complete Catalogue of the Library of Anthony Collins, Esq.* (n.p., 1731).

10 Samuel Clarke, *Collected Works* (London, 1738), III, 883. Collins is usually identified as the author of the pamphlet *A Discourse concerning Ridicule and Irony in Writing, in a Letter to the Reverend Dr. Nathanael Marshall* (London: J. Brotherton, 1729), which was probably inspired by Shaftesbury's earlier *Essay on the Freedom of Wit and Humour.* The basic argument was that wit and humor were the only weapons to be employed against hypocrisy, ignorance, and imposture in situations where full liberty to examine the truth was not granted; they have always been appropriate devices for even serious debates, such as those dealing with religious or other controversial matters. The pamphlet also presented a plea against censorship and in favor of open-mindedness. Whether or not Collins composed this work, he would have endorsed its sentiments.

11 O'Higgins, *Anthony Collins,* pp. 19-22, 91-92, 171-74, 179, 229-30, 234.

12 Locke to Collins, May 4, 1703. *The Works of John Locke,* X, 261.

13 Anthony Collins, *An Essay concerning the Use of Reason in Propositions, The Evidence whereof depends upon Human Testimony* (London, 1707), pp. 10, 30, 36, 39, 45.

14 The sharing of common religious attitudes and a common debt to Locke drew Toland and Collins together. The two men corresponded, and Toland visited Collins at the latter's country estate several times. Collins had a full set of Toland's works in his library. Toland, in turn, mentioned Collins in the preface of his *Nazarenus* (London, 1718) and dedicated both his translation of Aesop's fables (London, 1704) and the book *Adeisidaemon* (The Hague, 1709) to Collins; see O'Higgins, *Anthony Collins,* pp. 13-15.

15 O'Higgins, *Anthony Collins,* pp. 59, 67-68.

16 Ibid., p. 55. Rosalie L. Colie, "Spinoza and the Early English Deists," *The Journal of the History of Ideas,* 20 (1959), 23-46.

17 The book was *Some Considerations concerning the Trinity* (London, 1696).

18 Anthony Collins, *A Discourse of Free-Thinking, Occasion'd by the Rise and Growth of a Sect call'd Free-Thinkers* (London, 1713), pp. 61-65.

19 Collins, *Essay concerning the Use of Reason,* pp. 3-4.

20 D. J. O'Connor, *John Locke* (London: Penguin Books, 1952), pp. 33-39.

21 Collins, *Discourse of Free-Thinking,* p. 5.

22 See, for example, Richard Bentley, *Remarks upon a Late Discourse of Freethinking in a Letter to N. N. by Phileleutherus Lipsiensis,* 6th ed. (Cambridge: Cornelius Crownfield, 1723), I, 10-11. O'Higgins, *Anthony Collins,* p. 81.

23 Collins, *Discourse of Free-Thinking,* pp. 4-6, 14-15, 27.

24 Collins, *Essay concerning the Use of Reason,* pp. 4-7.

25 John Locke, *Essay concerning Human Understanding,* IV; 15; 4-5. I have used the text of the definitive and posthumous fifth edition of 1706 as it was printed in *The Works of John Locke,* ed. J. A. St. John (1877; rpt. Freeport: Books for Library Press, 1969). For the sake of simplicity, book, chapter, and section of Locke's *Essay* will be cited rather than page numbers.

26 Collins, *Essay concerning the Use of Reason,* pp. 7-9.

27 Locke, *Essay concerning Human Understanding*, IV; 18; 5.

28 Collins, *Essay concerning the Use of Reason,* p. 11.

29 Ibid.

30 Ibid., p. 27.

31 Locke, *Essay concerning Human Understanding,* IV; 19; 14.

32 Collins, *Essay concerning the Use of Reason,* pp. 25-28.

33 Ibid., pp. 28-30.

34 Ibid., pp. 30-38.

35 Ibid., pp. 12, 42–45.
36 Ibid., pp. 38-41.
37 Ibid., pp. 17-23.
38 Ibid., p. 24.
39 John Locke, *The Reasonableness of Christianity,* ed. I. T. Ramsey (Stanford: Stanford University Press, 1958), pp. 32-33.
40 Anthony Collins, *The Scheme of Literal Prophecy Considered; In a view of the Controversy, Occasion'd by a late Book, intitled, A Discourse of the Grounds and Reasons of the Christian Religion* (London: T. J., 1726), p. 62.
41 Ibid., pp. 225-71, 310-32.
42 Locke, *Essay concerning Human Understanding,* II; 17; 1.
43 Ibid., II; 17;16-17, 22.
44 Ibid., II; 21; 71.
45 Collins, *Essay concerning the Use of Reason,* pp. 50-55.
46 The longest chapter in Locke's *Essay concerning Human Understanding* was the one entitled "Of Power" ((II; 21), which dealt mostly with the question of freedom. It was one of the least satisfactory sections in the book.
47 Collins, *Essay concerning the Use of Reason,* pp. 48-49.
48 Anthony Collins, *A Philosophical Inquiry concerning Human Liberty* (1717; rpt. Birmingham: Thomas Pearson, 1790), pp. 52-53.
49 Collins, *Essay concerning the Use of Reason,* p. 56.
50 He stated precisely this in *Discourse of Free-Thinking,* p. 4., and in *Philosophical Inquiry,* p. xx.
51 Anthony Collins, *Priestcraft in Perfection* (London: B. Bragg, 1710), pp. 23-25.
52 Ibid., pp. 46-49.
53 Collins, *Discourse of Free-Thinking,* pp. 10-12.
54 Collins, *Priestcraft in Perfection,* p. 47.

Shaftesbury and Wieland: The Question of Enthusiasm

JOHN A. McCARTHY

In 1706 a small contingent of French Cévennois, commonly called Camisars, landed in England. They were refugees from religious persecution by the French government in the districts of Cévennes and Bas-Languedoc. In London the Camisars caused great commotion by their enthusiastic effusions, pretences to prophecy, and ecstatic convulsions.[1] Their gyrating street spectacles were for many a source of amusement, for many others an inspiration, for yet others a cause for serious concern. Among their more extreme English followers was a small group of Quakers near Manchester led by James and Jane Wardley who later became known as Shakers because during their worship they were often seized by

> a mighty trembling, under which they would express the indignation of God against all sin. At other times they were affected under the power of God, with a mighty shaking; and were occasionally exercised in singing, shouting, or walking the floor, under the influence of spiritual signs, shoving each other about—or swiftly passing and repassing each other, like clouds agitated by a mighty wind.[2]

Although England had produced many religious fanatics of her own in the seventeenth century and was continuing to do so in the eighteenth century (we need only think of the Methodist type satirized as Mr. Geoffrey Wildgoose in Richard Graves' *The Spiritual Quixote* [1773] or be reminded of the popular witch Moll White),[3] the advent of the Camisars in England was the immediate catalyst for Shaftesbury's treatment of religious fanaticism in his *Letter concerning Enthusiasm* (1708) to Lord Sommers.

About seventy years later, in 1775, a doctor from Vienna gained almost instantaneous notoriety on the continent for his reputedly miraculous healing powers. Through the induction of a catatonic state and the laying-on of hands he is said to have cured the neurotic, the lame, and the possessed. His subjects were also said to be able to read sealed letters and to prophesy events. The source of these miraculous powers lay in what he called the magnetism inherent in every animate being and inanimate object. This sensational doctor was Franz Anton Mesmer (1734-1815). He was but one of the most renowned practitioners of antirational theories in the 1770s and 1780s and served to draw the critical attention of the enlightened world more sharply into focus. (In 1784 the French government appointed a commission to investigate Mesmer's activities; one of the illustrious members of this commission was Benjamin Franklin.) The Augsburg miracle-working priest Gassner, the Lindauer doctor and alchemist Oberreit, and the charlatan Martin von Schlierbach were lesser-known fantasts; Swedenborg and Cagliostro were equally famous.[4]

The furor wrought among the "Aufklärer" by Mesmer and his kind was to continue for years, as is evinced by such writings as Kant's "Träume eines Geistersehers, erläutert durch Träume der Metaphysik" (1766), Karl Philipp Moritz' *Andreas Hartknopf* (1786), Schiller's *Der Geisterseher* (1787-89), Geothe's *Der Gross-Cophta* (1791), and Wieland's *Agathodämon* (1799). In November 1775 Christoph Martin Wieland printed excerpts from a lecture by Heinrich Meister on the phenomenon of "Schwärmerei" which seemed to be so widespread; Wieland added notes and a postscript commenting that the question of enthusiasm is a difficult problem in need of much further study.[5] Wieland was probably thinking of his acquaintance Johann Caspar Lavater when he wrote this, for Lavater, a sincere truth-seeker, thought he had found the key to his belief in the divineness of man and nature in Mesmer's concept of magnetism.[6] Neither Lavater nor Mesmer were considered charlatans by Wieland.[7] Wieland pursued the matter of enthusiasm by posing the question in the January 1776 issue of the *Teutsche Merkur*: "ob durch die Bemühungen kaltblütiger Philosophen und Lucianischer Geister gegen das, was sie Enthusiasmus und Schwärmerey nennen, mehr Böses oder Gutes gestiftet und in welchen Schranken müssten sich die Anti-Platoniker und Luciane halten, um nützlich zu sein?"[8] Implicit is a differentiation between beneficial and malevolent enthusiasm with the further implication that the questioner wants a defense of enthusiasm.[9] Yet on both sides of the English Channel and in both halves of the century the generally held opinion of enthusiasm in enlightened circles was negative, being heavily weighted in favor of reason. For example, in the October 10, 1711 issue of the *Spectator* Addison warns of devotional excess which, if unchecked by reason, "may disorder the mind" and "is very apt to degenerate into enthusiasm" which "has something in it of madness." Finally, he states that "enthusiasm and superstition are the weaknesses of human reason."[10] In 1726 an antienthusiastic engraving by Hogarth appeared. It depicted men and women in a frenzied state and a thermometer for measuring the temperature of a Methodist's brain. Its scale runs the gamut from raving madness through ecstasy and lust to despair and suicide.[11] An anonymous writer in *The Gentleman's Magazine,* January 1735, declares religious enthusiasm to be "any exorbitant monstrous Appetite of the human mind, hurrying the Will in Pursuit of an object without the Concurrence, or against the Light of Reason, and Common Sense."[12] In his dictionary Dr. Johnson defines enthusiasm as a "great heat of imagination"; an enthusiast as "one of a hot, credulous imagination, one who thinks himself inspired . . . ."[13] To Hume, enthusiasm was a "compound of hope, pride, presumption, and a warm imagination, together with ignorance."[14]

The Germans in the second half of the eighteenth century echo the same intellectually biased disparagement of the enthusiast, perhaps with a little more vehemence and pathos. In the aforementioned treatment of "Schwärmerei" Heinrich Meister refers to the ever-present danger of religious excess whereby he pompously declares,

> Dank sey es der Aufklärung des achtzehnten Jahrhunderts, schwerlich haben wir mehr St. Barthelemi, Kreuzzüge, Münzerische Aufrührer zu fürchten; gleichwol scheint das Feuer unaufhörlich unter der Asche zu glimmen. Gleichwie der Saame des Todes, so scheint der Saame der Schwermerey, und zwar beyde aus demselben Grunde, wegen der Schwäche und Blödigkeit unsrer Natur, in jedem Menschen zu liegen. Nur der Entzündung eines Pulverkörngens bedarf es, und die fürchterliche Mine wird springen![15]

Common to the English and German enlighteners is the strong prejudice against all irrational behavior. Thus the most frequently cited guard against fanaticism is the "exact employment of logic and physics" (Meister, p. 49) so that we accept nothing without rational consideration: "Was die Vernunft–nicht was die Sinnen, die Leidenschaften, die Einbildungen gut heissen, das allein sollen wir für würklich gut ansehen" (Meister, p. 142). It is not surprising that reason reigns supreme over the senses, the passions, and the imagination in the Age of Enlightenment.

However, it is astonishing that the Aufklärer would go to the noncharacteristic extreme of intolerance in their condemnation of "Schwärmerei." This is what the reviewer (signed Zp.) in the *Allgemeine Deutsche Bibliothek,* vol. 30, no. 1 (1777), is guilty of when he cursorily rejects Lavater's notion of man's magnetic moral community with God. It is beneath his dignity as an enlightened individual to examine the theory closely, because it strikes him as running contrary to reason. He haughtily asserts, "An der ganzen Gaukely an sich ist jetzt wahrlich! nicht [sic] mehr zu untersuchen."[16] This he declares, although he has not conducted any kind of investigation.

Just as Dr. Johnson had defined enthusiasm with a rational bias, so too does Johann Christoph Adelung in his dictionary. "Schwärmerei" is described as the "ability to make confused [i.e., "Einbildungen"] and vague [i.e., "Empfindungen"] ideas the criterion of one's judgments and actions." Specifically, religious "Schwärmerei" is the misconstruing of presumptions ("Einbildungen") and sensations ("Empfindungen") as divine operations and truths. A further classification bases "enthusiasm" on ideas, whereas "Fanatismus" arises from the emotions.[17]

Viewed through the spectrum of reason, religious enthusiasm (we are concerned here only with the religious, not the poetic connotations of the phenomenon) represented for a great number of enlightened thinkers an unhealthy imbalance of the human psyche. Not so for Shaftesbury and Wieland; at least not *in toto.* These two men were early advocates of a tolerant, objective assessment of individual cases of "Schwärmerei." Although Anglo-American scholars have often failed to recognize the central position enthusiasm occupied in Shaftesbury's thought, German scholars such as Cassirer and Windelband have paid due attention to its centrality.[18] More recently Heinrich Küntzel has formulated the fulcral function of enthusiasm in Shaftesbury's theories as follows: "Der Enthusiasmus wird innerhalb einer Ethik und Theologie ernstgenommen, die auf den Affekten basiert: 'passions' sind 'natural affections'."[19] The importance of Wieland's enduring preoccupation with the phenomenon of "Schwärmerei" in his personal and intellectual life has long been noted. His first biographer, J. G. Gruber, pointed out the error in thinking that Helvetius' materialism had replaced Plato's enthusiasm.[20] His most respected biographer, Friedrich Sengle, describes the "Schwärmer" motif as Wieland's "Kern," his "Urerlebnis."[21] Because both men, Shaftesbury and Wieland, had this penchant themselves for enthusiasm in moral, theological, and even aesthetic matters, they were perhaps more equitable judges of the phenomenon.

It is due in great part to them that the distinction between true and false enthusiasm was introduced into the public discussions of emotional extremism. Unfortunately, many of the lesser spirits took little notice of their differentiation and continued to condemn all enthusiasm as false and dissumulating. To be sure, Wieland and Shaftesbury were neither the first nor the only thinkers to point out the difference; but they appear to be the first to give effective lead in the commendatory use of the term in the eighteenth century. Shaftesbury, for his part, drew heavily upon Henry More's *Enthusiasmus Triumphatus; or a Brief Discourse on the Nature, Causes, Kinds, and Cure of Enthusiasm* (1656), whereas Wieland followed Shaftesbury rather closely.[22]

In his *Letter concerning Enthusiasm* Shaftesbury endeavors to widen and elevate the term which generally connoted, as we have seen, religious fanaticism. He begins by citing the accepted notion that fantasts and the so-called inspired are mere charlatans, intent upon deceiving others; yet, he continues, there is "a further mystery" to its occurrence, for man has a definite propensity to exaggerate his passions.[23] This latter point proves to interest Shaftesbury much more. His essay focuses in fact upon this "further mystery," although much of his deliberation is devoted to descrying means of curing men of their religious excesses. The cure proposed, and which reverberated throughout the century, is the "test of ridicule," for—as Shaftesbury asks—"what ridicule can lie against reason? " (*Enthusiasm,* p. 10). In keeping with the optimistic rationalism of his age the Englishman asserts that "the best security against enthusiasm is good humour"; it is in true alignment with "right thoughts and worthy apprehensions of the Supreme Being" (*Enthusiasm,* p. 17). The reference to good humor as a security against enthusiasm reflects Shaftesbury's awareness of the physiological stance taken by Henry More in *Enthusiasmus Triumphatus,* where false enthusiasm is seen to originate in "that *Flatulency* which is the *Melancholy* complexion" and which "rises out of the *Hypochondriacal* humour upon some occasional heat, as *Winde* out of an *Aeolipila* applied to the fire."[24] With the exception of true enthusiasm, which he tries to isolate—with limited success (pp. 44–45)—More reduces all other enthusiasms "in Complexion, or present temper, or rather distemper, of the body arising from natural causes" (p. 47). Whereas the term "enthusiasm" signified both the true (divine) and false (physiological) types for More, melancholy always denoted the purely physiological. This is also the case for Shaftesbury. Thus Shaftesbury argues that those who are truly inspired by God will not be grave and melancholy, since God as a rational Being cannot be ill humored. Shaftesbury even contends that is is ill humor alone that "can bring a man to think seriously that the world is governed by any devilish or malicious power." For him ill humor is the sole cause of atheism (*Enthusiasm,* p. 17). God "is either not at all [good], or truly and perfectly good" (*Enthusiasm*, p. 25).

By arguing that everything about God is godlike and that melancholy is not a godlike trait whereas good humor is, Shaftesbury seeks to justify his test or ridicule proposition. The effort to suppress enthusiasm would be fatuous and vain since the propensity for enthusiasm is innate in human nature (*Enthusiasm*, pp. 12, 14, 35) and must vent itself in some fashion. Thus our aim should only be to control it. In the last third of the essay, then, the true significance of the "further mystery" of enthusiasm comes to the fore. It is here that Shaftesbury admonishes man to introspection and explicitly makes a distinction between true and false enthusiasm. With the introduction of a positive evaluation of enthusiasm, a means must be located to differentiate between the true and erroneous states. This expedient is discerned in the principle of introspection. Before we may judge the spirit of others, we must first know our own, and discover to what extent our own ideas are based on sound reason or on a real feeling of the Divine Presence (see *Enthusiasm,* pp. 37, 39). In other words, we must be aware of our own weaknesses and strengths. Shaftesbury writes:

> Methinks, my lord, it would be well for us if, before we ascended into the higher regions of divinity, we would vouchsafe to descend a little into ourselves, and bestow some poor thoughts upon plain honest morals. When we had once looked into ourselves, and distinguished well the nature of our own affections, we should probably be fitter judges of the divineness of a character, and discern better what affections were suitable or

> unsuitable to a perfect being. We might then understand how to love and praise, when we had acquired some consistent notion of what was laudable or lovely. Otherwise we might chance to do God little honour, when we intended to do him the most. For 'tis hard to imagine what honour can arise to the Deity from the praises of creatures who are unable to discern what is praiseworthy or excellent in their own kind. (*Enthusiasm,* pp. 29-30)

Introspection thus serves as a guard against the rise of false enthusiasm in one's self as well as a guide to its recognition in others. Before we can recognize the sublime in others we must learn to espy the divine in ourselves. In a sense Shaftesbury leaves off just as he begins to unravel the intricacies of the phenomenon. But then he really can't be blamed, because—as he readily acknowledges—enthusiasm is "the hardest thing in the world to know fully and distinctly" (*Enthusiasm*, p. 37). His task, however, has been accomplished; he has carefully and eruditely argued for a commendatory evaluation of a widely disparaged phenomenon and taught others to view enthusiasm in a different light.

Shaftesbury's influence in Germany in the eighteenth century was considerable.[25] In the first half of the century his impact was felt by such men as Brockes, Hagedorn, Uz, Gellert, Justus Möser, and Mendelssohn in the areas of philosophy, poetics, and *belles lettres.* In addition to the direct influence there was also the natural affinity between the philosophies of Shaftesbury and Leibniz, the most representative German philosopher of the early century. Such was the similarity that Leibniz found the substance of his *Theodizee* (1710) prefigured in *The Moralists* (1709).[26] In the second half of the century Shaftesbury's "Weltanschauung" was most completely echoed by Christoph Martin Wieland, a student of both Leibniz and Shaftesbury, whom Goethe aptly called the Englishman's "Zwillingsbruder im Geiste."[27] Wieland freely acknowledged his intellectual debt to the moral philosopher, whose cardinal influence lay in the manner the individual elements of Wieland's eclectic philosophy jelled in his mature period.[28] It was Wieland's "Verdienst" to have reemployed the dichotomy of genuine and false enthusiasm in the continuing controversy on the continent. For almost fifty years the differentiation made by Shaftesbury had—despite his otherwise broad influence—been generally neglected. Kant, for example, in his "Versuch über die Krankheiten des Kopfes" (1764) discussed only the false types of enthusiasm which he too reduced to physiological causes. He did not accept arrogance, love, melancholy, and other emotional states as the occasion of mental disorders. The real source, he felt, lay rather in the body itself, more specifically in the intestinal tract: "Ich habe nur auf die Erscheinungen [der Krankheiten des Kopfes] im Gemüte acht gehabt, ohne die Wurzel derselben ausspähen zu wollen, die eigentlich wohl im Körper liegt und zwar ihren Hauptsitz mehr in den Verdauungsteilen, als im Gehirn haben mag . . . . Ich kann mich sogar auf keinerlei Weise überreden: dass die Störung des Gemüts, wie man gemeiniglich glaubt, aus Hochmut, Liebe, aus gar zu starkem Nachsinnen und wer weiss, was für einem Missbrauch der Seelenkräfte entspringen solle."[29] Although Kant did allow for true enthusiasm (p. 267), it is not stressed at all and is thus completely overshadowed by his physiological considerations.

In his essay Kant made no reference to Shaftesbury's *Letter concerning Enthusiasm*; others did, but only to the Englishman's disparagement of the phenomenon, not to his justification of it. A typical example of this persistently one-sided view of Shaftesbury's letter is Johann August Eberhard's discussion of the terms "Enthusiasmus, Begeisterung, Schwärmerey" in his *Versuch einer allgemeinen kritisch-philosophischen Wörterbuche der sinnverwandten Wörter der hochdeutschen Mundart* (1797). Between the terms there is only a quantitative difference, no qualitative one. In Eberhard's eyes they are all equally negative values worthy of disparagement. His concluding statement reveals in proper "Kleinaufklärermanier" a purely superficial understanding of the Englishman's thinking: "Shaftesbury hat die Methode empfohlen, diese Enthusiasten durch Witz und Laune zu bessern, indem ihre erträumten Ideen von der lächerlichen Seite dargestellt, und so ihre Ungereimtheit zeigt. Wenigstens kann man auf diese Art diejenigen davor bewahren, die noch unangesteckt und nüchtern sind. Am sichersten aber wird man der Schwärmerey vor bauen, wenn man die Vernunft bearbeitet und der Gefühlssprache der Schwärmer deutliche Begriffe unterzulegen sucht."[30] Even though Eberhard specifically refers to Shaftesbury, and elsewhere to Wieland, there is no mention of the dichotomy initiated by the Englishman and expounded by the Swabian; he uses the terms "Enthusiast" and "Schwärmer" apparently interchangeably.

There is no excuse for this capricious misuse of terminology, for Wieland was concerned solely with the qualitative differentiation between "Enthusiasmus" and "Schwärmerei" in the essay of 1775, which opens with the twitting line, "Mit den Worten muss es so genau nicht genommen werden—pflegt man zu sagen, und hat sehr unrecht."[31] The fact that the boundary between the two states in the same individual often vacillates should not deter us "from observing the fundamental difference between two dissimilar states of the soul . . . and from detailing this difference as far as possible." He adds that the attempt to define the difference has been sorely lacking heretofore (XLVII, 183).

"Schwärmerei" he defines as "an excitation of the soul by objects which either do not exist in Nature or are at least not that for which the intoxicated soul takes them" (XLVII, 181). Enthusiasm, on the other hand, is the "result of the immediate perception of the beautiful, the good, the perfect, and the divine in Nature and in our own souls, Nature's mirror" (XLVII, 181-82). The close relationship to Shaftesbury's thought is readily apparent in the formulation of "bonum, pulchrum, verumque" and their expression in nature as well as in human affections. Wieland consciously chooses "enthusiasm" as the most appropriate term for the positive state because of its etymology, which designated for the ancients inspiration by a god or by divine afflatus (XLVII, 182*n*).[32] Wieland justifies his choice with the statement: "Denn das, wovon dann unsre Seele glüht, ist göttlich, ist (menschenweise zu reden) Strahl, Ausfluss, Berührung von Gott; und diese feurige Liebe zum Wahren, Schönen und Guten ist ganz eigentlich Einwirkung der Gottheit, oder (wie Plato sagt) Gott in uns" (XLVII, 182).[33] The contrast between enthusiasm and "Schwärmerei" is pursued metaphorically: "Schwärmerei ist Krankheit der Seele, eigentliches Seelenfieber; Enthusiasmus ist ihr wahres Leben!" (XLVII, 183). Both the "Schwärmer" and the enthusiast are inspired; the difference lies in the source of inspiration. The enthusiast is inspired by a god, whereas the "Schwärmer" is excited by a fetish. It is high time to cease using the terms in a derogatory manner, Wieland argues, because enthusiasm is the best and noblest temper man is capable of whereas "Schwärmerei" is not really more damnable than a high fever (XLVII, 184).

In the process of differentiation between these conditions Wieland sets them apart from other popular terms such as fanaticism and "Begeisterung." Fanaticism designates specifically religious excesses and rightly so, because the word is derived from *fanum,* which means temple. "Begeisterung" is a more generic term for it connotes inspiration by any kind of spirit ("Geist"). Enthusiasm and "Schwärmerei" are thus sub-species of "Begeisterung" (XLVII, 181, 183-84).

Despite their close similarity the reason for the essays by Shaftesbury and Wieland is different. Shaftesbury wanted to draw the attention of his countrymen to the fact that all enthusiasm was not reprehensible. In order to make his point, he had first to discuss methods of reinstating order in the confused minds of the highly excited. Of course that position made the next step to self-inspection necessary, which in turn admitted the possibility of true Divine Presence. Wieland's purpose has been made somewhat simpler. He does not feel himself constrained to argue divine inspiration; he merely presents it as a *fait accompli* and thus concentrates on expounding the essential difference between true and false inspiration.

There is no need to assume that Wieland was influenced wholly by Shaftesbury concerning the concept of enthusiasm. The evidence does not support that position. Wieland had already thoroughly studied Pythagoras, Plato, Xenophon, Horace, and others: the same sources that Shaftesbury had used. This would explain why a positive appraisal of enthusiasm is accepted *à coup sûr.* In *A Letter concerning Enthusiasm* Shaftesbury is careful about maintaining a balance of man's intellectual and intuitive faculties. Time and time again he returns to the touchstone of reason as the criterion of true inspiration (*Enthusiasm,* pp. 10, 24, 31, 39). Pope's oft-quoted couplets accurately reflect Shaftesbury's standpoint:

> Two Principles in human nature reign:
> Self-love, to urge, and Reason, to restrain . . .
> Self-love, the spring of motion, acts the soul;
> Reason's comparing balance rules the whole.[34]

However, there seems to be a subtle shift of accent in Wieland's consideration. Whereas Shaftesbury was apparently concerned primarily with social behavior founded on common sense, Wieland appears to go beyond the social to the philosophical. Wieland is interested in the repercussions of true enthusiasm for the perception of ultimate truth. Reason as the touchstone of truth is not mentioned in the determination of the true state of enthusiasm. Here Wieland speaks of the epistemological qualities of enthusiasm which can know that which is truly beautiful and good (XLVII, 182). The beautiful and good have the tendency to include the true[35] and together they comprise the Shaftesbury-Wieland concept of Truth.[36] Twice Wieland refers to the fact that life without divine inspiration is dry and insipid (XLVII, 182-83, 184). He closes his remarks with a lightly veiled criticism of the too-skeptical enlighteners who will admit only what their craniums can contain. He explains: "Ich besorge also–doch Nein! Ich will nichts besorgen. Helfe, was helfen kann! Wenn wir immer besorgen, immer daran denken wollten, dass wir in die Luft bauen, ins Wasser säen, den Fischen predigen u.s.w. so würden wir zuletzt gar nichts mehr thun;–und das taugte noch weniger! " (XLVII, 185).

From the preceding elucidations it is obvious that the negatively depicted activities of "in die Luft bauen, ins Wasser säen, den Fischen predigen" are seen from the perspective of those contemporaries who immediately reject all nonrational theories as nonsense and adhere exclusively to the light of reason. The final coda ("und das taugte noch weniger") unmistakably reveals Wieland's bias for enthusiasm by placing it higher than reason. It is almost as if Wieland perceived in the intolerance of reason a serious threat to the totality of man with his sublime yearnings; in a sense he is defending the benefits of enthusiasm as Johannes Reuchlin once defended humanism against the infringing *odium theologicum* of the scholastics. In this light Wieland's position is no longer identical with Pope's and Shaftesbury's as expressed in the couplets from *An Essay on Man.* The passion of enthusiasm is for Wieland more than a mere driving force; it is now a guiding light as well, so that man can more completely fulfill his destiny.[37] This view of Wieland's position is astonishing when one considers that in the 1770s he was widely held to be a sworn enemy of enthusiasm, which he had seemed to mock in *Don Sylvio von Rosalva* (1764), *Komische Erzählungen* (1765), and *Musarion* (1768). In fact Gruber makes such a point of the fact that Wieland was not undisposed toward enthusiasm that it sounds rather like a vindication.[38] Although most of his contemporaries denied the possibility of the dual existence of skepticism ("Lucianische Geister") and enthusiasm in the same person, Wieland was fully convinced of their reconcilability. The proof of it was Socrates "whose every endeavor until his death gave evidence of the most intense and pure enthusiasm for the true and the good."[39]

In a period characterized by a search for philosophical, historical, and psychological truth, the call is heard for the augmentation of intellectual perspicuity through intuitive insight. Taken together, Shaftesbury's *A Letter concerning Enthusiasm* and Wieland's "Enthusiasmus und Schwärmerei" can be seen as an enlightened apology against narrow enlighteners for unreason in the so-called Age of Reason. Their explanation of true enthusiasm as a state of divine afflatus and their shift of emphasis from the social context to the solipsistic prepared the way as well for the Romantic interpretation of enthusiasm as an aesthetic-religious experience.[40]

NOTES

1 Sister M. Kevin Whelan, *Enthusiasm in English Poetry of the Eighteenth Century (1700–1774)* (Washington, D.C.: The Catholic University of America, 1935), p. 159.

2 Cited by George Rosen, "Forms of Irrationality in the Eighteenth Century," *Studies in Eighteenth-Century Culture*, vol. 2, *Irrationalism in the Eighteenth Century* (Cleveland and London: Case Western University Press, 1972), p. 260.

3 Whelan, pp. 15-18. Cf. the article dealing with Moll White and witchery in the English countryside in *The Spectator,* ed. with critical and explanatory notes by George Washington Greene (Philadelphia: J. B. Lippincott, 1876), I, 315.

4 For a discussion of the German interest in various enthusiasts see Mary Lavater-Sloman, *Genie des Herzens: Die Lebensgeschichte Johann Caspar Lavaters* (Zurich: Morgartenverlag, 1939), pp. 187, 210-14, 260-65. See also J. G. Gruber, *Wielands Leben* (Leipzig: Göshen, 1828), LII, 260ff. which appears as vols. 50–53 of *Wielands Sämmtliche Werke* (Leipzig: Göschen, 1818-28).

5 B. Seuffert, *Prolegomena zu einer Wieland Ausgabe* (Berlin: Akademie der Wissenschaften, 1909), V, 52; *Der Teutsche Merkur* (1775), IV, 134, 142, 146, 151-55.

6 See Lavater-Sloman, pp. 186-87.

7 Friedrich Sengle, *Wieland* (Stuttgart: Metzler, 1949), p. 481.

8 *Teutscher Merkur* (1776), I, 83, and compare *Teutscher Merkur* (1775), IV, 83-85. Hans Wahl, *Geschichte des Teutschen Merkurs* (Berlin: Mayer & Müller, 1914), pp. 110-12, discusses the effects wrought by the posing of this question.

9 Lessing remarked in answer to the question: "Weiss man wenigstens nicht, wer sie [die Frage] aufgegeben? Ein kaltblütiger Philosoph und Lucianischer Geist? Oder ein Enthusiast und Schwärmer? Der Wendung nach zu urtheilen, wol ein Enthusiast und Schwärmer. Denn Enthusiasmus und Schwärmerei erscheinen darin als der angegriffene Theil—den man auch wol verkenne—gegen den man zu weit zu gehen in Gefahr sey" (cited by Gruber, LII, 225–26). Elsewhere in his reply, which appeared only in 1789, Lessing acknowledges the fundamental difference between enthusiasm (true) and "Schwärmerei" (false), but leaves no doubt that even true enthusiasm must be subordinated to the judgment of reason (see Gruber, LII, 198–202). Two other responses to Wieland's question are not as sober or well considered and both appeared anonymously. The one appeared in the *Teutscher Merkur,* vol. 4, no. 3 (1776), 111–36. It was later determined that the author was a disciple of Lavater, Johann Kaspar Häfeli

(1754–1812). Wieland took exception to the rhapsodic tone of Häfeli's defense of enthusiasm and refused to publish any more of its kind. The second response was published in the *Teutsches Museum*, vol. 2 (August 1776), 785–87. Although less impassioned, this essay is still less than objective and barely advances beyond a discussion of mockery and "Schwärmerei" (see Gruber, LII, 195–98). Finally, an article titled "Philosophie und Schwärmerei–Zwo Schwestern" by J. G. Herder appeared in the last issue of the *Teutscher Merkur* for 1776 (vol. 4, 138–49). Herder's position lies between the rhapsodic defenses and Lessing's critical astuteness. He recognizes the need for both enthusiasm and common sense; nevertheless his essay does not really address itself to Wieland's question. In short, Wieland was somewhat disappointed with the general results. Had Lessing's insightful reply been known to Wieland, he might not have felt as frustrated in his endeavor to shed more light on the question of enthusiasm and reason as Gruber suggests (LII, 246).

10 Addison, *Spectator*, I, 482–83.

11 Rosen, pp. 257-58.

12 Quoted by Whelan, p. 3.

13 Samuel Johnson, *Dictionary of the English Language,* 3rd American ed., ed. Joseph Hamilton (Boston: West & Blake, 1810), p. 82.

14 David Hume, "Of Superstition and Enthusiasm," *The Philosophical Works of David Hume* (Boston: Little, 1854), III, 78.

15 Heinrich Meister, *Über die Schwermerei: Eine Vorlesung*, part I, "Über die Schwermerei," part II, "Aberglaube und Schwärmerey" (Bern: bey der typographischen Gesellschaft, 1775, 1777), I, 55-56.

16 *Allgemeine Deutsche Bibliothek,* 30 (1777, no. 1), p. 346.

17 Johann Christoph Adelung, *Versuch eines vollständigen grammatisch-kritischen Wörterbuches der Hochdeutschen Mundart mit beständiger Vergleichung der übrigen Mundarten, besonders aber der oberdeutschen* (Leipzig, J. G. I. Breitkopf, 1780), part IV: "Sche–V," column 334.

18 See the introduction by Stanley Grean, pp. xviii-xix, to Anthony Ashley Cooper, Third Earl of Shaftesbury, *Characteristics* (Indianapolis: Bobbs-Merrill, 1964).

19 Heinrich Küntzel, *Essay und Aufklärung* (Munich: Fink, 1969), p. 150. Stanley Grean, *Shaftesbury's Philosophy of Religion and Ethics: A Study in Enthusiasm* (New York: Ohio University Press, 1967), makes amends for the usual failure of Anglo-American critics to recognize the importance of enthusiasm for Shaftesbury by expressly placing the concept at the core of Shaftesbury's total philosophy.

20 Gruber, L, 506–7.

21 Sengle, p. 481.

22 Wieland is also known as the German Shaftesbury. Grean, *Shaftesbury's*

Philosophy, pp. 23–24, points out Shaftesbury's intellectual debt to seventeenth-century thinkers, particularly to Henry More, but also to Meric Casaubon, Ralph Cudworth, and John Dennis.

23 Shaftesbury, *Characteristics*, I, 6-7. Hereafter cited in text as *Enthusiasm*.

24 Henry More, *Enthusiasmus Triumphatus* (London: James Flesher, 1661; rpt. Los Angeles: The Augustan Reprint Society, 1966), p. 12. Cited hereafter in text by page number.

25 See Herbert Grudzinski, *Shaftesburys Einfluss auf Chr. M. Wieland* (Stuttgart: Metzler, 1913), who traces the philosopher's impact on pre- and post-1760 German letters.

26 See Grean, *Shaftesbury's Philosophy,* p. ix.

27 Johann Wolfgang von Goethe, *Werke,* ed. im Auftrage der Grossherzogin von Sachsen (Weimar: Hermann Böhlau, 1887-1912), XXXVI, 323.

28 Grudzinski, p. 51.

29 Immanuel Kant, "Vorkritische Schriften II," in *Gesammelte Schriften,* vol. 2 (Berlin: Akademie der Wissenschaften, 1905), 270.

30 Johann August Eberhard, *Versuch einer allgemeinen deutschen Synonymik in einem kritisch-philosophischen Wörterbuche der sinnverwandten Wörter der hochdeutschen Mundart* (Halle & Leipzig: Joh. G. Ruff, 1797), part II, D-E, p. 144.

31 Gruber, XLVII, 180. Hereafter this essay will be cited in text by volume and page number.

32 See also Whelan, p. 1.

33 Cf. Eugen Fink, *Vom Wesen des Enthusiasmus* (Essen: Hans V. Chamier, 1947), p. 16, who declares that enthusiasm is possible only with regard to the good (Fink writes "das Heilige"), the beautiful, and the true, because they are rooted in the triade of the *θειου*. Grean, p. 28, sees the concept of enthusiasm as "an important link between Shaftesbury's religious, moral, and aesthetic doctrines."

34 Alexander Pope, "An Essay on Man," in *The Poetry of Pope: A Selection* (New York: Appleton-Century-Crofts, 1954), p. 58.

35 Cf. Fink, p. 16.

36 See John McCarthy, *Fantasy and Reality: An Epistemologic Approach to Wieland* (Bern: Lange, 1974), chapter 1, "Aesthetics and Epistemology," pp. 17-41.

37 Fink, pp. 10-15, discusses the philosophical implications of enthusiasm which is "nicht ein vernunftloses Gefühl, eine Tollheit und ein Wirbelsinn . . ." (p. 14). Hermann Müller-Solger, "Zu neueren Publikationen über Christoph Martin Wieland (1970-71): Ein Forschungsbericht," *Archiv für das Studium der neueren Sprachen,* 209 (1971), 111, drew attention to this important point when he wrote, "Die Frage ist, ob in Wielands Werk

die empiristisch orientierte Aufklärung dominiert oder ob nicht doch die idealisierende Grundhaltung des Dichters den zentralen Fluchtpunkt seines Werkes ausmacht, ob nur der 'gesunde Menschenverstand' oder nicht doch die 'ursprünglich enthusiastische Natur," die Goethe in Wieland erkannte, sein Denken bestimmte."

38 Gruber, LII, 224–32.

39 Ibid., 229–30.

40 See Christa Karoli, *Ideal und Krise enthusiastischen Künstlertums in der deutschen Romantik* (Bonn: H. Bouvier & Co., 1968). She defines enthusiasm as the "existentielle Grundhaltung" of the Romanticists (p. 63), indicates Shaftesbury's role in redefining the concept (pp. 32–32), and mentions certain Romantic strains in Wieland (pp. 36–37).

A Classical Setting for a Classical Poem: Philidor's Carmen Sæculare

CHARLES MICHAEL CARROLL

The celebration of the secular games in Rome derived (according to Roman historians) from an Etruscan custom of sacrificing to the gods at the beginning of a new *saeculum* or century on behalf of the coming generation. In Roman tradition the custom became associated with celebrating the anniversary of the founding of the city of Rome in 753 B.C. Among the Etruscans the saeculum comprised a period of one hundred and ten years, but even this irregular period was not strictly observed in Rome. The games were given in 249 B.C. and again in 146. Augustus ordered them to be celebrated in 17 B.C., and they were given on seven later occasions at varying intervals by succeeding emperors. After A.D. 262 the custom was abandoned.

The festival lasted three days, marked by sacrifices to the gods, principally Apollo and Diana, who were the tutelary deities of Rome and also the patrons of Augustus. Processions, plays, and athletic competitions contributed their part to the festivities. The climax of the festival was reached on the evening of the third day, when a chorus of twenty-seven young men and a like number of maidens, chosen from the Patrician families, sang the "Secular Hymn" to Apollo and Diana in the temple of Apollo built by Augustus on the Palantine hill. It was for this event of the festival that Quintus Horatius Flaccus composed his *Carmen Saeculare* in 17 B.C., at the specific request of the Emperor Augustus.

The *Carmen Saeculare* has held an exalted place in poetry from that time, as one of the major creations of Horace, who has generally been revered in the West as the greatest Latin poet next to his contemporary Virgil. But exactly what constitutes the original poem has not been so well established. The work traditionally known as the *Carmen Saeculare* has consisted only of a poem of nineteen stanzas, beginning "Phoebe silvarumque potens Diana," which forms the fourth part of Philidor's musical setting. The first three parts derive from an arrangement by Noël-Etienne Sanadon, a Jesuit who in 1728 published his French translation of Horace.[1] In that edition Sanadon remarks that he found among the works of Horace several poems which were incongruous in their settings, but which seemed to refer to the celebration of the secular games. Specifically, these were Ode XXI of Book One, the first stanza of Ode I of Book Three, and Ode VI of Book Four, which he added to the traditional *Carmen Saeculare* in the following order:

Prologus: first stanza of Ode I of Book Three ("Odi profanum vulgus et arceo")
Prima Pars: lines 1-28 of Ode VI of Book Four ("Dive, quem proles Niobea magnae")
Secunda Pars: Ode XXI of Book One ("Dianam tenerae dicite virgines")
Tertia Pars: *Carmen Saeculare* ("Phoebe silvarumque potens Diana")
Quarta Pars: lines 29-44 of Ode VI of Book Four ("Spiritum Phoebus mihi, Phoebus artem")

To distinguish his arrangement from the traditional one, Sanadon called his "reconstituted" poem the *Polymetrum Saturnium in Ludos Saeculares*, or *Saturnian Poem for the Secular Games*. When

Philip Francis published his edition of the works of Horace in Dublin and London during the 1740s,[2] he adopted Sanadon's ideas but rearranged the sequence of verses, placing Sanadon's Part Four just after the Prologue, so that the order of verses in Francis' edition becomes:

Prologus: "Odi, profanum vulgus et arceo"
Prima Pars: "Spiritum Phoebus mihi"
Secunda Pars: Dive, quem proles"
Tertia Pars: "Dianam tenerae"
Quarta Pars: *Carmen Saeculare*

While this has the curious result of taking the latter half of Ode VI of Book Four and placing it before the first half, it must be admitted that in the sense of the words and in the mood of the poems the sequence is a logical one. If we admit the validity of Sanadon's "reconstitution" of Horace's work (a point by no means agreed on by classical scholars), we must likewise admit the wisdom of Francis' arrangement. In any event, this is the sequence followed by Philidor in his musical setting.

The idea of making a musical setting of the *Carmen Saeculare* was not Philidor's, however, but came from Joseph Baretti (Giuseppe Marc'Antonio Baretti, properly), the Italian-born writer and critic, friend of Samuel Johnson, and member of the Streatham coterie. In a brochure prepared for the first performance of the work in London, Baretti explains the genesis of the musical setting:

> In an age disposed, like this, to musical entertainments; and in a nation acquainted, like the English, with learned antiquity; I see no reason why literature and pleasure should not contribute to each other, and why the Odes of Horace should not find their way from the school and college to gayer scenes.
>
> Whenever I happened to look into those Odes, I have wondered at the inattention of our Composers, who, ever since the invention of modern Musick, have been hunting every where for harmonious verses, yet never bethought themselves of Horace's, which in point of harmony, as well as other excellence, are, by universal confession, superiour to any thing of the kind produced these two thousand years.[3]

These phrases have a ring that is decidedly Johnsonian. Indeed, R. W. Chapman has suggested, in an article in *The Times Literary Supplement,* August 16, 1941, that these opening paragraphs may have been written by Johnson himself rather than by Baretti, although Johnsonian scholars today do not accept this attribution.

The odes of Horace were obviously intended to be sung, Baretti reasons; many of them, the *Carmen* especially, specifically indicate a musical rendition. He notes that it is impossible to ascertain how these poems were originally sung, or to what music, but these facts should not deter composers from giving the words a musical setting. "Why then should we scruple to give them a modern musick as we do a modern pronunciation?" But having resolved that Horace's poem deserved musical treatment, Baretti found himself with another, graver problem.

> Having once conceived that the *Carmen Saeculare* was a very fit subject for such an entertainment, I looked about for a Composer, to whom I could impart my discovery, if I may so call it, and entrust the setting of it, without any fear of having it disgraced. . . . I was resolved not to have many of those common topicks and passages which every man, used to Italian Operas, has heard over and over, and can anticipate in his own mind as soon as the first bar is out of the singer's mouth; nor would I suffer a Chapel-master to give a singer many opportunities of splitting a vowel into a thousand particles. . . . I was resolved that he should avoid those full repetitions, which, under the name of *Ritornellos,* prolong an air beyond endurance, and fatigue the attention without adding to the energy of the words. In short, I wanted a man of sense, a man of taste, a man of enthousiasm, fertile in ideas and expedients, and able to temper alternately the solemnity of church-musick with the brilliancy of the theatrical. To light upon such a man was not an easy thing, and I went long in search of him without any success.[4]

While in Paris on one occasion, Baretti heard several operas by François-André Danican Philidor, and decided he was the composer who could meet the required specifications. However, Philidor was not in Paris at the time, and it was several years later when the composer and the man of letters finally met. Philidor was receptive to Baretti's suggestion, but took the precaution of discussing it first with Denis Diderot, who approved the plan and offered suggestions. Baretti in turn discussed the plan with Charles Burney, who was noncommittal, according to Dr. Johnson, who wrote to Mrs. Thrale, "Baretti has told his musical scheme to Burney, and Burney will neither grant the question nor deny. He is of opinion that if it does not fail, it will succeed, but if it does not succeed, he conceives it must fail."[5]

Philidor wrote the music to the *Carmen Saeculare* in Paris during 1778 and brought it to London early in 1779. Three performances of the work were given at intervals of one week, the first on February 26, the next two on March 5 and 12. All took place at the Free Masons' Hall. Wilhelm Cramer was the conductor.[6] The work was successful beyond the fondest hopes of those involved. The performances were attended by the Dukes of Gloucester and Cumberland, and the most distinguished literati of the island. Dr. Burney, writing a quarter-century after the event for Rees' *Cyclopedia,* noted that "the performance was attended by all persons of learning and talents, in expectation of a revival of the music of the ancients, and by many, of its miraculous powers."[7] Whatever the audience may have expected, they were pleased with the result. Several of the numbers had to be repeated immediately, and were applauded as vociferously the second time as the first.

Baretti's reaction to the concerts is contained in a notation in his copy of Hester [Thrale] Piozzi's *Letters to and from Samuel Johnson, LL. D.*, published in 1788. Next to the letter of November 21, 1778, cited previously, Baretti has written in the margin, "The musical scheme was the *Carmen Saeculare.* That brought me £150 in three nights, and three times as much to Philidor. It would have benefited us both greatly more, if Philidor had not proved a scoundrel."[8] The significance of Baretti's concluding remark is not known. With such a decided success, additional performances might have been profitable; perhaps

Philidor vetoed them for some reason. Or perhaps they fell out over the division of the profits. Or perhaps Philidor simply insisted on a share of the credit for the work; from Baretti's preliminary remarks it would appear that he would have preferred to reserve all the honor for the project to himself alone.

News of the success of the *Carmen Saeculare* soon reached France. In July, 1779, the *Mercure de France* carried a special article giving an account of Horace's poem and its original usage in ancient Rome, an account of the collaboration of Baretti and Philidor in the composition of the musical setting, and an analysis of the setting in relation to the demands of Latin prosody. The article ended with the hope that the work might soon be heard in Paris. This hope was realized in a limited way when the work was privately performed at Philidor's home in October. But it was not until January 19, 1780, almost a year after the first performance in London, that the *Carmen Saeculare* was performed publicly in Paris, in the Salle des Cent Suisses of the Tuileries Palace.

Philidor prepared for the event in every possible way to ensure the success of his work. A brochure giving the Latin text with a French translation was printed for distribution at the concert.[9] Feeling that the work would excite the interest of classicists, and of scholars in general, Philidor scheduled the performance on Wednesday afternoon, at a time when classes at the University of Paris were not in session. When the day of the performance arrived, interest centered almost as much on the audience as on the composition. Bachaumont reports that "although this musical composition, employing thirty-five strophes of the Latin poet, was expected by everyone to be monotonous and boring, it was an honor to attend such a performance. Such an assembly, both in numbers and elegance, is rarely seen. A throng of Ribbons, red, blue, and other colors, was to be seen. The boxes were filled with the most stylish women, and for the first time, perhaps, young ladies were not excluded."[10]

The expected boredom did not materialize; during a performance which lasted nearly two hours, the audience listened with attentive interest broken only at intervals by outbursts of enthusiastic applause. Two of the numbers had to be repeated immediately. The occasion was a triumph for the composer. Baron Melchior Grimm could not find language extravagant enough to praise the composer sufficiently:

> There was given on Wednesday, January 19, in the hall of the Tuileries an extraordinary concert in which the *Poème séculaire* of Horace, set to music by Philidor, was performed before a very large and very brilliant audience. This work does honor to the infinite talents of this celebrated composer. All were astonished at the art with which he was able to perceive all the variety of vocal themes of which the poem is susceptible, without ever straying from the sublime and religious tone which is its principal characteristic.[11]

Grimm further suggests that the vivid descriptive power of the music should be realized by a performance on the stage of the Opéra in a dramatized version. There is no record that such a project was ever undertaken, however, at least in France.

Additional performances were given in the same hall on March 14 and 17. Bachaumont states that the soloists executed their roles better than at the first performance, and the success of the composition was as great as before. The account ends with a panegyric to the composer:

> We no longer have reason to envy other schools. Our French composers can contrast with their dramatic music productions not less brilliant; with their church music works still nobler and more religious. It has remained for Philidor to equal them in the oratorio, and his first work in that genre can be placed beside the admirable compositions which have immortalized Handel, Hasse, and Jommelli.[12]

Baron Grimm remained enthusiastic about the *Carmen Saeculare.* He recommended the work to Catherine II of Russia, who was planning the celebration of the twentieth anniversary of her accession to the throne (June 28, 1762). The possibility was considered of including a performance of the *Carmen Saeculare* in the festivities. (There was much talk in the eighteenth century of Moscow as the "third Rome" and doubtless Philidor's work meshed with those ideas.) In May 1780, Catherine ordered Grimm to send her a copy of the score, for which she paid Philidor the princely sum of 5,000 livres. Grimm was permitted to make the transaction public in an open letter to Philidor which was printed in the *Mercure de France* in the issue of August 25, 1780.

> The success, Sir, which the *Polymetrum Saturnium* has had in London and Paris, has inspired the Empress of Russia to want to know a composition in which difficulty vanquished is the least of its merits, though that project might seem to present insurmountable obstacles.
>
> This great Princess, on whom all distinguished talents and works of genius, of whatever kind, have direct claims, does not stop at wishing to hear your work in concert. She has written to one of the most famous scholars of Italy for a program, so that the charm of your music may be heightened by the pomp of a dramatic performance and by the exact presentation of the religious ceremonies which have inspired you.

The famous Italian scholar was the Abbé Galiani; whether his program for this part of the festivities was ever submitted is unknown. In any event, plans for the celebration of Catherine's twentieth anniversary went awry and festivities were postponed until 1787, the twenty-fifth anniversary. Having already received his gratuity of 5,000 livres, Philidor requested (through Grimm) the privilege of dedicating the score to the Empress, and this was done when the work was published in 1788.

Although there was no production of the *Carmen Saeculare* in Russia during the eighteenth century, these circumstances have given rise to several spurious accounts of such a performance. The most remarkable is found in a Latin textbook which has been used in French schools for over a century:

> Catherine II had the *Carmen Saeculare* dramatized at Saint Petersburg, with costumes and scenery, exactly accurate. A temple was built in Tsarskoye Selo Park expressly for the

Title page of the *Carmen Saeculare*. The page bears approximate copies of two famous sculptures, the Artemis of Versailles and the Apollo Belvedere. Across the top, Catherine II is flanked by the poet Horace (on the left) and the composer Philidor.

> occasion. Soloists, choristers, and instrumentalists, dressed in Roman costume, walked through the sacred wood surrounding it, carrying tripods and censers from which Asian incense and perfumes spread their aroma, strewing flowers in their path, etc. Is there not opportunity for astonishment that in the eighteenth century, among so many nations long celebrated in the arts and letters, such a spectacle should have been given on the banks of the Neva, in the country of a still barbarous race, and at a court which was only beginning to be aware of elegant and polite manners?[13]

Despite the graphic detail of this account (and the rather remarkable chauvinism with which it concludes), it seems certain that there was no such dramatized performance, or indeed performance of any kind, of the *Carmen Saeculare* in Russia during the eighteenth century.[14]

Though the negotiations with Catherine did not result in a performance in Russia, Philidor's work was repeated in Paris on numerous occasions. About two months after the first Paris performance, it was given again on March 14 and 17 to the same enthusiastic reception. Presentations of the work were given on April 3 and 4, 1781, and on December 3, 1783. The latter concert inspired a poem by a M. Duchosal, an *avocat en parlement* (i.e., an attorney admitted to plead before the Parlement of Paris), which was printed in the *Mercure de France* of December 20:

> Quelle variété sublime!
> Ici, je dois verser des pleurs;
> Là, c'est la gaîté qui m'anime
> Par ses dioesis enchanteurs.
> Ces Romains qui vouloient prétendre
> Au sceptre de tous les talens,
> N'auroient pas consenti d'attendre
> Un intervalle de cent ans,
> Si Flaccus leur eût fait entendre
> Vos accords simples et touchans.
> Moi vous chanter! quelle folie!

Car pour célébrer les Concerts
Que modula votre génie,
Il foudroit mettre dans mes vers
Autant de grâce et d'énergie
Que vous en mettez dans vos airs.[15]

The last complete performance of the *Carmen Saeculare* took place on October 4, 1784; after that date, portions of the work were given in 1786, 1787, and 1788 at the *Concert spirituel*. (Evidently the administration of the *Concert spirituel* were reluctant to devote an entire program exclusively to the work.) An additional performance was given in London on May 30, 1788, organized by Philidor himself. After that date the *Carmen Saeculare* was forgotten. The Revolution put an end to concert-giving in Paris for almost a decade, and with its resumption a new style emerged. Philidor's work was neglected throughout the nineteenth century, to be rediscovered in the twentieth. In 1911 a performance was given in St. Petersburg sponsored by the Gymnasium of St. Catherine; another followed in Warsaw in 1925. After performances in Paris in 1925 and 1937, the work was given in several European cities. It has not yet been heard in the United States, nor anywhere in the Western Hemisphere.

Philidor's work is scored for chorus, orchestra, and four soloists: soprano, mezzo-soprano, tenor, and bass. Two numbers are designated for alto voice, but it would seem that this is a semantic rather than a musical matter. In the eighteenth-century performances only four soloists are listed, and in fact three of these are male names and only one female, indicating that the mezzo (or alto) role was sung by a male alto (or *haute-contre*), a common practice in French choral music and opera at the time. The thirty-five strophes of Horace's poem are converted into twenty-five musical numbers, mostly following a musical rather than a poetic or literary logic. For example, the Prologue and Part One of the poem are exhortations by the poet and Philidor preserves the hortatory nature of the poem by assigning all five strophes to a solo tenor. But in Part Two, which should be sung by the combined choruses of youths and maidens, and in Part Three, which should be sung by the two choruses in alternation, the composer sets the text in the most effective way for a musical or dramatic effect, without regard for the specific manner of rendition which Horace seems to have intended. The musical scheme is:

Overture	
Prologue	
1.	Recitative for Tenor: "Odi profanum vulgus"
Part I	The Poet Encourages the Youths and Maidens to Sing the Songs Well
2.	Aria and Recitative for Tenor: "Spiritum Phoebus mihi"
3.	Solo Quartet with Chorus: "Deliae tutela deae"
4.	Recitative and Aria for Tenor: "Nupta iam dices"
Part II	The Two Choruses Together Praise Apollo
5.	Chorus: "Dive quem proles"
6.	Recitative for Bass: "Ceteris maior"
7.	Bass Solo with Chorus: "Ille mordaci"
8.	Aria for Soprano: "Ni tuis victus"
9.	Chorus: "Doctor argutae"
Part III	The Two Choruses Sing the Praises of Apollo and Diana
10.	Duet for Soprano and Mezzo-Soprano: "Dianam tenerae"
11.	Tenor Solo with Chorus: "Vos laetam fluviis"
12.	Solo Quartet with Chorus: "Hic bellum lacrimosum"
Part IV	Prayer for the Preservation of the Empire and the Emperor
13.	Soprano and Mezzo-Soprano Duet with Chorus: "Phoebe silvarumque potens Diana"
14.	Bass Solo with Chorus: "Alme sol"
15.	Aria for Soprano: "Rite maturos"
16.	Chorus: "Certus undenos deciens per annos"

17. Aria for Bass: "Vosque veraces"
18. Soprano and Mezzo-Soprano Duet with Chorus: "Fertilis frugum"
19. Solo Quartet with Chorus: "Condito mitis"
20. Recitative and Aria for Alto: "Roma si vestrum"
21. Bass Solo with Chorus: "Quaeque vos bobus"
22. Recitative and Aria for Tenor: "Iam mari terraque"
23. Aria for Soprano: "Augur et fulgente"
24. Trio (Alto, Tenor, and Bass) with Chorus: "Quaeque Aventinum tenet Algidumque"
25. Chorus: "Haec Jovum sentire"

Although the literary division would indicate five parts, the work divides aesthetically and musically into two sections. The prologue and first three parts, comprising sixteen strophes, requires about fifty minutes for performance, and the fourth part, comprising nineteen strophes, takes about fifty minutes also.

From almost every musical aspect Philidor's setting of Horace's poem is *sui generis.* In terms of style and sonority it owes much to the oratorios of Handel, whose works Philidor almost certainly heard during his residence in London from 1747 to 1754. But in many other respects it is unusual if not unique. The oratorio was a musical form which was only beginning to be known in France, and its province, furthermore, was religion. There was no precedent for the musical treatment of a pagan poem. Indeed, the setting to music of Latin secular poetry had been singularly neglected by composers, as Baretti notes in his pamphlet. The *Weltanschauung* of the Enlightenment could not be illustrated better than by Baron Grimm's report that this pagan poem, set by an operatic composer and performed in the palace of His Most Christian Majesty, could be accepted by the audience in the same "sublime and religious spirit which the author had intended in 17 B.C. in imperial Rome. In that context there can be no question of its contemporaneous success, but in the long run its longevity will depend on its purely musical worth; and on that basis also it is clear that Philidor produced a masterpiece. The melodic invention and the harmonic richness of the work set it apart from much of the music of its time. It exhibits an intriguing mixture of Baroque procedure (including a masterful double fugue) and Classical texture, such as may be found in the Haydn oratorios of two decades later. The many excellent choruses probably reflect the influence of Handel, but Philidor adds a refinement seldom invoked by his contemporaries, that of adding a solo voice which is sometimes accompanied by the chorus, sometimes pitted against it. In sum, the *Carmen Saeculare* can stand comparison with the best choral music of its era, a work which deserves to be known and performed in our time.

NOTES

1 *Les Poésies d'Horace, disposées suivant l'ordre chronologique, et traduites en français, avec des remarques et des dissertations critiques* (Paris, 1728).

2 Dublin, 1742; London, 1743, 1745, 1747, and many subsequent editions.

3 Joseph Baretti, *The Introduction to the* Carmen Saeculare (London, 1779), p. 3.

4 Ibid., p. 8. Baretti's ideas are expressed in words remarkably similar to those of Gluck, whose preface to the opera *Alceste* (1769) states, "I did not wish to arrest an actor in the greatest heat of dialogue in order to wait for a tiresome *ritornello,* nor to hold him up in the middle of a word on a vowel favorable to his voice, nor to make display of the agility of his fine voice in some long-drawn passage, nor to wait while the orchestra gives him time to recover his breath for a cadenza. . . . In short, I have sought to abolish all the abuses against which good sense and reason have long cried out in vain."

5 Samuel Johnson, *The Letters of Samuel Johnson,* collected and edited by R. W. Chapman (London, 1952), II, 270-71 (letter of November 21, 1778).

6 Wilhelm Cramer (1745-99) was the son of a flutist in the orchestra at Mannheim, and first played in that orchestra. He went to London in 1772 and remained there the rest of his life, enjoying a distinguished career as the leading violinist and conductor then in England. He was the father of Jean-Baptiste Cramer (1771-1856), the pianist and composer.

7 Charles Burney, "André Philidor," *The Cyclopedia, or Universal Dictionary of Arts, Sciences, and Literature; by* Abraham Rees, with the Assistance of Eminent Professional Gentlemen (London, 1819).

8 James Boswell, *The Life of Samuel Johnson, LL. D.*, ed. G. Birkbeck Hill, rev. L. F. Powell (Oxford, 1934-50), III, 373*n*.

9 *Poëme séculaire d'Horace, mis en musique par A.-D. Philidor, avec la traduction françoise du P. Sanadon, qui doit être exécuté dans la salle des Thuilleries le mercredi 19 janvier 1780* (Paris, 1780). A similar brochure, with an English translation by Baretti, had been prepared for the London performances, but evidently was not printed in time. Boswell notes that it was still in manuscript on March 15, 1779 (Boswell, *Johnson*, III, 373*n*).

10 Louis Petit de Bachaumont et al., *Mémoires secrets pour servir à l'histoire de la république des lettres en France . . .* (London, 1777–89), XV, 28 (entry for January 23, 1780). The red ribbon (cordon rouge) was the badge of the Order of Saint Louis, the blue ribbon (cordon bleu) that of the Order of the Holy Ghost.

11 Frédéric Melchior, Baron Grimm, *Correspondance littéraire, philosophique, et critique de Grimm et de Diderot depuis 1753 jusqu'en 1790* (Paris, 1829), X, 259 (entry for February, 1780).

12 Bachaumont, *Mémoires secrets*, XV, 103 (entry for March 22, 1780).

13 Edouard Sommer and August Desportes, *Les Auteurs latins expliqués d'après une méthode nouvelle par deux traductions françaises* (1847; Paris, 1923), II, 310-11.)

14 See Robert Aloys Mooser, *Annales de la musique et des musiciens en Russie au XVIIIe siècle* (Geneva, 1948-51), II, 289; and Etienne [Stefan] Cybulski, "Le Carmen Saeculare d'Horace mis en musique par Philidor," *Munera Philologica Ludovico Cwiklinski* (Poznan, 1936), p. 184. Mooser was a Swiss-Russian who was a student of Balakirev and Rimsky-Korsakov in St. Petersburg, and from 1897 to 1909 was organist of the French Calvinist Church in St. Petersburg and music critic of the French-language *Journal de St.-Pétersbourg*. Cybulski, a native of Poland, was director of the Gymnasium of St. Catherine in St. Petersburg during the first decade of the twentieth century.

15 Translation: "What sublime variety! Now I want to cry, later I am moved to mirth by his enchanting quarter-tones. Those Romans, who claimed mastery of all skills, would never have agreed to wait another hundred years if Horace had let them hear your simple and touching harmonies. But for me to sing about you would be foolish. In order to praise the concerts which your genius fills with music I would need to put into my verses as much grace and energy as you put into your airs." Precisely what Duchosal may have intended by his obvious solecism "quarter-tones" is obscure.

Politics from the Outside: Mary Wollstonecraft's First Vindication

MITZI MYERS

With the publication of *Reflections on the Revolution in France* on 1 November 1790, Burke became England's leading spokesman for aristocratic conservatism, a figure epitomizing the establishment, orthodoxy, and authority whom scores of opponents rushed to confront. The pamphlet war between Burke's antagonists and supporters resembles a second battle between the ancients and the moderns; it raged two and a half years during which time some seventy works were published by the two sides. That a woman seems to have been the first to attack Burke's passionate defense of the status quo is unusual in the arena of eighteenth-century political controversy.[1] At this time, Mary Wollstonecraft was an obscure hack writer of thirty-one, but upon the appearance of *A Vindication of the Rights of Men* in the same month as the *Reflections,* she made her mark at once as a polemic writer. The book achieved, as Godwin notes, "extraordinary notice": the anonymous first edition apparently sold out immediately, and on 14 December a second edition was published with the author's name on the title page.[2]

Discussions of Wollstonecraft's eventful life far outnumber

those of her work, and most criticism of her writing centers on her most famous book, *A Vindication of the Rights of Woman* (1792). The first *Vindication* has received comparatively little recent attention despite its early success. Yet it is a seminal work for students of Wollstonecraft's later thought: *VRM* gave her confidence in her ability to articulate her ideas, established her stature as a commentator on morals, politics, and society, and laid the groundwork for the theories developed in subsequent works. Moreover, this earlier work merits consideration in its own right as a searching and sometimes compelling criticism of the *Reflections.*

From Godwin on, Wollstonecraft's critics and biographers have given the first *Vindication* a mixed press. On the one hand, the work has been highly praised for its uncompromising social criticism and its passionate humanitarian protest. G. S. Veitch, for example, calls *VRM* in some ways the best of the replies to Burke and the only one "adequate on the emotional side."[3] On the other hand, Wollstonecraft has been frequently censured for the vehemence of her attack on Burke and the seeming lack of organization and connection in her arguments. Some critics have rebuked her for relying too heavily on the appeal to reason as a corrective to Burke's theories while others have reproved her for overemotionalism. In addition, she has been faulted for sidestepping political science and constitutional theory: R. R. Fennessy remarks that she "accomplished the unlikely feat of writing an answer to Burke without treating at all either of the French revolution or of the English revolution of 1688" (p. 203). These criticisms must be examined and the grounds for praise elucidated before Wollstonecraft's achievement can be measured.

Neither Wollstonecraft's merits and defects nor her general mode of operation in the first *Vindication* can be understood fully without taking into account the position from which she writes. Since she is both a woman and a radical intellectual, she is doubly outside of and in protest against traditional social structures. This position she characterizes as being "the first of a new genus."[4] Wollstonecraft's coign of vantage is well described by Virginia Woolf: "If one is a woman one is often surprised by a sudden splitting off of consciousness, say in walking down Whitehall, when from being the natural inheritor of that civilisation, she becomes, on the contrary, outside of it, alien and critical."[5] The facts of Wollstonecraft's life and nature have their share in her approach: the unhappy, peripatetic childhood under the aegis of an improvident and authoritarian father, the long struggle to escape poverty, educate herself, and achieve a desperately desired intellectual and economic independence, and the deeply compassionate nature in which pity, as she herself remarks, was a prevailing passion.[6] As Eleanor Nicholes has noted, "to a remarkable degree hers was a mind shaped by personal experience, by contact with actual individuals, by involvement in events. . . . Her mode, her style, is intensely personal. There was the belief, upon which her practice was founded, that truth was to be discovered, or validated, by searching into one's own experiences and thoughts upon the meaning of those experiences. In this she anticipated much of the attitude and tone of the Romantic period."[7] Having developed her moral and intellectual values through prolonged individual effort, Wollstonecraft is always intransigent in her refusal to alter her personal vision in deference to any external authority.

Yet Wollstonecraft does not write blindly out of merely personal grievances, but rather out of identification with and commiseration for all those outsiders whom the established order oppresses. She typically moves from an awareness of the difficulties involved in her own exclusion from the power structure to a broader understanding of the powerlessness of all outsiders. For example, in the second *Vindication* she says:

> I may excite laughter by dropping a hint which I mean to pursue some future time, for I really think that women ought to have representatives, instead of being arbitrarily governed without having any direct share allowed them in the deliberations of government.
>
> But, as the whole system of representation is now in this country only a convenient handle for despotism, they need not complain, for they are as well represented as a numerous class of hard-

> working mechanics, who pay for the support of royalty when they can scarcely stop their children's mouths with bread. (*VRW*, p. 220)

Her social and moral criticism is based upon her recognition that such underprivileged groups as women and the lower classes can exist inside the structure of society only by obedience to authority and acceptance of their places as defined by current codes governing manners, rank, and wealth. Wollstonecraft's position outside the customary patterns of social existence often gives her a peculiar moral honesty and clarity of perception. Her sense of cultural distance allows her to view those received opinions about the social hierarchy for which Burke is the apologist *par excellence* without the comforting myths and "enchanting illusions" (*VRM*, p. 140) which sustained the conservatives and even many of the liberals. Like Paine, though for different reasons, Wollstonecraft stands out from the rank and file of the moderate reformers who answered Burke by virtue of the radicalism of her attack. Indeed, as in her denunciation of property, she sometimes outdoes Paine himself in drafting a ringing indictment against the extant social structure.

The form, tone, method of attack, and the nature and structure of the argument in *VRM* all partake of the strengths and weaknesses of Wollstonecraft's intensely personal mode. Formally, the *Vindication* is a letter: the reasons for this decision are not far to seek. Burke of course uses the letter format in the *Reflections*, no doubt for some of the same reasons which make it attractive to Wollstonecraft.[8] The looseness of the epistle allows her the freedom and ease of movement necessary to follow her antagonist's arguments, to touch on and interweave topics as she pleases, and to enlarge on important points of her own. Because Wollstonecraft wrote at great speed and glowing with indignation, as she tells us in the Advertisement, the letter is a natural choice to convey the spontaneity and vigor of her "effusions of the moment" (*VRM*, p. iii). Moreover, it is an appropriate technique for this initial stage of the controversy at which a stinging and even "hasty" (*VRM,* p. 153) rebuttal might be a more effective response than cold analysis.

Wollstonecraft's letter is addressed expressly to Burke, and, like many of Burke's critics, she often speaks directly to her opponent, usually as "Sir" or "you." Indeed, Burke almost invites a personal reply by emphasizing in his first paragraph that his own reputation must answer for his errors. The juxtaposition of that former reputation as a defender of liberty with Burke's current conservative manifesto puzzled his adversaries and led many of them, including Wollstonecraft, into occasional pointed abuse and *ad hominem* argument.[9] For example, Wollstonecraft frequently castigates Burke as the "slave of impulse" for allowing false sensibility to triumph over his reason, suggests his hatred of innovation would have led him to demand the crucifixion of a mere carpenter's son, and insinuates that he may have sold out his principles for a pension (*VRM,* pp. 56, 20-22). Burke's prestige was such that efforts to discredit him personally seemed valid and logical to many of his opponents. In Wollstonecraft's case, an aggressive tone may also have been a personal psychological strategy necessary for reducing a politician of such high stature to a size possible to confront. That occasional bitter irreverence of the female outsider toward politics and politicians led Godwin to charge *VRM* with "a too contemptuous and intemperate treatment of the great man against whom its attack is directed."[10]

But it is precisely this public great man, not the virtuous if sometimes weak private citizen, against whom Wollstonecraft must direct her "contempt, and even indignation": she maintains that she "war[s] not with an individual" but seeks to "separate the public from the private character" (*VRM,* pp. 2-3).[11] Burke's self-appointed role as the voice of the English people and his continual assumption of the magisterial "we" make it incumbent on his opponents to accept his arrogation of authority for purposes of refutation. Burke in his public role as the voice of English orthodoxy is thus the sounding board against which Wollstonecraft develops her criticism of what she sees as a moribund social and ethical system. Just as the mild and benevolent Dr. Richard Price, Wollstonecraft's friend and mentor, becomes in the *Reflections* a living symbol of the forces of social disintegration which Burke fights so fiercely to suppress, so Burke himself in his public aspect becomes for Wollstonecraft a unifying image emblematic of repressive authority in all its manifold forms. Burke is the "champion of property, the adorer of the golden image which power has set up" (*VRM*, p. 20). His respect for rank has obliterated the common feelings of humanity so that he expresses only contempt for the poor (*VRM*, pp. 32, 42). He is obsessed with a "servile reverence for antiquity" and demands an "implicit submission to authority" which would cut off all "capacity of improvement" (*VRM,* p. 23). Burke substitutes prejudice and prescription for reason. Moreover, he celebrates a meretricious code of manners based on a false ideal of sensibility and depraved notions of beauty. This merely aesthetic code of aristocratic manners is divorced from true morality and vitiates the social structure for which, according to Burke's theory, it is supposed to provide the foundation. In short, for Wollstonecraft, Burke represents the stifling of all human aspiration under "the iron hand of destiny, in the shape of deeply rooted authority" (*VRM,* p. 38).

In strong contrast with Burke's horrific presentation of the minister in the *Reflections,* Price in the *Vindication* stands for an expansive vision of human possibility.[12] Wollstonecraft no doubt felt some personal hostility against Burke for his virulent assault on her revered friend, but her spirited vindication of Price rises above the merely personal to establish him as her preeminent exemplar of those human attributes she values most highly. Wollstonecraft's defense of Price links him with reason, liberty, free discussion, mental superiority, the improving exercise of the mind, moral excellence, active benevolence, orientation toward the present and future, and the rejection of power and riches (*VRM,* pp. 32-39). Wollstonecraft's association with Price and the Dissenting community at Newington Green (1783-86) provided her with the philosophical rationale to buttress her personal belief that moral and intellectual truth was to be validated through the testing of one's own experience. The truths thus confirmed become for her the groundwork of her lifelong devotion to "the progress of knowledge and virtue" (*VRW,* Dedication). Wollstonecraft, like Price, sees a correlation between liberty and morality based on humanity's inherent right to freedom of inquiry.[13] Her confidence in human nature derives from man's unique possession of improvable faculties (*VRM,* pp. 22, 126). Hence the underlying concern of her work is always to elucidate the optimum conditions under which the greatest possible realization of all human potential, including that of society's outsiders like women and the poor, and even that of the idle rich, can take place. Like Price, who sees the revolutionary period as a great opportunity for "a general amendment beginning in human affairs," Wollstonecraft continually stresses the "glorious *chance* that is now given to human nature of attaining more virtue and happiness than has hitherto blessed our globe" (*VRM,* pp. 119-20).[14] This expansive vision of human self-realization is threatened by Burke's vatic denunciation of the revolution as a reversal of traditional values, as the crisis of European civilization (*Ref.,* p. 92). Price and Burke thus represent for Wollstonecraft two conflicting sets of values, and around these opposing poles she organizes the first *Vindication.*

The lack of organization imputed to Wollstonecraft's essay by some critics is greatly overestimated. Like Burke himself, Wollstonecraft is not writing a logical academic exposition of her theories, but questioning the assumptions of an adversary. Since her principles evolve as she follows Burke through the "devious tracks" (*VRM,* p. iv) of his disputation, her central argument may appear at first glance more discursive than it actually is. Wollstonecraft is virtually alone among those who answered Burke in eschewing a narrowly political approach for a wide-ranging critique of the foundation of the *Reflections* (*VRM,* pp. 7, 124). Wollstonecraft would agree with Burke that "the most important of all revolutions" is "a revolution in sentiments, manners, and moral opinions" (*Ref.,* p. 175). Her dissection of society must thus probe to the underlying premises upon which the whole social structure with all its interlocking codes is erected. Burke's role as the public enunciator of the meaning and function of these interlocking codes is most brilliantly and concisely demonstrated in the section of the *Reflections* which includes the famous apostrophe to Marie Antoinette. This passage has been rightly termed central to the work as a whole and an embodiment of Burke's political thought. [15]

> Never, never more, shall we behold that generous loyalty to rank and sex, that proud submission, that dignified obedience, that subordination of the heart, which kept alive, even in servitude itself, the spirit of an exalted freedom. . . .
>
> This mixed system of opinion and sentiment had its origin in the antient chivalry. . . . It is this which has given its character to modern Europe. . . . All the pleasing illusions, which made power gentle, and obedience liberal, which harmonized the different shades of life, and which, by a bland assimilation, incorporated into politics the sentiments which beautify and soften private society are to be dissolved by this new conquering empire of light and reason. . . . There ought to be a system of manners in every nation which a well-formed mind would be disposed to relish. To make us love our country, our country ought to be lovely. (*Ref.*, pp. 170-72)

This passage articulating Burke's fundamental assumptions reveals why Wollstonecraft's censure of the *Reflections* falls into two broad interconnected categories: the socioeconomic and the moral-aesthetic.

Burke and Wollstonecraft share an awareness of the alliance between manners and morals, and both perceive that the existing patriarchal, hierarchical system of society depends upon the maintenance of certain codes of feeling and conduct. But for Wollstonecraft, Burke's lengthy paean to the age of chivalry and ancient manners as the foundation of European civilization substitutes a factitious aesthetic vision of a beautifully ordered social structure for the existing society, which is in actuality exclusive, static, and repressive. Wollstonecraft admonishes Burke throughout the *Vindication* that "your politics and moral, when simplified, would undermine religion and virtue to set up a spurious sensual beauty, that has long debauched your imagination, under the specious form of natural feelings" (*VRM,* p. 121). This key quotation is reiterated in varied forms, for Wollstonecraft's effort is concentrated on stripping off the gorgeous drapery of tyrannic principles (*VRM,* p. 88) and exposing Burke's confusion of the aesthetically appealing and the truly moral. As she remarks in the second *Vindication,* "manners and morals are so nearly allied that they have often been confounded; but though the former should only be the natural reflection of the latter, yet, when various causes have produced factitious and corrupt manners . . . morality becomes an empty name" (*VRW,* Dedication).

Those critics who categorize Wollstonecraft's strictures on the *Reflections* either as a rationalist critique of Burke as an imaginative writer whose feelings are not controlled by reason and who is out of place writing political theory, or else as an economic condemnation of Burke for being the spokesman of the rich and propertied against the poor, miss the fundamental interconnection between her two main lines of attack.[16] Her socioeconomic and moral-aesthetic arguments against the manifold prevailing codes of authority in English society are closely correlated: each of the two broad areas of attack necessarily implies the other. Wollstonecraft structures her essay to bring out the interlocking nature of her two-part indictment against society. Sometimes she interweaves both lines of attack contrapuntally in a single section; at other times she alternates her socioeconomic examination with moral-aesthetic criticism. But whatever the mode of argumentative counterpoint she employs, she continually emphasizes the connection between corrupt manners based on false sensibility and a rigid social order which stifles the full moral and intellectual development of a majority of its members.

Wollstonecraft's whole intertwined argument evolves out of the implications she attaches to that key phrase, the rights of men. She does not convert the words into a code term signifying a radical republican alternative to Burke's conservative pronunciamento, as Paine does in *The Rights of Man* (I, 1791; II, 1792). Her usage is not specifically political, but broadly humane. She begins by linking "the *rights of men* and the liberty of reason" and quickly equates the rights of men with the rights of humanity (*VRM,* p. 2).[17] Her definition of these rights is simple and general: "The birthright of man . . . is such a degree of liberty, civil and religious, as is compatible with the liberty of every other individual with whom he is united in a social compact" (*VRM*, pp. 7-8). Wollstonecraft employs such terms as the rights of humanity, liberty, justice, truth, reason, and natural feeling throughout the *Vindication* as basic principles on which to erect what is essentially a humanitarian plea for the fullest possible moral and intellectual development of every individual. Since it is man's power of exercising his understanding which raises him above the brutes, whatever limits any person in the exercise of his god-given faculties and restricts his capacity for improvement works to the detriment of society as a whole (*VRM,* pp. 77, 37-38, 71). It is thus incumbent on the social order to provide the appropriate conditions in which those who are presently excluded from complete human development will be able to contribute fully to the "slow progress of civilization" (*VRM*, p. 75). Yet society continues in a state of "frozen inactivity" because of that entrenched authority of which Burke is Wollstonecraft's emblem; his principle of prescription serves as an "immortal boundary" against all beneficial social innovation. Burke's feelings for "venerable vestiges of ancient days" constitute "gothic notions of beauty—the ivy is beautiful, but, when it insidiously destroys the trunk from which it receives support, who would not grub it up?" (*VRM,* pp. 10-11). Wollstonecraft vigorously and consistently attacks the reigning codes of feeling and property derived from the past and shows how they interact to limit the rights of humanity.

Wollstonecraft's opening pages reveal the dual nature and interwoven texture of her polemic and exemplify the method which she follows throughout the *Vindication.* For instance, she begins with a depiction of Burke as the spokesman for the ostentatiously displayed ornamental feelings of the fashionable world and points out how artificial feelings and manners set up a barrier against the genuine natural feelings which would lead to social improvement: "Sensibility is the *manie* of the day, and compassion the virtue which is to cover a multitude of vices, whilst justice is left to mourn in sullen silence" (*VRM,* p. 5; cf. p. 133). Like the code of sensibility, "the demon of property has ever been at hand to encroach on the sacred rights of men, and to fence round with awful pomp laws that war with justice" (*VRM,* p. 8). The rights of humanity to justice, freedom, and self-development are severely restricted for those who do not belong to the propertied classes. The poor are not only cut off from self-realization and condescended to by the rich, but even the limited liberty and property they do possess is insecurely held. Legal codes derived from the feudal past are biased toward the property of the rich, but the poor are victimized by enclosures, impressment, game laws, and severe punishments for trivial offenses: "Security of property! Behold, in a few words, the definition of English liberty" (*VRM,* p. 24).

Such legal and ethical codes work to the detriment of the upper classes as well:

> The strong gained riches, the few have sacrificed the many to their vices; and, to be able to pamper their appetites, and supinely exist without exercising mind or body, they have ceased to be men. . . . Their minds, in fact, instead of being cultivated have been so warped by education, that it may require some ages to bring them back to nature, and enable them to see their true interest. . . . The civilization which has taken place in Europe has been very partial, and, like every custom that an arbitrary point of honour has established, refines the manners at the expence of morals, by making sentiments and opinions current in conversation that have no root in the heart, or weight in the cooler resolves of the mind.—And what has stopped its progress?—hereditary property—hereditary honours. The man has been changed into an artificial monster by the station in which he was born, and the consequent homage that benumbed his faculties. (*VRM,* pp. 10-12)

Wollstonecraft stresses the plight of those outside the social power structure, but she is also concerned with the poverty of mind and spirit of those whom society favors. The rich and the poor have one common nature, and both the "great and small vulgar, claim our pity; they have almost insuperable obstacles to surmount in their progress towards true dignity of character," as Wollstonecraft points out later in the essay (*VRM,* pp. 85, 68). The rich, restrained by their codes and station from the full development of their faculties, can only regard the "*inelegant* distress" of the poor with patronizing charity, the product of self-indulgent sensibility: "A *gentleman* of lively imagination must borrow some drapery from fancy before he can love or pity a *man*" (*VRM*, pp. 12, 26). And Wollstonecraft addresses Burke directly as the self-proclaimed spokesman for the "age of chivalry" and "manly sentiment" (*Ref.*, p. 170):

> Misery, to reach your heart, I perceive, must have its cap and bells; your tears are reserved . . . for the declamation of the theatre, or for the downfall of queens, whose rank alters the nature of folly, and throws a graceful veil over vices that degrade humanity; whilst the distress of many industrious mothers, whose helpmates have been torn from them [by the press gang], and the hungry cry of helpless babes, were vulgar sorrows that could not move your commiseration, though they might extort an alms. (*VRM*, p. 27)

This opening section of the *Vindication* is an epitome of Wollstonecraft's mode of integrating her socioeconomic and moral-aesthetic indictments of a society based on the values of the feudal past. Moreover, it indicates clearly how Burke becomes for Wollstonecraft an emblematic figure who is both the spokesman for and embodiment of those ancient values which inhibit individual and social development.

In her effort to "distinguish depravity of morals under the specious mask of refined manners" (*VRM,* p. 91), Wollstonecraft sets up a number of oppositions which range those qualities she associates with Price against those which Burke represents. Many of these oppositions necessarily derive from those which Burke establishes as central in the *Reflections.* For example, Burke's contempt for man's naked private reason and his consequent emphasis on sensibility, inbred sentiments, general prejudices, honor, inheritance, and tradition naturally stir Wollstonecraft to juxtapose reason and the passions, the understanding and imagination or fancy, personal validation and prescription, and innovation and tradition. Wollstonecraft approaches these topics from varied angles, but the gist of her argument is always her insistence that real wisdom must be the fruit of one's own laborious exertions (*VRM,* p. 104). Inherited codes, however noble, are not guarantors of individual worth: "talents, knowledge, and virtue, must be a part of the man, and cannot be put, as robes of state often are, on a servant or a block, to render a pageant more magnificent" (*VRM,* p. 106). The only valuable inheritance our forefathers could bequeath is the foundation of experience (*VRM,* p. 100). True dignity of character, solid personal merit, independence, and virtue result only from active individual acquisition (*VRM,* p. 70). Implicit submission to "arbitrary authority and dark traditions" produces servility and degradation of character, replaces respect for individual merit with veneration for rank and fortune, and "stifles the natural affections on which human contentment ought to be built" under a self-indulgent and passive code of sensibility (*VRM*, pp. 37, 52).

Wollstonecraft always connects the tyrannic spirit with factitious feelings as correlative manifestations of society's substitution of manners for morals (*VRM,* p. 142). In her critique of Burke's eulogium on feeling, Wollstonecraft strongly contrasts the active exertions of virtue with the vague and passive declamations of sensibility, and humanitarian sympathies with artificial delicacy of feeling (*VRM,* pp. 137, 70). Although she censures Burke in the name of reason, she would not limit man's faculties to reason alone any more than Burke himself would. Her ideal of fully developed human nature includes a key role for emotion (*VRM,* pp. 29, 70-73). For Wollstonecraft, the passions necessarily act as the instigators and auxiliaries of reason; and a complex union of the feelings and the understanding is at once the impetus toward social reformation and the ultimate goal of that reformation. She chides Burke as much for contrived or improperly directed sentiment as for neglect of reason.

Indeed, one of Wollstonecraft's heaviest charges against Burke and the social system he speaks for is a want of feeling for those who compose the "swinish multitude" (*Ref.,* p. 173): "Your respect for rank has swallowed up the common feelings of humanity; you seem to consider the poor as only the livestock of an estate, the feather of hereditary nobility" (*VRM,* p. 32). Burke as the voice of the inherited social creed notices the poor only in connection with public order, natural subordination, and preservation of property: the poor "must be taught their consolation in the final proportions of eternal justice" (*Ref.,* p. 372). Wollstonecraft's stinging reply terms such passages "contemptible hard-hearted sophistry, in the specious form of humility and submission to the will of Heaven.—It is, Sir, possible to render the poor happier in this world, without depriving them of the consolation which you gratuitously grant them in the next" (*VRM,* p. 144). One means of improving the lot of the poor is to ameliorate current codes governing property. Since Wollstonecraft is speaking from a position outside the conventional order, she regards the existing arrangement of property only in its relation to social welfare. First of all, property should be fluctuating. The entailed inheritance which Burke makes the basis of his theory of society and government is for Wollstonecraft a barbarous feudal relic; the only security of property should be a man's right to enjoy the fruits of his own acquisition (*VRM,* pp. 50-51).

Furthermore, the use of property for selfish or merely aesthetic purposes is an affront to the humanitarian sympathies:

> Why cannot large estates be divided into small farms? . . . Why are huge forests still allowed to stretch out with idle pomp and all the indolence of Eastern grandeur? Why does the brown waste meet the traveller's view, when men want work? But commons cannot be enclosed without *acts of parliament* to increase the property of the rich! Why might not the industrious peasant be allowed to steal a farm from the heath? (*VRM*, p. 148)

Wollstonecraft does not suggest that a simple redistribution of property will effect a radical regeneration of society. Socio-economic reform must be coupled with revision of the moral-aesthetic basis of aristocratic manners. Specious economics and aesthetics unite to make the lands of the rich only "*objects* for the eye," where "every thing on the estate is cherished but man." The rich turn their backs on the revolting sight of human misery and seek refuge in an "attractive Arcadia of fiction" where they complacently contemplate the beauty and order of an idealized social structure; they unite a want of natural affections for their fellow men with an excess of reverence for "ideal regions of taste and elegance" (*VRM,* pp. 144-45, 150).

Wollstonecraft criticizes Burke sharply for justifying society's rejection of true morality in favor of beauty because of his emphasis on the social value of pleasing and beautifying illusions in the *Reflections* and his manner of defining beauty in the *Enquiry into the Origin of our Ideas of the Sublime and the Beautiful* (1757). If beauty is associated with love, littleness, and weakness and dissociated from reason, respect, and such virtues as fortitude, justice, wisdom, and truth, then society must not encourage but "banish all enervating modifications of beauty from civil society" (*VRM,* p. 115). Wollstonecraft ironically turns Burke's remarks on the refinement and relaxing qualities of beauty into an indictment of his aesthetically ordered social system:

> Should experience prove that there is a beauty in virtue, a charm in order, which necessarily implies exertion, a depraved sensual taste may give way to a more manly one—and *melting* feelings to rational satisfactions. Both may be equally natural to man; the test is their moral difference. . . .
>
> Such a glorious change can only be produced by liberty. Inequality of rank must ever impede the growth of virtue, by vitiating the mind that submits or domineers. . . . you must allow us to respect unsophisticated reason, and reverence the active exertions that were not relaxed by a fastidious respect for the beauty of rank, or a dread of the deformity produced by any *void* in the social structure. (*VRM,* pp. 116-17; cf. *Ref.,* p. 246)

A culture based on aesthetic discrimination and social segregation and a pattern of life founded on domination and submission degrade both rich and poor, for virtue can flourish only among equals (*VRM,* p. 149).

What Wollstonecraft wants is no less than a new system of manners which will establish a different foundation for social interrelationships and provide an environment conducive to human self-realization. A viable social code must be based on inclusion and equality rather than exclusion and hierarchy; reverence for liberty, justice, and reason must replace devotion to the false sensibility and meretricious beauty of the old aristocratic codes derived from the outmoded past. In her envoy to Burke, Wollstonecraft demonstrates her passionate hatred of social injustice:

> Man preys on man; and you mourn for the idle tapestry that decorated a gothic pile, and the dronish bell that summoned the fat priest to prayer. You mourn for the empty pageant of a name, when slavery flaps her wing. . . . Hell stalks abroad;—the lash resounds on the slave's naked sides; and the sick wretch, who can no longer earn the sour bread of unremitting labour, steals to a ditch to bid the world a long good night. (*VRM,* pp. 152-53)

Such misery dramatizes the pressing need for a reconsideration of manners and morals. A truly moral society must be organized in terms of actual human needs; Burke speaks only as the voice of a cultivated minority intent on preserving an antiquated society based on chivalric manners and feudal authority:

> Our manners, you tell us, are drawn from the French. . . . If they were, it is time we broke loose from dependance. . . . for, if manners are not a painted substitute for morals, we have only to cultivate our reason, and we shall not feel the want of an arbitrary model. Nature will suffice; but I forget myself:—Nature and Reason, according to your system, are all to give place to authority. (VRM, pp. 156-57)

The vehemence of Wollstonecraft's attack here and throughout the *Vindication* stems from her conviction that the maintenance of traditional structures of authority and the full realization of the rights of humanity are fundamentally incompatible.

The *Vindication* is essentially a stringent moral criticism of a corrupt society and of Burke as its oracle. As such, Wollstonecraft's polemic is not a confutation of Burke's political theories, but an exposure of the cruel inequities which those theories presuppose. Wollstonecraft thinks primarily in terms of moral revolution in England rather than of political revolution in France. If her critique is sometimes weak in specific proposals for reform and detailed consideration of contemporary political issues, it is also undamaged by the vagaries of current events; much of her social criticism retains its power even today. Wollstonecraft paradoxically turns her original position of weakness as a political outsider into a certain kind of strength; if she lacks the training to make a contribution to constitutional theory, she is well-equipped to champion the cause of society's underprivileged because of her own hard experience. Wollstonecraft's reverence for the rights of humanity is an extension outward of her personal concern with human dignity and self-realization: "Sacred rights! for which I acquire a more profound respect, the more I look into my own mind. . . . the regard I have for honest fame, and the friendship of the virtuous, falls far short of the respect which I have for myself. . . . And this, enlightened self-love . . . forces me . . . to *feel,* that happiness is reflected, and that, in communicating good, my soul receives its noble aliment" (*VRM,* pp. 78-79).[18] The high valuation she places on self-respect, independence, and the development of individual capabilities combines with her powerful sympathies for all those who are debarred from participation in these values to explain her firm belief in egalitarian principles. Wollstonecraft's own position leads her to an early recognition of the justice of social equality between both sexes and among all groups of mankind. Although she expects no earthly millenium, Wollstonecraft does believe that a society founded on greater purity of morals is no mere poetic fiction (*VRM,* p. 76), and the *Vindication of the Rights of Men* offers a striking testimonial to the strength of that belief.

NOTES

1 Detailed accounts of the *Reflections* controversy appear in R. R. Fennessy, *Burke, Paine and the Rights of Man: A Difference of Political Opinion* (The Hague: Martinus Nijhoff, 1963) and James T. Boulton, *The Language of Politics in the Age of Wilkes and Burke* (London: Routledge and Kegan Paul, 1963). Wollstonecraft was censured by the *Gentlemen's Magazine* for her assumption that women might discuss political topics; see Ralph M. Wardle, *Mary Wollstonecraft: A Critical Biography* (1951; rpt. Lincoln: University of Nebraska Press, 1966), p. 121. For women as political controversialists, see also Eleanor Flexner, *Mary Wollstonecraft: A Biography* (New York: Coward, McCann & Geoghegan, 1972), p. 128. Catharine Macaulay Graham also answered Burke, but her name does not appear on the title page of *Observations on the Reflections of the Right Hon. Edmund Burke, on the Revolution in France, in a Letter to the Right Hon. the Earl of Stanhope* (London: C. Dilly, 1790).

2 William Godwin, *Memoirs of Mary Wollstonecraft,* ed. W. Clark Durant (1798; rpt. London: Constable, 1927), p. 51. For facts of publication, see Wardle, p. 120. *VRM* was originally published by Wollstonecraft's employer Joseph Johnson, the friend and publisher of many liberal writers and co-founder of the *Analytical Review*. Page references to *VRM* incorporated in the text refer to the reprint of the second edition, introduction by Eleanor Louise Nicholes (Gainesville, Florida: Scholars' Facsimiles & Reprints, 1960). For a brief account of Johnson, see *Minor Lives: A Collection of Biographies by John Nichols,* ed. Edward L. Hart (Cambridge: Harvard University Press, 1971).

3 George Stead Veitch, *The Genesis of Parliamentary Reform* (1913; rpt. London: Constable, 1965), p. 167.

4 Wollstonecraft's description of her situation comes from a letter to her sister Everina, in C. Kegan Paul, *William Godwin: His Friends and Contemporaries* (London: Henry S. King, 1876), I, 191.

5 *A Room of One's Own* (1929; rpt. New York: Harcourt, Brace & World, 1957), p. 101.

6 "I think I love most people best when they are in adversity, for pity is one of my prevailing passions," Wollstonecraft observes in a letter quoted in Paul, I, 175. Her passionate desire for independence colors many of the letters reprinted by Paul and Durant and is the keynote of the *Vindication of the Rights of Woman*: "Independence I have long considered as the grand blessing of life, the basis of every virtue—and independence I will ever secure by contracting my wants, though I were to live on a barren heath." Ed. Charles W. Hagelman, Jr. (New York: W. W. Norton,

1967), unpaginated dedication. Subsequent references to *VRW* incorporated in the text refer to this edition.

7 *Shelley and His Circle, 1773–1822*, ed. Kenneth Neill Cameron (Cambridge: Harvard University Press, 1961), I, 52-53. Wardle also notes what he calls Wollstonecraft's "pre-Romantic tendencies," pp. 254-56, 284-85, 312-13, 341.

8 Burke writes of his approach, "Indulging myself in the freedom of epistolary intercourse, I beg leave to throw out my thoughts, and express my feelings, just as they arise in my mind, with very little attention to formal method." *Reflections on the Revolution in France,* ed. Conor Cruse O'Brien (Harmondsworth: Penguin, 1969), p. 92. Subsequent references incorporated in the text refer to this edition. Fennessy, pp. 108-10, and O'Brien, pp. 49-50, discuss the letter form.

9 Burke himself is not guiltless in this respect, particularly with regard to Dr. Richard Price, whose famous Old Jewry Sermon (1789) goaded him into the fury which produced the *Reflections.* See, for example, Burke's identification of Price with the regicide Hugh Peters, *Ref.*, p. 158.

10 *Memoirs,* p. 51. That the attack on a venerable elder statesman took considerable courage on Wollstonecraft's part can be seen from Godwin's account of her faltering when the essay was half completed. Johnson's acceptance of her suggestion that she quit was a challenge that piqued her into finishing (*Memoirs,* pp. 52-53).

11 Cf. "Sacred . . . would the infirmities and errors of a good man be, in my eyes, if they were only displayed in a private circle" (p. 4; cf. p. 88).

12 For Burke's animus against Price and the Dissenters, see O'Brien's introduction and notes to the *Reflections,* pp. 25-30, 378-79. Burke writes to Francis: "I intend no controversy with Dr. Price, or Lord Shelburne, or any other of their set. I mean to set in full view the danger from their wicked principles and their black hearts. . . . I mean to do my best to expose them to the hatred, ridicule, and contempt of the whole world; as I always shall expose such calumniators, hypocrites, sowers of sedition and approvers of murder and all its triumphs." Quoted in Fennessy, p. 107.

13 Nicholes discusses Wollstonecraft's relation with Price in *Shelley and His Circle* and quotes Price's key statement on the correlation between liberty and morality: "To be *free* is to be guided by one's own will; and to be guided by the will of another is the characteristic of *Servitude,*" I, 57.

14 Price's phrase comes from the Old Jewry Sermon, "A Discourse on the Love of Our Country," quoted in *The Debate on the French Revolution 1789-1800,* ed. Alfred Cobban (1950; rpt. London: Adam & Charles Black, 1960), p. 64.

15 Boulton, pp. 127-33.

16 For an example of the former approach, see Boulton, p. 168, and for the latter, Fennessy, p. 203.

17 The use of man as a synonym for the species in *VRM* and *VRW* sometimes involves Wollstonecraft, as it has others, in linguistic difficulties. For a discussion of the problem, see Mary R. Beard, *Woman as Force in History: A Study in Traditions and Realities* (1946; rpt. New York: Collier, 1962), pp. 57-61.

18 Cf. *Ref.*, p. 123, "Respecting your forefathers, you would have been taught to respect yourselves," with *VRM,* p. 94, "What can make us reverence ourselves, but a reverence for that Being, of whom we are a faint image? "

The Cell and the Garret: Fictions of Confinement in Swift's Satires and Personal Writings

HOPEWELL R. SELBY

Reading Swift's satires is almost always to experience claustrophobia of a sort. Who does not gasp for air as Gulliver, imprisoned in the Lilliputians' temple, adds to its ancient pollutions new ordures of his own? Who does not gag as the Brobdingnagian monkey squeezes Gulliver with one paw and crams filthy food down his throat with the other? Or feel involuntary constrictions of the throat as he nearly drowns in Brobdingnagian cream? Or squirm as he wriggles in the marrow-bone? Few if any of us, I suspect, can read the *Travels* without feeling some if not all of these responses, which are almost involuntary reflexes. Similarly, few if any of us can experience the malodorous eructations in the *Tale of a Tub*'s cramped quarters without sharing, to some extent, the wish to rise above the crowd and breathe free. A common satiric procedure with Swift is to confine his reader within a narrow space—conventicle, dressing room, or crowd—and then let fly with a full-scale assault on the nose.

Typically, Swift yokes together his reader and satiric speaker in a fearful embrace which threatens to strangle, suffocate, and choke. Theirs is the kinship of fellow prisoners. My aim here is to explore—selectively and doubtless in what Swift would term "*Mignature*"[1] —the implications of this relationship as it appears in Swift's protean prisons. This exploration can help to clarify the relation between Swift's images of himself in the personal writings and their antitypes in the satires. The speakers of both kinds of writing have much in common beneath their apparent contrariety. Characteristically, Swift seeks to annihilate his satiric speakers—Gulliver, Partridge, the *Tale*'s mad scribbler—by imprisoning them and inflicting upon them the tortures of solitary confinement. But in the personal writings—including the *Journal to Stella*, the correspondence, and "autobiographical" pieces such as the *Holyhead Journal*—Swift presents himself, in the guise of Presto and Punsibi, Dean and Drapier, as a similarly trapped victim, who is tortured as a prisoner by his keeper, by Patrick's insolence, by his Dublin housekeeper's tyranny, by the rudeness of an innkeeper's wife. The two apparently different cases resemble each other in their common fictions of confinement, which are both psychological and epistemological in nature. Swift's fictive prisons express his fears of the human mind's tendency toward violent and anarchic disintegration, which results in its solipsistic alienation from the world of "outside" things.[2]

In this sense, Swift's confinements are more than just another of the "special effects" which the satirist pulls from his proverbial bag of tricks. The claustrophobia generated by Swift's satire has its nonsatiric counterpart in writings of the period as diverse as Pope's *Eloisa to Abelard,* Defoe's *Journal of the Plague Year,* and Richardson's *Clarissa,* to name only three well-known examples. All of these works treat the problems created by individuals whose minds are isolated not only from the minds of others but also from what the empiricists were fond of calling "external objects." All portray this isolation in the concrete image of the confined space: Eloisa's cell, Clarissa's closet, the small room through whose window H. F. observes the plague and his own ideas as well. It is not surprising that these fictions of confinement should proliferate in the age of Locke and the empiricists, who portray the mind, in the words of Sir Isaiah Berlin, as "a box containing mental equivalents of the Newtonian particles," and for whom "three-dimensional Newtonian space has its counterpart in the inner 'space' of the mind over which the inner eye—the faculty of reflection—presides."[3] In the nonsatirical writings of the period, this image of the mind appears in the external caves, grottoes, and other small spaces which are the setting for reflective contemplation and which may also represent one of the period's unconscious images of the mind itself.[4] But whereas many eighteenth-century closed spaces are the setting for a subjectivity that is creative, for Swift they provide the setting for a subjectivity that is ultimately both delusive and destructive. In Swift's satires, enclosures inevitably resemble the madman's Bedlamite cell. In this "tour" of his fictive prisons, I propose first to consider the behavior that occurs within them, and then to explore some of the broader epistemological concerns which I believe they suggest. Finally, I wish to examine some ways in which their physical unpleasantness offers both punishment and potential cure for the mind's omnivorous tendency to recreate the world in its image.

"The Life of a Spider"

With his professed hatred of elaborate types, fables, and symbols, Swift often spoke his truths in puns. Writing early in his career, presumably with his own uncertain future in mind, he observed that "it is a miserable Thing to live in Suspence: it is the Life of a Spider. *Vive quidem, pende tamen, improba, dixit.*"[5] Punning on his own suspense, and intuitively connecting it with Athena's sentencing of Arachne to the perpetual prison of her web, Swift here regards the spider's confinement as both the expression of, and the punishment for, the pride with which he repeatedly reproaches himself. Thus it is no surprise to find him, in a mocking but serious reiteration of Athena's decree, condemning his satiric victims to various forms of arachnoid life. The mad modern scribbler of the *Tale of a Tub,* spinning out of himself the allegorical tale which he enmeshes in an omnivorous web of digressions, reveals early on "that the shrewdest Pieces of this Treatise, were conceived in Bed, in a Garret" (*Tale,* p. 44). Similarly Bickerstaff, visiting Partridge on the "fatal" night of March 29, 1708, stays only long enough to record the astrologer's delirious revelations that he is both fool and fanatic, and then departs, "being almost stifled by the Closeness of the Room" ("An Account of Partridge's Death," *Prose,* II, 155). And Gulliver, having voyaged through the prisons of the Lilliputians, the boxes of the Brobdingnagians, and the stifling chambers of the Grand Academy of Lagado, concludes his travels, after his ludicrously timorous decision to quit his chamber in Don Pedro's house, in the solitary confinement of his room and his stable at Redriff.

All of these writers—Gulliver in his house, Partridge in his suffocating room, the *Tale*'s author in his garret—create their versions of past, present, and future out of themselves, and all, in this sense, resemble Swift's most completely realized fiction of confinement, that of the spider who dwells in his web above the books in St. James's library. Swift's treatment of the spider is curiously ambivalent. It is true that the spider's web is spun of venom and excrement and that the bee has the last word of their too-familiar argument. But the spider, unlike all of the constantly displaced books on the shelves below, is the only creature in the library to have a home of his own, even though it is spun from the dirt of his entrails. Our first view of the spider emphasizes the comparative security of his dwelling, "which had Windows fronting to each Avenue, and Ports to sally out on all Occasions of Prey or Defence. In this Mansion he had for some Time dwelt in Peace and Plenty, without Danger to his *Person* by *Swallows* from above, or to his *Palace* by *Brooms* from below" ("Battel," *Prose,* I, 148). In his meeting with the bee, what's striking about the spider is the contrast between his vitality—"*A Plague split you,* said he, *for a giddy Son of a Whore*"[6]—and the fragility of his "Cittadel, which, yielding to the unequal Weight, sunk down to the very Foundation" ("Battel," *Prose,* I, 148). The web, though spun of venom and excrement, is almost wondrous in its intricacy, and almost sympathetic in its fragility. Even the bee, who sardonically comments that its *"Materials are nought,"* admits that *"In that building of yours, there might, for ought I know, have been labor and method enough"* ("Battel," *Prose*, I, 149).

Swift created the spider out of his own professed rage to destroy all the attributes of "modern" culture which he hated most. In the *Bickerstaff Papers,* similar attitudes motivate Swift to "destroy" the astrologer Partridge, whose almanac is but a cosmic analog of the spider's fragile web. Partridge's predictions for the future are connected tenuously if at all. It is no accident that he is a freethinker. Bickerstaff's prediction of his death resembles the bee's invasion of the spider's web: the spider initially interprets the "terrible Convulsion" by supposing "that *Beelzebub* with all his Legions, was come to revenge the Death of many thousands of his Subjects, whom his Enemy had slain and devoured" ("Battel," *Prose,* I, 148), and Partridge considers his illness as a time "for repenting those Fooleries" which he agrees were "meer Impositions upon the People" ("An Account of Partridge's Death," *Prose,* II, 154-55). But Bickerstaff's prediction has more dire consequences, because Swift wishes to free Partridge's readers from the superstitious credulity that would leave them trapped in a universe of sheer destructive caprice. No wonder Bickerstaff envisages the end of the millenarian Camisards and their predictions of imminent Apocalypse. Partridge's own personality is so fragile that his mental stability is easily shattered by Bickerstaff's prediction of his death, which "affected and worked on his Imagination. He confessed he had often had it in his Head, but never with much Apprehension till about a Fortnight before; since which Time it had the perpetual Possession of his Mind and Thoughts; and he did verily believe it was the true natural Cause of his present Distemper" ("An Account of Partridge's Death," *Prose,* II, 154).

Swift "destroys" Partridge, but the astrologer attains in the process a curious kind of immortality.[7] Although eliminated from the Stationers' Register, he lives on in spirit as the butt of Swift's joke. Similarly (in a mock-vindication of Asgill's notions of immortality?), he lives on in body as well: Bickerstaff complains that "Neither had the said Carcass any Right to beat the poor Boy, who happened to pass it in the Street, crying, *A Full and True Account of Dr. Partridge's Death*, &c" ("A Vindication of Isaac Bickerstaff, Esq.," *Prose,* II, 162). In the same way, the spider becomes most "alive" when he is most threatened with destruction. Swift seems to wish to destroy these imprisoned creatures and yet preserve them too. In the Grand Academy of Lagado, he develops the covert sympathy implicit here, when Gulliver visits the "narrow Room, where the Walls and Ceiling were all hung round with Cobwebs, except a narrow passage for the Artist to go in and out." This insubstantial alchemist, seeking to turn his cobwebs into a rainbow of silks, feeds his spiders with "a vast number of Flies most beautifully colored," and lacks only "proper Food for the Flies, of certain Gums, Oyls, and other glutinous Matter, to give a strength and Consistence to the Threads" (*Travels, Prose,* XI, 180-81). Again, the flimsiness of the webs is paramount; it here becomes emblematic of the fragility of all art and of the preposterousness of the artist, whose benevolent scheme is as ludicrous and futile as Swift's other satiric and serious projects to benefit mankind.

In both fragility and vulnerability, Gulliver resembles these confined projectors. Even in Lilliput, he is forced to submit to being bound with "slender Ligatures" (*Travels, Prose,* XI, 21) and delicate "Chains, like those that hang from a Lady's Watch in *Europe*" (*Travels, Prose,* XI, 28). In Brobdingnag, where he is constantly under the threat of being squeezed, squashed, or trampled to death, Gulliver's box becomes both his prison and his refuge, which seems large enough to him but which repeatedly fails to defend him from rats, wasps, swallows, and other outside invaders. In the third voyage, by contrast, Gulliver often appears to be the only individual who is not confined by some form of imprisonment. But although he visits other prisoners, ranging from the Laputans trapped in their thoughts to the projectors confined in their cells, and although he seems less vulnerable and more substantial than they, he experiences in this voyage the terrors of the infinite, and the agoraphobic effects of both the Laputans and the Struldbruggs leave him relatively content to be confined to the world of material substance and to the short span of his life. This prepares for the fourth voyage, where he is initially imprisoned by the mutineers who fasten his leg with a chain that recalls his earlier confinement in Lilliput, and where he finally becomes his own keeper, confining himself to his cabin, room, and stable in a mad mixture of timidity and rage. At once vulnerable and vehement, perhaps the victim of a kind of cumulative calentures, his personality ultimately seems threatened with the disintegration that characterizes all the trapped speakers of Swift's satires.

Inmates that they are, these speakers inevitably tell tales of the imprisoned life, whose principal characteristic is violence. When the spider's web is invaded, he "stormed and swore like a Mad-man, and swelled till he was ready to burst" ("Battel," *Prose,* I, 148). Bickerstaff, refining upon Patridge's astrology, predicts overwhelmingly violent disasters, which include "the Death of the Dauphine, after a short fit of Sickness, and grievous Torments with the Straungery," and "the death of the Pope," "the swellings in his Legs breaking, and the Flesh mortifying" ("Predictions for the Year 1708," *Prose,* II, 146, 148). Similarly, all of the *Tale*'s Bedlamite cells restrain inmates who would do violence either to others or to themselves: they contain the student who is "tearing his Straw in piece-meal, Swearing and Blaspheming, biting his Grate, foaming at the Mouth, and emptying his Pispot in the Spectator's faces;" the paranoid who "talks much of hard Times, and Taxes, and the *Whore of Babylon*; bars up the woodden Windows of his Cell constantly at eight a Clock: dreams of *Fire,* and *Court Customers,* and *Privileged Places,*" and the "surley, gloomy, nasty, slovenly Mortal, raking in his own Dung, and dabbling in his Urine" (*Tale,* pp. 176, 177, 178, 179). Much of the irony in the "Digression on Madness" stems from the difficulty we have in distinguishing cause and effect in the relation between Swift's madhouse/prison and the violence that occurs within it. We are invited to assume that the hospital's inmates are imprisoned because they are violent, but Swift also suggests that they are violent because they are imprisoned: all of their energies "would . . . be very natural, in their proper Element" (*Tale,* p. 179). In its confusion of madmen and heroes, and in its abolition of the conventional distinctions between the prison and the world outside, the Digression is as close as Swift ever comes to writing what could be termed "Bedlam Pastoral." When Swift later asks Pope what he thinks "of a Newgate Pastoral, among the whores and thieves there?"[8] it comes as no surprise. In a sense, his own satiric career had produced little else.

Swift's fictions of confinement express his anxieties about what he views as the human personality's inevitable tendency toward violent and anarchic disintegration. In his satires, it is the human condition to be always, like the spider, "ready to burst." In the frail restraints which he imposes on his fictive prisoners, Swift expresses his pessimism about the futility of all efforts to "contain" the violence which leads people to destroy others and themselves as well. Like Partridge, whose incoherent personality disintegrates into penultimate delirium, the *Tale*'s speaker is a former inhabitant of Bedlam, who confesses himself to be "a Person, whose Imaginations are hard-mouth'd, and exceedingly disposed to run away with his *Reason,* . . . upon which Account, my Friends will never trust me alone, without a solemn Promise to vent my Speculations in this, or the like manner" (*Tale,* p. 180). Trapped in the garret, he resembles mad Jack, the hero of his "tale" who "hired a Taylor to stitch up his Collar so close, that it was ready to choak him, and squeezed out his Eyes at such a Rate, as one could see nothing but the White," and who pisses in the eyes of strangers, bespatters them with mud, and solicits from passers-by "a Basting sufficient to swell up his Fancy and his Sides" (*Tale,* pp. 198, 199). The coincidence of Jack's final "triumph" with the *Tale*'s ultimate disintegration reflects Swift's fear that all restraints, be they those of the madman's straitjacket, the tenets of religious belief, or the discipline of literary "form," are ineffective checks on the frenzied fragmentation that characterizes modern sensibility.

Given the fragility of the ligaments which hold together the primal anarchy of every human mind, Swift's fictive prisons appear as forms of punishment which are a kindness too. In all of them, punitive and curative measures are inextricably confounded. Gulliver's stable at Redriff is both a punishment and a refuge, the ironic embodiment of the mixed prison and hospital which Swift wishes for himself. "Drown the World," he writes to Pope shortly after finishing the *Travels,* "I am not content with despising it, but would anger it if I could with safety. I wish there were an Hospital built for it's despisers, where one might act with safety and it need not be a large Building, only I would have it well endowed."[9] In much of his correspondence of the 1720s, Swift portrays himself as a prisoner who is condemned to Ireland and to the narrow Dublin society which moves from drawing room to drawing room, and from drawing room to dining room. In a typical comparison of his own turbulence with Pope's serenity, Swift envies Pope that the translation of Homer will be bought by Whig and Tory alike, but claims that "I who am sunk under the prejudices of another Education, and am every day perswading myself that a Dagger is at my throat, a Halter about my neck, or Chains at my Feet, all prepared by those in Power, can never arrive at the Security of Mind you possess."[10] Swift's view of himself here suggests one reason why his satires and serious proposals both urge their readers to conserve what little coherence they possess, to hold their personalities together by time-tested systems of belief even if they should involve repression of individual doubt and oppression of collective dissent. Swift's well-known attacks on freethinkers are reflected in his complaint about the bad conversationalists who abound among Anglicans as well as Dissenters: "I say nothing here of that Itch of Dispute or Contradiction, Telling of Lies, or of those who are troubled with the Disease called the Wandering of the Thoughts, that they are never present in Mind at what passeth in Discourse; for whosoever labors under any of these Possessions, is as fit for Conversation as a Mad-man in Bedlam" ("Hints Toward an Essay on Conversation," *Prose,* IV, 94).

Swift hated freethinkers, but their style was precisely his talent. Even the *Contests and Dissentions* shows digressive tendencies. John Traugott has amply and eloquently discussed the parodic catachreses through which Swift speaks the *Tale*'s deepest truths in the tongues of his enemies.[11] It is enough to note here Swift's perennial fascination with the trapped mind's crazy connections among totally unrelated ideas. What else could have motivated Swift to have written the *Tritical Essay upon the Faculties of the Mind,* which comes as close as humanly imaginable to having absolutely no rational content whatsoever? What else could have inspired the *Compleat Collection of Polite and Ingenious Conversation,* whose characters say virtually nothing through an entire series of social engagements? Swift himself exhibits a delightfully disordered "wandering of the thoughts" in the *Journal to Stella,* a narrative of confinement permeated by a sense of the physically small spaces in which Swift writes as he paces his room and retreats to the smaller enclosure of his bed. Typically, the long sentences of these letters oscillate among casual gossip, serious reports on the progress of his career, jokes, sulks, and the intimacy of his "richar Gangridge." When the narrative comes closest to "stream of consciousness," it reveals Swift's tendency to connect his own thoughts in the illogic which the satires attack: "I have my mouth full of water, and was going to spit it out, because I reasoned with myself, how could I write with my mouth full. Han't you done things like that, reasoned wrong at the first thinking?"[12] The collective counterpart of this inanity surfaces not much later:

> Morning. *I have desired* Apronia *to be always careful, especially about the legs.* Pray, do you see any such great wit in that sentence? I must freely own that I do not. But party carries every thing now-a-days, and what a splutter have I heard about the wit of that saying, repeated with admiration above a hundred times in half an hour. Pray read it over again, and consider it. I think the word is *advised,* and not *desired.* I should not have

> remembered if I had not heard it so often. Why—aye—You must know I dreamt it just now, and waked with it in my mouth. Are you bit, or are you not, Sirrahs? (*Journal,* 8 February 1710/11, I, 182)

The "bite," encapsulating in its idiotic sentence all the learning of Lagado's political projectors, takes in the reader and Stella as well, and identifies individual and collective insanity in a mock-Lucretian *clinamen* of disordered ideas. For Swift, the Lucretian model applies not so much to outer as to inner space. The problem with digressions is that their ubiquity suggests that all thoughts (and hence all systems of belief) are related only in a chance collision not merely of words but of sounds. No wonder Swift devotes such energy to puns. The universe of the *De Rerum Natura* is a strangely insubstantial cobweb, infinite in extension and utterly incoherent in shape. Like the narratives of Swift's arachnoid victims, it is held together only within the consciousness of whatever mad projector would be induced to "spend tranquil nights in wakefulness" (*Tale,* p. 123, my trans.) in revealing the heart of its mysteries.

Metaphors of the Mind

The inevitable tendency of the Lucretian Universe is to dissolve, to reduce all of its creations into "the Notions of *Atoms* and *Void,* as in the Originals of all Things" (*Tale,* p. 167). It is the void which threatens Swift most, as satirist and as diarist. On January 4, 1710/11, he wakes from a nightmare that is rare in the absolute clarity of its terror: "Morning. Morrow, little dears. Oh Faith, I have been dreaming; I was to be put in prison, I don't know why, and I was so afraid of a black dungeon; and then all I had been dreaming of Sir Andrew Fountain's sickness I thought was of poor Stella" (*Journal,* I, 152). Atoms and void, derangement and disappearance. These twin nightmares define the fears which animate Swift's satires and personal writings alike. Portraying himself in the *Journal* as a foolish rogue supping milk porridge, itching, scratching, and dying of the heat, Swift seeks to bring Stella to sympathy with his supposed misfortune of having to remain in London. Here, as in the correspondence where he frets over the construction of Naboth's vineyard and the contents of his cellar, Swift seeks the reassurance that since his departure he has not suffered what he fears, in his verses on his death, as "No further Mention of the Dean; / Who now, alas, no more is mist, / Than if he never did exist."[13] A similar fear animates the *Holyhead Journal,* a prison record which can only be viewed as a narrative of nonbeing. Its pages record Swift's fear that he will disappear from his own consciousness, literally drop out of his own mind. With nothing to read, and nothing to write, and nothing decent to eat, he walks the rocks for endless vacant hours, disdains the others at the inn, and waits for the voyage which never seems to start. In what can be regarded as a mock reversal of the Cartesian *cogito,* Swift does not think, and therefore almost ceases to be.

Swift's fictive prisons seem to invoke less anxiety about the gallows than about the possibility of disappearing behind their walls and simply vanishing. This, at least, is what seems to happen to the *Tale*'s productions of modern wit which disappear in the jakes, bawdy-house, and oven, "hurryed so hastily off the Scene, that they escape our Memory, or delude our Sight" (*Tale,* p. 34). It is also what happens in Brobdingnag, when Gulliver is repeatedly on the point of vanishing into the marrow-bone, or gravy, or cream, or (as finally) into thin air. In this voyage, Gulliver is threatened with an annihilation that is more epistemological than physical. He fears that he will be extinguished because he will vanish from the minds of others who simply don't see him, don't notice. Implicit here is a version of the Berkeleian *Esse est percipi* which (at least as Berkeley seems to have been understood) locates the individual's existence in the perceptions of others.

In describing the *Tale* as "an Experiment very frequent among Modern Authors; which is, *to write upon Nothing*" (*Tale,* p. 208), Swift parodies Berkeley in advance. In his *Principles of Human Knowledge,* Berkeley argues against his fictive opponent's desire to retain the notion of an abstract substance which "underlies" appearances. When the opponent makes a last-ditch attempt to retain the idea of matter as "an unknown *somewhat,* neither substance nor accident, spirit nor idea, inert, thoughtless, indivisible, immoveable, unextended, existing in no place," Berkeley grants his wish by allowing that "You may, if so it shall seem good, use the word *matter* in the same sense as other men use *nothing,* and so make the terms convertible in your style."[14] Viewed in this context, Papist Peter's proclamation that his twelvepenny loaf of bread is a shoulder of mutton becomes a blasphemously catachrestic pun upon the "lamb of God" which presents transubstantiation in bizarrely contemporary philosophic dress. Unlike Jack, who relies on his sense perceptions to proclaim that *"I can only say, that to my Eyes, and Fingers, and Teeth, and Nose, it seems to be nothing but a Crust of Bread"* (*Tale,* p. 118), Peter deduces his interpretation of the loaf entirely from within the confines of his mind.

One of Swift's recurring prison images is that of the pulpit, whose confinement of the preacher is emblematic of the dilemmas faced by whatever individual would try to interpret the scriptures. In the *Tale,* the pulpit is an emblem of pride, one of the machines by which orators seek to exalt themselves above the crowd. It is clearly a kind of prison, whose "Degree of Perfection and Size, I take to consist in being extremely narrow, with little Ornament, and best of all without a Cover" and an instrument of torture as well, bearing "a near Resemblance to a Pillory" (*Tale,* p. 58). A similar image of the pulpit (which suggests another association of the priest and the spider) appears two years after the *Tale,* in Swift's portrayal of the transformation of Baucis and Philemon's cottage into a church: "The groaning Chair began to crawll/Like a huge Insect up the Wall,/There stuck, and to a pulpitt grew,/But kept it's Matter and it's Hue" ("The Story of Baucis and Philemon's Cottage" [1706], *Poems*, I, 93, ll. 105-10). Apparently responding to Addison's strictures, Swift later replaced the simile by the lines "The groaning Chair began to Crawll/Like a huge Snail along the Wall;/There stuck aloft, in publick View/And with small

Change, a Pulpit grew" ("Baucis and Philemon" [1708/9], *Poems*, I, 113, ll. 85-88). Unlike most of the revisions, which sacrifice vitality in the interest of visual "decorum," this change intensifies the image of the pulpit as a house-within-a-house,[15] at once "containing" and displaying its occupant.

By the time Swift wrote these lines, the figure of the snail was a cliché, a battered remnant of earlier emblem books. There, as in Lovelace's euology of this "Wise emblem of our Politick World/ Sage Snayle, within thine own self curl'd,"[16] it had usually represented the felicities of self-containedness. In the seventeenth century, as the near-innumerable emblems on snails, tortoises, and other self-housed creatures testify, the notion of confinement inspired wonder rather than terror. But many of these poems (George Withers' celebration of the tortoise is a good example) contain a moral purpose as well: to encourage their audience to be content with little rather than much, and to learn to live with the companionship of their own thoughts. This sentiment finds its darker echo in Pascal's familiar diagnosis of the human condition: "Tout le malheur des hommes vient d'une seule chose, qui est de ne savoir pas demeurer en repos, dans une Chambre." In his catalog of the futile diversions which human beings seek in their effort to escape their metaphysical malaise, Pascal's dialectic moves from a lament over our inability to remain in the room to an indictment of our refusal to stay there: "De là vient que les hommes aiment tant le bruit et le remuement; de là vient que la prison est un supplice si horrible; de là vient que le plaisir de la solitude est une chose si incompréhensible."[17] For Swift, however, the problem is more ominous: we cannot find repose within the room, but that is where we are trapped. Worse yet, the room is a prison within our very minds, its fetters the ways of reason itself:

STRANGE to conceive, how the same objects strike
At distant hours the mind with forms so like!
Whether in time, deduction's broken chain
Meets, and salutes her sister Link again;
Or hunted fancy, with a circling flight,

Comes back with joy to its own seat at night;
Or whether dead imagination's ghost
Oft hovers where alive it haunted most;
Or if thought's rolling glove her circle run,
Turns up old objects to the soul her sun.[18]

Although these conceits are supposed only to introduce a comparison with an earlier ode written in Temple's praise, they dominate the entire poem. Swift's real interest is (and remains) in the processes by which the modern mind, succumbing to rampant subjectivity, ceases to look "outside" and concentrates instead only on the ideas which it has stored within itself. In the *Tale,* Swift transforms Locke's distinction between ideas of sensation and reflection into an elaborately satirical "progress piece," in which the speaker's digressive commentary shows an increasing preoccupation with the manner in which his own mind works. After undergoing a bizarre metamorphosis, the metaphors of the ode reappear in the *Tale*'s universalizing meditation in which the speaker formulates a similarly unresolved series of conjectures about the proximity of "the frontiers of Height and Depth" within the confines of the imagining mind. Here, the poem's metaphoric bird of "hunted fancy" reappears as the "dead Bird of Paradise," which, instead of completing its circular flight, "becomes over-shot, and weary, and suddenly fails . . . to the Ground." The ode's image of "thought's rolling globe" reappears in the *Tale* with a new emphasis, not on its ability to "turn up old objects," but rather on the way in which "Reason reflecting on the sum of Things can, like the Sun, serve only to enlighten only one half . . . leaving the other half, by Necessity, under Shade and Darkness" (*Tale*, p. 158). For the ode's images of completion and fulfillment, the *Tale* substitutes notions of partial blindness, precipitous descent, and violent death. The difference between the two passages consists precisely in how much more closely the mind's prison walls press inward in the second. In the earlier ode, the objects of past and present mental experience bear at least some resemblance to each other; in the *Tale,* they coexist only in the ironic symbiosis of opposites—height and depth, God and Devil, reason and madness.

Like the spider's web, with its "windows fronting to each Avenue," many of the epistemological prisons in both the *Tale* and the *Travels* can be viewed as satiric metamorphoses of Locke's familiar architectural model of the mind, which takes the *camera obscura* of Cartesian dioptrics and makes of it a model for the human understanding. When Locke's *Essay* employs the shell-topos of the century, it becomes clear just how much of a prison his model of the mind really is. Discoursing of the similarities among human and animal faculties, Locke speculates that "we may, I think, from the make of an oyster or cockle, reasonably conclude that it has not so many nor so quick senses as a man, or several other animals." In their limited faculties, Locke's shellfish resemble the old people whose afflictions are so terrifyingly portrayed in Swift's Struldbruggs: "Take one in whom decrepit old age has blotted out the memory of his past existence, and clearly wiped out the ideas his mind was formerly stored with, and has, by destroying his sight, hearing, and smell quite, and his taste to a great degree, stopped up almost all passages for new ones to enter; or if some of the inlets are yet half open, the impressions made are scarcely perceived, or not at all retained. How far such an one (notwithstanding all that is boasted of innate ideas) is in his knowledge and intellectual faculties above the condition of a cockle or an oyster, I leave to be considered."[19]

Swift, in a riddle on the five senses which I think may be considered his, assimilates and recreates this metaphor and portrays the mind as but a shell in every age of life:

> All of us in one you'll find
> Brethren of a Wondrous Kind,
> Yet among us all no Brother
> Knows one Tittle of the other;
> We in frequent Councils are,
> And our Marks of Things declare,
> Where, to us unknown, a Clerk
> Sits, and takes them in the Dark.

He's the Register of All
In our Ken, both great and small;
By us forms his Laws, and Rules,
He's our Master, we his Tools;
Yet we can, with greatest Ease,
Turn and wind him where we please.[20]

In his portrayal of the trapped "clerk" (an endlessly self-replicating figure in any empirical model of the mind)[21] who is at the mercy of the senses, the riddle synthesizes the rogueries of Swift's Dublin servants with the tricks played on Gulliver's senses in so much of the *Travels.* When Gulliver finally stuffs up his nose with lavender and rue at the end of his voyages, he becomes an ironic embodiment of the Lockean cockle, a self-created counterpart of the Laputans who are literally "insensitive" in so many different ways. In his room with its symbolic mirror, he is trapped within the conception of himself that is to be both his punishment and potential cure.

Pandora's Box

In his *Verses on Gulliver's Travels,* Pope demonstrates just how clearly he understands the dual implications of Gulliver's self-imposed confinement. Mary Gulliver, lamenting her husband's indifference, complains that "Your Eyes, your Nose, Inconstancy betray;/Your Nose you stop, your Eyes you turn away." Gulliver, she fears, is literally out of his senses, alienated from the physical realities of life in a manner which the reader perceives as both contemptible and ludicrous:

I've no red Hair to breathe an odious Fume;
At least thy Consort's cleaner than thy *Groom.*
. . . .
Some think you mad, some think you are possest
That Bedlam and clean Straw will suit you best:
Vain Means, alas, this Frenzy to appease!
That *Straw,* that *Straw,* would heighten the Disease.[22]

To the extent that he has insisted upon denying the realities of his physical being, Gulliver is mad indeed—as mad as any of the Bedlamites in the *Tale* or in the vitriolic eulogy "The Legion Club." Trapped within the speculations which result from his sojourn with the Houhyhnhms, Gulliver punishes himself by confronting the horror of his own physicality: he resolves "to behold my Figure often in a Glass, and thus if possible habituate my self by Time to tolerate the Sight of a human Creature" (*Travels, Prose,* XI, 293). Punishment this is indeed, but Swift seems to see within it at least a potential cure for the disease of pride which, in his satires and serious writings alike, is the essence of the human condition. Like Rabelais, who locates the *"substantifique moelle"* of his *Gangantua and Pantagruel* in tripe, codpieces, bacon, bungholes, geese, cabbages, and weeds, Swift ultimately directs his satire at the ways in which we all risk madness by seeking to deny the physical necessities without which life would cease. But unlike Rabelais, who offers his book as a draught to cure the world's diseases, Swift portrays life's physical necessities as inherently repugnant, and thus betrays his pessimism about the possibility of curing the madness whose ultimate etiology he never completely explains. Gulliver, almost as isolated as the Laputans, would be tragic if his end were less terrifyingly ridiculous.

The heroine of Laputa is clearly the "great Court Lady" who repeatedly steals down to the land below, where she is found "in an obscure Eating-House all in Rags, having pawned her Cloths to maintain an old deformed Footman, who beat her every Day" (*Travels, Prose,* XI, 116). She returns to him again and again because his beatings confirm her reality. Unlike her fellow citizens who remain trapped within their own speculations, and unlike most of Swift's satiric speakers, she escapes from the prison of her mind. Her liberation, however, only delivers her to the pain of her physical being. Her escape epitomizes the procedure of Swift's satires, which portray human beings straining toward the heights of sublimity only to plunge into the depths of physicality. In what is surely a parody of Descartes' oxymoronic *"esprits animaux,"* the fanatics in the *Mechanical Operation of the Spirit* seek the heights of spirituality by confining their heads in *"quilted Caps,"* which

> stop all Perspiration, and by reverberating the Heat, prevent the Spirit from evaporating any way, but at the Mouth . . . . For, it is the opinion of Choice *Virtuosi*, that the Brain is only a Crowd of little Animals, but with Teeth and Claws extremely sharp, . . . That all Invention is formed by the Morsure of these Animals, upon certain capillary Nerves, . . . Further, that nothing less than a violent Heat, can disentangle these creatures from their hamated Station of Life, or give them Vigor and Humor, to imprint the Marks of their little Teeth.[23]

Like the *Tale*'s mad Jack, who rails against his eyes as *"blind Guides, . . . who fasten upon the first Precipice in view, and then tow our wretched willing Bodies after You, to the very Brink of Destruction" (Tale,* p. 193), the fanatics in the "Fragment" fix their eyes on the constellations only to be seduced by their lower parts into a ditch. Swift's "ditch" is inevitably the privy, the ubiquitous jakes whose metamorphoses determine the shape of many of his fictive prisons. Its omnipresence is mortifying (denying, as Norman O. Brown has noted, the sublimities), but it is paradoxically comforting too. Given Swift's agoraphobic speculations on the ultimately meaningless vacuity of the universe, there is comparative security in the *Mechanical Operation of the Spirit*'s concluding admonition "that however Spiritual Intrigues begin, they generally conclude like all others; they may branch upwards towards Heaven, but the Root is in the Earth. Too intense a Contemplation is not the Business of Flesh and Blood; it must by the necessary Course of Things, in a little Time, let go its Hold, and Fall into *Matter*" ("Fragment," *Tale*, p. 289).

For Swift, the bed is a fictive prison which embodies both the comforting reassurances and the horrors of physicality. In the *Journal,* Swift secures himself within the confines of his bed, drawing the curtains against the cold (January 1710/11, I, 171) and even, on an earlier occasion, addressing Stella's letter as though it were a "prisoner" like himself: "Come out, letter, come out from between the sheets: here it is underneath, and it won't come out. Come out again, I say: here it is" (1 June 1710, I, 126). Advising the upstairs maid in his *Directions to Servants,* he tells her that when she makes the bed in the summer and sweats, she should feel free to wipe her perspiration on the sheets. Wrapped in the bed's confinement, we dream and wake, and come to terms with the intimate realities of the mind and the body alike. "Is that tobacco at the top of the paper, or what?" Swift asks Stella as he wakes in bed with his letter, "I don't remember I slobbered. Lord, I dreamt of Stella &c. so confusedly last night, and that we saw Dean Bolton and Sterne [sic] go into a shop, and she bid them call to her, and they proved to be two parsons I knew not; and I walked without till she was shifting, and such stuff, mixt with much melancholy and uneasiness and things not as they should be, and I know not how, and it is now an ugly gloomy morning" (*Journal,* 14 October 1710, I, 56). The stain on the paper brings Swift back to himself, reconfirming his reality and banishing the oneiric derangements of sleep.

Sharing the chamber pot in bed on their wedding night, Strephon and Chloe drop their illusions and establish for the first time the basis of a genuine and more realistic intimacy. The illusions won't last long anyway, says Swift, warning the young Lady on the occasion of her marriage to cultivate her mind because her beauty will soon decay. Strephon and Chloe fail to realize their opportunity because they do not learn the value of the illusions that they should strive all the harder to preserve after glimpsing the horrors they conceal. Strephon and Chloe do find intimacy, but it is the companionship of the chamber pot, which they subsequently share "And, by a beastly way of Thinking,/Find great Society in Stinking" ("Strephon and Chloe," *Poems*, II, 590, ll. 210-11). Their tragedy is that they have both condemned themselves to the prison of their bodies, for "Love such Nicety requires,/One *Blast* will put out all his fires" (*Poems,* II, 588, ll. 135-36).

But Swift's final attitude toward them is not entirely hostile, just as his attitude toward Celia's dressing room is not entirely condemnatory. The trickery and independence of the senses is finally salutary too: even the effects of a tour of the dressing room could be overcome "When Celia in Her Glory shows/If Strephon would but stop his Nose" ("The Lady's Dressing Room," *Poems,* II, 530, ll. 135-36). In London, Swift seems able enough to recover from a similar experience: "I was to see Lady ——, who is just up after lying-in, and the ugliest sight I have seen, pale, dead, old, and yellow, for want of her paint. She has turned my stomach. But she will soon be painted, and a beauty again" (*Journal*, 21 October 1711, II, 443). Strephon is punished for his "grand survey" because he makes it in the same spirit as the *Tale*'s readers (and Swift's contemporaries) visit Bridewell and Bedlam. We go to Bedlam and behold its freaks only to learn that they are us. A visit to any of Swift's prisons only reveals the criminality in ourselves; a tour of his Augean stables only leaves us covered with filth.

In a riddle entitled "The Gulph of all Human Possessions" (which I think could only be Swift's), the reader is advised to "Come hither, and behold the fruits,/Vain man, of all thy vain Pursuits" (*Poems,* II, 921, ll. 1-2). At the bottom of the jakes lies a noxious mass compounded of books, bribes, perjuries, frauds, and fees, whirled round by "the combat of opposing Winds" and serving as "the food of worms, and Beasts obscene,/Who round the Vault luxurious reign." Its shape is the ultimate form assumed by all of Swift's satiric prisons, in which all human accomplishments either suddenly burst forth in a blast of wind, or fall to earth. *Inter faeces et urinas nascimur*, said Augustine (and innumerable others thereafter); to the jakes we all return, says Swift. At the end of the riddle the privy becomes a grave, "Sad Charnal House! A dismal Dome;/For which all Mortals leave their Home;/The young, the Beautiful, and Brave,/Here buried in one common Grave" (*Poems,* II, 922-23, ll. 51-54). This is proto-graveyard poetry with a vengeance, conjuring up as it does the twin nightmares of the stench of the Augustans and the horrors of the mid-century tomb. Here as elsewhere, the satirist and his reader are finally imprisoned together in its confines, left stopping their noses with Strephon's only alternative—"The Bottom of the Pan to grope,/And fowl his Hands in search of Hope" (*Poems,* II, 528, ll. 93-94). It is not a pleasant choice. Swift's prisons stink. As jailer-Jove-jokester, he leaves us confined within their walls, to face the punishment that could cure us at last, if we would but attend to the delirious lunacies which proliferate in their depths and define the realities we live. [24]

NOTES

1 *A Tale of a Tub, to which is added The Battle of the Books and the Mechanical Operation of the Spirit,* ed. A. C. Guthkelch and D. Nichol Smith, 2nd ed. (Oxford: Clarendon, 1958), p. 38. Subsequent parenthetic references to the *Tale* are to this edition.

2 Solipsism is the subject of A. D. Nuttall's *A Common Sky: Philosophy and the Literary Imagination* (Berkeley: University of California Press, 1974). Nuttall's first chapter, "The Sealing of the Doors," discusses the way in which the British empiricists actually deny the validity of "external" experience; subsequent chapters treat the theme in Sterne, Wordsworth, and later writers. Probably the most comprehensive phenomenological treatment of a wide variety of confinements and enclosures is to be found in Gaston Bachelard, *The Poetics of Space,* trans. Maria Jolas (New York: Orion, 1966).

3 Introduction to his edition of *The Age of Enlightenment: The Eighteenth-Century Philosophers* (New York: New American Library, 1956), pp. 18, 19.

4 In a similar way, the Lascaux cave, according to Bertram D. Lewin's *The Image and the Past* (New York: International Universities Press, 1968) may function, with its numerous animal paintings, as a collectively "externalized replica of the internal cephalic image, in which our 'pictures' are stored and concealed." Lewin speculates that if his conjecture about the cave is correct, it holds "not only the earliest visual images but is also the first model of the memory and the mind" (p. 39).

5 "Thoughts on Various Subjects," (1699) in *The Prose Works of Jonathan Swift,* ed. Herbert Davis, 13 vols. (Oxford: Clarendon, 1938-67), I, 252. Subsequent short-title references to *Prose* are to this edition.

6 John Traugott quotes the spider's outburst, in a somewhat different context, on p. 87 of his essay "*A Tale of a Tub*" in *Focus: Swift,* ed. C. J. Rawson (London: Sphere, 1971). For a discussion of the spider web as a

"striking image . . . of an external periphic world, incessantly felt and rethought by a central consciousness," see Georges Poulet, *The Metamorphoses of the Circle*, trans. Carley Dawson and Elliott Coleman (Baltimore: Johns Hopkins, 1966), pp. 54-57.

7 See W. B. Carnochan, "Swift's *Tale*: On Satire, Negation, and the Uses of Irony," *ECS*, V (1971), 136.

8 Swift to Pope, 30 August 1716, *The Correspondence of Jonathan Swift*, ed. Harold Williams, 5 vols. (Oxford: Clarendon, 1963), II, 215. Subsequent references to the *Correspondence* are to this edition.

9 Swift to Pope, 26 November 1725, *Correspondence*, III, 117.

10 Swift to Pope, 20 September 1723, *Correspondence* II, 465.

11 See the essay on the *Tale* cited above, esp. pp. 89-93.

12 *Journal to Stella*, ed. Harold Williams, 2 vols. (Oxford: Clarendon, 1948), 9 November 1710, I, 89. Subsequent parenthetic references to the *Journal* are to this edition.

13 "Verses on the Death of Dr. Swift, D.S.P.D." in *The Poems of Jonathan Swift*, ed. Harold Williams, 2nd ed. in 3 vols. (Oxford: Clarendon, 1958), II, 562, ll. 246-48. Subsequent references to the *Poems* are to this edition.

14 *A Treatise Concerning the Principles of Human Knowledge*, ed. Colin M. Turbayne (New York: Library of Liberal Arts, 1957), p. 61.

15 I thank Max Byrd for pointing out to me John Summerson's *Heavenly Mansions* (London: Cresset, 1949), whose title essay traces the early development of the aedicule, the architectural "house-within-a-house" which proliferates in gothic churches and expresses what Summerson terms (p. 10) "a desire to transform the heavy man-made Romanesque temple into a multiple, imponderable pile of heavenly mansions." British pulpits of Swift's age—both the one in St. Patrick's Cathedral and those in Hogarth's prints—seem to me to display their aedicular heritage.

16 "The Snayl," reproduced in *Natural Magic*, Kitty W. Scoular's anthology with commentary (Oxford: Oxford University Press, 1965), p. 78, ll. 1-2. A richer treatment of both emblematic background and contemporary politics in the poem is Randolph L. Wadsworth, Jr., "On 'The Snayl' by Richard Lovelace," *MLR*, 65 (1970), 750–60.

17 *Pensées*, no. 80, "*Divertissement*," in *Pascal: Pensées*, ed. Louis Marin (Paris: Didier, 1969), pp. 90-91.

18 "Occasioned by Sir W— T——'s Late Illness and Recovery" (1693), *Poems*, I, 51, ll. 1-10.

19 *An Essay concerning Human Understanding*, ed. Alexander Campbell Fraser, 2 vols. (1894; rpt. New York: Dover, 1959), II.ix.14, I, 191.

20 "Another," *Poems*, III, 931, ll. 1-14. On the questionable authenticity of the riddles in this section, see Williams's introductory note on p. 914 of

this volume. Grounds for considering the riddle Swift's may be found in the resemblance between its "clerk" as one whom the senses can "turn and wind" at will and Swift's similar portrayal of himself in "The Dean's Reasons for not Building at Drapier's Hill" (1730). In "The Dean's Reasons," written during the period to which Faulkner assigns the riddles, Swift jokingly describes himself as "The greatest Cully of Mankind:/The lowest boy in Martin's school/May turn and wind me like a fool" (III, 899, ll. 12-14). For a graphic analog to this poem, see Huet's engraving *"Le Palais des Facultés"* (1635), which portrays the mind's faculties as women arrayed in front of a Parisian palace. At the left of the engraving is the woman entitled *"le sens commun,"* who holds in her hands the strings which lead to puppets of the disembodied hand, ear, eye, nose, and partial face which represent the senses.

21 For a pellucid discussion of this aspect of empiricism, see Nuttal, *A Common Sky,* ch. 1.

22 "Mary Gulliver to Captain Lemuel Gulliver," *The Poems of Alexander Pope,* vol. VI, ed. Norman Ault and John Butt (London: Methuen, 1964), pp. 276-77, ll. 6-7, 35-39.

23 *The Mechanical Operation of the Spirit* is reprinted in the Guthkelch-Smith edition of the *Tale,* pp. 259-89. This passage appears on p. 277. The subsequent reference to the "Fragment" is to this edition.

24 I wish to express my appreciation to the Librarian of the William Andrews Clark Memorial Library, who asked that I read this essay in a program on August 1, 1975. The essay was originally written for the workshop "The Prison in Literature and Art," held on July 15 during the Fourth International Congress on the Enlightenment, Yale University.

Conflict and Declamation in Rasselas

FREDERICK M. KEENER

My Lord, forsake your Politick Utopians,
To sup, like Jove, with blameless Ethiopians.
Pope

"It seems to me, said Imlac, that while you are making the choice of life, you neglect to live."[1] Readers of Samuel Johnson's *Rasselas* have tended to regard this reflection, from Chapter xxx, as just; have from time to time proceeded to remark that only when Pekuah is abducted in Chapter xxxiii do the travelers cease to be mere spectators of life and begin to participate in it—although that harrowing degree of participation was not what Imlac had in mind three chapters before.[2] Indeed, so wise is Imlac, so often do his sayings correspond with those of the narrator, and with those uttered by Johnson elsewhere, that a reader has trouble sustaining disbelief that all three persons are not, for practical purposes, one. So natural is the trinitarian assumption that criticism, while alert to other possibilities of interpretation, has seemingly been restricted in its examination of them.[3] I hope to cast light on Imlac's relation to the narrator as well as to Rasselas, but first it will be necessary to question the validity of Imlac's "you neglect to live." Although the characters have only tentatively involved themselves with complete strangers to this point more than midway through the tale, whether or not Imlac wishes to acknowledge it they have seriously become engaged not just in life but also in conflict, with each other.[4] Although the book is not a full-fledged novel as we have come to understand the meaning of that term, its account of the main characters' disagreement, anger, and estrangement from each other deserves recognition.[5]

To emphasize the prominence of this chain of events, a chain linking together more than a third of the tale, I shall summarize the main details before looking into them. By Chapter xiii, Rasselas is pleased to have found a friend in Imlac, who, while differing from him in the expectations they entertain about the world outside the Happy Valley, will help him escape. But by the twenty-third and twenty-fourth chapters, the prince and his sister, Nekayah, have come to distrust Imlac, to feel that he disapproves of their "search, lest we should in time find him mistaken." Imlac disappears for several chapters while brother and sister alone pursue the choice of life. By Chapter xxix, however, Rasselas and Nekayah have themselves fallen out, she tending to agree with Imlac and thinking Rasselas has now questioned *her* honesty: "I did not expect, answered the princess, to hear that imputed to falshood which is the consequence only of frailty" (Ch. xxviii).

Then, after six or more chapters' absence, Imlac reenters to suggest living, specifically an instructive visit to the pyramids. Rasselas resists the suggestion but relents with—not eagerness but acceptance on principle: "I am willing, said the prince, to see all that can deserve my search" (Ch. xxx). Almost immediately, by denying the possible existence of ghosts, he provokes Imlac's stern disagreement, accompanied by a gratuitous slap at the doubts of some "single cavillers." And when news of Pekuah's abduction reaches the party, Imlac abruptly questions Rasselas' order for pursuit of the bandits. Rasselas does not respond, has difficulty controlling himself; he wants to accuse "them"—the Turkish guards, maybe others as well—of cowardice (Ch. xxxiii). Not until the end of the thirty-fifth chapter does the prince show any sign of willing cooperation with his mentor, when comforting Nekayah. It has been thirteen chapters since Rasselas' disaffection was announced to us, nearly a third of the book, and it will be longer still before Rasselas shows another sign of reconciliation. In Chapter xxxvii Imlac refuses to let the prince accompany him in ransoming Pekuah. Only in the fortieth chapter, with fewer than ten chapters to go and very few episodes, mainly that of the astronomer, is there evidence of renewed affection between the younger man and the older.

But the nature of their conflict and of their means of resolving it is more important than the fact of its existence, for the reader's giving their competition its due weight will reveal new depth, almost a new dimension, in the meaning as well as the drama of the tale, which has more fictional and rhetorical force than is usually acknowledged. It is a philosophical *tale*, not just philosophy superficially decorated by a story. The chain of events, faintly drawn as it is in places, holds together; in part it is a chain of development in the character of the prince and in his relationship with his mentor.

The critic who, to my knowledge, has faced the basic generic question most squarely and specifically is Sheldon Sacks, in *Fiction and the Shape of Belief.*[6] Very briefly: Sacks argues that *Rasselas* is neither a novel nor a philosophical dialogue but an "apologue," which, as it progresses, formulates and refines a set of abstract propositions about its subject, in this case the possibilities of human happiness; thus "Johnson's task was to increase our interest in the agents [the characters, as plausible persons] to the greatest degree possible short of obscuring the relation of the episode to the controlling theme" (p. 57). This is a helpful distinction, but it does not settle the question fully, and Sacks only sketchily comments on the degree to which characters of an apologue must be conserved, must remain consistent (pp. 59-60). The aforesaid distinction would permit too much inconsistency in characterization from episode to episode. Moreover, it seems to encourage a priori underestimation of the fullness of characters; to refer to Sacks's main example, he remarks that "Rasselas' contempt for the meretricious teacher of morality [the stoic of

Chapter xviii, defeated by his daughter's sudden death] does not reveal his emotional reaction to human suffering" (p. 60; see also p. 14). Yet neither the passage nor its context warrants so strong a word as "contempt" to describe the feelings of "the prince, whose humanity would not suffer him to insult misery with reproof." He could perhaps have stayed and comforted the devastated, mistaken philosopher, but Rasselas is emotionally young, in this early episode has his own fish to fry—and has just been badly burned himself, having accepted the philosopher at face value against Imlac's advice. The prince's reaction here, like that of the man who has disappointed him, is unphilosophical but human.

Sacks, in addition, implies by his statement an overall conviction of the young man's customary humaneness; like other readers who insist on the difference between *Rasselas* and novels, Sacks tends pleasantly to take the characters more seriously than not. His not fully explained impression that the thwarted search for the happiest state of life is still somehow consoling, not unreassuring about the human condition, may, indeed, derive from the advantages he sees the characters discovering in virtue and the hope of eternal joy (pp. 52-55). But it may arise also from the resiliency, penetration, and generosity the characters display as, over the course of the story, they convincingly take disappointments in stride and come to understand each other, the consolations of companionship and education, and the universality of their condition, better than they did at the beginning. The consolations I mention are for the most part enacted rather than talked about and thus apparently tend to escape readers who take up the book expecting discursive propositions rather than evocative fiction. More than Sacks recognizes, *Rasselas* gives fullness to its characters as well as to its moral teachings; it may be that such an equilibrium best defines the apologue, rather than stress on propositions at the expense of the characters. Such a formula would, in any event, preserve the distance between Johnson's tale and *War and Peace* without giving too much away.

The question may also invite more historical understanding

than it has received. How fully, a hundred years before Tolstoy, did fictional characters need to be developed in order to "seem real"? (The question is not unlike that of how much Pope's persona in the later moral and satirical epistles is and was designed to be, realistically, Pope himself.) Consider the inclusiveness of this generalization about the early history of English prose fiction, from an exceptionally literate eighteenth-century reader well acquainted with the minds of the contemporary book-buying and borrowing public, Benjamin Franklin: "Honest John [Bunyan] was the first that I know who mix'd Narration and Dialogue; a Method of Writing very engaging to the Reader, who in the most interesting Parts finds himself as it were brought into the Company, and present at the Discourse. Defoe in his Cruso, his Moll Flanders, Religious Courtship, Family Instructor, and other Pieces, has imitated it with Success. And Richardson has done the same in his Pamela, &c."[7] Or consider how seriously Fanny Burney took Johnson's story as well as his moral (the italics are mine): "Oh, how dreadful, how terrible is it to be told by a man of his genius and knowledge, *in so affectingly probable a manner,* that true, real, happiness is ever unattainable in this world! –Thro' all the scenes, publick or private, domestick or solitary, that Nekaya or Rasselas pass, real felicity eludes their pursuit and mocks their solicitude."[8] The eighteenth-century threshold for judgments about the seemingly real in fiction was decidedly lower than later criteria—as ecumenically receptive as, in that time, anything approaching precise discrimination between apologue and novel was rare.[9] I can simply touch on such large historical issues, however, before returning to my main topic, the contests and dissensions in Abyssinia and Egypt.

From Imlac, Rasselas wants help in choosing a station in life attended by constant happiness. Yet within a chapter of what W. K. Wimsatt calls Imlac's "curiously abrupt" entry into the book[10] —that strangely inconspicuous entry, to which I shall return— Rasselas begins to be disappointed. As Imlac opens his autobiographical account, he mentions his father's fear that the governors of the province would take away his riches, and Rasselas is appalled that his own father, the emperor, permits such villainy.

> "Sir, said Imlac, your ardour is the natural effect of vertue animated by youth: the time will come when you will acquit your father, and perhaps hear with less impatience of the governour. Oppression is, in the Abissinian dominions, neither frequent nor tolerated; but no form of government has been yet discovered, by which cruelty can be wholly prevented. Subordination supposes power on one part and subjection on the other; and if power be in the hands of men, it will sometimes be abused. The vigilance of the supreme magistrate may do much, but much will still remain undone. He can never know all the crimes that are committed, and can seldom punish all that he knows."
>
> "This, said the prince, I do not understand, but I had rather hear thee than dispute. Continue thy narration." (Ch. viii)

Rasselas is inexperienced, Imlac wise, yet as the story continues, Imlac shows a tendency to generalize about the world in a manner which if not utterly disproved by the prince's later, disillusioning experience, is not wholly corroborated by it either. Imlac draws his contrasts too sharply, for example in these early words, from Chapter xii: "The world, which you figure to yourself smooth and quiet as the lake in the valley, you will find a sea foaming with tempests, and boiling with whirlpools: you will be sometimes overwhelmed by the waves of violence, and sometimes dashed against the rocks of treachery. Amidst wrongs and frauds, competitions and anxieties, you will wish a thousand times for these seats of quiet, and willingly quit hope to be free from fear." The speech, like others in the book, is spoken not only about something but also to someone, with various potential intentions behind it.

Here Imlac may be fulfilling the role assigned to sages in the Happy Valley, who, as we are told in Chapter ii, did everything possible to induce contentment in the pent sons and daughters of Abyssinia, including exaggerating the miseries and calamities of the world outside. That world, Rasselas will find, never becomes quite so malevolent as Imlac promises; the prince will later rebuke his sister for "producing, in a familiar disquisition, examples of national calamities, and scenes of extensive misery, which are found in books rather than in the world, and which, as they are horrid, are ordained to be rare" (Ch. xxviii). In books like *Candide,* he might have said; in his own story, evil, though heard of, for the most part keeps its distance or enters in its Sunday clothes, as in the person of the kidnapper whose surface gentility almost rivals Imlac's. But to cite Imlac for exaggeration is to recognize not only that he is a sage of the Valley but also that he is human, and to understand that he speaks not in a vacuum but in the company of a young man with distressingly optimistic expectations. He is replying to Rasselas, evidently replying passionately, disturbed by his companion's attitude and exerting himself to change it by head-on verbal assault.

Ostensibly about civil government, what Imlac says in Chapter viii has broader application, and the subject will be pursued, discursively and dramatically, throughout the book. Nekayah, for example, will later remark, "If a kingdom be, as Imlac tells us, a great family, a family likewise is a little kingdom, torn with factions and exposed to revolutions" (Ch. xxvi). The analogy is reminiscent of the *Lettres persanes,* with some comparable irony. Rather than addressing the subject of their own relationship, Imlac and Rasselas talk about their fathers—one of whom happens to be an emperor, but both fathers are governors of their children, and it begs no question to point out that Rasselas is seeking paternal guidance from Imlac. Indeed, Rasselas probably expects at first that Imlac, after listening to his complaints, will rummage through his own experience of the world and pick out just the choice of life to suit the young man's needs—Imlac, who has met with indifferent success in making his own choice. Would Imlac tell him if he could, or Rasselas heed him? Again Nekayah speaks later to the purpose: "An unpractised observer expects the love of parents and children to be constant and equal, but this kindness seldom continues beyond the years of infancy: in a short time the children become rivals to their parents. Benefits are allayed by reproaches, and gratitude debased by envy" (Ch. xxvi). She pursues the topic: there is a natural difference of perspective separating young and old: "The opinions of children and parents, of the young and the old, are naturally opposite, by the contrary effects of hope and despondence, of expectation and experience, without crime or folly on either side." And, most appositely in so sententious a book as this, she adds, "Few parents act in such a manner as much to enforce their maxims by the credit of their lives. The old man trusts wholly to slow contrivance and gradual progression: the youth expects to force his way by genius, vigour, and precipitance." But despite her maxims and examples, the prince cannot agree with her. "Surely . . . you must have been unfortunate in your choice of acquaintance: I am unwilling to believe, that the most tender of all relations is thus impeded in its effects by natural necessity." In this obduracy he is not simply naive, as the book will show; he is not finally just Imlac's rival.

Yet what Nekayah has said perfectly fits the case of Rasselas' relations with Imlac through the middle of the tale, although Rasselas may not see it. Rasselas has grown impatient with his mentor, especially it seems with Imlac's wanting to tell young people what to think, and to tell them at length. As a poet of his own description, Imlac is not simply intolerant of youthful impetuosity; he yearns to play "the interpreter of nature, and the legislator of mankind"; he has maxims by the dozens, likes delivering them, has indulged himself in the fit of enthusiasm about poetry that culminates in Chapter xi, is seldom without a string of universal opinions on any topic that arises. Soon Rasselas grows unwilling to raise any. Through the beginning of Chapter xxiii Imlac speaks a great deal, mostly to depress the prince's high expectations of happiness. "Do not seek to deter me from my purpose," Rasselas protests in Chapter xii. After another exchange he exclaims, "surely happiness is somewhere to be found" (Ch. xvi).

When Imlac reappears after the seven chapters in which the two young people have conducted their search without him, his suggestion of a tour of the pyramids meets with a declamatory refusal from the prince.[11] "My curiosity, said Rasselas, does not very strongly lead me to survey piles of stone, or mounds of earth; my business is with man. I came hither not to measure fragments of temples, or trace choaked aqueducts, but to look upon the various scenes of the present world" (Ch. xxx). The princess, however, replies in a slightly different fashion. She too resists the suggestion, forcefully, but her statement ends with a question to Imlac about why they ought to be concerned about old monuments, a question which, needless to say, Imlac is prepared to answer quite fully. Rasselas simply protests, then gives in; but albeit backhandedly, Nekayah asks for information and gets it, to her satisfaction. "I, said the princess, shall rejoice to learn something of the manners of antiquity."

The distinction, though apparently small, is worth making because of what had occurred during the chapters just preceding this, in which Rasselas and Nekayah had searched alone, then become disappointed with each other. They had fallen out over the question of marriage, Nekayah refusing to take its disadvantages lightly, Rasselas holding out for its advantages. The end of their debate naturally focuses on the relation of parents to children, that constant theme of the book. While Rasselas wants to believe in the possibility of some mediating bond between young and old, Nekayah insists that "those who marry late are best pleased with their children, and those who marry early with their partners." Says Rasselas, "The union of these two affections . . . would produce all that could be wished. Perhaps there is a time when marriage might unite them, a time neither too early for the father nor too late for the husband" (Ch. xxix). Still Rasselas dreams of a condition supplying "all that could be wished"! Still he resists the opinion that nothing sufficiently positive can be expected.

The princess not only disagrees, perhaps too forcibly; she also reassociates herself with the person whom she and her brother, in a happier moment, had allied themselves to evade. "Every hour . . . confirms my prejudice in favour of the position so often uttered by the mouth of Imlac, 'That nature sets her gifts on the right hand and on the left.'" And she amplifies the point as

Rasselas' rejected mentor would. "Flatter not yourself with contrarieties of pleasure. Of the blessings set before you make your choice, and be content." These cryptic imperatives she confirms, like the poet's poet,[12] with "general and transcendental truths," truths decorated and emphasized by ideas drawn from the "awfully vast" and "elegantly little" in nature ("the plants of the garden" and so forth, as stipulated by Imlac in Chapter x). "No man," she says, probably feeling some "complacence in her own perspicacity" like that felt by Rasselas in Chapter ii, "can taste the fruits of autumn while he is delighting his scent with the flowers of the spring: no man can, at the same time, fill his cup from the source and from the mouth of the Nile."[13] She propounds her beliefs as if she possessed the wisdom of ages and the tongue of an angel, and she leaves poor doubtful Rasselas to pursue his increasingly forlorn search all by himself.

Her speech is inflated, insensitive. Everyone speaks with relative formality in the book, but in different voices at different times, as Carey McIntosh has noted.[14] Imlac speaks *Rambler* essays, whenever he has the chance—or so it seems up to this point. We know Imlac's ruling passion is his love of speech poetic and authoritative, and we know, since Chapters x-xi, that it can run away with him. Moreover, he is not the only major figure in the book with a tendency that way, but I am not thinking now of Nekayah as she, on the occasion just described, emits her master's voice. The other major figure with an inclination for grandiloquence is, of course, the narrator, nowhere more so than in the first sentence of the book, the monitory tones of which rumble as if they emanated from some primordial chamber deep within the most ancient of pyramids or the catacombs of Cairo, rumble and creak. "Ye who listen with credulity to the whispers of fancy, and persue with eagerness the phantoms of hope; who expect that age will perform the promises of youth, and that the deficiencies of the present day will be supplied by the morrow; attend to the history of Rasselas prince of Abissinia." Not merely chronologically does this speaker have a place between Milton's God and Blake's Nobodaddy, obliterating all distinction between the assertive and the authoritarian, holding forth about "gates of iron, forged by the artificers of ancient days, so massy that no man could, without the help of engines, open or shut them." Some sort of "two-handed" engines no doubt.

To Rasselas' credit, he seldom speaks that way, doing so only in the first half of the book, when complacent about his perceptions or when about to be more directly deflated, as when he futilely preaches sobriety to the Young Men of Spirit and Gaiety (Ch. xvii). Rasselas grows quieter as the book progresses. His encounter with the would-be stoic in Chapter xviii leaves him, we are told, "convinced of the emptiness of rhetorical sound, and the inefficacy of polished periods and studied sentences," a typical overreaction. The next time he meets a sage of that sort, the advocate of a Life Led According to Nature, he does not stay to haggle. "The prince soon found that this was one of the sages whom he should understand less as he heard him longer. He therefore bowed and was silent" (Ch. xxii). His debate with his sister provokes from him statements not free of the "errours of exaggeratory declamation" and "quer[u]lous eloquence" he finds in hers (Ch. xxviii), but after the unhappy impasse with her, he says very little.

When he does speak between Chapters xxx and xxxix, he continues to be at cross-purposes with Imlac. After consenting on principle to visit the pyramids, he is quiet for two chapters while Imlac discourses on the "hunger of imagination," until, hearing of Pekuah's misfortune, he announces his resolve to pursue the abductors, saber in hand. But Imlac quashes the idea with cool, or cold, common sense. (As Nekayah had said, "The old man trusts wholly to slow contrivance and gradual progression: the youth expects to force his way by genius, vigour, and precipitance.") Two chapters later we again hear something about Rasselas—that he tried to console his sister, and after being quoted then he is not again heard from until, four chapters later, Pekuah is finishing the account of her adventure. Back in Chapter xxxv, however, attempting to comfort Nekayah, he had reasoned in a spirit as appropriate to his condition as to hers: "At least, said the prince, do not despair before all remedies have been tried: the enquiry after the unfortunate lady is still continued, and shall be carried on with yet greater diligence, on condition that you will promise to wait a year for the event, without any unalterable resolution." Then the narrator gives us a highly significant piece of information, not sufficiently emphasized to strike the casual reader, that Rasselas had extracted this promise from his sister on Imlac's advice. Rasselas has once more turned to Imlac, accepted his guidance. How much time the prince had sat sulking in his tent—he has evidently been sulking—we are not told. His contention with Imlac, now active for thirteen chapters and more, is over.

When Rasselas speaks again, his sentences are not declamatory, are in fact seldom declarative; instead of asserting himself, he asks questions, his tone enquiring, reflective, his words beginning with an "I could not" (Ch. xlvii) or comparably self-effacing phrase. His response to the astronomer's suggestion of a visit to the catacombs—"I know not, said Rasselas, what pleasure the sight of the catacombs can afford; but, since nothing else is offered, I am resolved to view them, and shall place this with many other things which I have done, because I would do something" (Ch. xlvii)—this response, in contrast with his declamatory reply to Imlac regarding the pyramids, though tinged with plaintiveness, is not arrogant. That Rasselas' character has changed seems possible; another indication comes in the younger persons' various attitudes toward Imlac's account of the old, crazed astronomer, Rasselas seeming more profound than the others.[15] "The prince heard this narration with very serious regard, but the princess smiled, and Pekuah convulsed herself with laughter." Imlac scolds the two women. "Rasselas," we are told, "more deeply affected, enquired of Imlac, whether he thought such maladies of the mind frequent, and how they were contracted" (Ch. xliii). The young man's one outburst toward the end of the book is in temporarily successful opposition to the women's plan of deceiving the astronomer (Ch. xlvi).

There is a plausible explanation for Rasselas' greater sympathy, since he had induced Imlac to describe the astronomer by his own immature and enthusiastic declaration, at the start of Chapter xl, that he meant to devote himself to a life of learning, a life like the astronomer's. Imlac's tale speaks directly to Rasselas' new fantasy. I think, however, that there is an indirect and deeper cause for the prince's sympathy. Alone among the young people in the book he seems to have experienced a change of mind affecting his whole sense of himself. Nekayah was recovered from solitary misery by an external, chance event, the return of Pekuah.[16] Rasselas, having broken with Imlac and then with his sister, himself moved—moved himself—toward recovery from potential solipsism. I would not want to make too much of this reorientation: the book remains too schematic to be read primarily as psychological fiction—yet at the same time is too provocative, psychologically, to be read as a set of philosophical propositions in disguise. Unobtrusively, consistently however, the change has occurred: the Rasselas who had professed to be an enquirer at the beginning of the book has begun to enquire in earnest, and has ceased to insist that the world conform to untested expectations. Instead he will become more conscious of his preconceptions, most notably when a few chapters later he and Nekayah and Pekuah, as if members of an encounter group, confess their favorite daydreams. Rasselas' own "fantastick delight" has been "to image the possibility of a perfect government, by which all wrong should be restrained, all vice reformed, and all the subjects preserved in tranquility and innocence" (Ch. xliv).[17] That the world will not permit realization of that dream for state or family is the recognition he has been resisting throughout the book, since in the Happy Valley he began to differ with Imlac, refusing to accept the seemingly contradictory facts that there are some bad governors in Abyssinia and that his father is not to blame. Although entering the wide world, he has insisted on bringing the Happy Valley with him.

One could now introduce the psychological extrapolation that Rasselas' wish to make the world perfect, as his father has not, masks a wish to do away with his father and to rationalize and atone for parricide by excelling him in good works. But one need introduce nothing, for Johnson, with characteristic insight, has Rasselas both judge his utopian fantasy rightly, as "more dangerous" than his companions', and begin to understand it by approaching consciousness of his deep motives: ". . . I start, when I think with how little anguish I once supposed the death of my father and my brothers." This remarkable statement bears also on Rasselas' relations with Imlac, whose reply is a model of order and discretion. He selectively addresses himself not to Rasselas' surprising conclusion but to the general theme of all three young persons' confessions, and he has the grace to include himself in his generalization: "Such, says Imlac, are the effects of visionary schemes: when we first form them we know them to be absurd, but familiarise them by degrees, and in time lose sight of their folly." The main subject of the chapter is the way in which solitary imaginings may begin to affect a person's actions, interfering with his perception of reality and his comportment of himself within it. Pekuah, Nekayah, and Rasselas all give instances of that tendency in their own past behavior; Pekuah, for example, in her desire for sovereignty, has at times nearly forgotten to be properly obedient to the princess. But only Rasselas begins to answer the consequent, disturbing problem: what practical realization of the dream would entail. Although Pekuah's dream would call for more havoc than his, and Nekayah's for evasion of a princess's responsibilities, the two women do not venture so far as to acknowledge these "side effects." Rasselas, to be sure, could go further. Insightful as his disclosure is, he does not see the true longings satisfied by his fantasy. He is, however, very much on the right track, more so than his sister or her maid.

Time, experience, solitude, suffering, and the company of Imlac have brought about the change in Rasselas, although it is difficult to specify what each has exactly contributed. What Imlac has certainly not done is give in to Rasselas' opinions, despite the prince's opposition and withdrawal. Imlac has, however, not withdrawn himself, and events have drawn the two of them back together—chiefly, the event of Rasselas' change in attitude. But a still more subtle trait distinguishes Imlac's behavior toward the prince, the gist of which a reader may discern in what Imlac says to Nekayah when she blames herself for not having commanded

Pekuah to enter the pyramid, out of real harm's way: "Do not reproach yourself for your virtue, or consider that as blameable by which evil has accidentally been caused. Your tenderness for the timidity of Pekuah was generous and kind" (Ch. xxxiv). He labors the point, but not beyond recognition; and that respect for Pekuah he praises in Nekayah is a general attitude toward others which Imlac himself, in action if not in every word, always maintains (by contrast, Nekayah in the next chapter will summon him to attend her against his will). Imlac's conduct unflaggingly exemplifies a point made by Rasselas in the marriage debate: "We will not endeavour to modify the motions of the elements, or to fix the destiny of kingdoms"—again the fantasies of Rasselas and the astronomer. "It is our business to consider what beings like us may perform; each labouring for his own happiness, by promoting within his circle, however narrow, the happiness of others" (Ch. xxviii).[18]

From the beginning, Imlac tends to behave as if he has seen it all and wants to save Rasselas the trouble, assuming that the prince will in the long run come to see everything as his mentor already does. But in the course of the book Imlac tempers this attitude somewhat, complementing the change in Rasselas. With time Imlac tends to adopt a tone less of pronouncement than of statement—statement, moreover, in which he ranges himself with rather than above or against his young companions. The tonal contrast is sharp in Chapter xxx, for Rasselas ("rather pretentiously," according to Walter Jackson Bate[19]) has just delivered himself of a pronouncement himself, the "My business is with man" passage, and his sister has asked, not entirely in the tone of someone seeking an answer, "What have I to do with the heroes or the monuments of ancient times? " Here is Imlac's reply.

> To know any thing . . . we must know its effects; to see men we must see their works, that we may learn what reason has dictated, or passion has incited, and find what are the most powerful motives of action. To judge rightly of the present we must oppose it to the past; for all judgment is comparative, and of the future nothing can be known. The truth is that no mind is

> much employed upon the present: recollection and anticipation fill up almost all our moments. Our passions are joy and grief, love and hatred, hope and fear.

To the young persons' reactive first-person singulars, Imlac answers in the first-person plural. Like the narrator with his "Ye," Imlac has tended to speak as if the member of a species outside and above the conditions occupied by the prince and his sister, but here he pointedly speaks otherwise. And although there is a "we" which flatters or coerces, and a neutral editorial "we," Imlac's in this passage is arguably neither aggressive nor toneless but conciliatory, for he is speaking not of the limitations peculiar to the young or remotely affecting abstract mankind, heretofore his usual, sometimes fruitless topic, but of the limitations he, Imlac, shares with his companions. In the first-person plural he is speaking directly about the force and burdensomeness of his own as well as others' emotions.

Not that he maintains this position unfailingly thereafter; he is too much drawn to the declamatory, as we have seen, and, before quitting the pyramid, he will make it ring with—it has been noted[20]—an echo of the narrator's first sentence: "Whoever thou art, that, not content with a moderate condition, imaginest happiness in royal magnificence, and dreamest that command or riches"—and so on (Ch. xxxii). But this apostrophe, at this point, relates only quite indirectly to any of his companions, and after his tempered tone has brought him somewhat closer to them, near the end of the book, there comes a chapter in which he joins their search not simply as philosopher and friend but because he shares their longings. Like a guide passing the boundary of the tract he knows, the older man becomes an explorer again, in his suggestion that the party question a very old man, "that we may know whether youth alone is to struggle with vexation, and whether any better hope remains for the latter part of life" (Ch. xlv). For Imlac the questions are not purely speculative. Like Rasselas on so many previous occasions, he resists the old man's despondency. He even tries to place in the old man's mouth the words he himself needs to hear: "You may at least recreate yourself, said Imlac, with the recollection of an honourable and useful life, and enjoy the praise which all agree to give you." In vain; the old man goes on to summarize "The Vanity of Human Wishes." The narrator for the first time in the book draws all the travelers together in a single reaction to an intellectual experience, commenting that the old man left "his audience not much elated with the hope of long life." This episode and the evening end with each of the young people's finding a characteristic defense against the old man's unpalatable words—Rasselas showing less resistance than the others.[21] Imlac, who has already bared his feelings, does not declaim; he, "who had no desire to see them depressed, smiled at the comforts which they could so readily procure to themselves, and remembered, that at the same age, he was equally confident of unmingled prosperity and equally fertile of consolatory expedients. He forbore to force upon them unwelcome knowledge, which time itself would too soon impress."

There are so many dichotomies in *Rasselas,* so many cases of things set either on the right hand or on the left, that one may come away from the book with a sobering sense of the unalterable discreteness, if not the downright contrariety, of everything and everyone. It is, in fact, hard to see how one may not; yet to emphasize this point may be to miss another equally important, that exists in a state of constant tension with it. For the contrariety of persons, at any rate, a contrariety which becomes emphatic midway through the book, does not sum up their relationship, nor does discreteness, important as it is. Had Pekuah not been restored to Nekayah, it is doubtful whether the princess would have recovered fully from her loss. Rasselas is a more stable, more phlegmatic figure, never as close to despair as his sister can be and perhaps incapable of her degree of attachment. The book may seem without any sort of mediation between the terms of its dichotomies, yet that is too one-sided a view. There *is* mediation, or a measure of it; there is, in fact, a mediator, namely Imlac, who does something to join past, present, future, and other discrete entities, including Rasselas and himself. He does not fuse them; he cannot, nor can any mediator, at least in nature as the book presents it and as Johnson evidently saw it. But through trial and error, error and trial, Imlac, with increasing cooperation from Rasselas, seems to guide his pupil and himself to a state of self-knowledge and mutual understanding that—the action of the tale implies—people do not find ready-made even by traveling from China to Peru.[22] Moreover, through participating from near the beginning of the tale in what seems a heuristic, educational process for himself as well as Rasselas (who is not merely Imlac's pupil), the older man helps the prince acquire not a new sort of dependency but the capacity to make, independently, his own moderate contentment beyond the illusions of blind desire. Something is concluded, I think readers will agree, at the famously inconclusive conclusion of the tale: Rasselas' pressing need for Imlac's guidance.

The main characters readjust themselves, and so—very subtly, yet at one point very awkwardly—does the book as a whole. First the subtle readjustment: I have described the way in which the hortatory, declamatory, even accusatory tone which Imlac sometimes favors resembles that taken by the narrator at the outset of the tale. The narrator of *Rasselas* speaks as if omniscient in the fullest sense, not only as if privy to everything in the world, including the workings of the characters' minds, but also as if privy to what is finally right and wrong in the world. The narrator is omniscient in the conventional narrative sense of the word, and in the theological sense as well, an energetically judgmental narrator, a pantocratic overseer.[23] Not, however, as much as he seems to be; he seems more judgmental than he is because he is so much so at the beginning of the book with his booming exordium, his so formal setting of the scene, his propensity for dry maxims ("But pleasures never can be so multiplied or continued, as not to leave much of life unemployed") and valetudinarian wisdom ("But in the decline of life shame and grief are of short duration"—Ch. iv), and his ironies against Rasselas' gropings, in which the initial thunder may seem more forceful for being held in check. With his "but's" and his palpable assurance, he is more overbearing than

Imlac in his emphasis on human limitations, particularly because he seems subject to none himself. He enjoys totalitarian freedom.

Until Imlac enters the book. With Imlac's awkward entrance, the narrator subtly changes his tone, even his ironies almost entirely vanishing. He settles down to being omniscient only in the conventional narrator's way, and the burden of judgment is assumed by Imlac. From then on, the narrator describes, Imlac prescribes. To Rasselas, Imlac's burdensome prescriptions must seem utterly, oppressively weighty, heavier than the reader finds them; after hearing the narrator's voice of doom, the acute reader cannot help but find less authority in Imlac's voice, no matter how imposing his declamation. The effect is that judgment itself becomes emphasized as limited and nontranscendent, a matter of exertion and expression by specific, limited persons under a mute sky, and any potential agreement now appears to be a matter not of unilateral submission, although it seems so to Rasselas and will continue to seem so for some time, but of common understanding in so far as such can be established and maintained. The change in the posture of the narrator turns the universe of the book inside out: from a place where everyone seems required to know absolutely everything (as does Imlac's poet and, by implication, the poet Imlac), it changes to a place where everyone must learn to tolerate vast reaches of uncertainty. The change parallels Rasselas' experience of his quest, as he goes from imagining he need only choose the best of all possible lives, to wondering gloomily whether a suitable choice exists anywhere, to acknowledging his desire and simultaneously expecting that it could not "be obtained" (Ch. xlix). The tale, with fallible, human Imlac unobtrusively taking over the judgmental function of the superhuman narrator, enacts for the reader the fall into reality and relativity that Rasselas endures.

In closing, I return to the question of Imlac's strange entrance—the awkward readjustment of the book. Unlike the unnamed sage of Chapter ii or the also unnamed would-be aviator of Chapter vi, unlike Rasselas too, Imlac first turns up (in Chapter vii, "The Prince Finds a Man of Learning") unheralded by any description of his character, as if he had already been introduced, and by name. New readers must commonly pause and glance back at the preceding chapters, like the woman rebuked by Tristram Shandy, to see if they have somehow overlooked his introduction. It seems, though, that he is already known to us in some manner, being the dramatic, diminished, earthbound surrogate of the sublime narrator, who remains above and out of the hearing of prince, mentor, and, in life, the grown-up reader, who here must reenact the experience of his own leap from the nest of absolutely valid guidance. "The transition from the protection of others to our own conduct," wrote Johnson in a letter which Paul Fussell has brought to bear upon *Rasselas,* "is a very awful point of human experience."[24]

"Highly episodic," superficially exotic, *Rasselas* nevertheless "refuses" to be fully an Oriental tale.[25] Not anachronistically realistic, its plot not amounting to that of a *Bildungsroman* as later writers would develop the form, the tale is yet much more than a staged philosophical disquisition. It is also, in large measure, a serious representation of human life, novel-like in sensitivity to its characters and their chain of growth.

NOTES

1 All quotations from *Rasselas* are from Samuel Johnson, *Rasselas, Poems, and Selected Prose,* ed. Bertrand H. Bronson, 3rd ed., enl. (San Francisco: Rinehart, 1971), pp. 607-709.

2 Gwin J. Kolb, in an important early critical study of the tale, qualifies that opinion, saying that the characters "become more active participants by taking a trip to the pyramids" ("The Structure of *Rasselas,*" *PMLA,* 66 [1951], 710). But such qualification is rare. Frederick W. Hilles says "the observers become participants" with Pekuah's abduction and the consequent suffering of her friends ("*Rasselas,* an 'Uninstructive Tale,'" *Johnson, Boswell, and Their Circle: Essays Presented to Lawrence Fitzroy Powell* [Oxford: Clarendon, 1965], p. 113). Alvin Whitley remarks, "Up to this point we have been viewing a pure comedy of ideas; now we are faced with a comedy of emotion and behavior as well" ("The Comedy of

Rasselas," *ELH,* 23 [1956], 63). According to Carey McIntosh, "Quite suddenly the travelers are living in earnest, transformed from observers to participants. In the first half of *Rasselas* they had examined the actions and sufferings of others; now they act and suffer themselves" (*The Choice of Life: Samuel Johnson and the World of Fiction* [New Haven and London: Yale University Press, 1973], p. 190). Emrys Jones says, more simply, that with the abduction the travelers become "actively involved with other men," but does not comment on their prior emotional involvement with each other ("The Artistic Form of *Rasselas*," *RES*, 18 [1967], 397). The list of such statements could be lengthened. At issue, really, is the generic classification of the tale, and especially the question of how seriously the characters should be taken as people.

3 Earlier studies took Imlac as Johnson's spokesman, or at least as the complete spokesman for the message of the work, until C. R. Tracy's comic interpretation ("Democritus Arise! A Study of Dr. Johnson's Humor," *Yale Review,* 39 [1949], 306-9). Agostino Lombardo singles Imlac out as Johnson's hero, adding that Imlac's "essays interpolated into the body of the novel are . . . justified also in relation to narrative structure, in that they are phases in the development of Rasselas, the means by which his *éducation sentimentale* is achieved" ("The Importance of Imlac," *Bicentenary Essays on* Rasselas, ed. Magdi Wahba, *Supplement to Cairo Studies in English* [1959], p. 39). But the particular stages of that development and education are not enumerated, nor is the conflict between Rasselas and Imlac recognized, beyond Imlac's function as the destroyer of Rasselas' illusions. W. K. Wimsatt amusingly likens the Imlac of one passage to "a wound-up automaton, a speaking toy-philosopher" ("In Praise of *Rasselas*: Four Notes (Converging)," *Imagined Worlds: Essays on Some English Novels and Novelists in Honour of John Butt,* ed. Maynard Mack and Ian Gregor [London: Methuen, 1968], p. 127). J. P. Hardy, defending Rasselas as Johnson's hero, cites the aimlessness of Imlac's final disposition in the book (*The History of Rasselas Prince of Abissinia* [Oxford: Oxford University Press, 1968], p. xxiv). Howard D. Weinbrot has carefully distinguished Imlac's theory of poetry from Johnson's ("The Reader, the General, and the Particular: Johnson and Imlac in Chapter Ten of *Rasselas,*" *ECS,* 5 [1971], 80-96), but see also the rejoinder by Donald T. Siebert, Jr. ("The Reliability of Imlac," *ECS,* 7 [1974], 350-52).

4 McIntosh, more than any other commentator, has noticed the way in which "Chapters 23-29 develop in a mounting atmosphere of doubt and distrust" (p. 190). Lombardo, taking Imlac as the author's spokesman, in sketching the action of the book repeatedly skips over the crucial Chapters xix-xxix (pp. 40-41, 44-45). One might keep in mind a remark

of Johnson's at an early meeting with Boswell: "Sir, a father and a son should part at a certain time of life. I never believed what my father said. I always thought that he spoke *ex officio,* as a priest does" (*Boswell's London Journal,* 1762-63, ed. Frederick A. Pottle [New York: McGraw-Hill, 1950], p. 284).

5 That, as Hilles says, "we do not read *Rasselas* for the story" (p. 114) is an axiom of most *Rasselas* criticism, expressed earlier by Bronson in a postscript dated 1958 (p. xx). But Wimsatt discerns in Hilles "a warmer affection for the story (character and plot)" than may be found in Kolb (p. 124), though Kolb too remarks that "the prince and his companions have definite characters" and their actions have "at least a superficial resemblance to the parts of a real story" (p. 714). Jones, noting that "critics of *Rasselas* have tended to stress the philosophy at the expense of the fiction," broadly describes one meaning inherent in the story: "Rasselas loses his insularity, his state of innocent isolation from ordinary living . . ." (pp. 392, 397). Despite the axiomatic unimportance of the story, readers have continually responded to the characters as if the latter were interesting persons; I give examples in my text and subsequent notes.

6 *A Study of Henry Fielding with Glances at Swift, Johnson and Richardson* (Berkeley and Los Angeles: University of California Press, 1964; rpt. 1967); page references in parentheses are to this edition.

7 *The Autobiography of Benjamin Franklin,* ed. Leonard W. Labaree et al. (New Haven and London: Yale University Press, 1964), p. 72.

8 *The Early Diary of Frances Burney, 1768-1778,* ed. Annie Raine Ellis (London: George Bell, 1889), I, 14-15, quoted in part by William Kenney, "Johnson's *Rasselas* after Two Centuries," *Boston University Studies in English,* 3 (1957), 89.

9 Commenting on late-eighteenth-century reviewers, Ioan Williams says that "while they often stated that the romances of Mrs. Radcliffe were in a different class from the novels of Fielding, the basis of their distinction was merely the degree to which either writer imitated nature, a criterion which had been used so often, in so many contexts throughout the century, that it had lost its precision and usefulness" (*Novel and Romance 1700-1800: A Documentary Record* [New York: Barnes & Noble, 1970], p. 23). To what extent does *Rasselas* imitate real life? Bernard L. Einbond comments that "*Rasselas* criticism is far more allegorical than *Rasselas*" and that the characters are "individuals or types, not metaphors" (*Samuel Johnson's Allegory* [The Hague and Paris: Mouton, 1971], pp. 83-84), and proceeds to take a general position like A. R. Humphreys'—that "to overstress the general and abstract would be misleading. . . . The tale chooses a middle ground between abstract and

concrete, on which morality can be embodied as an impression of real life adequately but not obtrusively maintained" ("Johnson," *From Dryden to Johnson*, vol. IV of *The Pelican Guide to English Literature*, ed. Boris Ford [Harmondsworth, Middlesex: Penguin, 1957], p. 412).

10 Wimsatt, p. 131.

11 "Declamation" and cognate words, as employed here, in my title, and elsewhere in this essay, are intended to convey the sense set forth by Johnson not only in the *Dictionary* ("A discourse addressed to the passions; a harangue; a set speech; a piece of rhetoric"–1st ed.) but also, quite pejoratively, in *Ramblers* 172 and 202 and the "Preface to Shakespeare": "His declamations or set speeches are commonly cold and weak, for his power was the power of nature; when he endeavoured, like other tragick writers, to catch opportunities of amplification, and instead of enquiring what the occasion demanded, to show how much his stores of knowledge could supply, he seldom escapes without the pity or resentment of his reader" (*Johnson on Shakespeare,* ed. Arthur Sherbo, *The Yale Edition of the Works of Samuel Johnson,* VII [New Haven and London: Yale University Press, 1968], 73). Cf. Johnson on the chief disease afflicting eighteenth-century tragedy: "From Bard, to Bard, the frigid Caution crept,/ Till Declamation roar'd, while Passion slept" ("Prologue Spoken by Mr. Garrick . . . 1747"), and note that the canting stoic of *Rasselas,* Ch. xviii, who suffers the sharpest reversal of the book, is discovered in a "hall or school of declamation."

12 Hugo M. Reichard, "The Pessimist's Helpers in *Rasselas,*" *TSLL,* 10 (1968), 60. This essay is remarkably severe about the intellectual shortcomings of the characters, who are called "boobies" (p. 63). Truly flat characters would provoke neither hot disdain nor, as is more customary in critics of *Rasselas,* positive affection.

13 After writing the present essay, I came upon an informative and provocative study by the late Earl R. Wasserman ("Johnson's *Rasselas*: Implicit Contexts," *JEGP,* 74 [1975], 1-25). I note it here rather than earlier (like the critics mentioned in note 2, Wasserman upholds the spectator-participant distinction [p. 23]), because, in order to deny the possibility of any stable "mean between extremes" in the tale, he cites the speech by Nekayah which I have just quoted, insisting that it be seen in the context of the tale's numerous comments on the stream-like nature of life, comments including Imlac's description of the world outside the valley as "a sea foaming with tempests," etc. (pp. 10-12). But if, as I am arguing, Nekayah seems to be imitating Imlac, too hastily making up her mind, and if Imlac seems to be exaggerating the world's normal perils, then explicatory recourse to allusion (Wasserman here sees negative allusion to the familiar eighteenth-century concept of *concordia discors*)

must commence with more attention to equivocal elements in Johnson's text.

14 Many commentators have noted the presence of, in Hilles' words, the "Grand Style" (p. 113). McIntosh usefully observes that the "sublime and majestic gloom" of the "pseudo-oriental sage," echoed by Imlac and other of the characters, is subverted by the events of the tale, while the less overbearing voice of the "confident teacher of true pessimism" is not; he distinguishes other voices as well (pp. 168-74, 186).

15 "His nature is deeper than his sister's," wrote G. B. Hill in his edition of *Rasselas* (Oxford: Clarendon, 1887), p. 29. Elsewhere Hill faults Johnson's characterization of Nekayah, who is "sometimes Rasselas, sometimes Imlac, sometimes undisguised Johnson" (p. 31), but there is good reason to suppose that Hill has discovered Nekayah's problem rather than Johnson's mistake.

16 Sheridan Baker's comment ("*Rasselas*: Psychological Irony and Romance," *PQ*, 45 [1966], 258) that time cures Nekayah's grief is overstated. Time lessens it, but at the end of the crucial chapter (xxxvi) she says she will "henceforward fear to yield my heart to excellence, however bright, or to fondness, however tender, lest I should lose again what I have lost in Pekuah."

17 Both Reichard (p. 63) and Whitley (pp. 69-70) cite Rasselas' continued longing for a kingdom as evidence of his unteachability, as if once a person had learned not to expect something he would necessarily stop desiring it.

18 Martin Price's opinion that Imlac participates in Rasselas' search "as if being the spectator to another's desire were a palliative to the absence of his own" (*To the Palace of Wisdom: Studies in Order and Energy from Dryden to Blake* [Garden City, N.Y.: Doubleday, 1964], p. 318) implies the characters' progression to infinity on parallel, untouching lines. More faithful to the spirit of Imlac and the book is Mary Lascelles' reminder that the whole—especially the account of the curing of the astronomer—enjoins readers, "do not withdraw yourself," "acknowledge your kinship with your fellow beings" ("*Rasselas*: A Rejoinder," *RES*, 21 [1970], 54).

19 *The Achievement of Samuel Johnson* (New York: Oxford University Press, 1955; rpt. 1961), p. 63.

20 Wimsatt, p. 119.

21 E. L. McAdam, Jr., reaffirming the judgment of Hill (note 14, above), writes of this passage: "Once more Johnson uses a character to point up the relative maturity of the three young people, and the order is the same as before . . ." (*Johnson and Boswell: A Survey of Their Writings* [Boston: Houghton Mifflin, 1969], p. 59).

22 Back in Chapter xiii, Rasselas, upon coming to know Imlac, had "thought that even the *happy valley* might be endured with such a companion, and that, if they could range the world together, he should have nothing further to desire"; he expected too much, as usual, but—also as usual—there was something to be said for his expectations when tempered. Less ardently drawn to the "choice of eternity" than his sister, Rasselas seems at home in the world by the end of the tale, like Imlac; from a high level of generalization, Harold E. Pagliaro nicely describes the "illusion that Imlac-Rasselas exists eternally" ("Structural Patterns of Control in *Rasselas,*" *English Writers of the Eighteenth Century: Essays in Honor of James Lowry Clifford,* ed. John H. Middendorf [New York: Columbia University Press, 1971], p. 215). Unlike the exemplary personages of "The Vanity of Human Wishes," Rasselas and Imlac seem capable of making the happiness they "do not find."

23 As such, the condition of the narrator could be said to realize the deepest desires of Rasselas, perhaps of Imlac the poet as well. The stoic of Chapter xviii seemed at first, in Rasselas' enthusiastic words, "a man who can teach all that is necessary to be known, who, from the unshaken throne of rational fortitude, looks down on the scenes of life changing beneath him." Only such a person could accomplish the perfect choice of life, or perfectly legislate for mankind.

24 To John Taylor of Ashbourne, April 13, 1775, *The Letters of Samuel Johnson,* ed. R. W. Chapman (Oxford: Clarendon, 1952), II, 24, quoted by Paul Fussell, *Samuel Johnson and the Life of Writing* (New York: Harcourt, 1971), p. 225. Fussell's perception that the various fantasies of the characters expressed in Chapter xliv are alike in revealing the wish for domination (pp. 241-43) provides another example of Rasselas' competitiveness.

25 Wimsatt, pp. 115, 117.

Imlac and Autobiography

CATHERINE N. PARKE

Let me begin by commenting briefly on the title of this essay, "Imlac and Autobiography." A title better reflecting my aims here, though an unwieldy one, would be "Imlac and the Relation Commonly of Most Value in Which the Writer Tells His Own Story." This title, borrowing Johnson's definition of autobiography from *Idler* No. 84,[1] written a few months after *Rasselas*, places the emphasis where I will be placing mine throughout the paper: on the way Johnson's thinking about the first-person form of biography helps us better to read Imlac's story of himself.

The story one man writes of another man and the story he writes or tells of himself are not different kinds for Johnson, or at least he does not choose to place his emphasis here, as have the nineteenth and twentieth centuries. If, however, they are not different kinds, they are importantly different. And the difference he focuses on between the two is their probable truthfulness. The life of another man, his motives and sentiments, are all conjecture to us. And conjecture, says Johnson, is easily modified by fancy or desire. It is a simple but profoundly important moral fact that the writer of his own life knows the truth about himself as no other man can know it. And this certainty of knowledge, Johnson writes in the

Idler essay, "not only excludes mistake but fortifies veracity." Such a statement as this makes it little wonder that Johnson esteemed autobiography. Though I would hasten to add that this encouraging statement of a cause and effect relationship between knowledge of the truth and the strength to tell it is no simple one, but is rather a coincidence of description and prescription, a way of teaching familiar to us throughout Johnson's works.[2] Johnson's solid trust in the story a man tells of himself would make us anticipate the importance of Imlac's autobiography in *Rasselas*, a work whose opening paragraph addresses the reader on the very grounds of self-delusion and fanciful conjecture which autobiography corrects.

Because we know how highly Samuel Johnson valued biography, particularly autobiography, for moral instruction and delight, it seems entirely reasonable to assume that the very paradigm of instruction in his moral tale *Rasselas* should be embedded in the five-chapter autobiographical account of the poet Imlac. Like Prince Rasselas, however—and this is no accident, I think—we critics have tended to focus on one of the chapters of this longest segment of the book, the "Dissertation upon Poetry."[3] And although only one of us has been willing to say that Imlac's narrative is "too long in proportion to the whole book,"[4] the history of critical readings makes much the same statement.

I would like to offer two suggestions about the function of Imlac's narrative. First, that its length, five of the forty-nine chapters, is one of the ways Johnson argues for the moral importance of this kind of biography in the tale as a whole and therefore in each man's life. And second, that in this episode Johnson clearly locates the two major and connected problems which the characters spend their time and energies trying to solve; attempts for which the form itself offers important help. The moral sequel to Imlac's autobiography comes in the last chapter when Rasselas, Nekayah, and Pekuah share their recent histories, repeating from first-hand experience the same kind of lesson about the impossibility of finding earthly happiness in any thing, taught by the tale's other autobiographies, Imlac's the most important and lengthy among them.[5] But exactly thereby they succeed, at least in part, in making the happiness they do not find. The two problems I have just alluded to are, what are the possibilities for real happiness, and what are the possibilities for successful teaching and learning? In brief, I would suggest that the episode of Imlac's story is a radical enactment of the difficulties and limited success we can reasonably hope for gaining knowledge and for achieving happiness.

Now, as we know, Johnson was skeptical about the possibility for one man's successfully teaching another man, a skepticism in no way lessening his commitment to the attempt. He most simply states this skepticism in *Rambler* No. 87: "It is not often that any man can have so much knowledge of another as is necessary to make instruction useful."[6] And as we also know, Johnson defined secular happiness as relational. Our wishes and achievements make us happy only as we see them reflected in the eyes of another. Like our knowledge of Johnson's moral commitment to autobiography, our knowledge of his skepticism about teaching and his understanding of the way happiness works lead us to anticipate the importance of the Imlac episode. By having Imlac, the teacher, speak his own story to his student, Rasselas, Johnson makes converge the problems of knowledge and of happiness for an elegantly compact examination with at least in theory a hopeful-looking solution. If you cannot know another man well enough to teach him anything, you can perhaps bypass that difficulty by teaching him, literally, yourself.

But as a preliminary to exploring this convergence, let me speculate briefly on our partiality as critics, together with young Prince Rasselas, for one chapter out of the five of Imlac's account. For here lies evidence not only of the continuing truth of the tale's accurate vision of human nature, the first requirement Johnson would ask us to make of any literary work; but also of the real problems of moral and philosophical perception which, as *Rasselas* teaches us, autobiography is especially good at exposing and correcting. For as readers we must finally discover, with Imlac and the prince, how very difficult is autobiography to tell and to listen to properly.

We critics and the prince are no exception to the troubling fact Johnson repeatedly remarks in his works. We all see what we expect to see, perceive only what we have in mind to look for. The matter is not, of course, entirely one of prejudice, though it may sometimes be. The problem is also the fundamental problem of knowledge and of how men learn. In his Preface to Baretti's *Guide Through the Royal Academy* Johnson writes: "He who enters, not knowing what to expect, gazes a while about him, a stranger among strangers, and goes out, not knowing what he has seen."[7] A man, in other words, must know what he is going to see in order to see it. In his biographical preface to *Christian Morals* Johnson notes that because Sir Thomas Browne loved the quincunx, he discovered this shape dominating man's architectural, military, and landscape achievements throughout history. Here Johnson is pointing out the reverse perceptual phenomenon. Browne knows what he is looking for and therefore finds it alone. And in *A Journey to the Western Islands* Johnson studies autobiographically the complicating effects of a traveler's nationality, residence, occupation, and other variables on the sights he sees and the reflections he can make. In summary, then, our minds conform to familiar objects. And we need to recognize this fact of perception so we can use it, as Johnson will instruct us to use it in autobiography. With our own business as critics in mind we do, not surprisingly, see Chapter 10 particularly clearly, because it is what we know, what we are looking for and like to find.

This natural conformity of our minds to familiar objects and the fact that we can only judge of what we do not know by what we know combine, Johnson shows us time and again, to make learning very difficult. So difficult, in fact, that Rasselas spends all his time, after Imlac's story, repeating for himself all the lessons Imlac has taught him—a repetition which the autobiography predicts when the poet confesses his unhappiness in the Happy Valley and his resolve to escape. This repetition is not, however, either for Rasselas or for Imlac mere repetitiousness. First, because my doing something and telling you I did it is never the same as your doing it. And second, because Imlac's decision to return to the world, as a teacher conducting students, is not identical with his earlier entrance as a young man in search of his first experience and the choice of life. As Johnson characterizes the effects of autobiography, every listener finds his mind naturally conforming to its "parallel circumstances and kindred images." And this conformity would make autobiography seem likely to be particularly effective for moral instruction, because it appeals to the listener and to the teller on the grounds of their knowledge and prejudice. Shortly in some of Rasselas's responses to Imlac's story, however, we shall see contradictions to this ideal description of the way autobiography works. For this description does not take into account the motives and emotions involved in the relationship between any teacher and student. Indeed, this description turns out to be another of Johnson's prescriptions.

As we critics find a mirror for self-reflection in Rasselas's particular attention to Imlac's "Dissertation upon Poetry," so we find another image of our response in his reaction to Imlac's story as a whole. By the end of the narrative, the prince is cheered considerably, his imagination is no longer deadlocked and, the narrator tells us, "Much of his uneasiness was now removed."[8] Knowing as we do Johnson's repeated endorsement of any innocent activity temporarily easing the pain of existence, we must judge Imlac's story a moral success. Johnson would, I think, have us start with this observation. For as we see time and again in the tale, one man's doing this sort of real good for another man happens seldom enough. But if we and the prince are finally cheered by this story—although Rasselas is annoyed and threatened along the way—it is certainly not on account of what Imlac says. Instead, Johnson encourages us by making implicit promises in the poet's autobiography that because we live in a world of meaningful repetition, not inescapable repetitiousness, we are safe from the graver risk of hopelessness. Like Emerson in *Representative Men*, Johnson persuades us to take the risks of education,[9] with its voluntary uncertainty and vulnerability, by having us take heart in the belief that "the history of the universe is symptomatic, and life is mnemonical." The remainder of my remarks will set out a few of those lesser risks taken by teachers, students, and seekers after happiness when they tell and listen to a man's story of himself.

Rasselas and Imlac begin their acquaintance with a poem. And that poem is mentioned only in passing, a fact important in itself. The prince does not interrupt Imlac's reading—indeed, he commands a repeat performance—but he will soon repeatedly interrupt his autobiography. By this contrast Johnson dramatizes a fundamental human weakness, the main stumbling block between man and his moral education: we all want to learn, but we do not like to be taught. And the two are, of course, inseparable, though we all try to invent ways to have it otherwise. Unlike his first-person history, Imlac's poem does not threaten or anger Rasselas, since it offers both teacher and student a kind of reciprocal safety and, no doubt, pleasure. The prince likes the poem enough to request it again, and Imlac has a listener for the first time since he entered the Happy Valley. One suspects, unhappily, that the poem fails to teach either man as much as the autobiography will, for rarely does Johnson show anyone learning comfortably.

Now moral autobiography can hardly fail to bring out some defensiveness in even the best of student-listeners, because by the simple act of offering example and advice repeatedly in the first person, the narrator asserts himself, however kindly, wiser than the listener. We are all hostile to moral teaching from our contemporaries, a psychological truth Johnson preserves in the *Rambler* No. 87 aphorism "dead counsellors are safest." Concluding the survey-poem and beginning his first-person moral travelogue, Imlac finds his formerly appreciative and delighted student becoming by degrees an adversary who interrupts the poet's life history with a series of objections. These objections begin quietly in Chapter 8 and reach their climax in Chapter 11. In this sequence of objections Johnson dramatizes the natural progress of a student's discomfort and antagonism when faced with knowledge less and less familiar and finally with the impossible. You will remember that Rasselas retracts his first objection to

Imlac's story of his father, who continued to seek wealth beyond both need and luxury, when he recalls that he has experienced a similar psychological need for "some desire to keep life in motion." Interrupting Imlac a second time, he questions Imlac's interpretation of why his caravan companions delighted in exploiting his innocence. But he allows his teacher to continue, still preferring knowledge to debate. But his third objection—this time to Imlac's speech on poetry—halts the narrative. This interruption is no wonder, for Imlac is here guilty of the most severe error in teaching, one which Johnson exposes elsewhere in his works: making the difficult seem impossible. I will return to this matter shortly.

I have been commenting on Imlac's autobiography from the listener's point of view. Let me turn now to the speaker's and then return finally to them both. Imlac begins his story by announcing to the prince, "Sir, my history will not be long." The autobiography does, however, turn out to be much longer than this opening remark would lead either the prince or the reader to expect. Imlac tells of occupations in distant lands, small fortunes possessed and lost, betrayals, and other diverse, if not extraordinary, events. This elaboration is both humorous and serious, because it reverses the classic joke pattern in the mechanic flyer's fiasco, the preceding episode. The flyer's long prepared for and wordily defended attempt to rise above the Happy Valley resolves itself into a single sentence punch-line: "He waved his pinions a while to gather air, then leaped from his stand, and in an instant dropped into the lake." Imlac's autobiography turns around that pattern, beginning tersely, then continuing for five chapters. As Imlac's history shares, though reverses, the joke of the flyer's failure, so at the beginning of Chapter 11 it also shares the pattern of recovery. When the flyer falls from his stand, the narrator recounts that his wings did at least support him in the water. It is useful to notice here that the very instrument of the man's error turns around into his salvation, a real instance of the hopeful, if in this episode comic, relation between error and its correction which Johnson shows us elsewhere in his work. In the Proposals for

Shakespeare,[10] for example, he states that in editorial work it very often happens that a wrong reading has affinity with the right. This doctrine of the affinity of error to truth is not simply another way of saying through tight, resigned lips that we learn from our mistakes. It is a significantly more accepting, expansive, even cheerful belief in the positive uses of error.

Imlac's recovery from error in his autobiography occurs in Chapter 11 when Rasselas interrupts the poet's enthusiastic speech. Correcting the serious teaching error of making the difficult seem impossible, Imlac replies simply, "To be a poet is indeed very difficult." Readers have tended not to give the poet's kind and economical reply its full moral weight; the weight which Johnson gives this succinct revision by its context. Here in the midst of five chapters of so much other talk, it is refreshing, indeed, and a model of teacherly patience.

By showing Imlac revising his autobiography Johnson applies visibly in his fiction the central lesson of *Rambler* No. 4. In that March 31, 1750, issue Johnson instructs novelists to teach credible moral lessons giving, particularly to their young readers, "the most perfect idea of virtue; of virtue not angelical, nor above probability, for what we cannot credit we shall never imitate." Rasselas, and the Rasselas in each of us, cannot credit Imlac's speech on poetry; it seems too hard. And as long as it seems too hard, neither the prince nor the reader can begin to apply the dissertation's most important moral lesson—one we shall examine later—that "to a poet nothing can be useless." So Johnson has his teacher recover carefully, amending his story of himself when the current version begins defeating its primary purpose: useful, practicable, enjoyable moral instruction. He returns immediately to simple, sequential narration, proof for Johnson of a healthy mind. He also enacts two rules which Johnson states for teachers in his 1748 preface to the *Preceptor.* The first is that whenever a student finds a lesson too difficult, really too difficult and discouraging, he should be allowed by his teacher to abandon it temporarily. And second, that all teachers should for the most part assume that their students' unruliness and inattention express fear of unfamiliar knowledge, of things considered too difficult to master, and should be handled accordingly with patience. Imlac acts out this imperative. And it is important for us to notice what he does not say in reply to his student; the many, easy, hasty and harmful responses he avoids. I think that we can feel comfortable in reading this omission because we know how often Johnson teaches us that men can on a daily basis do positive good simply by refusing to do evil.

With a brief sentence, then, Imlac betrays himself neither into foolishness nor into that tyranny which is for Johnson the worst of all teaching faults and which, unhappily, teaching of all occupations most severely tempts us to commit. And he proves himself capable of another difficult achievement Johnson has already described in *Adventurer* No. 85:

> It is difficult to imagine, with what obstinacy truths which one mind perceives almost by intuition, will be rejected by another; and how many artifices must be practised, to procure admission for the most evident propositions into understandings frightened by their novelty, or hardened against them by accidental prejudice.

When Imlac instantly modifies his long argument in the dissertation into that simple, unassuming correction, he demonstrates the self-control Johnson discusses here. Instead of multiplying a single point into comprehensible versions, Imlac contracts the many into a single modest one; but the principle is the same. Quickly responding to the new situation, he does what needs to be done in order to calm the prince's anger and reverse his dismay. Men need different truths or, as here, different versions of the same truth, at different times, and Imlac acts out this uncommonly good sense.

This error of tyranny is obviously related to the other error I mentioned earlier: making the difficult seem impossible. The teacher can easily tyrannize over the novice by exaggerating the lesson's difficulty. If in theory such easy exploitation of superior knowledge seems to offer little gratification, the sheer number of

Johnson's recurring reminders instructs us that men's taste for power over others is seldom delicate. Imlac's error may be, in fact, primarily one of timing—of testing his listener's tolerance for perfection too soon. But error it is, and he corrects it immediately. That correction, I would argue, depends as certainly upon its very source, autobiography, as the flyer's recovery depends upon those wings which got him into trouble in the first place. The way autobiography both tempts Imlac into error and helps to get him out of it again will be the subject of the last section of this essay.

At the end of Chapter 10 and the beginning of Chapter 11, then, Imlac significantly improves his telling of his own story. Here he undergoes the crucial test of every teacher's imagination: his capacity, first, to remember the time when he did not know what he now knows and teaches, and second, to use this retrospective imagination to place himself in the mind of his student, a man who knows fewer or, at any rate, different things from his instructor; in short, to use his past autobiography to imagine his student's current biography. Such is the moral capacity for pity, the capacity which the narrator pointed out to us in the poet when Imlac answered Rasselas's first joyful and excited questions about his poem. But Imlac soon undergoes a series of more severe tests of his pity for the prince's contentious ignorance. He succeeds here, too, although Johnson will locate the final proof of his success in the last chapter, when the students pay their teacher the high compliment of imitation.

The Imlac episode shows us that telling one's autobiography is not without its risks. Certainly no one likes to be talked to as Imlac is talked to by the prince. No one likes to be interrupted repeatedly and finally to have his narrative cut short and another topic ordered resumed. But having said this, one must then go on to point out the important gains resulting from these necessary risks. By his own admission Imlac has been recently melancholy in the Happy Valley. Finding no one there who wants his instruction, he for a time silently reviews his knowledge only to find its memory sadly dimming, until the prince, an eager student, enters fortuitously. Once again we see that Imlac's autobiography is long because it needs to be long. What we hear in the poet's history is the joyful release of knowledge made once again useful to another man. Not surprisingly, Imlac expatiates in that renewed freedom. There are prisons in *Rasselas* more subtle and more formidable than the mountains and gates enclosing the Happy Valley. A mind like Imlac's, having busied itself for a lifetime collecting images and ideas, is imprisoned by uselessness, until Rasselas's request for that knowledge frees him.

At this point I would ask you to recall two earlier comments I have made: one about *Rasselas* and one about all of Johnson's works. First, *Rasselas* tells the tale of men's search for happiness, as the young characters mistakenly try to find it in the proper choice of life. Second, Johnson shows us time and again that happiness (secular happiness, at least) is relational. It is unavilable to man alone, and it is not in things. Only as we see ourselves, our words, our achievements reflected in the eyes, heart, and mind of another can we be happy. Imlac's growing unhappiness in the Happy Valley illustrates this point. Now the odds for happiness, as shown by the prince and the poet's relationship, are these: We are surely damned to unhappiness without another person, but not reciprocally assured of happiness with one. Given this fact, Imlac can do no better than to avoid certain unhappiness. For when the odds show negative certainty in one direction and unknown possibilities in the other, the choice seems clear, because no risk is actually involved. But there is, of course, another kind of risk, felt if not actual, involved in any attempt to relate oneself to another, to give praise or criticism, to show one's work, to offer aid. And Johnson's works give many examples of such habitual, ordinary risks we all take. Given the nature of happiness, we can now begin to see that autobiography, the formal relation of self to another, is for Johnson the generic embodiment of the psychological fact of happiness. Occurring early in the tale, Imlac's autobiography is rightly long, because in a narrative whose theme is the search for happiness, it offers a crucial demonstration of how happiness works. Happiness is for Johnson what truth is for William James: a verb not a noun. And Imlac, the poet, the traditional maker, the teller of truth, teaches this lesson by the form of his narration. While the content of his autobiography instructs the prince in the impossibility of achieving earthly happiness, its form significantly modifies that lesson.

I have said that Imlac's story of himself helps to get him into and then out of trouble. I would like now to explore the implications of that statement. A man's own history is potentially the most full of all the literary kinds. Its capacity is the capacity for the full truth and, according to Johnson, this very capacity compels the possibility into existence. But here a problem arises, one not unique to autobiography but one which autobiography dramatizes with particular clarity. The problem is, once again, the problem of knowledge, not this time the problem of perceiving it, discussed briefly at the beginning of this paper, but rather of relating it. Autobiography reminds us formally that we speak to others from within our own minds. It continuously reminds us that we cannot escape the near-sightedness of familiarity with our own assumptions all too easily mistaken for the nature of things, our own vocabularies thought to be commonly available, our own collection of images and ideas thought to be every man's. In telling the self we struggle head on and undisguisedly with two principal difficulties: first, with approximating our minds to the minds of other men; second, with admitting our participation in the human condition. The very form of Imlac's story contradicts (or, to take the long view, complements) Rasselas's plan for a detached, empirical study of human nature, although the prince's mistaken method happily offers another instance of an error involving material for its correction. The object of Rasselas's repeated inquiries, other men's accounts of themselves, will finally help to correct his observer's detachment.

Imlac speaks as a partaker in the human condition, his autobiography teaching the demanding and risky lesson of epistemology. Experimenters cannot get outside their own experiments. When one's own life is "the experiment, when the elements of all life . . . are the acting and reacting agents . . . there can be no question of the experimenter being either outside the system or in control of its conditions."[11] Not surprisingly, Imlac encounters just the kinds of problems he encounters with the prince. He is teaching a hard lesson, asking his student to admit uneasy knowledge about our radical and shared human limitations. And yet Imlac offers Rasselas an important safety in return for the risky admissions his autobiography implicitly requires. He offers him the safety of many new objects of attention, a temporary cure for the prince's deadlocked imagination and one which Johnson often recommends as a cure for melancholy. Annoying as the prince may find parts of Imlac's story, he does actively renew his plan and finally escape the Happy Valley after hearing that story.

Halfway through his dissertation in Chapter 10 Imlac says, "To a poet nothing can be useless." This statement about the poet's admirable economy, his capacity for accepting and using everything, does suggest that autobiography would appeal to him. It also suggests that a good poet would tell a good autobiography as, to judge from its effects on Rasselas, Imlac does. And finally this statement suggests that because autobiography exercises the poet's ideally characteristic capacity for using everything, it is an especially useful recreation for a poet between poems, offering him the opportunity to practice for his primary task. Such is the kind of coincidence between description and prescription we have come to expect from Johnson. If to the poet nothing, really nothing, can be useless, then here we find a general statement of the positive uses of error already shown us in the flyer's fall and in the prince's mistaken plan for a detached study of human nature. If by telling an autobiographical narrative the poet can maintain his strength for using everything and can assimilate, as Imlac does, even harsh corrections into that practice, he becomes a teacher in the best sense of the word: a model whose life offers his student the unusual force of its example.

Becoming a teacher, while remaining an active student, of the positive uses of error, Imlac follows Johnson's directions for learning the courage of curiosity. In *Rambler* No. 150, two years after *Rasselas*, Johnson quotes Seneca's advice for how to contemplate and thereby strengthen ourselves against adversity. We should consider the risks of adversity just another study from whose pursuit we will "return . . . with encrease of knowledge, with enlarged views, and multiplied ideas." This autodidactic method for turning adversity into alluring knowledge should remind us of Rasselas's reply to his former teacher early in the tale. The teacher tries to discourage his student's escape by telling him about worldly misery. Rasselas reads the lesson differently than the teacher intended, but he reads it right, according to *Rambler* No. 150. The prince replies to his teacher, "Now, you have given me something to desire; I shall long to see the miseries of the world, since the sight of them is necessary to happiness." Rasselas knows this lesson from the beginning, but he must make a journey to reenact and thus prove its truthfulness in a full range of particular experiences. And Imlac's story, showing Rasselas a version of what he himself will soon learn, prepares him, like those students entering the Royal Academy, to know what he is looking for so he can see it.

That the young students share their first-person travel narratives in the last chapter of *Rasselas* is the moral sequel to that long autobiography Imlac told the prince early in the tale. Exercising themselves in this morally useful genre, where psychological difficulties are equal to epistemological ones, they share their experience for one another's instruction, acting out the lesson which Rasselas first learned from Imlac. Seeing themselves, their recent histories and current ideals reflected in the minds of one another, they enact the happiness they have sought, before resolving to return to Abissinia. And if the last chapter of *Rasselas* is meant to leave us partially unsatisfied by concluding, as the title tells us, "nothing," it does offer an important moral satisfaction in the young students' very act of telling their recent histories while Imlac and the astonomer, the figures who tell the tale's longest and most important stories of themselves, remain silent. The episode presents a model of pedagogical symmetry, as each of the young students assumes, in turn, the role of autobiographer.

NOTES

1 *Idler and Adventurer*, ed. W. J. Bate, J. M. Bullitt, L. F. Powell, vol. II in The Yale Edition of the Works of Samuel Johnson (New Haven and London: Yale University Press, 1963). All subsequent references to these works are from the same edition and are cited in the text by the essay's number.

2 See Paul Kent Alkon, *Samuel Johnson and Moral Discipline* (Evanston: Northwestern University Press, 1967) for an extended study of "the descriptive and prescriptive aspects" of Johnson's works.

3 For example, see Howard D. Weinbrot's "The Reader, the General, and the Particular: Johnson and Imlac in Chapter 10 of *Rasselas*," *ECS*, 5 (1971), no. 1, 80-96, and the recent reply by Donald T. Siebert, Jr., "The Reliability of Imlac," *ECS*, 5 (1974), no. 3, 350-52. Of the critics who do address themselves to Imlac's story, Alvin Whitley and Gwin J. Kolb speak most fully, but still briefly. In "The Comedy of *Rasselas*," *ELH*, 23 (1956), 48-70, Mr. Whitley points out that Imlac's story, foretelling everything Rasselas will learn, is but another version of such interpolated moral biographies as Fielding's Man of the Hill and Goldsmith's Mr. Burchell. But neither Mr. Whitley nor Mr. Kolb, in "The Structure of *Rasselas*," *PMLA*, 66 (1951), 698-717, discusses the psychological and moral effects of autobiography so as to give Imlac's story its due importance in the tale as a whole. The autobiography, you will recall, comprises a full five of the forty-nine chapters.

4 W. K. Wimsatt, "In Praise of *Rasselas*: Four Notes (Converging)," in Maynard Mack and Ian Gregor, eds., *Imagined Worlds: Essays on Some English Novels and Novelists in Honour of John Butt* (London: Methuen & Co, 1968), p. 116.

5 Many figures in the tale tell partial stories of themselves: Rasselas, the astronomer, the ruler of the small endangered state, the old man, to name a few. Only Imlac and the hermit tell their stories from birth to the present. And Johnson has the hermit's story repeat the pattern of Imlac's life: worldly success, misery, voluntary confinement, discontent, decision to return to the world. For the purpose of this essay, to locate Johnson's instructional paradigm in *Rasselas*, I am limiting my attention to Imlac's autobiography, because it is the longest personal narrative, requiring the gravest risks and offering the prince more knowledge than any other single episode. For the future one might usefully try to make distinctions among the other personal narratives and their respective contributions to Johnson's examination of the problems of happiness and knowledge. Most useful, I think, would be a consideration of the astronomer's story,

second in importance only to Imlac's. One could begin by thinking about why Johnson presents this life in part biographically from the man's former student, Imlac, and in part autobiographically from the astronomer himself.

6 *The Rambler,* ed. W. J. Bate and A. B. Strauss, vols. III, IV, V of The Yale Edition of the Works of Samuel Johnson (1969). All subsequent references to these works are from the same edition and are cited in the text by the essay's number.

7 *Samuel Johnson's Prefaces and Dedications*, ed. Allen T. Hazen (New Haven: Yale University Press, 1937), p. 12.

8 *The History of Rasselas Prince of Abissinia*, ed. Geoffrey Tillotson and Brian Jenkins (London: Oxford University Press, 1971), p. 38. All subsequent references to this work by chapter number are from the same edition.

9 See Liane Norman, "Risk and Redundancy," *PMLA*, 90 (1975), no. 2, 285-92, for a discussion of speech act theory in relation to the reader's risk and the author's reciprocal assurances of safety whenever the reader learns and the author teaches.

10 *Johnson on Shakespeare*, ed. Arthur Sherbo, vols. VII and VIII in The Yale Edition of the Works of Samuel Johnson (1968); VII, 55.

11 James Olney, *Metaphors of Self: The Meaning of Autobiography* (Princeton: Princeton University Press, 1972), p. 331.

The Friendship of Johnson and Boswell: Some Biographical Considerations

IRMA S. LUSTIG

Though the friendship of Boswell and Johnson is important in the lives of both men, a just and comprehensive view of it is essential to the biography of Boswell. The relationship universally employed to illustrate Johnson's moral and psychological strength is still, on the other hand, one of the sticks used to beat Boswell. Now critics renew the Macaulayan paradox by invoking not just the *Life of Johnson* but also the very journals which should refine our understanding of its author. They praise the *Life*—at least most of them do—but caricature Boswell by exaggerating his deference and his dependence. Thus they separate the talent from the person.

I am not an apologist for Boswell's character. On the contrary, I wish to speak frankly about actions which trouble most of us still. But I hope that by making his friendship with Johnson the subject of close examination I will contribute proportion and perspective both to it and to the figure we make of Boswell. I do not presume to advise Professors Brady and Pottle, the authors of the definitive biography; they do not need my help. But as students and teachers of literature, we are necessarily also continuing if informal biographers.

The cornerstone of my argument is modern orthodoxy: the teachings of Chauncey Tinker, Geoffrey Scott, Bertrand Bronson, and Frederick Pottle. I wish also to acknowledge the pre-Isham perceptiveness of George Mallory. It is generally agreed that an austere and demanding father had accustomed Boswell to authority, but provoked resistance to his own guidance by disapproval and a caustic tongue. Boswell's rebellion against Lord Auchinleck was troubled, on the other hand, by respect for his father's virtues and accomplishments. A feudal landowner of stern self-discipline, a good classicist, and most significantly, a Lord of Session and of Justiciary (appointment in the highest courts of Scotland), Lord Auchinleck was a man highly esteemed in the community. It is understandable, therefore, that the paternal figures to whom Boswell turned for sympathetic guidance were also distinguished men of strong character. Among his famous friends and confidants of Lord Auchinleck's generation—Rousseau, Voltaire, General Paoli, Lord Kames, for example—Samuel Johnson was the father-surrogate supreme.

I believe that Boswell's reverence for Johnson as moral and intellectual hero never failed. It is a fixed element of the friendship, and the motive and theme of the *Life*. Boswell came to see Johnson's imperfections, and to express resentment when Johnson tyrannized—directly, in the journal, and obliquely or even pointedly to Johnson himself. Others complained more bitterly than Boswell about Johnson's severity toward "weaker minds than his own."[1] Knowing his own frailties, Boswell was generally tolerant of those he found in others. He was aware, moreover, that he incited Johnson's wrath by persisting because of his own needs at disquieting topics like death and futurity. Finally, Johnson's superiority of mind and of character overrode all minor criticism.

Evidence of Boswell's reverence, and of its basis, is both public and private, and abounds from the first to the last years of their association. One of Boswell's particular talents is the ability to evoke the *feeling* of past experience. When he described his introduction to Johnson in Tom Davies' back parlor a quarter-century after the event, he transmitted his awe and panic to the reader of the *Life* by comparing Johnson's approaching figure with the ghost of Hamlet's father ("Look, my Lord, it comes"). That vivid metaphor is not found in Boswell's journals, but the reaction is. On 19 March 1778, fifteen years later, he read in proof a portion of Johnson's life of Cowley, and recorded the observation that "I really *worshipped* him, not *idolatrously*, but with profound reverence, in the ancient Jewish sense of the word."[2] On 2 May 1780 he wrote to the Earl of Pembroke, "I own I feel stately now from my consciousness of having been so warm against the American War notwithstanding Dr. Johnson, whose authority is so great, I may say so awefull over my mind upon most occasions."[3] And ten days after Johnson's death, he lamented in a letter to Sir Joshua Reynolds that "I have lost a Man whom I not only revered but loved, a Man whose able and conscientious Counsel was ever ready to direct me in all difficultys."[4]

Were we to know only the *Life* we would have ample testimony of what Johnson wrote to Boswell: "We know as well as man can know the mind of man, that we love one another, and that we wish each other's happiness."[5] The edited exchange of their letters, which Boswell printed to show Johnson's tenderness and generosity, also reveals both his pride in that great man's love and the depth of his own special need. Boswell's natural father was cold to all his children. It was James who repeatedly visited the second son, John, brought him oranges and sang songs with him in the private Yorkshire sanatorium for the mentally ill which Lord Auchinleck avoided, and Boswell who as master of Auchinleck restored his brother to the ancestral home, although John was gloomy and perverse, and a trial to all. It seems clear, however, that despite his father's characteristic distance, Boswell believed he had withered Lord Auchinleck's affection for him by his own unworthiness, and he longed to be reclaimed emotionally as first child and heir. Restrained by his stepmother from the bed where his father expired, "Wept [he wrote], for alas there was not affection between us" (26 August 1782, *BP*, XV, 121). Small wonder that all his life Boswell sought proof of love regardless of behavior from the same admired figures who pomised him authority.

The deliberate silences and prolonged delays in answering Johnson's letters when Boswell was depressed, lethargic, and guilt-ridden in Scotland were open tests of affection. Messages rebuking him for unmanly "affectations of distress," or for failing to overcome the hypochondria by study and routine, hurt him by their lack of understanding, and especially provoked him to tricks. When Johnson responded with conciliatory inquiries (though he suspected sullenness), or declared his unchanging regard, an elated Boswell replied in turn with effusions of love and gratitude, and promised never again to indulge his fears. But he did, as we know—painfully, to the very end—and this pattern in their correspondence makes Boswell's quest for an absolute affection a minor and disquieting theme of the *Life*.[6]

Surely it is not just their roles as mentor and proselyte but also the emotional relationship I have reviewed which validates Bertrand Bronson's warning in the seminal essay, "Boswell's Boswell": "There is never any question," Professor Bronson wrote, "in the mind of either [Johnson or Boswell], of equal status in their friendship, or on what basis it is founded."[7] But I wish to qualify Professor Bronson's important conclusion, to give argument to the major thesis of this paper, that though the friendship of Johnson and Boswell is not equal, it is more balanced than many have assumed.

To dispose of easy matters first, let us review the advantages to Johnson of Boswell's friendship, aside from the exercise of his great talent as teacher. Genuine admiration obviously nourished Johnson—whom does it not?—and Boswell's ardent kindnesses on his behalf (see *H-P*, III, 80, 105, for acknowledgments) finally moved him to tears. I refer, of course, to the efforts to increase Johnson's pension so that he might winter in Italy. Contemporaries were agreed, moreover, that Boswell was good-humored and enlivening company. The initiative and exuberance which could be so troublesome were powerful antidotes to gloom. They brought

Johnson adventure and new associations on the Scottish mainland and in the Hebrides, and proved his vigor and adaptability to his own satisfaction. In expanding Johnson's world, Boswell helped counter his dread of age.

The ground bass of their friendship was a shared intellectual passion: literature as an art, and as their craft. Professor Pottle demonstrated in "Boswell's University Education" that Boswell was a well-educated man.[8] The literary topics he started, the new works and authors he introduced to Johnson, and the Scottish scholars and writers for whom he acted as intelligent intermediary suggest the extent of his reading. We know that Johnson prodded Boswell to write, and that he appraised the results seriously, without condescension or equivocation, though he was sometimes prejudiced by his own tastes. What has been little remarked, however, is the correlative service Boswell rendered Johnson. The journals have shown us that Boswell's conscious goal was political office and a conventional public success, but his enormous output, from youth, of all kinds of writing attests that in steadily honing his literary skills he was faithful to a basic drive. Pottle's bibliography in the *NCBEL* is striking verification. Long practice and early success led Boswell to speak with more assurance about literature than about any other subject. He was only twenty-eight years old when *An Account of Corsica* made him famous. Published in defiance of Johnson's opinion, in a little over a year it went to three editions published by the Dillys, and three of an unauthorized Irish reprint, and was translated into Dutch, German, Italian, and twice into French.[9] In maturity, therefore, Boswell was respectful and admiring of Johnson, but not idolatrous, and he too nagged and criticized, praised and emended. To cite a few examples readily discovered in the *Life*: he successfully proposed another meaning of the word *side* for the revised *Dictionary*, and argued, this time unsuccessfully, for including *civilization* as well as *civility* in order to distinguish meanings (*H-P*, II, 155). At Boswell's objection to close repetition, Johnson substituted *burns* for *spread* in "The Vanity of Human Wishes" (*H-P*, III, 357-58).

More important, Boswell solicited materials for the *Lives of the Poets*, thus contributing that "minute accuracy" to which, he tells us in an aside, Johnson "was by no means attentive" (*H-P*, III, 359, *n* 2). Johnson's fury over the quiet negotiation with Lord Marchmont for the Life of Pope tends to obscure the sequel, that in the following year Johnson sent the nobleman the first published volumes of the *Lives of the Poets*. The proud writer who had originally rebuffed Lord Marchmont's proposed visit called on *him* now, in company with Boswell (*H-P*, III, 342–45, 392).

The Life of Pope also owes to Boswell Hugh Blair's letter on the poet's knowledge of Greek, and on his indebtedness to Bolingbroke in the "Essay on Man" (*H-P*, III, 402–4). At Johnson's request, Boswell twice interviewed the sister of the poet Thomson, and obtained three letters, one of which Johnson included in the biography (*H-P*, III, 116-17, 359-60). That Johnson assigned Boswell responsibility, and accepted his contributions (all subjected, of course, to his own superior judgment), signifies the respect he accorded Boswell as literary man.

I believe it not impertinent to add that Boswell stimulated the exercise of Johnson's intellect generally, by testing on his mentor the new ideas that attracted him. Most of these discussions were easy, because on the whole the friends were ideologically compatible. But it is in the nature of things that the younger man thought himself more modern, philosophically, politically, and artistically. When he pressed his views, moreover, he felt himself supported by other friends of stature—Burke, on the American colonies, for example—and finally by events. More sophisticated with years, he was also emboldened in argument by his successes, from the *Account of Corsica* to the *Letter to the People of Scotland*, 1783. The static view of Boswell which some critics hold, that of a limited and naively questioning youth, *must* be unrealistic, though it is owing in part to Boswell's literary techniques.

We remember chiefly Johnson's triumphant rejoinders at Boswell's expense, because of his extraordinary intellect, of course, but also because the biographer generally gave his subject the last word. Thus Boswell was true to the announced design of the *Life*—keeping the hero, like Odysseus, always in view—and to his appraisal of Johnson's powers. There are sufficient exceptions to this famed structure of scenes to keep Johnson human and relationships representative. The stature of Sir Joshua Reynolds, and Johnson's respect for his independence of mind (see *H-P*, I, 246), are fully communicated by Sir Joshua's retorts, for example. Occasionally Boswell deleted Johnson's rebukes to himself, like part of the conversation of 19 October 1769 (*H-P*, II, 95). Johnson had advised him not to feel guilt regarding persons who seemed to be more feeling than Boswell himself. " 'You will find these very feeling people are not very ready to do you good. They *pay* you by *feeling*.' " Originally this conclusion was followed by another exchange. "*Boswell*. 'But I am uneasy that I do not feel enough.' *Johnson*. 'Why then keep better company, and read melancholy stories.' "[10] But Boswell's journals, and the manuscript of the *Life*, which I have studied closely in all its stages of composition, from draft to printer's copy, reveal that he also cancelled responses *topping* Johnson. An impressive number of these conclusions which would have dimmed Johnson's lightning brilliance by anticlimax are Boswell's.

A striking example of self-effacement is the scene of spring 1768 in which an individual identified only as a "poor speculatist" insisted on the unorthodox doctrine of the future life of brutes. I quote the entire conclusion: " 'But really, Sir, when we see a very sensible dog, we don't know what to think of him.' Johnson, rolling with joy at the thought which beamed in his eye, turned quickly round, and replied, 'True, Sir: and when we see a very foolish *fellow*, we don't know what to think of *him*.' He then rose up, strided to the fire, and stood for some time laughing and exulting" (*H-P*, II, 54). Boswell cancelled an additional sentence: "The Gentleman did not shrink; but when the merriment had abated gravely persevered saying, 'But you Sir do not know what to think of a very sensible dog.' "[11]

It may be charged that by deleting retorts such as I have just restored Boswell exaggerated Johnson's savagery. My evidence for a generally even acceptance of each other's views would support instead the thesis of Percy Fitzgerald, and now Donald Greene, that the *Life* is not an act of love and homage, but post-mortem revenge for years of subordination and suppressed resentment.[12]

Such an interpretation ignores the overwhelming approval in which, Ralph Rader pointed out, Boswell envelops Johnson's faults.[13] And how explain then the cancellation of dialogue possibly injurious to Johnson? One cannot have it both ways. Marshall Waingrow, who as editor of the forthcoming complete manuscript of the *Life* surely knows it better than any other scholar, tells us that what Boswell suppressed in the draft, he finally revealed elsewhere in the biography, another way.[14] I have found this true not only of damaging information, but also of matter cancelled for self-protection which, on the other hand, ennobled Johnson.

Boswell reports, for example, that at a tavern supper on Friday, 31 March 1775, one of the company teased Johnson intolerably about having attended a benefit for Mrs. Abington. Did he see? Did he hear? To both these impertinent questions Johnson answered no. Why, then, did he go? " 'Because, Sir, she is a favourite of the publick; and when the publick cares the thousandth part for you that it does for her, I will go to your benefit too,' " Johnson replied (*H-P*, II, 330). Three final words in the manuscript are struck through, "This quieted me."

The text of the published account is pasted to the top of the manuscript at page 451, and replaces a full explanation of the provocation. Lord Mountstuart was determined to prevent Boswell from attending this meeting of The Club, or at least to send him there drunk. Unable to resist "the generous wine," Boswell went to supper "in exuberant spirits," and, of course, "would needs encounter the great man." Standing by Johnson's chair, he rallied him on his presence at the theater; the dialogue which Boswell printed in the *Life* follows here. We learn from a cancelled sequel that he also expected a severe reprimand the next day. But Johnson was gentle, merely advising him not to go into new company when drunk because he would not be "in unison" with it. Somebody meaning Boswell harm asked Johnson if he had seen him the day after his drunken appearance. " 'Yes, sir,' Johnson replied. 'And what did he say?' 'Sir, he said all that man should say. He said he was sorry.' " You will find this story transferred to 16 March 1776 (*H-P*, II, 436) as evidence of Johnson's forgiveness of wine-drinking, though he himself was an abstainer, and of his practicality. The offender is anonymous, and revealing circumstantial details are muted, properly so, because self-victimization here served no biographical or artistic purpose.

For three years I have carried in my mind a question from Philip Daghlian which followed the publication of my article "Boswell at Work: the 'Animadversions' on Mrs. Piozzi." Professor Daghlian thought that I had explained convincingly Boswell's *publication* of the "Ode by Dr. Samuel Johnson to Mrs. Thrale upon their supposed approaching Nuptials" four years after Johnson's death,[15] but why, he asked, did Boswell compose the parody in the first place? It was almost certainly written at Sir Joshua Reynolds', perhaps even with his encouragement, 12 April 1781, only eight days after Thrale's death, and the day after he was buried. (See the appendix for the text of the verses.)

Professor Daghlian's question implies the general one: what accounts for Boswell's lapses of decency respecting Johnson if, as I argue, the delicate balances of the *Life* prove that he enjoyed a loving relationship with him, and a more dignified one than is generally supposed? Were the vulgarities retaliation for anguish reminiscent of what Lord Auchinleck had made him suffer? Perhaps. Boswell recorded episodes when Johnson, too, checked him as if he were a child. But to Johnson he could express his hurt at the time, if not verbally, then by a significant absence, after which Johnson apologized or otherwise rewon his gratitude and affection.

I think that a particular answer to Daghlian's question is also important to understanding the relationship between Boswell and Johnson. It has been speculated that writing the nuptial ode was therapeutic. Perhaps, the argument goes, Boswell feared subconsciously that Mrs. Thrale would indeed marry his friend, and thus shatter his intimacy with Johnson, as, he believed, the second Lady Auchinleck had widened the distance between his father and himself. The ode enabled him to discharge his anxiety and anger harmlessly. In support of the hypothesis, one can point to Boswell's own statement, that while writing an admittedly personal essay on hypochondria he had "by some gracious influence been insensibly relieved from the distress under which I laboured when I began it."[16]

There is no wholly satisfying answer to a reductive theory, and the analogy on which this one is based lingers in the mind. The circumstances surrounding the composition of the nuptial ode throw up obstacles to formula, however, as particulars frequently do. I don't pretend to grasp wholly the incongruities of Boswell's behavior, but I think he generally acted upon recoverable patterns. He was not angry at Johnson or Mrs. Thrale when he wrote the parody, and he had liked and respected Thrale, though obviously he was not mourning him. Johnson, however, had found a home with the generous brewer and his family, and grieved deeply. His place in the Thrale household was now awkward and uncertain. If there were no hostility, how could Boswell sit down at such a time and write prurient verses making his noble friend a figure of fun?

Boswell's quick sense of comic incongruity was aroused, I think, by a serious speculation. Mary Hyde reports in *The Impossible Friendship* the indecent haste with which Mrs. Thrale was both wooed and talked about. Gossip named Johnson among her suitors.[17] On considered judgment, when Boswell wrote the *Life*, he denied that his revered friend wished to marry Thrale's widow, though he had seen him "pleased to be rallied" upon the speculation. That a woman could find Johnson sexually attractive seemed impossible, Boswell later told Lucy Desmoulins in tête-à-tête; there was "something in his figure so terribly disgusting." (Mrs. Desmoulins' hesitation is instructive: "Yet, Sir, one cannot tell. His mind is such."[18]) But only three days after Boswell wrote the ode, he and Sir William Scott agreed that it "was possible Mrs. Thrale might marry Dr. Johnson, and we both wished it much. He [Scott] saw clearly the Doctor's propensity to love *the vain World* in various ways" (*BP*, XIV, 198, 15 August 1781).

Boswell's own marriage had been a love match, but marriages of convenience, among them the Thrales', were common enough. Like other, more discreet intimates, Boswell saw advantages to the ill and lonely Johnson of union with Hester Thrale, and there is incontrovertible evidence that his friend's well-being concerned him greatly. Boswell was acute enough, moreover, to recognize the element of passion in Johnson's attachment. I doubt that he gave much thought to Mrs. Thrale's desires, until she was known to favor Gabriel Piozzi, of whom he disapproved. Johnson genuinely liked women, was sensitive to them, and delighted in their charms. Boswell's attitude was gross: he had little appreciation of women as independent or intellectual beings. His proposal to Zélide's father for her hand was preposterous because of the demands meant to tame her. It is not alien to a Boswell to speculate, as others seem to have done, that Mrs. Thrale might capitalize permanently on the preeminence Johnson gave her. His own report contradicts the charge now made that he opposed such a union.

Boswell has provided the world with more than enough evidence, moreover, that he could not forego gossip and burlesque. He thought the ode not hurtful, but "humorous." Though his behavior was licentious, Boswell did not engage in bawdy *talk*. There is none in his private letters, and one is hard put to recall it in his journals. Wilkes wrote to him on 22 June 1765, "You too like the thing almost as well as I do, but you dislike the talk and laugh about it, of which I am perhaps too fond."[19] But Boswell loved to sing at masculine parties, where he was roundly applauded. Professor Pottle points out in a forthcoming volume of journals the tradition in British and Irish folk song of combining exquisite airs with dirty, or at least earthy, words, as the lyrics of Gay, Ramsay, Burns, and Moore exemplify. Boswell took pleasure in composing as well as delivering ribald verses, especially those intended for music. He called the "sportive lay" a "song," and endorsed it for his archives as an "epithalamium." "Too much intoxicated," he recited or sang it to Edward Eliot (later First Baron Eliot of Saint Germans) and his family two days after its composition (*BP*, XIV, 197). He also showed it to John Wilkes.[20]

The latter's teasing threat to tell Johnson alarmed Boswell, for he had felt Johnson's anger when he previously linked his name with Mrs. Thrale's.[21] Boswell saw no harm in indulging his "gaiety of fancy" (which even in his letter of condolence to Mrs. Thrale he said he could not restrain), so long as its victims were ignorant of the scurrilities. We may think the line he drew reprehensible, but it is certainly not foreign to the private world of eighteenth-century England. David Garrick and Sir Joshua parodied Johnson as awkward young husband and as dogmatist, to the delight of his friends.

Fortunately for Boswell, Johnson did not learn of the lampoon in which he figured. But the *Life* and the journals are so abundant with incident where Boswell confronted him directly with his faults and made him look at his own soul that I need not point them out. If he phrased the criticisms discreetly or blended them with praise, how could he have done otherwise, recognizing as he did Johnson's inner disquiet, the disparity in years, wisdom and stature, and the skill of an opponent who needs, in the words of that astute observer, Sir Joshua, "no formal preparation, no flourishing with his sword; he is through your body in an instant" (II, 365)?

What I believe remarkable is not the explosions, but the quiet candor of the friends' conversations. Consider Boswell's daring in raising the ugly story of Johnson's ingratitude to a friend, and the monumental poise with which Johnson rebutted it (III, 194-96). He answered straightforwardly and with a thoughtful logic, like a man who knows himself to be a biographical subject, and wishes honestly to meet the obligations to his public. There had to be differences, even occasional friction, in the evolution of this friendship as in all others. But one must acknowledge its *basic* qualities: enduring respect, sympathy, and harmony. Without them, Boswell could not have asked such personal questions as he did, and Johnson answer so often without offense.

APPENDIX

EPITHALAMIUM ON DR. J. AND MRS. T.*

1

If e'er my fingers touch'd the lyre
In satire fierce or pleasure gay,
Shall not my Thralia's smiles inspire?
Shall Sam refuse the sportive lay?

2

My dearest darling, view your Slave,
Behold him as your very Scrub,
Ready to write as Author grave,
Or govern well the brewing tub.

3

To rich felicity thus rais'd
My bosom glows with amorous fire;
Porter no longer shall be prais'd;
'Tis I myself am Thrale's entire.

4

Desmoulins now may go her ways,
and poor blind Williams sing alone;
Levet exhaust his lungs in praise,
And Frank his master's fortunes own.

5

Congratulating crowds shall come
Our new-born happiness to hail,
Whether at ball, at rout, at drum;
Yet human spite we must bewail.

*MS Yale M302. The verses which follow are Boswell's original composition, written on both sides of a discarded wrapper addressed to Sir Joshua Reynolds, and on the recto of a second leaf. They are endorsed with the title I give them here, and the year 1781. I have not included the two stanzas Boswell added when he printed the ode in 1788, though I have adopted the later order; the sequence in the manuscript is 2, 3, 11, 1, 4 (margin), 5, 6, 12, 8, 9, 10.

6

For though they come in pleasing guise,
And cry, "The wise deserve the fair! "
They look askance with envious eyes,
As the fiend looked at the first pair.

7

From thee my mistress I obtain
A manumission from the power
Of lonely gloom, of fretful pain,
Transported to the Blissful Bower.

8

Charming Cognation! With delight
In the keen aphrodisian spasm,
Shall we reciprocate all night
While wit and learning leave no chasm?

9

Nor only are our limbs entwin'd,
And lip in rapture glued to lip;
Lock'd in embraces of the mind
Imagination's sweets we sip.

10

Five daughters by your former spouse
Shall match with nobles of the land;
The fruit of our more fervent vows
A pillar of the state shall stand.

11

Greater than Atlas was of yore,
A higher power to me is given;
The earth he on his shoulders bore,
I with my arms encircle heaven!

NOTES

1 Boswell to Bennet Langton, 25 February 1779, MS Yale L846.

2 *Private Papers of James Boswell from Malahide Castle in the Collection of Lt.-Colonel Ralph Heyward Isham*, 18 vols. (Mt. Vernon, New York: privately printed, 1928-34), XIII, 110. References to this work will be cited hereafter as *BP*, within parentheses in the text.

3 MS Yale L1044.

4 Somervell Papers, National Library of Scotland. This letter, like the one above, is quoted from the forthcoming volume in the Yale Editions of the Private Papers of James Boswell: *The Correspondence of James Boswell with Certain Members of The Club*, ed. Charles Fifer (London: Wm. Heinemann, 1976).

5 *Boswell's Life of Johnson*, ed. George Birkbeck Hill, rev. L. F. Powell, 6 vols. (Oxford: Clarendon Press, 1934-50), III, 442. Referred to hereafter as *H-P*.

6 See, for example, *H-P*, II, 380-84; III, 86-89, 101, 104-5, 215-16, 362-63, 435-36; IV, 379-80.

7 *Johnson Agonistes and Other Essays* (Berkeley: University of California Press, 1965), p. 75.

8 In *Johnson, Boswell and Their Circle: Essays Presented to L. F. Powell* (Oxford: Clarendon Press, 1965), pp. 230-53.

9 Frederick A. Pottle, *The Literary Career of James Boswell, Esq.* (Oxford: Clarendon Press, 1929), p. 62.

10 MS Yale M144, p. 346. "Nay, Sir, how can you talk so?'" (*H-P*, II, 195, ll. 19-20) read originally, ". . . how can you talk so foolishly? " MS, p. 363.

11 MS Yale M144, p. 329. The dog is also featured in one of Boswell's victorious metaphors. On Wednesday, 27 March 1776, he and Johnson talked of Andrew Stuart's *Letters to Lord Mansfield*, which arraigned Mansfield for an unjust decision. Johnson argued that the book would not trouble the Chief Justice, for he was either protected by his conscience, or if deliberately dishonest, glad to see the man who attacked him so much vexed. Here the published dialogue is ended. There is a final exchange, however, in the manuscript. Johnson: " 'And after all, Sir, those letters are the wailings of a dog who has been licked.' – 'But, Sir,' said I, 'a dog may bite' " (p. 549). For a more available example of Boswell's self-effacing cancellations, compare *Life*, *H-P*, II, 60 (May 1768) and *BP*, VII, 190, on the subject of "popular liberty."

12 *Boswell's Autobiography* (London: Chatto and Windus, 1912); "Reflections on a Literary Anniversary," *Queen's Quarterly*, LXX (Summer

1963), 198-208; "Johnson without Boswell," *Times Literary Supplement*, 22 November 1974, pp. 1315-16.

13 "Literary Form in Factual Narrative," in *Essays in Eighteenth-Century Biography*, ed. Philip B. Daghlian (Bloomington: Indiana University Press, 1968), pp. 3-42.

14 *The Correspondence and Other Papers of James Boswell Relating to the Making of the Life of Johnson* (London: Wm. Heinemann, 1969), p. xxxvi.

15 *Modern Language Review*, LXVI, 1 (January 1972), [11]-30.

16 *The Hypochondriack*, ed. Margery Bailey, 2 vols. (Stanford: Stanford University Press, 1928), II, 46.

17 Cambridge: Harvard University Press, 1972, p. 66.

18 "Extraordinary Johnsoniana—Tacenda," MS Yale J88.

19 Written from Napes, to Boswell at Venice. MS Yale C3089.

20 Chauncey B. Tinker, *Letters of James Boswell*, 2 vols. (Oxford: Clarendon Press, 1924), II, 314-15.

21 To David Boswell: "Anxious lest my Epithalamium in an hour of pleasantry has been maliciously told to Dr. Johnson and he offended being very irritable. Begging him in confidence to call on the Dr. and sound him about me and let me know what passes. But to give no hint of my fear." Register of Letters, 6 November 1781. MS Yale M254, p. 110.

The Ironic Mode in Autobiography: Franklin and Rousseau

JEAN A. PERKINS

As many critics have pointed out, autobiography as a genre is a product of the late eighteenth century; it came into full flower with the Romantic movement and has remained an important literary resource ever since.[1] Whether the reasons for this are sociological, philosophical, or psychological shall not concern us here, but we do need to look back briefly at the traditions on which both Franklin and Rousseau drew before turning to the main theme of this paper.

In France the major autobiographical work before Rousseau was Montaigne's *Essays*, which form part of that series of egotistical and moralistic writings of the Renaissance distinguishable from autobiography by the fact that they are not narrations of a life but syntheses of an intellectual nature. The *mémorialistes* such as Saint-Simon were more in the nature of historians, commenting upon the events of the era in which they played a privileged part. And finally there were authors such as Mme. Guyon who concentrated upon their own religious experience in an attempt to convey the quality of this exceptional phenomenon. In the case of

Rousseau it is obviously the Renaissance tradition of intellectual biography which is of most importance. In his *Dialogues*, Rousseau produced a moral and intellectual self-portrait very much in line with this tradition. However, this is not the form of the *Confessions*. Nor does Rousseau follow the well-established method of the historical memoir; he recounts very few of the important political, economic, or sociological events of the eighteenth century; he observes himself, not the world. In contrast to the religious tradition, Rousseau does not concentrate on his adult life, nor does he limit his reflections to those sentiments and experiences which can be related to his religious convictions.[2] He is concerned to show himself as fully as possible to his reader, calling for incursions into areas of life, both intellectual and emotional, where few authors had strayed in the past. Rousseau announces himself as an exception to all rules about humanity, and his choice of incident certainly shocked his eighteenth-century public when the first part of the *Confessions* was published in 1782. They were also impressed by the emotional overtones which clearly distinguish Rousseau's self-searching from Montaigne's skeptical inquiries.

In English literature, both in England and America, many of the same literary trends were noticeable. Political memoirs have been written in every country in every age; the didacticism of the French *moralistes* is echoed in Addison's *Spectator* and Lord Chesterfield's *Letters to His Son*, but the literary development most pertinent to Franklin springs directly from the Puritan Revolution and involves spiritual autobiography. The concept of using the life of one man as a guide to everyone's spiritual growth was particularly apparent in the Puritan and Quaker tradition, witness John Wesley and John Woolman. In addition, there developed a large number of so-called conduct books, works in which fathers addressed putative sons and gave them practical hints on how to make progress in this world in such a way as to ensure entrance into the world to come. There is no doubt whatsoever that Benjamin Franklin was aware of these books and that to a great degree, the attitude he affects in the opening pages of his own work is directly imitative of such writers as Cotton Mather and William Penn.[3] Franklin's *Autobiography* has a totally different tone, however, most particularly in the first part. Franklin's choice of incident did not shock his readers, but they did find his tone much lighter and more worldly than that of the writers of conduct books.

If we accept this eighteenth-century view that both Rousseau's and Franklin's self-portraits were distinguished from previous autobiographical works by their tone, we can look at developments in other literary genres in which tone played an important role. The novel is the immediate candidate for close examination. Here we find both the emotional heightening so characteristic of Rousseau and the didactic but witty style contemporaries singled out in Franklin. The picaresque tradition gave way to the much more closely constructed and realistic story of a young person's progress from poverty to riches or from innocence to knowledge. The sentimental novel moved from a discontinuous series of incidents, each of which exemplifies an emotional attitude, to the history of emotional growth in a given individual. In terms of technique, the novel moved away from third-person narration to first-person or epistolary forms. It does not take a great deal of critical acumen to put these developing themes and techniques into context with the *Confessions* and the *Autobiography*. They were both drawing on this new storehouse of literary devices and thereby transforming and molding autobiography into something much closer to its contemporary form than are the *Confessions* of Saint Augustine or the *Autobiography* of Benvenuto Cellini.

Both Franklin and Rousseau were fully aware of these developments in the novel. In his account of his early reading, Franklin puts more stress on the philosophical, religious, and practical books which came his way, but does note that Bunyan was the first to combine narration and dialogue in *Pilgrim's Progress*, and that Defoe and Richardson use the same technique.[4] Rousseau read novels before he read anything else,[5] and his own epistolary novel *La Nouvelle Héloïse* (1762) revolutionized the genre in France.

Sentimental, realistic, or cynical, the novels of the period all participated in that great eighteenth-century fashion of searching for the origins of things, whether they be society, language, animal behavior, or human knowledge. It no longer sufficed to give a complete description of a mountain chain or a love affair; what must be explored was the background of these phenomena. Even epistolary novels so tightly tied to current activities as *Les Liaisons dangereuses* or *Clarissa* found space to delineate the way in which the protagonists had arrived at their present state. The memoir novel such as *La Vie de Marianne* and *Robinson Crusoe* deliberately juxtaposed the voice of the narrator and that of the young actor who eventually becomes the narrator.

Autobiography follows this fictional mode, and the relative distance between older narrator and young actor is crucial to the tone and the meaning. Both Rousseau and Franklin had to face the question of how they became what they were at the time of composition. Neither of them could afford a total identification of writer-narrator with actor-hero; the young hero is not the same person as the older writer, and yet the first cannot be totally divorced from the second, since he will, given time and experience, actually become the latter. Both Franklin and Rousseau adopted a particular point of view which enabled them to divorce themselves from their youth and yet show how the one led to the other.

The device they both used was irony, a humorous approach to their childhood and youth, which enabled them, first, to create a real distance between these two facets of themselves, and second, to elicit enough sympathy for the young hero to make his development into the wiser and older narrator both plausible and necessary. Rousseau is more troubled by the personality conflict inherent in his life, and he agonizes over those evil deeds performed during his youth which continue to haunt him in his maturity. Franklin is also concerned about his youthful "errata" but for the most part indicates how he made up for these misdeeds. As a scientist, Franklin was also preoccupied with the question of origins, convinced that at some level every detail does indeed fit into a larger whole. So he too was determined to show how Fame and Fortune can come from very dubious origins.

In superficial terms, the life stories of the two authors have remarkable similarities: they were both born of artisan parents; they were both apprenticed at an early age and objected to their subservient position; they both ran away from their apprenticeship; they both eventually established themselves in another city after a long series of adventures; they both became famous. Certain incidents chosen from their childhood and adolescence are almost parallels; however, other incidents occur which are not at all comparable, and it should be noted that the dissimilarities are in many ways greater than the similarities. For instance, Rousseau's predilection for incidents either overtly or covertly sexual is in marked contrast to Franklin's preference for incidents either overtly or covertly moralistic.

To convey the quality of their childhood, both authors recount a comic incident with moral overtones. During the period spent with the Lamberciers, Jean-Jacques and his cousin became involved in planting a willow tree on the same terrace on which M. Lambercier had just planted a walnut tree. The motivation was good: shade was needed on the terrace and two trees would be better than one. Unfortunately water was scarce, and in order to give their tree a sufficient supply, the boys built a channel from the walnut to the willow tree and in so doing drained off most of the water destined for the first. When this was discovered M. Lambercier cried out, "An aqueduct! an aqueduct! " and destroyed the structure. He then retreated to the house from which the boys heard "his full-throated laugh ring out shortly afterwards" (pp. 31-34).[6] The boys were ridiculous but at the same time admirable and were encouraged to plant another tree in a different place. As a youth, Benjamin Franklin became a leader of a group of boys who loved to go fishing in the salt marsh but found that the bank they stood on had become a quagmire. Seeing a heap of stones gathered nearby for a new house, Benjamin organized his gang to build a wharf. When the workmen discovered the loss the next day, the boys' fathers all reprimanded their offspring, Benjamin's pointing out that "nothing was useful which was not honest" (pp. 53-54). The conditions are much the same in the two incidents: young boys wishing to imitate their elders and to create something for themselves but being forced to use a subterfuge which is harmful to the adults.

Rousseau describes in great detail the building of the aqueduct, and he builds up the suspense by concentrating on the almost unbearable agony suffered by the boys until the moment they saw the water flowing towards their own tree. It is the boys themselves who betray their activity by their shouts of joy. The humor of the situation is emphasized by the fact that M. Lambercier did not reproach them afterwards but reacted with laughter to their escapade.

Franklin's portrait of himself as the leader of a group forever getting into scrapes is also presented in a comic way, but he does not rely on the reaction of an adult to convey the humor. Indeed, the adults involved are all severely reproachful, and the humor has to be seen in the activities of the boys themselves, who are compared to a group of ants:

> Accordingly in the Evening when the Workmen were gone, I assembled a Number of my Playfellows, and working with them diligently like so many Emmets, sometimes two or three to a Stone, we brought them all away and built our little Wharff. (P. 54)

The comic aspect of the situation is conveyed by a comparison which reduces the significance of the boys' activities to a point of diminishing returns. Such a minor incident could not have major consequences, and so the quality of leadership displayed by Benjamin could be sympathetic even though the activity itself was reprehensible.

As adolescents, both Rousseau and Franklin resented the terms of their apprenticeship and suffered under the harsh regimen imposed on them by their masters. Eventually both of them ran away from their servitude, Jean-Jacques after he had returned from a Sunday outing to find the gates of the city closed for the night. Had he returned to his master the next day, he would have been severely punished, since it was not the first time he had been caught in this way. So he set off happily with no idea of where he was going or what he was going to do, full of the illusions of youth. The narrator presents this likeable but ridiculous young man, impressed with his independence, travelling across the countryside like a knight in a romance:

> I did not see a castle on the left or the right without setting off to seek the adventure which I was sure awaited me there. I neither dared to enter nor yet to knock, for I was exceedingly timid. But I sang under what looked the likeliest window, and was very surprised after singing my loudest for a considerable time to see no ladies or maidens appear, attracted by the beauty of my voice or by the wit of my songs.[7] (P. 54)

Benjamin's leaving is presented in much less romantic terms. He tricks his master, his own brother, by using the discharge his brother had been obliged to sign in order to permit his newspaper to continue publication under Benjamin's name. Since there was another secret set of indentures, Benjamin was not really free to leave his brother's employ, and so he passed himself off as a young man escaping from an undesirable marriage. During this adventurous journey to Philadelphia, Benjamin manages to rescue a drunken Dutch sailor in a storm, suffers from a fever, meets a number of interesting people in New York and New Jersey, and helps to row the river boat from Burlington to Philadelphia. At one inn, he is mistaken for a runaway servant, a suspicion a little too close to reality for comfort.

The best known scene in Franklin's *Autobiography* is his arrival in Philadelphia. This incident is developed at some length with far more detail than in any other section. Franklin introduces the young adventurer in a brief portrait:

> I was in my Working Dress, my best Cloaths being to come round by Sea. I was dirty from my Journey; my Pockets were stuffed with Shirts and Stockings; I knew no Soul, nor where to look for

> Lodging. I was fatig'd with Travelling, Rowing and Want of Rest. I was very hungry. (P. 75)

Benjamin sets off up Market Street and enters a bakery, where, not knowing either the prices or the types of bread available, he asks for "three penny worth of any sort." What he gets in return are the three famous rolls which become the emblem of his innocence and ridiculousness:

> He gave me accordingly three great Puffy Rolls. I was surpriz'd at the Quantity, but took it, and having no room in my Pockets, walk'd off, with a Roll under each Arm, and eating the other. Thus I went up Market Street as far as fourth Street, passing by the Door of Mr. Read, my future Wife's Father, when she standing at the Door saw me, and thought I made as I certainly did a most awkward ridiculous Appearance. Then I turn'd and went down Chestnut Street and part of Walnut Street, eating my Roll all the Way. (P. 76)

In this passage, Franklin, like Rousseau in the aqueduct incident, has recourse to an outside observer who records the comic element of the situation. However, the ridiculous young man is not wholly comic; his next move is to share his rolls with a woman and child who have travelled with him from Burlington. Continuing his walk, Benjamin is again portrayed in a comic vein as he follows the crowd into meeting, it being Sunday morning:

> Thus refresh'd I walk'd again up the Street, which by this time had many clean dress'd People in it who were all walking the same Way; I join'd them, and thereby was led into the great Meeting House of the Quakers near the Market. I sat down among them, and after looking round a while and hearing nothing said, being very drowzy thro' Labour and want of Rest the preceding Night, I fell fast asleep, and continu'd so till the Meeting broke up, when one was kind enough to rouse me. This was therefore the first House I was in or slept in, in Philadelphia. (P. 76)

The picture of a tired and dirty young man, his pockets bulging with underwear, mingling with the sombrely dressed Quakers is amusing enough in itself, but Franklin develops the comic aspect by playing up the atmosphere of the Quaker meeting. Letting the silence settle did nothing for Benjamin's spirit except to put him to sleep, conduct usually frowned on in meeting.[8]

Franklin's reasons for developing this scene at such length are delineated at the start by the following remark:

> I have been the more particular in this Description of my Journey, and shall be so of my first Entry into that City, that you may in your Mind compare such unlikely Beginnings with the Figure I have since made there. (P. 75)

The young hero is not yet the wise narrator, far from it, but he must also participate in the process which will eventually lead him to fame. Paying for his passage on the river boat even though he had helped with the rowing is passed off as a form of vanity; people with very little money are sometimes more generous "perhaps thro' fear of being thought to have but little" (p. 75). Sharing the rolls is presented partly as generosity and partly as a desire to get rid of an unbecoming burden. Finally, his choice of activity is eminently proper: young men should indeed attend divine service on Sunday, and despite his inability to profit from it, Benjamin's activity conforms to those standards of prudence and industry which Franklin insists will lead to fame and fortune.

In the *Confessions* the scene of an innocent and ridiculous young man turned loose in a large city is much less developed. Jean-Jacques has just completed his stay in the seminary at Turin and is delighted at his newly refound freedom. He has only twenty francs in his pocket and he is carrying his clothes wrapped in a small bundle. Rousseau gives a rather sympathetic portrait of a young man with no place to sleep, roaming the streets of Turin as a tourist, gawking at the sights:

> The first thing I did was to satisfy my curiosity, or perhaps to celebrate my liberty, by making a complete tour of the town. I went to see the posting of the guard, and was highly delighted by their military band. I followed processions, fascinated by the mumbling of the priests. I went to see the royal palace, and approached it with awe. But, seeing other people go in, I followed

> them and no one prevented me. Perhaps I owed my immunity to the little parcel under my arm. However that may be, I conceived a great opinion of myself when I found myself in the palace, I felt almost as if I lived there. In the end, after so much trotting about, I grew tired. I was hungry and it was hot. So I went into a dairy, and was given some *giuncà* (cream cheese) and two sticks of that excellent Piedmontese bread that I prefer to any other.[9] (P. 75)

The similarities with Franklin's account are striking: the unassuming dress of the young hero, his joining the crowd to enter any building they did, his making a meal of fairly simple food and enjoying it fully. But at this time Jean-Jacques has not yet reached the point at which he will "find himself" and so he is portrayed as still totally committed to romantic illusions which will not lead to the future, whereas Benjamin is getting closer to his goal and Franklin emphasizes the reality of the situation.

Both young men soon do find the means to earn a living. Franklin settles in Philadelphia as an associate in a printing shop and is tapped by the Governor as his future official printer. Not realizing that Governor Keith's word is not to be trusted, Benjamin sets off for Boston in an attempt to convince his father to underwrite the expenses of a new printing press. While there, Benjamin pays a visit to his brother's printing shop in order to show off his new grandness:

> I was better dress'd than ever while in his Service, having a genteel new Suit from Head to foot, a Watch, and my Pockets Lin'd with near Five Pounds Sterling in Silver. He receiv'd me not very frankly, look'd me all over, and turn'd to his Work again. The Journey-Men were inquisitive where I had been, what sort of a Country it was, and how I lik'd it? I prais'd it much, and the happy Life I led in it; expressing strongly my Intention of returning to it; and one of them asking what kind of Money we had there, I produc'd a handful of Silver and spread it before them, which was a kind of Raree-Show they had not been us'd to, Paper being the Money of Boston. Then I took an Opportunity of letting them see my Watch: and lastly, (my Brother still grum and sullen) I gave them a Piece of Eight to drink and took my Leave. (Pp. 81-82)

Nothing about the young hero is presented in a sympathetic light; not only has he let his vanity get the better of him, but the very basis on which he is flaunting himself to his brother is fallacious. Governor Keith will never actually live up to the promise made to Benjamin. This time he is ridiculous without the saving grace of innocence or generosity. He is pretending to be something more than he actually is, and circumstances will eventually show him his error. The narrator does not moralize openly but quite obviously does not approve of Benjamin's actions in this scene.

In the *Confessions*, Rousseau presents a similar scene during the period of his life when he was passing himself off as a music master. Jean-Jacques assumes a false name and claims to be a composer. To further his musical career, he actually composes a piece, scores it for orchestra, and conducts a performance of it himself. In view of the fact that he had almost no knowledge of music, the results can be imagined:

> Attention! All was quiet. Gravely I began to beat time. They began. No, throughout all the history of French opera never was there heard such a discordant row. Whatever they might have thought of my pretended talents, the effect was worse than anything they seem to have expected. The musicians were choking with laughter; the audience goggled their eyes, and would gladly have stopped their ears; but they had not the means.[10] (Pp. 145-46)

In this case, the young hero is aware that his performance is ridiculous, but he is driven by shame to continue his masquerade. The gap between reality and appearance cannot be acknowledged in public.

This juxtaposition of appearance and reality, of disorder and order, of role-playing and sincerity is at the base of the techniques of irony and comedy of both authors. The necessary distance can be arranged, the reader can be let into the secret, but at the same time the integrity of the young hero can be preserved so that he can eventually go on to better things.

Secure in his mature personality and sure that his public and private images coincided, Franklin could afford to continue his irony right up to the moment of conversion from young actor-hero to industrious business man and beneficent public servant. This rite of passage is condensed by Franklin in his description of his famous Project of Moral Perfection. The section has been a difficult one for critics, because it does mix a serious moral lesson with an ironic presentation.[11] Franklin outlined thirteen virtues on a tablet, marked off columns for each day of the week, and then set himself the task of working on one of the virtues for each of thirteen weeks, repeating the process four times a year, in an attempt to habituate himself to Temperance, Silence, Order, Resolution, Frugality, Industry, Sincerity, Justice, Moderation, Cleanliness, Tranquility, Chastity, and Humility. Order gave him the most trouble at first, but he made some progress in all but the final virtue, Humility, which had been added to his original list on the advice of a Quaker friend. Franklin finally acknowledged that moral perfection is not possible, since at the last moment pride in one's achievement destroys the result (pp. 148-60). An individual can better himself by practicing the virtues listed, however, and it is only the belief that moral perfection is attainable that is treated ironically. The older and wiser narrator can thus smile at the follies of youth but present them in an extremely sympathetic light, since he knows that life itself is a series of scenes, comic or tragic according to the position of the observer.

For Rousseau, the problems of personality are much more distressing; one of his main reasons for writing the *Confessions* is to correct the public image which does not correlate with his own self-image.[12] Therefore, as Jean-Jacques approaches the stage at which he will blossom forth into the mature Rousseau, the identification between the young hero and the narrator becomes closer and closer. The rite of passage in this case occurs during the conversion on the road to Vincennes (pp. 327-28), followed by Rousseau's resolution to abandon his quest for fortune and advancement and to live modestly on what he earns copying music (pp. 337-38). Both of these moments are described as moments of ecstasy or delirium followed by rational decision; the emotional stage is not treated ironically but is presented as a necessary concomitant to any important moral choice. Hereafter Rousseau may undergo reverses, but he is no longer ridiculous to himself, even though the public may view him as a comic figure. For Rousseau the comedy is over, and the crucible of sincerity will be the test of all his actions.

NOTES

1 The two works which I found most useful on autobiography as a genre are Philippe Lejeune, *L'Autobiographie en France* (Paris: Colin, 1971), and Roy Pascal, *Design and Truth in Autobiography* (Cambridge, Mass.: Harvard University Press, 1960).

2 Lejeune, *L'Autobiographie*, pp. 65-66.

3 Both Bruce I. Granger in his book *Benjamin Franklin: An American Man of Letters* (Ithaca: Cornell University Press, 1964) and J. A. Leo Lemay in his essay "Benjamin Franklin" in Everett Emerson, ed., *Major Writers of Early American Literature* (Madison: University of Wisconsin Press, 1972) discuss the debt of Franklin to his English and American predecessors, stressing the role of the conduct book.

4 *The Autobiography of Benjamin Franklin*, ed. Leonard W. Larabee et al. (New Haven: Yale University Press, 1964), pp. 57-58, 72. All future references to Franklin's *Autobiography* will be to this edition. It is interesting to note that Franklin was the first to publish Richardson's *Pamela* in America, in 1744.

5 Jean-Jacques Rousseau, *The Confessions,* tr. J. M. Cohen (Baltimore: Penguin Books, 1954), pp. 19-20, and *Les Confessions,* in *Œuvres complètes* (Paris: Pléiade, 1959), I, 8. All future references to Rousseau's *Confessions* will be to these editions.

6 ". . . nous l'entendimes même un peu après rire auprès de sa soeur à gorge deployée, car le rire de M. Lambercier s'entendoit de loin" (I, 24).

7 "Je ne voyois pas un château à droite ou à gauche sans aller chercher l'avanture que j'étois sur qui m'y attendoit. Je n'osois entrer dans le château ni heurter; car j'étois fort timide. Mais je chantois sous la fenêtre qui avoit le plus d'apparence, fort surpris, après m'être longtems époumonné, de ne voir paroitre ni Dames ni Demoiselle qu'attirât la beauté de ma voix ou le sel de mes chansons" (I, 48).

8 In the alternate version of this incident which A. O. Aldridge discovered in the *London Chronicle* for October 1, 1778, none of these qualifying details are present and the scene is hardly amusing at all (A. O. Aldridge,

"The First Published Memoir of Franklin," *William and Mary Quarterly*, ser. 3, vol. 24 [1967], 624–28).

9 "La prémiére chose que je fis fut de satisfaire ma curiosité en parcourant toute la Ville, quand ce n'eut été que pour faire un acte de ma liberté. J'allai voir monter la garde; les instrumens militaires me plaisoient beaucoup. Je suivis des processions; j'aimois le faux bourdon des prêtres. J'allai voir le Palais du Roi: j'en approchois avec crainte; mais voyant d'autres gens entrer je fis comme eux, on me laissa faire. Peutêtre dus-je cette grace au petit paquet que j'avois sous le bras. Quoiqu'il en soit je conceus une grande opinion de moi-même en me trouvant dans ce Palais: déja je m'en regardois presque comme un habitant. Enfin à force d'aller et venir, je me lassai, j'avois faim, il faisoit chaud; j'entrai chez une marchande de laitage: on me donna de la Giuncà, du lait caillé, et avec deux grisses de cet excellent pain de Piemont que j'aime plus qu'aucun autre" (I, 71).

10 ". . . *prenez garde à vous.* On fait silence, je me mets gravement à battre la mesure, on commence . . . non, depuis qu'il existe des Opera françois, de la vie on n'ouit en semblable charivari. Quoi qu'on eut pu penser de mon prétendu talent, l'effet fut pire que tout ce qu'on sembloit attendre. Les musiciens étouffoient de rires; les auditeurs ouvroient de grands yeux et auroient bien voulu fermer les oreilles, mais il n'y avoit pas moyen" (I, 149). The fact that Rousseau's initial entry into French society would be through his musical talent adds piquancy to the scene.

11 The ironic tone of this section has been commented on by numerous critics, including J. S. Leo Lemay, "Franklin and the Autobiography," *ECS*, 1 (1967-68), 185-211, David Levin, "The Autobiography of Benjamin Franklin," *Yale Review*, n.s. 53 (1963-64), 258-75, James A. Sappenfield, *A Sweet Instruction: Franklin's Journalism as a Literary Apprenticeship* (Carbondale: Southern Illinois University Press, 1973), pp. 185–92, Robert F. Sayre, *The Examined Self: Benjamin Franklin, Henry Adams and Henry James* (Princeton: Princeton University Press, 1964), pp. 27-31, and John W. Ward, "Who Was Benjamin Franklin? " *American Scholar*, 32 (1963), 541-53.

12 This interpretation of the *Confessions* is stressed by such critics as Lester Crocker, *Jean-Jacques Rousseau*, 2 vols. (New York: Macmillan, 1968-73), Ronald Grimsley, *Jean-Jacques Rousseau: A Study in Awareness* (Cardiff: University of Wales Press, 1961), and Jean Starobinski, *Jean-Jacques Rousseau, la transparence et l'obstacle* (Paris: Plon, 1957).

Lessing on Liberty: The Literary Work as Autobiography

FRANK G. RYDER

This essay, which urges a radically unorthodox view of Lessing as man and writer, also takes autobiography in a somewhat "liberated" sense, to include any self-revelation of the subject's essential attitude toward the central issues of his life and times.[1] Of life and times it concentrates on the latter, being part of a larger study devoted to questions of social justice and human rights, of personal liberty and the claims of authority, as they occupy the attention of writers in Germany of the late eighteenth and early nineteenth centuries. Lessing serves as a case in point, but directly comparable approaches lead to similarly heterodox views of Goethe, Schiller, and other literary figures of the period.

Not only because the devotion of such writers to formal autobiography varies—only with Goethe is it extensive—but because autobiographical statement is, like other kinds of language, camouflage as well as communication, we need to widen the frame of evidence to encompass the lines, and the spaces between the lines, in letters, in recorded casual utterances, and especially in literary works—whatever the difficulties inherent in treating the last as autobiography. We will not profit much from the traditional identification of the author with one of his fictive heroes. True, Werther is somehow Goethe, Posa speaks for Schiller, Nathan is Lessing on the rivalry of religions. But these evocations of personality are tenuous and unreliable. They are often adulterated by pathos—the persona as idealization of the self—or obscured by the tension between revelation and mask. The work of biographers is too often distorted by *their* attitudes, usually hagiographical, toward such ambiguities. What we are after in the case at hand, is the surest possible access to the "deep structure" of the writer's mind, the deep structure which generates, at any given time, all the explicit utterances at the surface level.

Remarkably, we will find ourselves turning often in such a search to the literary work, relying (with due caution) less on ostensible meaning and the received interpretation, more on the elusive but genuine evidence of contradictory stances in related works or inconsistencies in the inner logic of plot or character, inconsistencies which can be explained only by reference to the author's own divided mind or to feelings he might overtly deny. Even the fact that a work is left fragmentary may reveal the threat of a similar, more palpable inconsistency, as if the author had found himself in danger of taking or seeming to take a position he was not prepared to sustain, of revealing more than he had intended to reveal.

Above all, and especially in the case of Lessing, we shall have to question both traditional pieties and modern apologetics. I see Lessing (at least in the present context) neither as the staunch hero of Reason *engagée,* "Streiter für Wahrheit," exemplary scion of yet another of the obligatory Lutheran pastorates, nor yet as the cool tactician of the mind—Alan Menhennet's Lessing as the "intellectual's intellectual," for whom discussion and controversy are all and whose plays are problem-solving. I should rather see him as a man complexly involved in the essential political and social divisions of his time, aware of the discontinuity between the demands of reason and the practices of society, but himself of seriously divided convictions and allegiances, on the one hand dedicated to the principles of freedom, on the other still persuaded of either the rightness or the inevitability of the absolutist state and princely rule.

Instead of representing either position in more or less unalloyed form he tended in his earlier writing to leave the statement unfinished, in his mature work to maintain both positions in uneasy, contradictory, or shifting balance in the same document, sometimes in the dramatic form of a dialectic exchange which permits us to identify him with either, both, or neither of the poles represented. The frames of mind that can normally be adduced in explanation of such a posture are few: honest indecision? fascination with contraries? irony? caution? evasiveness?

That Lessing was concerned with the issues of human rights, constitutional government, and the oppressiveness of autocracy is no matter of conjecture. Of the relatively few plays that stand out against the generally conventional subject matter, the stock characters and situations of his earlier oeuvre, two are centrally occupied with liberation and revolution—and one of these is both utterly *au courant* and promisingly subversive. But that one remained a fragment and the other is only a sketch.

The rebellion of Samuel Henzi against the stultifying patrician oligarchy of Bern and the two acts of Lessing's dramatic fragment *Samuel Henzi* fall in the same year, a tribute of intense contemporaneity scarcely seen in German literature since Gryphius' *Carolus Stuardus.* The newspapers of the time were filled with the story of Henzi, a rebel who seems fully to have deserved the name of patriot, since what he rebelled against was an increasingly concentrated oligarchy—four families in possession of half the city offices—a stultifying neglect not only of the arts and sciences but of trade and industry, and the high-handed abrogation of existing constitutional limitations upon special privilege, plus the suppression of traditional electoral rights.

Add to this the demonstrable merits of Henzi as a man—like Lessing, the son of a pastor, he was also an officer and city official, a cultivated man, artistically inclined, energetic and dedicated—and Lessing's empathy for both the cause and the person is fully comprehensible. What is more, Lessing was personally attacked for his treatment of the sensitive topic and the play, should it ever be finished, was the object of a resolution by the City of Bern, of anticipatory suppression.

From this sympathy and involvement stems the essential pathos of the play, obviously a tribute to a good man in a just cause, betrayed by wicked co-conspirators who use for personal revenge what was designed as a legitimate and limited uprising. The potential of *tragic* flaw exists, and not only in the trusting nature of Henzi, his "weiches Herz," but also in his bitterness and loss of composure (in the face of false accusations that he has betrayed the plot). Although the fragment ends with such a scene, one feels that the potential flaw it represents will not be capitalized upon, that the sustaining mode will be the pathos of a good man savagely brought down, a noble cause thwarted; that the end was to be as the end was in fact, the maiming and execution of the three leaders, with drums ready should the rebels try to speak to the citizens.

Pathos of character and situation, and personal involvement of the author, are qualities which do not necessarily make for great literature. What they do make for is, in a quasi-autobiographical sense, powerful and unambiguous evidence of the author's stand—in this case concerning human rights and their fate under authoritarian rule of whatever persuasion. The entire complex of urgent contemporaneity and utmost clarity of issue justifies our regarding the position of Henzi as described in his words in the play as Lessing's own position at the age of twenty, audacious and unsubtle no doubt, but also untarnished by the compromising wisdom of experience and the muffling cautiousness of reputation and position, those aspects of "maturity" that in this context characterize Lessing more than we might care to admit.

Henzi's stand, in the abstract (but via direct paraphrase of Act I, Scenes 1 and 2, and Act II, Scene 2, *LM,* V, 98-110, 117-18) is this:

> When guaranteed freedoms are abrogated by the power drives and the selfish personal aggrandizement of a few, controlled revolutionary action in the interest of the common welfare is justified. Violence and personal revenge are unworthy motives, endangering the just cause, and they must be banished from any such undertaking (I,1). The governing institutions must be given one more chance to desist from their perversion of authority (I,2), but such a challenge must be backed by the willingness to use force and that force should be not putative but at the ready. (Henzi in fact has armed the *Landvolk*; I,1.) Men do not deserve to be free unless they recognize civic duty and virtue, mutual responsibility, the certainty of honor and truth independent of what is "preached" to them, charity to the less privileged, the happiness of fighting for one's land and not for a king's vanity. *Such* men are heroes, not rebels. (II, 2)

It is a remarkable statement of libertarian ideals, a fine chapter—or paragraph—in Lessing's intellectual credo. But it is to some degree vitiated by the fragmentary quality of its matrix, and alas, it is one of the last times such an ideal is expressed with clarity and courage.

The vigorous awareness of the logical imperative of individual freedom, the painful awareness of its precarious state under absolutism, surfaces explicitly in a few detached utterances of the older Lessing, such as the familiar letter to Nicolai twenty years later: "Let someone try to do what Sonnenfels did in Vienna, let him be tempted to tell the truth to the aristocratic mob at court, let someone step forward in Berlin and raise his voice for the rights of subjects, against exploitation and despotism . . . and you will soon find out what country is to this very day the most slavish land in Europe."[2] Sonnenfels, although he advanced the claims of secular education against prevailing church control, was in other contexts (and perhaps even in this one) a thoroughgoing bureaucrat of absolutism, scarcely capable of the democratic exertions implied in Lessing's challenge. Yet even in the limited appropriateness of its point of reference, this is a drastic statement, implying the gravest verdict upon the quality of political life in Lessing's own adopted home, the domain of the "first servant of the state."

Lessing may have disagreed with Winckelmann about Greece but perhaps not about Prussia: "the greatest despotism that has ever been conceived."

The precise nature of Lessing's *mature* attitude toward absolutism is hard to fathom. If it were not for fragmentary outbursts like that to Nicolai we might assume either that he had ceased to care or that he no longer considered the issue of personal liberty in the political sphere to be one of his central concerns, preferring to exercise his intellectual gifts in religious controversy and literary criticism. Given these exceptions, however, we must start from the premise that he cared very much, at least "deep down," and must therefore seek some mediating key to his later silence or ambivalence.

Lessing's own brief sketch of his proposed play "Das befreite Rom" (*LM,* III, 357-59) may furnish or approximate such a key. The suggestion is admittedly radical, but the material is in itself so striking that it demands attention in any examination of Lessing's politics *or* psychological makeup. The sketch presumably originates not long after *Henzi,* a temporal bond which alone is significant. It is so short that for present purposes I shall translate it substantially in full:

> Act I Brutus alone. In a brief speech he reveals his dissembling, which is beginning to weigh on him. Two Romans enter, conversing about the tyranny of Tarquinius. They catch sight of Brutus but pay no attention to him, considering him mad. They mention Tarquin's most recent crime, against Lucretia. Lucretia appears, accompanied by a crowd of people and two slave women. She is beside herself, tells the people of her shame, and stabs herself before their eyes, casting the dagger among them, with the cry, "To my avenger." She is carried off, dying. Brutus seizes the dagger, since no one dares pick it up. The crowd laughs to see that it has fallen into *his* hands, but mourns the fate of Lucretia.
>
> Act II Brutus's ambiguous and suggestive mockery, as he speaks to various of the people, concerning the dagger and the deed committed with it. The lictors come . . . but the people drive them away. . . . Tarquin himself appears. . . . The people

disperse and leave Brutus alone on the square. The king exults over their fear. He takes up a conversation with Brutus, listening to him as he would to a fool. The people stand at a distance. Brutus stabs the king and exits, as if mad. Tarquin is carried off, dying.

Act III Collatinus appears and speaks to the populace of his claims to the vacant throne. Another crowd rushes in, crying "Freedom! Brutus! "

Collatinus: How long is this madman to confound the city?

Brutus: Listen to me, Romans. I am no madman, no fool. He declaims against kings and Collatinus is compelled to leave. Enter Publicola, recognized as the husband of Lucretia. Brutus gives him the reins of government, but not as king, rather as counselor of the people. He declares that he, Brutus, cannot take over, because his dissembling has rendered him incapable [unworthy; "untüchtig"] of doing so.

The thematic and motival affinity with *Emilia Galotti* is obvious. Transferring from this fragment to *Emilia* certain aspects of the parallelism of sexual affront and the symbolic dagger would result in a fascinating and radically different reading of the later tragedy, a reading which, I hasten to add, it does not in its own context bear or deserve.

From our point of view the essence of the fragment is this: An insufferable tyranny prevails. The one person aware of the necessity of drastic change has disguised his intent, Hamlet-like, in a mask of follies, but he takes up the symbolic challenge of remedial action. By "ambiguities and pregnant mockery" he sustains both the outward show and the inner conviction until the occasion is ripe; then the fool kills the tyrant. But disingenuousness and the cultivation of ambivalence render one unsuitable for the charge of government under freedom, and that charge is given over to another.

It is my suggestion that the fragment *Das befreite Rom* may be seen, obviously in modified form yet in essential ways, as an autobiographical *parodos* of Lessing himself, that it represents a sort of intermediate stage between the overt revolutionary sympathies of *Henzi* and the later, increasingly cryptic or vitiated statements of freedom. Absolutely essential, however, is a sober awareness that neither *Henzi* nor the Brutus fragment represents more than a tentative and passing stance. Lessing retreated farther and farther into true ambivalence and nothing can make such works as *Ernst und Falk* or *Emilia Galotti* into arguments *in tyrannos,* whatever discrete bits and pieces may be taken out of context, from his life or works, to urge such a point.

To judge from the evasiveness and contradiction with which Lessing surrounds the genesis of *Emilia* one might assume almost the opposite: either that the play *was* written *in tyrannos,* an intent which the author however had no mind to acknowledge, or that it contained, by inadvertence or in balanced ambiguity, elements which might be interpreted as subversive, a danger which the author meant at all costs to forestall. The story is familiar. In 1758 Lessing reports that "a young tragedian" is working on a play concerning a middle-class Virginia, to be called Emilia Galotti, but has eliminated from Livy's original all elements which concern the state as such, since there is quite sufficient dramatic fascination in a father's slaying of a daughter to whom virtue is more important than life. So the play is domestic, not political.

But the actual writing of the final version brought the ironic danger of being attacked for the wrong reasons, when it was not even certain that any true ones existed. Lessing was now writing, in Erich Schmidt's words (II,14), as the employee of a ducal house (Brunswick) with many romantic intrigues on its escutcheon, and by a singularly uncomfortable coincidence finished the play just in time for production as a birthday present for the Duchess. Lessing now felt compelled to clear the production with the head of state: It was an old play, really, and might not fit the present occasion, so it was up to the Duke to decide; really the play was just the ancient Roman story of Virginia, of course, done in modern dress. Lessing covered for himself in Berlin too, in precisely the same way. He also covered by directing the play himself—some say it was the only time he did such a thing— and as Eschenburg (the translator of Shakespeare) reports, indicating for all doubtful passages the proper intonation. One would like to know in what sense doubtful, and in particular how he treated certain crucial (and moot) episodes such as the last scene. In any event, all these denials and coachings apparently were insufficient to allay Lessing's own worries, because he ignored special personal invitations from on high to attend the premiere.

In plain fact, the Duke was accidentally right in his casual judgment that the play could be produced without offense, and this not by dint of Lessing's adept maneuvering but because the play is not *in its own terms* revolutionary or even subversive. (Believing it so is the seemingly inescapable fallacy of wishful thinkers of the Left, from Mehring on.) Whatever libertarian implications the play does have are for the most part carefully suppressed, qualified, or negated, in the tragic counterpart of Brutus's disabling harlequinade—or they exist in a context so wide as to include the unhappy circumstances which forced a great man to write in this fashion. *Emilia* is not a revolutionary document, and it poses little revolutionary threat.

I have argued elsewhere at length and in detail (and beg leave to repeat here) that the basic contradiction of the play lies in the proffered justification for the catastrophe. Two allocations of fault are suggested and they are at variance. One is political or social and suggests that the blame falls on the Prince. The other is psychological and much of the "fault" is Emilia's. The introduction of psychological considerations is the wedge which sunders political consistency. No matter how it is assessed, in Aristotelian terms or as self-punishment or as the result of filial disillusionment, the more psychologically plausible Emilia's death becomes, the less the play is political. The more literally we take Emilia's protestations of sexuality, the more nearly her death becomes comprehensible, appropriate, tolerable. And the less it matters whether the would-be seducer is a prince or a petty clerk. The two causal factors, however, are not consistently sustained through the course of the action. The play begins (apart from the disquisition on art) with predominantly social-political emphasis and ends with psychological; it begins by establishing the responsibility of the Prince and increasingly exculpates him or removes him from the scene; it begins by portraying Emilia as innocent and, increasing though ambiguously, reveals flaws in her character.

The Prince is allowed to shift initiative and blame to his counselor Marinelli. The Prince is the speaker of the last words of the play and his world is intact, while all other worlds (with the exception, ultimately, of Marinelli's) are in ruins. To assume he has a mortified conscience is in my opinion the purest sentimentality.

Odoardo, in the received view a man of rigorous virtue, the harsh but just *paterfamilias,* is by witness of his own words and actions less a true father than a selfish and anxious man, a person of shocking instability, whose mind audibly crumbles as he turns against his own child the weapon explicitly intended for the Prince or Marinelli or both. He is a model of intrapunition, and as such one of the most significant and frightening political models of the play. (He also may have a great deal to say about the father-son relationship in the pastorate at Kamenz.)

The lines of contradiction meet, clash–and disappear–in Emilia. Lessing has seen to it that we know little about her and hear from her almost nothing. She has no monologue. She appears in only seven of the forty-three scenes of the play whose name she bears. Yet as the blame shifts gradually from the Prince it moves explicitly to her and at the end we are asked to believe unbelievable things about her. For all this, Lessing scatters throughout the play subtle hints, in imagery and structure, of Emilia's innocence and the Prince's guilt.

And, remarkably, in one figure he creates the exemplary response of a free man to tyranny. Appiani defies the hireling and disobeys the master, scorns obsequious pretexts, repels cynical intrusion, meets insinuations with counterattack, willingly matches each escalation of violence with equal force, and literally scares away the cowardly agent of tyranny by suggesting a confrontation without delay. He may be a stuffy fiancé but he is a model of political courage. In words spoken after the encounter with Marinelli–"That did me good . . . I feel better"–he will say something no one else in the play does or could. He also dies, as no one else in the play does, just once.

In sum, *Emilia* shows Lessing demonstrably aware of the injustice, corruption, and oppression of petty tyranny, and aware of the appropriate answer to it. But it also shows him, even in the drastic circumstances of his own fictional creation, unprepared to generalize the imperative of refusal or rebellion. Whether out of conformism or indecision or disinclination to draw drastic consequences, he was moved to leave the Absolute State fundamentally unshaken, suggesting personal psychological factors as the downfall of the subject, weakness or evil counsel as palliation for the monarch. But, once again, he was a man of too great honesty and insight to give full rein to such extenuations. His play is, in the view urged here, an ironic monument to a divided political conscience.

To the end of his life and work, Lessing maintained this (it would seem) corrosive ambivalence, at once suggesting the need for drastic change in the name of human dignity and avoiding the logical consequences, in actual or recommended action, of that perception, or placating the autocratic hand which lay heavy on freedom.

Ernst und Falk is an instance. Freemasonry was widely recognized in Germany as a progenitor of liberal political thought, a dangerous haven for egalitarianism. Even the hierarchical adornments of the Strict Observance could not entirely eliminate the danger of subversion. The paradigm of both biographical fact and revelation of ambivalence is the same as with *Emilia.* The locus of placable authority is the same Duke Karl Ferdinand of Brunswick, this time in his dual capacity as monarch and as head of the Strict Observance. The strongest challenge is in the dedication from the unnamed "most submissive servant of his Excellency": "Most excellent Duke: I too was at the wellspring of truth and I drank. How deeply I drank can be judged only by him whose permission I hope to have that I may drink even more deeply—The people has languished for long and is about to expire of thirst."[3]

If the foreword following this dedication pretends to more or less innocent anonymity, the *"Vorrede eines Dritten"* heading the appended fourth and fifth conversations is informed by the evasion of Brutus:

> The author of the first three Conversations had this continuation ready in MS when he was asked, by suggestions from above, not to publish it.
>
> Previously however he had imparted [the material] to friends, who without his permission had copied it. One of these copies fell by curious chance into the hands of the present editor. He regretted the suppression of so many glorious truths and decided to have the manuscript printed. . . .

For all this, the fourth and fifth conversations are more historical curiosities than matters of substance. The direction of the first three by contrast is anything but harmless. The egalitarian and liberal tendencies of the Freemasons are prominent, and isolated quotations can be found that have a strongly anti-authoritarian tone: "When each individual knows how to govern himself no government is needed." "The state is for man, not man for the state." "The state joins men together to secure their happiness . . . and any other happiness within the state which is associated with the suffering of individual members of it . . . is the mask of tyranny."

But all of this is vitiated in several quarters. The dialogue between Falk and Ernst, one nominally enlightened, the other nominally an apprentice, permits issues to be clouded, as if Falk were afraid to reveal too much to the uninitiated Ernst. Or Ernst may be maneuvered into taking the ideological initiative and saying things he does not fully understand and is therefore not responsible for—which exculpates Lessing too. But the more serious evisceration of the argument is explicit or overtly implied in the logic of the piece itself. When Falk has worked Ernst, Socratically, into agreeing that Nature must prefer the happiness of any actual individual to the happiness of an abstract conception (like the state), and that constitutions are means not ends, indeed means invented by human minds and therefore not infallible but often countereffective, he has in essence set the groundwork for the negation of unjust authority.

The metaphor that follows, designed to clarify for Ernst this notion that constitutions may achieve the opposite of their purported goal, reduces a substantial point almost to triviality. Falk: "Ships and navigation are means of travel to distant lands but they also become the cause of men never getting there." Ernst is allowed to think he has guessed the connection–as apparently he has, for he is not contradicted–when he identifies as such causes shipwreck and drowning. But shipwreck and drowning, one assumes, are accidents or the result of negligence. The failure of constitutions, however, tends to be a matter of suppression or abrogation or denial, therefore no matter of coincidence but an act of somebody's will.

Later in the same Conversation Falk concedes that differences of religion, class, and wealth are inevitable in any organized society but he says that this does not make them sacred. "In what sense [do you mean] sacred?" asks Ernst. "Not so sacred that one is forbidden to lay hand on them." Again, the virtually explicit suggestion of forcible reform vanishes in Falk's answer to Ernst's question: "[Lay hand on them] with what aim in mind?" Falk: "With the aim of not allowing [these gaps or differences] to widen more than necessity commands. With the aim of making their consequences as harmless as possible." Whoever retreats this far has generally lost the battle.

Or, in the third conversation, this exchange: Ernst: "From what you say I assume Freemasons to be people who have voluntarily taken it upon themselves to work against the unavoidable evils of the state." Falk: "All right, but not of this or that particular state. Not the unavoidable evils which . . . follow necessarily from a given constitution. The Freemason never deals with these, at least not as a Mason. The amelioration and healing of these [evils] he leaves to the citizen to deal with at his risk, in accord with his insight and his courage. Evils of a very different and much higher sort are the object of his activity."

Either we must work this around to the notion that Masons are to be viewed as the higher guides of the common citizen—a leap nowhere made by Lessing, at least not in connection with the state—or we must recognize in it the crucial disabling act of Lessing's political thinking, and see in his removal of the best minds to other spheres of thought and action Lessing's own form of the diversionary maneuver by which responsibility for individual action is averted, an escape related to Schiller's moral-aesthetic education of the individual as prior to—or increasingly the substitute for—collective political and social action.

It is perhaps risky to apply the language of the couch to the analysis of political attitudes and doubtless presumptuous to do so in the case of greatness, but how far removed is Lessing's "political subconscious," thus demonstrated in his own works, from one of the modal postures of the eighteenth-century German intellectual and man of letters?

> "I see and resent the evils of Absolutism, in its frequent denial of liberties which are, in elementary humanity and by the dictates of reason, the due of the individual. But I recognize the power and in many ways the established right of princes and the state—or at the very least the definitive danger, especially to me, inherent in striking out against it. I am therefore not willing to suggest rebellion against social or political injustice—though as a younger person I was close to advocating it—but I shall hint at it, by suggestion and tentatively in essays or dialogues, and through models of anti-authoritarian behavior, more or less hidden but implicitly praised, in fiction or drama. In the latter I may identify, even more subtly, my essential sympathies, using images, metaphors, and structural devices. However, lest I be either misunderstood or open to damaging attack, I prefer to qualify all direct public utterances and make certain that in the indirect statement of fictive situations my own ambivalence or indecision is reflected in alternative patterns of motivation and action."

If this seems to cultivate irreverence when we should rather praise famous men, then we ought perhaps to accustom ourselves to viewing the writers of eighteenth-century Germany not against an imagined backdrop of Light, Reason, and *Humanität*, but in the context of that almost universal stultification of libertarian thought so well documented by such scholars as Aris and Epstein, weighing then, but without sentimentality, both the enormous difficulty of asking to be free and the modest credit that accrues to a writer for even raising the question in the first place, however muted his answer.

NOTES

1 The present text represents a slight revision of a talk given in July, 1975, at the Sixth Annual Meeting of the American Society for Eighteenth-Century Studies at Yale University, in the section "Autobiography and Biography." Conclusions here derived from Lessing's works are strikingly similar to those derived by my colleague Ruth Angress from reexamination of biographical evidence and presented in a talk at the concurrent session of the Lessing Society: "On the Need for a New Lessing Biography." Both of us obviously hope for a quite different "Lessing-Bild," long overdue, less worshipful and simplistic than the accepted one—and far more interesting.

The Lessing edition used is that of K. Lachmann and F. Muncker, *Lessings sämtliche Schriften,* 3rd ed., 21 vols. (Leipzig: Göschen, 1886-1907), here abbreviated as *LM.*

Also referred to: Alan Menhennet, *Order and Freedom* (London: Weidenfeld and Nicolson, 1973); Erich Schmidt, *Lessing,* 4th ed. (Berlin: Weidmann, 1923); Franz Mehring, *Die Lessing-Legende,* reprinted as Ullstein Buch 2854 (Frankfurt, 1972); Klaus Epstein, *The Genesis of German Conservatism* (Princeton: Princeton University Press, 1966); Reinhold Aris, *History of Political Thought in Germany from 1789 to 1815* (London: Allen & Unwin, 1936). The handiest collection of material on the historical Samuel Henzi is in *Lessings sämtliche Werke in zwanzig Bänden,* ed. Hugo Göring (Stuttgart and Berlin: Cotta, n.d.), V, 14-38.

2 "Lassen Sie es aber doch einmal einen in Berlin versuchen, über andere Dinge so frey zu schreiben, als Sonnenfels in Wien geschrieben hat; lassen Sie es ihn versuchen, dem vornehmen Hofpöbel . . . die Wahrheit zu sagen . . . ; lassen Sie einen in Berlin auftreten, der für die Rechte der Unterthanen, der gegen Aussaugung und Despotismus seine Stimme

erheben wollte . . . und Sie werden bald die Erfahrung haben, welches Land bis auf den heutigen Tag das sklavischste Land von Europa ist" (*LM*, XVII, 298).

3 The German of this and the remaining citations from *Ernst und Falk* may be found in *LM,* XIII, 341-68 and 389-411.

A Matter of Competence: The Relationship between Reading and Novel-making in Eighteenth-Century France

RONALD C. ROSBOTTOM

"Ce lecteur, il faut que je le cherche, (que je le 'drague'), sans savoir où il est."

Roland Barthes, *Le Plaisir du Texte*

The Enlightenment saw the introduction of a new and problematic concept into the relatively stable context of neoclassical esthetic theory: the function of the reader in the creative act. More generally, the whole process of perception had become integral to a new esthetic based on the theory that art's effect was not indivisible, and subsequently that taste was a relative and individual matter. Of course, the post-Lockean, post-Quarrel (r)evolution in esthetics was extraordinarily complex,[1] but for our purposes, let it suffice to say that the subjectivization of the esthetic moment created significant changes in verbal art which would not be fully realized or formalized until the Romantic (r)evolution. Perception, then, and more specifically, the cognitive functions of the reader, became a dominant, persistent topic, not only in esthetic treatises but in the fictional works of the writers themselves.[2] In this essay, I will concentrate on the effect this issue had on the appearance and development of the so-called "modern novel."[3] The essay is a prolegomenon to a study which, when completed, should skirt the boundaries of affective stylistics and literary sociology and lead into the domain of what has been referred to as "literary competence";[4] however, for now, I would like to sketch a few theories and conclusions that a more detailed analysis should substantiate.

The thesis of this essay, once the initial premise is accepted, is two-fold: the relatively sudden appearance of the modern novel ruptured the generic expectations of an increasingly sophisticated reading public; as a result, the novelists themselves began to wonder if there were more than a few people who knew how to read their works. This lack of certainty about the constituency of a readership is one of the unique components of novel-formation in the Enlightenment. Without considering it, one risks misunderstanding the appearance, development, and eventual disintegration of pre-Romantic, first-person narrative fiction. Nothing is new in the observation that reading novels written in the eighteenth century necessarily forces one to consider the role of the reader in their creation. The "dear reader," "cher lecteur" interruptions of most novelists have been analyzed and codified in many studies of the novel, both here and abroad.[5] The hypostatization of a "reader" and the attention to the demands of an "audience" form consistent leitmotivs in the history of literary theory. Yet, it is my contention that the novelty of first-person narrative fiction in the Enlightenment, its unexpected success, and more important, on the ethical plane, its seductive aspects imposed very quickly on those who chose it as a felicitous form a need to invent and persuade a readership for it. The development of the form, then, is inextricably linked to this discovered need for a sympathetic, expectant, and competent audience. Though I would agree, in principle, with Lionel Gossman's observations that "communication was not yet a severe problem for the [eighteenth-century] writer," I would not go so far as to agree that "the eighteenth century attained a happy equilibrium between writer and public."[6] I hope to show that there was a preoccupation about finding such an equilibrium; whether or not it was found is still a very moot point.

The Enlightenment was the first book-centered age of man. It was the first age where literacy was widespread enough to serve as a backdrop to experimentation in the psychology and criticism of written narrative. It was the first age where the printed word became dominant and the oral tradition, and all of its attendant disciplines, lost its hold on man's conceptual capacities. The *Encyclopédie* is more than a compendium; it is the *coup de grâce* to mnemonics as a data storage and retrieval system. And, as one critic has recently shown, *Candide* is as much an encyclopedia of the techniques of the written norms of narrative as it is a critique of philosophical patterns.[7] In the late seventeenth and early eighteenth centuries in France, many writers (among them Fontenelle, Fénelon, Voltaire, Marivaux, and Montesquieu) exhibit a marked tendency to reexamine narrative discourse. The natural place to turn for direction was of course to that large and dominant field of theory called rhetoric. Perhaps one of the most significant legacies of the Quarrel of the Ancients and Moderns was the revaluation of the province of rhetoric. Hugh Davidson, in his excellent analysis of the crisis of rhetorical theory in the seventeenth century, has depicted the attempt made to restore to rhetoric all its former prerogatives. This attempt, however, was thwarted by the extraordinary influence and success of the *Logique de Port-Royal*, Arnauld's and Nicole's apology for logic. Though anti-Ramist, the *Logique* still insinuated that rhetoric was an insidious series of devices which seemed "to ally themselves with duplicity, with insincerity, with willingness to *faire flèche de tout bois*, so long as the end is achieved."[8] The result of this reexamination would be ultimately the rejection of rhetoric as a means of argumentation (though not as a list of techniques), as well as a final solution to the traditional problem of uniting the author-audience-work triad. Consequently, novelists of the early part of the century, especially Marivaux, looked to traditional rhetoric for help, and found it wanting. Whether this was because of the great debates over post-Ramusian rhetorical theory, mentioned above, or because of a new incursive cultural ideology which began to see words and language as detrimental to the discovery of truth, or because rhetoric was essentially an oral science are questions which must be answered elsewhere, but which imply that the agony of rhetoric had a definite impact on the formation of the modern novel. In a recent study on rhetoric and neoclassical literature, Kibédi Varga puts it quite succinctly: "Le roman pose des problèmes insolubles dans notre [étude] : de tous les genres littéraires, c'est le roman au sens moderne du terme qui semble s'éloigner le plus des conceptions et méthodes traditionnelles de la rhétorique. . . . Dans une littérature d'inspiration rhétorique, il n'y a pas de place pour le roman."[9]

Yet what happened when the contracts of traditional literary competence proved insufficient? What happened when generic understanding, based on accepted notions of *vraisemblance*, became blurred, unintelligible? What did an author do who wanted to go beyond the superficial structure of the picaresque, romantic, historical, fabulous traditions? How did the so-called, elusive "average reader" adjust himself and his conceptual habits to such works as *La Vie de Marianne, Le Paysan parvenu, Les Egarements du coeur et de l'esprit,* and *La Nouvelle Héloïse*? No other type of literature demands more creative energies from a more heterogeneous public in a more sustained way than does this ambiguous form which we call the novel. It does not proceed from the confidence of a well-defined and easily isolatable "public" or "audience." It is a type of story-telling, of re-creation of experience, of reification of process and change *which appeared before its audience was defined*. To be tautological, just as there were no novels before the eighteenth century, there were no readers of the novel, either. As a result, one finds contained in or attached to most successful novels of the period, even more than now, a discernible text which could have been entitled "how to read me." For the remainder of my remarks, I want to glance at a number of these directives for reading, these hints and not-too-subtle intimidations. I will concentrate on those prefaces, annexes, essays, and dialogues which are isolatable from the texts of the novels themselves, though most of the novels I will mention contain within them a discernible code for readers which itself needs evaluation.[10]

Most of the texts to which I will refer are familiar to anyone who has even cursorily studied fiction in the French Enlightenment. They were written over a period of fifty years, and form essential signposts to the understanding of how the novel developed. They are Diderot's "Préface-Annexe" to *La Religieuse* (1760; 1781) and "Eloge de Richardson" (1762); Rousseau's "Préface à *Julie* ou Entretien sur les romans" (1758-60) and the "Quatrième Promenade" (1777); Laclos' "Avertissement de l'éditeur" and "Préface du rédacteur" which precede *Les Liaisons dangereuses* (1782). However, there is a text of Marivaux's which is not as well known as these and with which I would like to begin. Marivaux was the first novelist of the Enlightenment to break away from much of the prose tradition of the Renaissance and the classical period and to develop successfully the type of narration which defines the novel of the eighteenth century. In the summer of 1733, while he was writing *La Vie de Marianne* and probably already creating the story of the *paysan parvenu*, Marivaux wrote a series of essays which he collected in his third *journal* called *Le Cabinet du philosophe*. This latter work is one of the most important commentaries on practical esthetics, and especially prose narrative, of the first half of the century. About one-half of the *Cabinet* contains an apologue entitled "Le Voyageur dans le nouveau monde" which calls for a new type of reader.[11] In this story, Marivaux concludes almost two decades of writing on the need for new forms and new signs to explain and contain a new ideology, even a new epistemology. This story (and the other short apologue it contains, which has been named "La Veuve et le magicien" [pp. 419-26]) explains how Marivaux wants *La Vie de Marianne* to be read, or, more specifically, it shows how it can be read. He also confronts other problems that will preoccupy writers of the eighteenth century: the false distinction between the *vrai* and the *vraisemblable*; the standard acceptance of two types of language, one for the expression of reason, the other for passion; the moral and esthetic questions surrounding the apparent ambiguity of language; and, finally, the desire to sensitize a new type of perceiver, a new type of reader. This apologue-essay is one of the first, and certainly the most pragmatic, to demand that the reader cooperate in an active and consistent way in the creation of a text, thereby de-emphasizing the exploitation of the reader which had previously characterized so much art, as well as the science of rhetoric itself.

Briefly, "Le Voyageur dans le nouveau monde" is the story of a young man who has been jilted by his mistress and best friend. Devastated, he leaves France and wanders aimlessly. On his travels, he meets an older man who promises to tell him how to read into the hearts of others, so that his life will not be a continuous string of disillusionments. The *philosophe* gives him books to read, including one entitled *l'Histoire du coeur humain*, and prepares him for a voyage to a new world where the duplicity of everyone's discourse—the difference between what they say and what they mean—will be manifest to the educated, newly sensitized hero. To make a long apologue short, the young man's credulity is maintained by the "magicien," as Marivaux names the *philosophe* at one point, and they return to France, though the youth continues to believe that it is a "new world," which only looks like France, where there are exact duplicates of all his friends and acquaintances, and where "les hommes . . . disent la vérité, . . . disent tout ce qu'ils pensent, et tout ce qu'ils sentent; . . . en vivant ensemble, ils se montrent toujours leur âme à découvert, au lieu que la nôtre est toujours masquée" (p. 389). Soon, the voyager notices that he hears and sees another extralinguistic as well as linguistic discourse which shows through the formal, apparently simple discourse of everyday conversation. The effect is not unlike movies or film cartoons where a character says one thing but an off-stage voice or a dialogue balloon shows what is really being thought or said. The narrator repeatedly reminds us: "Je rapporte sa pensée; . . . voilà . . . ce qu'il voulait dire" (p. 399), etc. The voyager, at first credulous, is soon demystified: "que toute illusion cesse," he is told (p. 418). You really are in France; nothing has changed but your perception of reality. Now that you have acquired these new techniques of perception, you can live a life as a spectator, neither judge nor victim, of your fellow men and women.

The complexity of this apologue must be examined in detail elsewhere. I chose to mention it in the context of an essay on readers and readings because it reflects the concern that an important writer had about the perception of his texts. Not unlike the voyager's older and more worldly friend, Marivaux wanted to teach his readers how to read, how to discern the distinct levels of codes which make up man's interpersonal and, by inference, written discourse. He calls the voyager's friend a magician several times, a term which is often used in the eighteenth century to refer to the fictioneer (e.g., Prévost in his preface to *Le Monde moral* says "l'art [du romancier] doit être une vraie magie"). And what is magic but the art of controlling the spectator's perception, of causing him to accept the magician's interpretation of reality. The magician teaches us to mistrust our own senses, to widen our range of acceptable phenomena. And we are never quite sure that it is all only a matter of sleight-of-hand, nor is the magician ever quite confident that he has fooled us.

Marivaux's apologue raises some fundamental questions about the nature of fiction. He was interested in evolving a new type of fictional discourse which would tend to control the ambiguity of language (an eighteenth-century preoccupation): "Langue, qui n'admet point d'équivoque; l'âme qui la parle ne prend jamais un mot l'un pour l'autre . . ." (p. 401). He was perhaps searching as well to remove the stubborn barrier that separates reader from writer, thereby establishing an intersubjectivity between the reader and the narrator.[12] "Le Voyageur dans le nouveau monde" is a companion text to Marivaux's two successful novels, *La Vie de Marianne* and *Le Paysan parvenu,* and like them, it is unfinished. Says the narrator of *Le Cabinet du philosophe* at the end of the *journal*: "Apparemment que le philosophe, à qui l'idée de ce Monde était venue, n'a pas cru qu'il fût nécessaire de la pousser plus loin; attendu sans doute que cette idée une fois donnée, tout le monde peut l'étendre, et s'en imaginer toutes les suites. Passons à autre chose" (p. 437). This is a final ironic challenge to Marivaux's reader to cooperate: don't expect generic certainty, he admonishes; do with fiction (and fiction about fiction) what you do with your own incomplete life. It is not the "story" that counts as much as the "organizing," the "telling" of the story; it is not the relationships of the fictional characters that count as much as that between the artist and his reader. *La Vie de Marianne* was a novel that caused readers to refamiliarize themselves with the process of reading. By stopping his story, and his novels, before they were formally "finished," Marivaux challenged and frustrated his reader; but such an action confirmed the reader's own self-image, and in effect, created him.

Such was the unarticulated but gradually perceived power of narrative fiction that Rousseau spent the last months of his life worrying with the subject. In the Fourth Promenade of *Les Rêveries du promeneur solitaire*, he warns his readers of the frightening seductiveness of fiction, a warning made all the more poignant by our—and his—knowledge that he had himself written and published one of the most popular fictions ever composed. In many ways similar to Diderot in his "Eloge de Richardson," written fifteen years earlier, Rousseau thinks the term *roman* too anodyne for the type of writing which he describes. Those types of fiction, "dépouillées de toute utilité morale, ne peuvent s'apprécier que par l'intention de celui qui les invente" (that is, the author and *not* the reader).[13] This whole essay is a tortuous, at times embarrassing attempt at justification, but it is a document which reveals how significant Rousseau believed the ethical relationship between fiction and its reader to be. This concern is perhaps most successfully articulated in the "Préface de *Julie*, ou Entretien sur les romans" (1760). It is in this text that Rousseau effectively neutralizes the traditional appeal to rhetoric. Again, he carefully differentiates between *roman* and *fiction*, but the whole essay is a simultaneous effort to hypostatize a reader and to formulate a reading of his novel. This text pays homage to the expected discussion of the conflicting concepts of *vérité/vraisemblance*, *fiction/mensonge*, illusion/reality, society/solitude, and so forth, and in so doing it arrives at some significant conclusions about the nature of fiction and its role in the propagandization of truth. Leaving aside the complexity of the ethical questions that Rousseau raises, here are a few of the conclusions that one reaches after having read this key to *Julie*. First, the premise of the entire dialogue is centered on the question, Who will read *La Nouvelle Héloïse*? In an attempt to guide his imagined reader, Rousseau shades the distinction between fictional and nonfictional discourse. Fiction, as a concept, exists through what he refers to as an "échange imaginaire," [14] a sort of creative misprision of reality, which the reader willfully makes. (We are close here to the concept of "reading as misprision" which such critics as Harold Bloom and Jonathan Culler have recently enunciated.) Jean-Jacques demands that the reader's uncertainty about the actuality of the *recueil* (is it a real correspondence or not is a question which forms a leitmotiv of the dialogue) be integral to the correct interpretation of the novel. He seems to be very much aware that reading a text as fiction and reading that same text as non-fiction demands a different set of competencies on the part of the reader. And yet, he hesitates about telling his reader which approach to take with *Julie*. Perhaps, in conformity with his preoccupation about the moral effects of the novel, he thought it best to let the "socialized" reader and the "ruralized" one pick their own readings, thereby absolving Jean-Jacques of any complicity in "lying" to an unsuspecting public. A second conclusion is that the novel, whose subject is passion, is essentially an antirhetorical genre. Consequently, a new type of eloquence is needed, one which is based on disorder ("son éloquence est dans son désordre," p. 742). Such a disorder will force the reader to activate his conceptualizing processes in order to make intelligible the chaotic. Third, novel-reading is a solitary and thereby antisocial activity (see, for example, pp. 751-52); however, and paradoxically, it is also a powerful socializing device, since as recent critics have affirmed, "learning to read is an interpersonal experience." [15] Finally, Rousseau's text emphasizes that cooperation between the writer and the reader is essential to the creation of an ethically significant work. The power of the artist is awesome, especially in a culture with an increasingly large but unsophisticated readership, yet

Rousseau seems to hint at a control to that power when he carefully delineates the reader's function in the ongoing creation of a fictional text. The "Préface de *Julie*" says much more about the quality of fiction, but these elements are the most pertinent to the purposes of our discussion.

Before we analyze Laclos' part in the creation and education of the novel reader, we should take a brief look at another novelist who needed to invent a readership: Diderot. Much has been written about Diderot's fascination with the relationship between fiction and reality, especially in terms of his masterpiece, *La Religieuse.*[16] In fact, the "Préface-Annexe" to that novel, written in 1760 and heavily revised in 1780-81, is a capital text in the history of the invention of the "modern-novel reader." As Dieckmann has pointed out, Diderot "anticipated and almost created the reader of his narrations."[17] Diderot's anxiety over who would read his works and how they would be read most likely was instrumental in his decision not to publish widely many of the best known (including *Le Neveu de Rameau*, the *Contes, Jacques le fataliste*, and *La Religieuse*) during his lifetime. This problem of readership led Diderot to look to the future, to posterity, rather than to his peers and contemporaries for a "fit" reader.[18] The most significant text in terms of this essay is his "Eloge de Richardson," which was published in early 1762, and which was written on the occasion of the English novelist's death in 1761. This essay is so rich in its implications about the relationship between reading and writing fiction that one could say that the golden age of the novel began with the death of Richardson.

Like Rousseau, Diderot recognized the emotive power of such fictions as Richardson had written. He likewise recognized that the response of the reader could be predicted and used by the writer. "O Richardson! on prend, malgré qu'on en ait, un rôle dans tes ouvrages, on se mêle à la conversation, on approuve, on blâme, on admire, on s'irrite, on s'indigne."[19] A novel cannot succeed if the reader does not respond while the book is being read, while the pages are being turned. He who reads a novel dispassionately, closes the book, and reflects calmly on the artistry and lessons of the novel has not "read"; he has failed to unleash the novel's power. Diderot warns that reading a novel is hard work; it demands intense concentration, a certain amount of time, and a commitment to the "magical" powers of an Other, unknown to the reader. Novels are frightening because they are so "real": "Le monde où nous vivons est le lieu da la scène" (p. 30). The solitary reader does not have the comfort of solidarity which he has, for instance, in a theater audience; he is alone, with himself, and with the Other, who can also be himself. Again, it is this conscious or unconscious assimilation of the Other which so intrigued novelists like Marivaux and Diderot. The novel, according to Diderot, tends to humiliate the reader by reminding him of his pettiness. Yet as long as he turns the pages he does not have to confront the consequences of this recognition; it is only when the last page is turned that the anxiety begins: "A la fin, il me sembla tout à coup que j'étais resté seul" (p. 31). Reading is not necessarily a pleasant pastime, either for the reader or for the author, who also reads his own book.

Diderot goes on to explain that a novel's verisimilitude is created in the reader's mind, or rather in that space between the text and the reader's apprehension of it, not in the text alone. Richardson's success as a "realist" did not come from his minute recreation of the picturesque but rather from the combined readjustment of perception on the part of the novelist and his reader. Diderot concludes his discussion with a demand for a new kind of reader—or reading: "Les ouvrages de Richardson plairont plus ou moins à tout homme, dans tous les temps et dans tous les lieux; mais le nombre des lecteurs qui en sentiront tout le prix ne sera jamais grand: il faut un goût trop sévère; et puis, la variété des événements y est telle, les rapports y sont si multipliés, la conduite en est si compliquée, il y a tant de choses préparées, tant d'autres sauvées, tant de personnages, tant de caractères! " (p. 39). So read, says Diderot, but know that reading is as intellectually distinctive and demanding as writing. It is hard to avoid concluding that this awareness of the problems of reading and being read is why Diderot hesitated to publish much of his own fiction while he was alive.

So far in this essay, I have been concentrating on those pieces which show how an awareness of the processes of reading became integral to the creation of the modern novel. And yet, I have skirted an issue which should have become obvious by now to those who have studied eighteenth-century fiction. One of the dominant narrative sub-genres of the Enlightenment incorporated the process of reading in its form; this was, of course, the epistolary novel. There is no other form of narration which so obviously draws attention to the role of the reader as creator, and it is not a coincidence that it knew its greatest vogue during the period when the modern novel first appeared. The significance of the act of reading to the successful functioning of a letter novel has been recently examined by Janet Altman.[20] In her chapter entitled "The Weight of the Reader" she explains how the two acts of reading and writing are internalized. The result is a reflection, a *dédoublement* of the real author and the real reader (us), and the struggle to form an intelligible world from the mosaic of letters that make up the novel as the real reader "watches" the protagonist(s) do the same. Another aspect of this phenomenon is that the real reader soon becomes a critic of the letters he reads; and, often, fictional letter-writers (Lovelace in *Clarissa*, Claire in *La Nouvelle Héloïse*, Merteuil in *Les Liaisons dangereuses*) become exegetes themselves, criticizing, judging, willfully and sometimes naïvely misinterpreting the letters written to them or which happen to fall into their hands. As Altman says, "portrayed readings, rereading, and even proofreading constitute part of the epistolary subject" (p. 150). A quick glance at the most successful of all epistolary novels will perhaps be the best way to end an essay on the importance of reading to the invention of the novel.

Laclos, like those who had preceded him, was aware that the success of a novel was relative to the degree of literary competence of its reader. By 1782, the so-called dilemma of the novel had been solved, or at least replaced by other dilemmas. The creative relationship between novelist and reader was now accepted theory.

The reader was no longer seen as an inert receiver of the novelist's signals but as an active, cooperative participant who, over the past half-century, had been cajoled and taunted into participating in the creation of the fictional text. *Les Liaisons dangereuses* (a novel about novel-making which could have been just as easily entitled *Les Lectures dangereuses*) is a work which comes out of the process of reading, and which entices by detailing the dangers and exhilaration of this activity. It is a book which challenges the reader to *dis*believe.

Rousseau's coy, nervous warnings and Diderot's taunting laughter are gone in the two prefaces which introduce *Les Liaisons dangereuses*: the "Avertissement de l'Editeur" and the "Préface du rédacteur," both written by Laclos. The novelist is confident enough to say in the *avertissement* that the collection "n'est qu'un roman," a throwaway line which illustrates how cocky the genre and its practitioners had become.[21] The *éditeur*, the apocryphal publisher of this novel, is the first noninvolved reader of the collection, and as such is the standard against which we, the "real" reader(s), are supposed to measure ourselves.[22] He is pompous, moralistic, and motivated by two conflicting drives: to make money by publishing the collection and to protect himself by warning the unprepared reader of the collection's "immorality," implying that maybe it should not be published at all. Thereby is the novel called a novel; its *in*authenticity is immediately established, and the reader is thrust into the realm of ironic fiction. This brief "warning" is, like Bartholo's speech against the "siècle barbare" in Act I of the *Barbier de Séville*, a conservative reinterpretation of the century which had produced "la liberté de penser, . . . l'*Encyclopédie*, et les drames."[23] In the final paragraph of this warning, the publisher *bien pensant* questions the verisimilitude of the novel's plot, "pour préserver . . . le lecteur trop crédule de toute surprise . . ." (p. 1). No one ever hears today, he tells us, of young women with incomes of 60,000 pounds becoming nuns, nor of young and pretty wives of magistrates dying of broken hearts. By insisting on the fictional status of the collection, on its *invraisemblance*, Laclos' *éditeur* effectively neutralizes the problem which so bothered Rousseau's interlocutor: is this correspondence real or not? Attention will now be placed, by Laclos' *rédacteur*, on how the novel is composed, not on its veracity.

The "préface du rédacteur" is an important essay on the formation of fiction, and it is the Enlightenment's last commentary on the *vraisemblance/vérité* dichotomy which had led the novel into innumerable theoretical culs-de-sac. It will be remembered that the first collator of this almost incredible collection of letters had been Mme. de Rosemonde, Valmont's aunt and Mme. de Tourvel's confidant. Through a series of blatantly fortuitous circumstances, she comes to possess all the letters of the protagonists. However, *we* do not have all the letters because Laclos' editor has presented us with only those which he felt were "nécessaires, soit à l'intelligence des événements, soit au développement des caractères" (p. 3). He has already read the collection, edited it, reorganized the sequence of letters, and so forth. In other words, the editor has created a fiction from his reading of the Rosemonde collection; and, he challenges "tout lecteur raisonnable" to do the same with the results of this compilation. Respecting the reader's desire for generic certainty, he affirms that his preface will lead the way: "Ceux qui, avant de commencer une lecture, sont bien aises de savoir à peu près sur quoi compter . . . peuvent continuer; les autres feront mieux de passer tout de suite à l'ouvrage même; ils en savent assez" (p. 4). The generic expectations of his readers should be respected; however, he is suggesting that a leap of faith is perhaps more conducive to a successful reading of the *recueil.*

Laclos concludes his preface with a traditional warning: "Loin de conseiller cette lecture à la jeunesse, il me paraît très important d'éloigner d'elle toutes celles de ce genre" (p. 5). Yet he is giving only passing attention to the argument of the novel's moral utility. What he is saying here, and what his caricature of the upright publisher had hinted at, is that reading fiction is not a neutral or safe activity. It is dangerous because it brings into play the most powerful conceptualizing forces of the reader, calling on him to help create such a world as that in the *Liaisons*, a world of articulate evil and attractive vice. "Il me semble toujours que ce recueil doit plaire à peu de monde" (p. 6), he supposes, but it will not leave them indifferent. It is a novel calculated to disperse ennui; however, its publication is dangerous, as is its reading, because together these activities give intelligible and frightening form to what Mme. de Rosemonde had already referred to as an "amas d'horreurs" (p. 388). Read with care, he warns; misreading is no small error. Valmont and Merteuil misread, and *Les Liaisons dangereuses* is not only about the disintegration of their relationship but of their personalities as well.

Reading, as a process of creation and as a key to the decoding of narrative texts, is increasingly the subject of imaginative critical activity. And yet we still know so little about *how* one reads fiction; all we do know is that the activity of reading has been seen from the first great age of literacy as integral to the success of fiction. Vivienne Mylne alludes to this significant phenomenon in the conclusion to her book on eighteenth-century fiction: "The rôle of the observer, we can now see, is neither as passive nor as predictable as many early writers on the subject supposed. His response is, or should be, an active participation; and it is conditioned by his expectations, including his ideas concerning the kind of thing a picture, play or novel may be."[24] Despite such observations made occasionally by critics of the novel, the interpretation of fiction has been consistently obsessed by the muse of mimesis, by the fascination with the relationship between fiction and "reality." Increasingly, however, and I believe that this may be the most significant legacy of the so-called structuralist impulse of the past fifteen years, the poetics of reading has become the object of criticism, and "reality" is seen more and more as the special construct which the reader makes while he reads. Critics as diverse as Stanley Fish, Roland Barthes, Harold Bloom, Jonathan Culler and Philippe Sollers are directing our attention with impatient persistence to this intractable area. It is not an analysis which is easily pursued or a critical model which is easily established. We know little of how people read or misread, how they make intelligible constructs from fictions, what processes of conceptualization they employ. Novels are by nature problematic, and yet paradoxically they are, as Culler has stated, "the primary semiotic agent of intelligibility."[25] Not unlike the author, the reader, to use Harold Bloom's term, suffers the "anxiety of influence": the influence of his predecessors and their residue of tradition, and the influence of his contemporaries and their imposition of taste. He learns to read through a process which involves the exchange of ideas on and methods of reading and misreading. A "poetics of readership" must include the study of how cultures define and formalize experience as well as how that experience is efficiently exchanged. We read our cultures like we read our novels: with ideological, psychological, and esthetic bias. And we want to impose readings of our culture, as novelists try, in the knowledge of certain failure, to impose readings of their work.

To return to my initial thesis, let me conclude by reiterating that the eighteenth century saw the eruption of a new form of narrative which demanded adhesion to the contemporary call for a new way of perceiving. For several reasons writers felt, and rightly so, that it was obligatory for them to "create" a readership and plausible readings for these narrations. Among these reasons was their uncertainty about the literary competence of the contemporary public. As a result, the preoccupation with reading, and with the scribal aspects of narrative fiction, informed the "modern novel" and became one of its most distinctive characteristics. The novel was a melodramatic form concerned with depicting the sensitive contact of the self and society, but, because of a demonstrated need to find and define its readership, it also became a genre that repeatedly and inescapably confronted the problem of its own reception. This concern was internalized by the best novelists and became integral to the genre's uniqueness.

The study of the novel demands, as David Goldknopf has said, "an excursion into the history of ideas" (p. 124). This statement has special application to the novel of the eighteenth century, for the primary impulses of the Enlightenment—antitraditionalism (especially as seen in the neutralization of a rhetoric based on oral discourse), empiricism, self-reflexiveness, and the refinement of the techniques of collecting, organizing, and presenting data—gave form to the novel and made it the key agent of cultural expression it remains today.

NOTES

1 Jacques Chouillet, in his *L'Esthétique des lumières* (Paris: Presses Universitaires de France, 1974), cogently outlines the esthetic debates of the period.

2 There are myriad reasons for the occurrence of this phenomenon, deriving primarily from the effect of the "new science" (Descartes, Newton, Locke) on the conceptual activities of eighteenth-century man, but here is not the place to examine them in detail. For an intelligent analysis of the relationship between the history of ideas and the appearance of the "modern novel," see David Goldknopf's *The Life of the Novel* (Chicago: University of Chicago Press, 1972), especially chapters 1–4, 5–6.

3 I recognize the dangers of basing my remarks on such an indefinite term as "modern novel," but the accepted terminology of literary history leaves me little choice. For the purposes of this essay, the term will refer to that type of fictional narrative in prose which was obviously and often substantially distinct from the great European traditions which had informed prose narrative up until the eighteenth century, especially the picaresque, fabulous, and historical impulses. The modern novel was that new narrative genre which subjectivized the confrontation between the individual and his society and which led, as Goldknopf has argued, to an equilibrium "between self-awareness and world-awareness" (p. 21).

4 For an analysis of this important concept, see chapter 6 of Jonathan Culler's *Structuralist Poetics* (London: Routledge and Kegan Paul, 1975).

5 Among the most influential are the works of such Chicago critics as Wayne Booth and Sheldon Sacks; a recent example of this trend is John Preston's *The Created Self* (London: Heinemann, 1970). Studies on Diderot, and such approaches as that of Jean Rousset's *Narcisse romancier* (Paris: Corti, 1973) have analyzed the problem in French fiction. Moving toward a more definite sociological approach, the Constance school of German criticism, and especially the work of Wolfgang Iser and Hans Jauss, have told us about the "implied reader." More recently, in this country, Stanley Fish's call for a "new affective stylistics," especially in his *Self-*

Consuming Artifacts (Berkeley: University of California Press, 1972), has caused many critics to refocus their attention on reading. Walter Ong recently published a paper entitled "The Writer's Audience Is Always a Fiction" (*PMLA*, 90 [1975], 9–21) which sketches some of the directions in which those who wish to examine the creative effect of reader-writer interaction on narrative art must go. He in effect calls for a "poetics of readership." He sees the history of written narrative as the concomitant history of the "fictionalization of readers" by the author as well as by the reader himself. "Time is ripe," he intones, "for a study of the history of readers and their enforced roles" (p. 10). Ong is careful not to opt for any specific approach—psychological, sociological, structural, semiotic, etc.—as the best to discern this history, and as a result of this neutrality, the article, though helpful in elucidating an important problem, unfortunately leaves us with little to go on as we try to distinguish from one another the many types of readers—and readings—which the story of written literature has left behind. Ong does, however, carefully distinguish between the reception of oral and written literature, and reminds us of the significance of oral residue in written narrative. He also makes allusion to a complex though essential relationship which gives a clue to the puzzle of "readership" and creation: "If the writer succeeds in writing, it is generally because he can fictionalize in his imagination an audience he has learned to know not from daily life but from earlier writers who were fictionalizing in their imagination audiences they had learned to know in still earlier writers, and so on back to the dawn of written narrative" (p. 11).

6 Gossman, *French Society and Culture* (Englewood Cliffs, N.J.: Prentice-Hall, 1972), pp. 125, 131.

7 Michael Danahy, "The Nature of Narrative Norms in *Candide*," *SVEC*, 114 (1973), 113-40.

8 Davidson, *Audience, Words, and Art* (Columbus, Ohio: Ohio State University Press, 1965), p. 63. See also, on rhetoric and its "agony," Peter France, *Rhetoric and Truth in France* (Oxford: Clarendon Press, 1972); Oscar Haac, "Theories of Literary Criticism and Marivaux," *SVEC*, 88 (1972), 711-34; W. S. Howell, *Eighteenth-Century British Logic and Rhetoric* (Princeton: Princeton University Press, 1971).

9 Kibédi Varga, *Rhétorique et littérature: Etudes de structures classiques* (Paris: Didier, 1970), p. 98. On rhetoric and the novel, see especially pp. 96-99, 124-39.

10 See Culler, *Structuralist Poetics*, especially chapter 9, "Poetics of the Novel." Also, Gerald Prince, "Introduction à l'étude du narrataire," *Poétique*, no. 14 (1973), 178-96.

11 *Journaux et oeuvres diverses*, ed. Deloffre-Gilot (Paris: Garnier, 1969), pp. 389-437. Future references to this edition will appear in the text.

12 On this "false distinction," see Paul de Man's article "Semiology and Rhetoric," *Diacritics*, 3 (1973), 27-33, especially p. 32.

13 Rousseau, *Rêveries du promeneur solitaire*, ed. Raymond (Geneva: Droz, 1967), p. 59.

14 Rousseau, *La Nouvelle Héloïse*, ed. Pomeau (Paris: Garnier, 1960), p. 748. Future references will be to this edition and will appear in the text.

15 Culler, "Stanley Fish and the Righting of the Reader," *Diacritics*, 5 (1975), 28.

16 See especially Vivienne Mylne, "Truth and Illusion in the Préface-Annexe to Diderot's *La Religieuse*," *MLR*, 57 (1962), 350-56; H. Dieckmann, "The Préface-Annexe of *La Religieuse*," *Diderot Studies*, 2 (1952), 21-40 (plus a photocopy of the manuscript); and Jean Parrish's introduction to her edition of *La Religieuse, SVEC*, 22 (1963).

17 "The Préface-Annexe of *La Religieuse*," p. 29.

18 See on this point Herbert Dieckmann's excellent essay, "Diderot et son lecteur," *Mercure de France*, 329 (1957), 620-48.

19 "Eloge de Richardson," in *Œuvres esthétiques*, ed. Vernière (Paris: Garnier, 1959), p. 30. Future references will be to this edition and will appear in the text.

20 In her unpublished dissertation, "Epistolarity: Approaches to a Form," Yale, 1973.

21 *Les Liaisons dangereuses*, ed. Le Hir (Paris: Garnier, 1961), p. 1. Future references will be to this edition and will appear in the text.

22 This indication came first to me after reading Irving Wohlfarth's very good essay on Laclos, "The Irony of Criticism and the Criticism of Irony: A Study of Laclos Criticism," *SVEC*, 120 (1974), 269-317.

23 Beaumarchais, *Théâtre*, ed. Rat (Paris: Garnier, 1964), p. 45.

24 In her *The Eighteenth-Century Novel* (Manchester: Manchester University Press, 1965), p. 270.

25 Culler, *Structuralist Poetics*, p. 189. See especially his chapter on the poetics of the novel, which points the way for what he calls "the theory of the practice of reading" (p. 259).

Social Realism in the Dialogue of Eighteenth-Century French Fiction

VIVIENNE MYLNE

One element of French novels which shows a marked change during the eighteenth century is that of dialogue. The simplest and most obvious way of describing the change is to say that, in a significant number of novels, dialogue becomes more "realistic" in manner and presentation: the style of conversations in a work by Balzac is more like the way people talk in real life than is, say, the dialogue style of *La Princesse de Clèves*. However, once we try to go beyond simplistic statements of this kind, the criterion of "realism" becomes less satisfactory. There are problems in applying the criterion (some of which involve conflicts between different types of "realism"); and in any case, "realism" alone cannot serve as a criterion of literary excellence.

In this essay we shall consider the theoretical problems as they arise in the course of discussing our examples, while the question of the evaluation of literary merit will be left until the end.

In order to keep the discussion within manageable limits, I shall concentrate here on the kinds of realism which can be most easily identified. These are the cases where a novelist indicates—by grammar, vocabulary and even spelling—that the character in question does not use the language of well-educated Parisians. Such divergences from standard French thus carry implicit information about the character's social class, level of education, and place of origin.

Before considering eighteenth-century developments, however, we need to look briefly at some of the conventions concerning dialogue which were in force toward the end of the seventeenth century. There are two main points which should be mentioned here. The first is merely one aspect of the more general question of levels of style: the concept of literary genres, and of maintaining a style consonant with each genre or type of work. This "rule" was followed in fiction as well as in drama and poetry, and it covered not only passages where the voice is that of the narrator, but dialogue too. Thus, in France, it was only in comic fiction, and more especially in burlesque novels or *anti-romans*, that one found common characters talking in a low style. Far more frequent were novels in which the protagonists were noble and the dialogue was presented in correct and fairly formal language. Commenting on the style of such works, Henri Coulet says:

> Sa politesse amortit toute violence, toute crudité, son absence d'élan est propre à insinuer la tristesse; les conversations sont très souvent rapportées au style indirect, dans le même but d'atténuation, et quand elles sont transcrites au style direct, toujours très éloignées de la phraséologie baroque, elles ne sont pas moins éloignées du dialogue familier.[1]

This regular correlation between certain identifiable kinds of fiction and their corresponding stylistic registers is one that begins to break down in the eighteenth century; and dialogue, as we shall see, is one of the elements which contributes to the breakdown.

Coulet's remark about the frequency of reported speech brings me to my second point concerning conventions. In this case we are dealing with a specific device or technique. Besides using indirect speech liberally, seventeenth-century writers also had frequent recourse to what one might call narrated speech, which presents the gist of what was said—sometimes fully, sometimes in a compressed form—but without supplying the actual words of the speaker. Narrated speech is often combined with reported speech, and this mode of presentation continued throughout the eighteenth century. In the hands of a skillful writer the technique can be quite lively and effective. The following passage, by Louvet de Couvray, relates a scene in which the Count is teasing the Marquise, in her husband's presence, about her guilty secret ("Mlle Duportail" is in reality young Faublas himself, disguised as a girl):

> Préludant avec la Marquise par de légeres épigrammes, il protestoit qu'elle seule, jusqu'à présent, savoit précisément combien Mademoiselle Duportail méritoit d'être aimée. La Marquise, également adroite et prompte, répondoit vîte et toujours bien; mesurant la défense à l'attaque, elle éludoit sans affectation ou se défendoit sans aigreur; déterminée à ménager un ennemi qu'elle ne pouvoit espérer de vaincre, aux questions pressantes elle opposoit les aveux équivoques, elle atténuoit les allégations fortes par les négations mitigées; et repoussoit les sarcasmes plus amers qu'embarrassans, par des récriminations plus fines que méchantes.[2]

Narrated speech offers several advantages: it can convey the sense of a long conversation economically; and it can save the novelist the trouble of trying to invent witty or subtle remarks. It may also be used to outline utterances which would, in direct speech, be out of keeping with the context. Thus when the young Dupuis, in *Les Illustres Françoises*, asks a prostitute if trade is brisk, the reply is, "Toujours de pis en pis, me dit-elle." The narrator then continues:

> Elle invectiva ensuite contre le Lieutenant de Police et contre le Lieutenant Criminel, et contre les Commissaires, et contre le bon ordre qu'ils établissoient dans Paris.[3]

Her exact words would, presumably, have gone beyond even the fairly ribald tone of Dupuis's reminiscences.

Reported and narrated speech serve a further purpose, which is connected with the status of direct speech. It seems to me that for the majority of novelists in the seventeenth and eighteenth centuries, direct speech was felt to be a privileged and peculiarly forceful kind of discourse. As such, it was not a feature to be used indiscriminately. Instead, these early novelists frequently proceed as though direct speech can be introduced only after the way has been duly prepared. The transition between narrated actions and dialogue is made by means of reported and/or narrated speech. And once the conversation has begun it is quite usual, after a few exchanges in direct speech, to find reported or narrated speech brought in again. In this way certain remarks, those in direct speech, are highlighted. The modern reader, accustomed to long stretches of direct speech at any and every juncture, may well fail to perceive these effects of added immediacy and vigor.

Some writers seem also to have related the importance of direct speech to the social importance of certain characters; the words of a servant or peasant are narrated or put into reported speech, while the utterances of nobles are given in the direct form. A case in point is the episode in *Manon Lescaut* where Des Grieux is helping Manon to escape. His command to the coach driver and his promise of a *louis d'or* are given in direct speech; but it is in reported speech that the driver's doubts are expressed, as also his final threat: "Celui-ci . . . s'enfuit de peur, . . . en criant que je l'avais trompé, mais que j'aurais de ses nouvelles."[4]

What emerges from all this is that even when a novelist does introduce characters who are uneducated or of humble social rank, he can still, if he chooses, avoid the "realism" of low or vulgar expressions by transmitting all their remarks in the form of reported or narrated speech. With this in mind, let us turn to our eighteenth-century examples.

Les Illustres Françoises is clearly worth discussing from the point of view of dialogue. Apart from the third-person narrator who provides the framework passages, the book consists entirely of conversations and of stories supposedly told in direct speech. Chasle's handling of dialogue is very skilled, and much could be said about the way he controls the various levels and types of conversation. The first six tales are largely serious in tone, and the protagonists are aristocrats or prosperous bourgeois. Their usage is of course correct and cultivated, though Chasles can also descend to a register of familiar speech which now seems wholly "natural."

With the last tale, that of the younger Dupuis, we move into a different world, one of youthful follies, escapades, and sexual intrigues. The earliest detailed review of the book expressed the opinion that this story was "fort inférieur à toutes les autres," adding: "On ne trouve pas ce récit trop bien à la suite du précédent" (II, 576). The grounds for complaint are thus that Chasles has sinned by juxtaposing different genres. We should note, however, that he has not allowed himself the full range of comic effects which a tale of this kind could, according to the conventions, include. He does not make the many low-life characters who come into these pages express themselves in low language. We have already seen how the prostitute's invective is attenuated. Similarly, when a *savetier* protests over being asked to carry out an unwelcome errand, we are simply told: "Cet homme fit quelque difficulté" (II, 419). The most noticeable instance of uneducated speech is a piece of mockery from Dupuis's brother. Word had got around that Dupuis meant to marry Célénie, and over dinner he was teased about this:

> J'avois soutenu en homme qui entendoit raillerie toutes celles qu'on m'avoit faites; mais je fus assommé de celle que mon frère fit mal à propos. Comme il ne regardoit Célénie que du haut de sa fortune, & qu'en effet ce n'étoit pas un bon parti pour moi, elle lui paroissoit tout à fait au-dessous de lui. Il la traita comme une gueuse & une misérable Je lui répondis d'une manière à lui imposer silence, s'il avoit eu quelque égard pour moi; mais il continua ses airs de mépris qu'il finit par me dire, en prenant un ton de village: Palsangué, puisque j'allons entrer dans son alliance, faut que j'allions lui faire la révérence. (II, 445)

I have supplied the whole of the passage leading up to this remark, because it makes clear the extent of the insult and the attitude of contempt implied by the imitation of countrified speech. Chasles does not attempt to create comic effects by making his uneducated Parisians use their equivalent "jargon," and to this extent he keeps within the norms of a correct, if sometimes familiar, style.

There are no grounds for supposing that he ever contemplated taking a more "realistic" approach in this story. But had he done so, we can see an objection which might have restrained him. This involves realism of a different order: Dupuis is supposedly an educated man, telling his story to a group of well-bred people, including some ladies. In such a setting a real-life storyteller might be expected not to utter vulgarisms or incorrect French. Thus we can see that realism about the narrator's situation could sometimes, in theory at least, inhibit realism in the dialogue which he or she quotes.

Turning now to *Gil Blas*, we find that Lesage is somewhat more generous in the quantity of direct speech he attributes to characters of humble origins. In the episode of the brigands' cave (Book I, chapters IV-X), the old Negro hostler, Domingo, and the cook, Léonarde, both have quite a lot to say. They have in common the use of familiar forms of address when talking to Gil Blas, and an otherwise "polite" style, with overtones of irony. Léonarde shows Gil Blas the cemetery-cum-cellar where he is to sleep:

> Voilà votre chambre, mon petit poulet, me dit-elle en me passant doucement la main sous le menton: le garçon dont vous avez le bonheur d'occuper la place y a couché tant qu'il a vécu parmi nous, et il y repose encore après sa mort. Il s'est laissé mourir à la fleur de son âge; ne soyez pas assez simple pour suivre son exemple.[5]

And when Gil Blas tries to escape, only to be caught by Domingo:

> Ah! ah! dit-il, petit drôle, vous voulez vous sauver! oh! ne pensez pas que vous puissiez me surprendre; je vous ai bien entendu. Vous avez cru trouver la grille ouverte, n'est-ce pas? Apprenez, mon ami, que vous la trouverez désormais toujours fermée. Quand nous retenons quelqu'un malgré lui, il faut qu'il soit plus fin que vous pour nous échapper. (I, 25)

These and other remarks by Domingo and Léonarde create an effect which is closer to sophistication than to naïveté. It is almost as though Lesage were writing with double satire, or antiburlesque, intentions. Instead of parodying an inflated serious style by using exaggeratedly vulgar dialogue, he turns the joke around and makes his vulgar characters talk with a neat correctness and even elegance.

In the last volume of the novel, which appeared in 1735, Gil Blas seeks the hand of Antonia, a farmer's daughter. The conversation between Gil Blas and this farmer does suggest a more straightforwardly realistic approach to uneducated speech. When Gil Blas says he wants to be quite sure that Antonia is willing to marry him:

> Oh dame! dit Basile, je n'entends pas toutes ces philosophies: parlez vous-même à Antonia, et vous verrez, ou je me trompe fort, qu'elle ne demande pas mieux que d'être votre femme. (II, 217)

Here the interjection, and the phrase "Je n'entends pas toutes ces philosophies," do have an air of simple rustic speech; and Basile's sentences are markedly simpler in construction and vocabulary than those of Gil Blas. There is also a fresh tone in the context: Lesage has now dropped the ironic detachment with which the narrator spoke of his early adventures. Gil Blas is sincerely attached to Antonia—his first sight of her leaves him "étonné, troublé, interdit." And it is appropriate to this atmosphere of frankness and sentiment that the simple approach of Basile should be reflected in his turns of speech. If we laugh over the style of these remarks, it is as much with Basile as at him.

Lesage's "realism" in this last quotation is in any case a slight and not very noticeable effort. The reverse is true of our next example, probably the best-known single instance of vulgar dialogue in eighteenth-century French fiction. It is of course the dispute between Mme. Dutour and the cab driver in *La Vie de Marianne.*[6]

Frédéric Deloffre has already provided an authoritative discussion of the linguistic aspects of this scene.[7] Among the points he makes is one that creates yet more difficulties with the notion of "realism": although Marivaux's presentation of this quarrel is doubtless more like real life than, say, the speech habits of Léonarde in *Gil Blas*, yet the language of Mme. Dutour and the cab driver is also highly conventional, even stylized. Patterns of demotic speech, as used by dramatists such as Cyrano de Bergerac, Molière, and Dancourt, had established a repertoire of typical vocabulary and grammatical forms. So a writer did not need to go out and listen to street quarrels in Paris. The educated man would have, in his mind's ear, an accepted model of vulgar speech, much as an English-speaking man of our own day knows the turns of speech associated with the stage Irishman.

Even within these limits, Marivaux's practice here is quite restrained. The cab driver is made to use "Palsambleu! " rather than "Palsangué! " or "Palsanguienne! ," the coarser forms. And Marivaux does not indicate any lapses from received pronunciation; some writers would have put, for instance, "Faut-y pas" or "Faut-i pas" for "Faut-il pas."

Yet this limited excursion into realism attracted, as we know, the blame of several critics. As Deloffre remarks, "Ce qui était permis au théâtre dans une pièce comique ne l'était pas dans un roman"[8]—or at least, not in a novel which is supposedly written by a countess, and which begins in the tone of the sentimental life story. What displeased the complaining critics was the shock of flouted expectations. Jacob, in *Le Paysan parvenu*, would not provoke the same protests over his occasional slips into countrified speech, because he *was* of peasant stock and because, from its opening pages, the book offers an atmosphere much closer to that of the conventional comic novel, in which vulgarisms are tolerated.

The adverse criticisms of the demotic dialogue in *La Vie de Marianne* rest on assumptions not only about the correlation of genre and style but also about the inherently comic or ridiculous nature of uneducated speech. This latter assumption had never, of course, been as widely accepted in England; and many English novelists of the eighteenth century introduce into more-or-less serious fiction a range of stylistic effects, including familiar and even low turns of speech, which would have offended French standards of literary *bienséance*. The difference of attitudes can be aptly seen in the English translations of *La Vie de Marianne*. Take the following sentences:

> Jarnibleu! ne me frappez pas, lui dit le cocher qui lui retenait le bras; ne soyez pas si osée! je me donne au diable, ne badinons point! Voyez-vous! je suis un gaillard qui n'aime pas les coups, ou la peste m'étouffe! Je ne demande que mon dû, entendez-vous? il n'y a point de mal à ça.[9]

The first translator, generally thought to be John Lockman, produced the following:

> Damn you! don't strike me, said the Coachman, laying hold of her arm:—Don't be so pert as that comes to! For—the Devil take me! —if you won't be quiet—I will shew you a Fellow that won't be beat. Pox take you! I don't ask a Farthing more than my due, you rotten Jade. And is there any Thing wrong in that?[10]

In Mrs. Collyer's version, which appeared in 1743, we find the euphemistic spelling, "D——n you," but the rest of the paragraph follows Lockman fairly faithfully. The final gratuitous insult, however, is intensified to become: "You stinking good-for-nothing jade."[11] A desire for vigor and liveliness, at the expense of refinement, appears in both translations.

Once the language of dialogue moves away from standard correct usage, it is of course notoriously difficult for a translator to strike and maintain the exact corresponding level. The eighteenth-century translator's free approach to his task is apt to produce further variations. So it is perhaps not surprising that, after comparing about fifty French versions of English novels with the original texts, I should feel obliged to admit that, at least until a more comprehensive review is carried out, it is impossible to discern any clear trends or tendencies in the handling of dialogue in this domain. It is perhaps slightly more common for the translator to tone down vulgarisms, as Prévost did on occasion, than to attempt a faithful equivalence. But there are also cases where the French writer has exaggerated, in his translation, some merely familiar English turn of phrase. In *Zoriada*, by Mrs. Hughes, we find: "Lo and behold, after a hasty rap at the door, in comes a gentleman in blue and gold, and advances towards me".[12] This is conveyed as: "Voilà-t-il pas qu'on frappe à enfoncer la porte, et voyez-vous, vlà que j'vois entrer un Monsieur vêtu de bleu et d'or, qui avance à moi."[13] Willingness to use "incorrect" forms in French seems to vary according to the individual translator's whim. And since other factors are involved, such as the degree to which the translator grasps the nuances of English usage, one would be rash to generalize about the way in which dialogue is translated.

Returning to novels by French authors, we can find an obvious parallel to *La Vie de Marianne* in Mouhy's *La Paysanne parvenue* (1735-37). To judge by the number of re-editions, these two works were equally popular: *Marianne* went into nineteen re-editions before the Revolution, and *La Paysanne* had seventeen for the same period. (These figures suggest, incidentally, that the public did not concur with the disapproving critics of *La Vie de Marianne*.) Like Marivaux, Mouhy has mixed his styles and tones; but he is far less competent in maintaining the various levels at which he appears to aim. This is apparent, as one might expect, in the dialogue. By the time she writes her memoirs, Jeannette has become a Marquise, though she started life as a woodcutter's daughter. Mouhy does allude to her naîve country speech when she was a girl: "Ce que ce brave monsieur m'avoit dit (car c'étoit mon expression dans ce tems) me revenoit souvent."[14] However, when the royal hunting party passes, and she gets one of the riders to point out the King, her exclamations are less convincing: "Oui, oui, c'est le roi; repris-je avec transport; mon Dieu, qu'il est beau! Ah! s'il n'alloit pas si vîte, que je serois heureuse! O ciel! il est déjà bien loin" (I, 19). Is this the talk of a Fontainebleu *paysanne* of thirteen? We might suppose that Mouhy had decided not to attempt any realistic speech effects. But when Jeannette talks to Colin, her village suitor, we can see how, in successive conversations, the young man's remarks become more and more "rustic." Here is part of his first contribution:

> Tenez, Jeannette, je vous aime, et je vois bien que vous commencez à me rendre le réciproque; mordienne! si cela étoit, je ne sais ce qu'il en arriveroit. Je sais bien que vous n'avez rien; mais n'importe, ce n'est pas là l'histoire pour vivre contens: vous êtes gentille et blanche comme neige, vous avez des yeux comme une souris, vous êtes droite comme un cierge, et cela vaut bien quelques écus de plus. Mon père ne pense peut-être pas comme moi: comment faire? Il faudra bien cependant qu'il se mette à la raison; autrement, jarni, j'irai m'engager. (I, 33-34)

Apart from the interjections (and this part of speech is a universal resource for cheap-and-easy local color in dialogue), the *paysan* quality of this passage seems to depend rather more on content than on manner.

A few pages later, Colin discusses how a village girl should answer a courting letter from a nobleman (he does not know that the letter in question was actually addressed to Jeannette):

> Non, sans doute, reprit Colin, qui refuse, muse; s'il parle à bon escient, it faut tout droit l'accepter, et ne faire point tant de raisonnemens; c'est ce qui perd la plus grande partie de nos filles. Elles font les réservées; chipotons, lanternons, qu'en arrive-t-il? le gaillard prend parti ailleurs, il en trouve de moins difficultueuses; elles en enrageons, zeste, l'oiseau est déniché; ils n'en voulons plus, et dame, ce sont les regrets, n'est-il pas vrai, Jeannette? (I, 37-38)

For the reader who notices this progressive countrification of Colin, the effect is the reverse of that which realism should ideally produce. One can no longer be absorbed in the world of the story, since one is reminded of the author's role, as an artist touching up his picture.

The plot of *La Paysanne parvenue* continues in a fairly sombre and sentimental vein: Jeannette and the young Marquis are in love, but are kept apart by family opposition and the machinations of various malicious characters. However, occasional touches of the comic, or even the grotesque, do break in. One of these is the irruption, when Jeannette is leading a secluded life in Paris, of a blind army officer who believes, because of the false name she has adopted, that she must be his wife. The officer is accompanied by a valet who remarks "dans un langage allemand: *Nous ferons, nous ferons si fou mocque long-tems de fotre mari; men Goth! men Goth!* ajouta-t-il, . . . *que les femmes sont toubles, et qu'on est malhéré de se laisser bercer par sté chienne d'enchance*" (IV, 130, the italics are in the text).

Now during the second half of the century, peasants and working-class folk in general ceased to be automatic subjects for laughter when they appeared in literature. But up to and beyond the Revolution, some touch of comedy appears to be intended whenever a foreign accent is indicated by an attempt at phonetic spelling. The inability of anyone from outside France to converse adequately in the language of civilization is bound to seem ridiculous. Conversely, any foreign character in French fiction who is *not* meant to be ridiculous will have a perfect command of French, however unrealistic this may seem. For example, Mme. de Grafigny's Peruvian princess, after only a few months in France, can speak fluently and correctly (the "je" of this dialogue is the princess herself):

> —Vous m'étonnez, repris-je; d'où naît votre défiance? Depuis que je vous connais, si je n'ai pu me fair entendre par des paroles, toutes mes actions n'ont-elles pas dû vous prouver que je vous aime?
> —Non, répliqua-t-il, je ne puis encore me flatter: vous ne parlez pas assez bien le français pour détruire mes justes craintes; vous ne cherchez point à me tromper, je le sais: mais expliquez-moi quel sens vous attachez à ces mots adorables, "je vous aime." . . .
> —Ces mots, lui dis-je, . . . doivent, je crois, vous faire entendre que vous m'êtes cher, que votre sort m'intéresse, que l'amitié et la reconnaissance m'attachent à vous; ces sentimens plaisent à mon coeur, et doivent satisfaire le vôtre.[15]

It seems on the face of it unlikely that anyone could define some senses of "aimer" in this way without being aware of the further sense, that of a "love" which goes beyond friendship.

Perhaps we may find it more realistic for foreign characters like Wolmar in *La Nouvelle Héloïse*, or the Polish nobles in *Les Amours du chevalier de Faublas*, to speak perfect French. After all, history books tell us that French was the language of the upper classes in Russia and Poland. But one may still wonder whether, in real life, all these people spoke such pure, fluent, unaccented French as the novels of the time would suggest. It would not, I think, be difficult to assemble enough evidence to support the notion that, in literature, noble birth was assumed to carry with it the ability to speak elegantly in any language. (Theodore, in Walpole's *The Castle of Otranto*, would certainly be a case in point.)

The earliest novel in which I have found any practical comments on the problems and advantages of speaking in a foreign language is *Adolphe*. The hero says of Ellénore:

> Elle parlait plusieurs langues, imparfaitement à la vérité, mais toujours avec vivacité, quelquefois avec grâce. Ses idées semblaient se faire jour à travers les obstacles, et sortir de cette lutte, plus agréables, plus naïves et plus neuves: car les idiomes étrangers rajeunissent les pensées, et les débarrassent de ces tournures qui les font paraître tour-à-tour communes et affectées.[16]

But however imperfectly Ellénore spoke other languages, there is never any suggestion in the dialogue of *Adolphe* that her command of French is limited. It is only later in the nineteenth century that we find a foreign accent brought into novels to contribute to the sinister effect of some characters, or the charm of others.

Before we return to our virtuous peasants, we should perhaps spend a moment on a less reputable type of fiction. From the 1740s onwards, there is a small but steady flow of stories about girls who have become prostitutes or courtesans. Such novels are often narrated in the first person, and the "heroine" is always of humble origins. The titles of a few of these works (which tend to be omitted from histories of literature) will indicate their scope: Antoine Bret, *La Belle Allemande ou les galanteries de Thérèse* (1745); Paul Baret, *Mademoiselle Javotte, ouvrage peu moral écrit par elle-même* (1757); *La Belle Cauchoise, ou mémoires d'une jolie Normande devenue courtisane célèbre* (1783). Stylistically, they range from the merely suggestive to the pornographically precise. Although gaiety often prevails during much of the narrative, these works generally offer an edifying conclusion, sometimes with a somber turn of events in which the woman suffers for her sins. Thus they cannot all be classed, in any simple sense, as "comic" novels. In certain cases the narrator maintains a level of correct language. In others, the dialogue presents linguistic forms which may recall the heroine's social origins. Thus Mademoiselle Javotte, a Parisian, revisits her "quartier natal" and is greeted by remarks such as, "Eh quoi donc, est-ce que j'ai la barlue? c'est-y là Javotte Godeau?" and, "Parguienne oui, c'est elle; et comme te v'là brave, Mameselle Javotte." Refusing to put a crude name to Javotte's new way of life, one of her friends adds, "Tu m'entends. Je n'ons pas la manigance du parlementage; mais je savons minager un queuquesun."[17]

These *poissard* turns of speech had become familiar to many members of the reading public through works by Caylus, Vadé, and others. *Poissard* was generally exploited only for crude comic effects. We may admit that, for all its conventions, it does entail some effort to convey the sounds produced by the proletariat of Paris. But it also illustrates another of the pitfalls of "realism," on the aesthetic level: even apart from the triviality of content, most *poissard* writing is manifestly tedious to read.

Tedium of another kind, from works aspiring to greater value as literature, awaits the twentieth-century reader who pursues the lower classes into the *conte moral*. Marmontel, whose set of *Contes moraux* can be said to have launched the vogue, plumed himself on the naturalness of his dialogue:

> Quand je fais parler mes personnages, tout l'art que j'y emploie est d'être présent à leur entretien, et d'écrire ce que je crois entendre. En général, la plus naïve imitation de la nature dans les moeurs et dans le langage, est ce que j'ai recherché dans ces *Contes*. S'ils n'ont pas ce mérite, ils n'en ont aucun.[18]

The condition of this last sentence is all to unfortunately fulfilled, and more particularly so of Marmontel's rustic characters. We can see, from what they say, that literary attitudes have changed, to the extent that peasant naïveté is now meant to be admirable rather than ridiculous. But a story such as *La Bergère des Alpes* is still likely to provoke laughter, unintentionally.

Some travellers passing through the mountains of Savoy hear a shepherdess talking to herself: "Que le soleil couchant brille d'une douce lumière! C'est ainsi (disoit-elle) qu'au terme d'une carrière pénible, l'âme épuisée va se rajeunir dans la source pure de l'immortalité" (II, 44). When this young woman leads the travellers to her humble abode, they find there an old couple (compared, inevitably, to Baucis and Philemon), who explain that she is not their daughter, but that she arrived four years ago "en habit de paysanne," and offered to look after their flocks. "Nous nous doutâmes qu'elle n'étoit pas une villageoise," the old woman goes on, "mais nos questions l'affligeoient et nous crûmes devoir en abstenir" (II, 49). After some more dialogue of this sort, we the readers do more than suspect that the old couple do not sound like villagers either. As Marmontel was brought up in a small hamlet until the age of about eleven, he must have had some notion of how country people might talk. But obviously he assumed that naturalness of this kind would impair our respect for these characters. In any case, they remain subsidiary personages. The *bergère* of the title turns out, to no one's surprise, to be of noble birth. As for Marmontel's other tale about shepherds, *Annette et Lubin*, this is a modern version of *Daphnis and Chloé*. Here the protagonists speak a French which is self-consciously simple, but is also clearly literary rather than naturalistic.

In *Jacques le fataliste*, Diderot too refrains from the cruder and more obvious ways of indicating how speech reflects social levels, though his portrayal of lower-class speakers does of course have the convincing quality so markedly lacking in Marmontel's *contes*. I shall not make any further comments on *Jacques*, partly because its general tone is comic, so that some realism of dialogue is not unexpected, and partly because Diderot's handling of direct speech is too varied, complex, and idiosyncratic to be adequately discussed in a few paragraphs.

We have now reached the period when Restif de la Bretonne's works began to appear. Restif, of course, was an author who deliberately advocated the use of dialect words as one way of enriching French, and who lived up to his own advice. There is no need to engage here in a detailed discussion of his range of styles in dialogue, as various critics have already covered the ground.[19] We may merely note some general points in order to relate Restif to his contemporaries. The main fact to keep in mind is perhaps that much of Restif's handling of lower-class dialogue is still influenced either by a tendency to idealize (in the case of *paysans*), or by the convention that vulgarisms are laughable (as regards town dwellers). However, in any discussion of the development of a realistic dialogue manner in French, Restif must always occupy, and deservedly, a place of honor. It is also a place apart, for no major author can be said to have adopted him as a model, and the minor writers who might be thought to have followed in his tracks are the palest of imitators in this respect.

(As a brief parenthesis on the fiction of the 1790s, we may observe that some of these imitators now treated the poor of Paris seriously as characters, and indicated their vulgarisms of speech without scorn. Gorgy's *Blançay* provides some examples. But as we might expect, such portrayal has swung towards an unrealistically favorable view of the lower classes in towns.)

In spite of his interest in regional differences, Restif never achieved a work which could properly be called a regional novel. The honor of writing "the first regional novel in English, and perhaps in all Europe" has been attributed to Maria Edgeworth, for *Castle Rackrent* (1800).[20] In French, if not in France, Mme. de Charrière may be said to have been breaking the same ground when she brought out her *Lettres neuchâteloises* in 1784. And this work owed something to a Dutch novel, *Histoire van Mejuffrow Sara Burgerhart* (1782), by Betje Wolff and Aagje Deken. Discussing the composition of the *Lettres neuchâteloises*, Mme. de Charrière said:

> Je venais de voir dans *Sara Burgerhart* . . . qu'en peignant des lieux et des moeurs qu'on connaît bien, l'on donne à des personnages fictifs une réalité précieuse. . . . Ne peignant personne, on peint tout le monde.[21]

In spite of its relative shortness, this novel builds up a surprisingly complete and coherent picture of life in Neuchâtel. And in the letters from Julianne C—, the little seamstress, we have a persuasive sketch of a working-class girl. Although shown as a victim of social conditions, she is not sentimentalized and does not accept uncritically her own unfavorable situation. Comparing herself with the ladies of Nauchâtel society, she says:

> —et peut-être ne sont-elles seulement pas aussi braves qu'une pauvre fille qu'on laisse pleurer en faisant son ouvrage, et qui n'a pas été à toutes leurs écoles et leurs pensions, et n'a pas appris à lire sur leurs beaux livres; et elles ont des bonnets, et des rubans, et des robes avec des garnitures de gaze, qu'il faut que nous travaillions toute la nuit et quelquefois les dimanches.[22]

Elsewhere Julianne uses various local words—*jaublâmes, un pierrot*—which accentuate her social origins. Thus she expresses herself in a convincingly colloquial way. But these turns of speech come to us in letters she wrote, rather than as her spoken words. It is no easy matter to decide whether, and if so how far, the style of a given character's letters can be equated with a spoken style; for this reason I have refrained from discussing here the question of what the characters say in letters.

If we now look onwards to Balzac, as the first great exponent of "realistic" dialogue in the nineteenth century, we find that his approach stems from the kind of work foreshadowed by Mme. de Charrière rather than from the rich confusion of Restif. Balzac's vivid impressions of the speech habits of the poorer classes first appear as an element in the local color of an historical novel, *Les Chouans*. Apart from a few attempts at medieval pastiche, the eighteenth-century historical novel generally produces correct and colorless speech for its largely aristocratic characters. It was not, of course, from works like these that Balzac learnt social realism in dialogue, but from the historical novels of Sir Walter Scott. And the first such work, *Waverley* (1814), was written according to Scott, "so as in some distant degree to emulate the admirable Irish portraits drawn by Miss Edgeworth."[23] However, even if we see Scott and Edgeworth as Balzac's immediate literary forebears in this aspect of his work, it is also true to say that the general tendencies of eighteenth-century French practice would in all probability have led him in the same direction.

What has emerged from this review of the development of dialogue is that we can indeed observe an increase in realism in the practice of a number of novelists, but that it is impossible to define the nature and degree of this realism with any accuracy.[24] Moreover, realism can, in any case, provide no more than a descriptive standard. If we wish to evaluate the literary effectiveness of a given author's dialogue, mere faithfulness to real-life speech habits is an inadequate criterion. Instead we must consider the congruence of the dialogue style with a range of elements inside the novel, and notably with the tone and the mode of literary expression which the novelist has established right from the beginning of the novel in question. Such factors may be extremely complex, and the critical verdict will inevitably depend in part on subjective reactions. But it is more satisfactory, and more honest, to recognize this personal factor in our judgments than to suppose that "realism" constitutes a yardstick which will allow us to measure objectively the novelist's skill in presenting his dialogue.

NOTES

1 Henri Coulet, *Le Roman jusqu'à la Révolution* (Paris: Armand Colin, 1967), I, 210.

2 Louvet de Couvray, *Une année de la vie du chevalier de Faublas* (London and Paris: L'Auteur et les Marchands de nouveautés, 1787), I, 103–4.

3 Robert Chasles, *Les Illustres Françoises* (1713), ed. Frédéric Deloffre (Paris: Société d'édition "Les Belles Lettres," 1959), II, 466. This edition is cited for other quotations from the work.

4 Prévost, *Manon Lescaut*, ed. Frédéric Deloffre and Raymond Picard (Paris: Garnier, 1965), p. 107.

5 Lesage, *Histoire de Gil Blas* (Paris: Garnier, 1955), I, 23-24. This edition is cited for other quotations from the work.

6 Marivaux, *La Vie de Marianne*, ed. Frédéric Deloffre (Paris: Garnier, 1957), pp. 92-97.

7 Frédéric Deloffre, *Une préciosité nouvelle: Marivaux et le marivaudage,* 2nd ed. rev. (Paris: Armand Colin, 1967), pp. 177-85, 225-27. See also the introduction to *La Vie de Marianne.*

8 Deloffre, *Une préciosité nouvelle*, p. 226.

9 *La Vie de Marianne*, p. 94.

10 *The Life of Marianne*, trans. John Lockman (?) (London: Charles Davis, 1736), I, 144.

11 *The Virtuous Orphan . . .* , trans. Mrs. Mary Mitchell Collyer (1743), ed. William Harley McBurney and Michael Francis Shugrue (Carbondale: Southern Illinois University Press, 1965), p. 72.

12 Mrs. Ann Hughes, *Zoriada, or Village Annals*, 3 vols. (London: Extell, 1786), I, 17.

13 *Zoräide* (translator unknown), 3 vols. (London and Paris: Buisson, 1787), I, 17.

14 Mouhy, *La Paysanne parvenue,* 4 vols. (1735-37); (Paris: Prault, 1777), I, 37-38.

15 Mme. de Grafigny, *Lettres d'une Péruvienne* (1747), in *Œuvres choisies* (Paris: Caille et Ravier, 1819), I, 146-47 (Lettre XXIII).

16 Benjamin Constant, *Adolphe*, ed. Gustave Rudler (Manchester: Manchester University Press, 1919), p. 14.

17 Paul Baret, *Mademoiselle Javotte* (1787; Bicêtre, 1788), pp. 56-57.

18 Marmontel, *Contes moraux*, 3 vols. (Paris: Merlin, 1765), I, xiii. All references to the *Contes* are from this edition.

19 See Charles A. Porter, *Restif's Novels* (New Haven and London: Yale University Press, 1967), pp. 392-407. (Porter supplies references to a

number of other works relevant to Restif's style.) See also Raymond Joly, *Deux études sur la préhistoire du réalisme* (Quebec: Presses de l'Université Laval, 1969), pp. 119-84.

20 Maria Edgeworth, *Castle Rackrent*, ed. George Watson (London: Oxford University Press, 1964), Introduction, p. vii.

21 Quoted by Philippe Godet in his edition of Mme. de Charrière, *Lettres neuchâteloises* (Geneva: Jullien, 1908), p. x.

22 *Lettres neuchâteloises*, p. 59.

23 Scott, *Waverley*, chap. lxxii, quoted by George Watson in *Castle Rackrent*, p. vii.

24 This final paragraph presents, in a necessarily brief form, the conclusions I reached after hearing the discussion which this paper prompted at the Congress of the International Society for Eighteenth-Century Studies.

From Marmontel to Berquin: The Dynamic Concept of Morality in Eighteenth-Century French Fiction

ANGUS MARTIN

The notion of moral usefulness, during the second half of the eighteenth century, comes to be one of the criteria of excellence adopted by critics and novelists alike. This common viewpoint represents a curious reversal of values, if one considers the bitter hostility directed against fiction before this time in the name of morality.[1] "Les Romanciers de nos jours," reads a preface of 1767, "ont cru avec raison qu'un Livre d'agrément peut devenir un Ouvrage essential."[2] Another novelist of the sixties can exclaim with perhaps excessive sincerity, "C'est toi, douce Vertu, dont la bénigne chaleur vient animer mon imagination peu féconde! "[3] Modern critics have not required such damning confessions in order to regret the general mediocrity of the novel, which, after Rousseau, developed in the grip of an all too sincere didacticism. They speak of "une véritable stérilisation du roman,"[4] or write that "le genre triomphe, mais se dissout."[5]

In this climate of newly respectable moralism, what became of those genres where morality had long been of prime importance:

edifying works and, above all, children's literature? Publication statistics allow us to make two basic observations: first, that children's reading material appeared regularly at this period and began to proliferate at the end of the century,[6] and second, that the success in this area of certain authors, whose popularity was maintained well beyond the end of the eighteenth century, suggests that some of them at least had found original and promising formulas.[7] If my purpose here is to examine aspects of this upsurge of children's fiction, it is not solely because of the interest of the phenomenon as such. I shall also venture somewhat further and propose certain hypotheses that, although based on a limited study of this microcosm of eighteenth-century fiction, do seem capable of illuminating and enriching our understanding of the evolution of the genre as a whole.

Children's Literature and the "Conte Moral"

It is not possible to attempt any sort of historical overview of French didactic fiction within the confines of this article.[8] "Tout le monde sait," runs a text of 1765, "que de tout tems on a employé les fables pour instruire les Enfans, & que Platon vouloit qu'on les leur fît succer [sic] avec le lait. Cet usage est encore assez en vigueur."[9] There were, of course, sterner observers who at times condemned a practice that consisted–paradoxically–of teaching virtue by means of the vice that the "untruth" of fiction was seen to be. Others expressed the view that it merely made a moral point harder to grasp if one incorporated it in a story. "Les lumieres des Enfans," the text just quoted also states, "sont ordinairement trop foibles, pour percer le voile de l'allusion; & le plus souvent ils s'arrêtent à l'écorce, sans découvrir ce qu'elle cache."[10]

But worthy churchmen like Jean-Pierre Camus in the seventeenth century or Fénelon on the threshold of the eighteenth were not afraid to use the novel and the tale to teach a lesson. A disciple of Camus, starting in 1744, is the prolific Minim father

Michel-Ange Marin, who up until 1766 published a series of novels bordering on hagiography that offered a constant model of the Christian life.[11] An author who is commonly considered to be one of the pioneers of children's literature as understood today, Madame Leprince de Beaumont, found her inspiration in principles that were essentially just as pious as those of Marin, both in writing for adults and for children.[12] But the great novelty of her work was that she made every effort to adapt her writing to her juvenile public in particular and to adopt pedagogical methods that would be as effective as possible. In the preface of her *Magasin des enfans* in 1756 we read that she apparently made a practice of testing out her work, by giving it to her pupils to read. She tells us of her delight in observing that "l'enfant de six ans s'en est divertie aussi bien que celle de dix & de quinze."[13] The technique used in most of her works is that of a dialogue between a governess and her charges, interrupted by short tales of all kinds.[14] Madame d'Epinay, practicing the same method in her *Conversations d'Emilie* (1774), seems to have solved, at least to her own satisfaction, the old dilemma of the "untruth" of fiction. "Est-il vrai ce conte?" asks Emilie; and her mother replies with aplomb, "Autant que peut l'être un conte de Fée; la morale n'en est point exagérée, elle est vraie; la fable ne l'est pas."[15]

Such explanations become less necessary as the fairy story and the fable progressively fall from favor in children's literature. In 1774 there appeared a collection of tales by Madame Leprince de Beaumont that is devoid of the dialogue framework habitually used by this author. The title given the work is indicative of changing tastes: *Contes moraux,* and the collection is followed in 1776 by a continuation, *Nouveaux contes moraux.*[16] The "moral tale" as practiced by Marmontel, with its simplicity, its economy, its realistic effects, is soon adapted to the requirements of edifying and juvenile literature.

In spite of reproaches often directed against Marmontel for having allowed himself too many voluptuous scenes or for having chosen an uninspiring and undemanding kind of moral code to illustrate, it is nevertheless tempting to speculate on the models that the author of the *Contes moraux* may well have found in certain forms of "moral" literature.[17] In England, for example, the periodicals of Addison and Steele as early as 1709 gave rise to a tradition of didactic stories, pursued in particular by such writers as Mrs. Haywood, Samuel Johnson, and John Hawkesworth towards the middle of the century.[18] This English example was soon imitated with considerable enthusiasm in Germany: the *moralische Wochenschriften* were an important inspiration for early juvenile writers in that country, especially in the case of the numerous periodicals for children of which Weisse's *Kinderfreund* in 1774 is certainly the most celebrated example.[19] If Marmontel's foreign debts remain obscure, there is no doubt of the cosmopolitan influences that existed in the realm of children's literature. A large part of Berquin's published work, for example, is made up of translations, from English, German, and even Dutch sources;[20] and the commercial methods of this same author (who was for a time his own publisher) were inspired both by the German children's periodicals and by the remarkable success of juvenile publishing in England, right from the beginning of John Newbery's career in 1744.[21]

In this period of renewal, tried and tested formulas of children's literature were not abandoned overnight. The didactic journey in the style of Fénelon's *Télémaque* still found admirers and imitators, especially towards the end of the century in the form of veritable fictionalized encyclopedias;[22] edifying biographies still appeared, although the heroes offered as models to young readers were considerably less saintly than formerly and far closer to everyday reality.[23] Nevertheless it is the formula of the collection of "moral tales" that appears to have attracted the greatest favor.[24] Sometimes these collections are made of very short and simple texts intended as elementary reading practice, while containing models of good conduct; sometimes they are presented as a course of religious instruction translated into a series of examples.[25] Very frequently Madame Leprince de Beaumont's favorite method lingers on: the dialogue framing a series of anecdotes,[26] with, at times, pretensions of being a complete program of education.[27]

The methodical illustration, through writings for children, of entire theories of education is best represented by the work of Madame de Genlis.[28] In spite of her hostility towards Marmontel, Madame de Genlis did not disdain to use the "moral tale." Her *Veillées du château,* for example, in 1784, were published as a "cours de morale à l'usage des enfans";[29] but this course of moral instruction is carried out by means of stories set in the framework of a dialogue between a mother and her children. The three tales of the third volume of this work were even published separately in 1785 under the title *Contes moraux,*[30] obviously in the hope of taking advantage of the reigning vogue for the "moral tale." Whereas Madame de Genlis always played the governess and kept her distance from her young readers, the other great name in the children's literature of the end of the century, Arnaud Berquin, proceeded in a far more familiar way, presenting himself as "l'Ami des enfants," as a sort of kindly and affectionate elder brother. Berquin's success, both with his contemporaries and during at least the first half of the following century, was a consecration of the short "moral tale" for children and was a fitting reward for this author's continuous search for subjects and techniques of presentation suitable for his readers. Berquin certainly does not deserve that his name should have become synonymous with a kind of watered-down sentimentality: in his day, his work possessed a fresh and novel quality to whose destruction the familiarity of overwhelming success largely contributed.

It should be borne in mind that amidst this flowering of moralizing fiction, treatises and works of a more austere nature continued to appear, and that many fashionable titles were more promising than the texts that they headed: *L'Ami des filles* in 1761, *L'Ami des jeunes gens* in 1764, *L'Ami des enfants* in 1765 are imitations of Mirabeau's *Ami des hommes* rather than precursors of Berquin. We may also note that not all works published for the juvenile market were written for children; a certain number of anthologies, for example, offered a selection of tales (and extracts from novels) that were taken from adult literature. The editor of *L'Almanach des enfans,* published in 1776 and 1777,[31] writes: "J'ai cru . . . lorsque je conçus l'idée de ce Recueil qu'un choix d'Anecdotes historiques, de traits de Bienfaisance, de petits Contes très-moraux, &c, pourrait intéresser la jeunesse, lui former le coeur, & l'occuper utilement dans ses momens de loisir."[32] This kind of compilation is, as it were, a monument to the very close links that existed between the "moral tale" in the Marmontel tradition and the didactic tale for children; transfers from one level to the other are effected with little difficulty in such anthologies, and borrowings of this sort are by no means rare.[33]

The Dynamic Concept of Morality and the Literary Techniques of Children's Fiction

One essential motivation of eighteenth-century writers of children's stories appears to have been a quite literal belief in the moral effectiveness of the tale. This notion—that example can influence an individual's behavior—is an ancient one and was abundantly exploited in the numerous defenses of fiction that early French theorists produced. During the second half of the century, however, the idea of the effect produced by example finds in Rousseau's pedagogy a new and powerful theoretical justification.

Emile's education is, of course, carried out with a considerable use of "pseudo-experience," of situations arranged by his tutor, so that the pupil may learn not by abstract rules, but by his personal reactions to circumstances that are perhaps artificially contrived but are nevertheless concrete.[34] Leaving aside Rousseau's hostility to reading as a mode of instruction,[35] children's writers took what in *Emile* is a type of real experience and transposed it into a written text. An example from Madame de Genlis's *Adèle et Théodore* manifests an obvious debt to Rousseau.[36] A mother who has devoted herself to her children's education is teaching her daughter to read by writing for her a series of short works; in order to give these productions greater prestige in the girl's eyes, the mother has them printed and brought to the house by a book peddler. On top of all this, she stage-manages her daughter's choice, so that the stories read will have a direct relationship with actual incidents that have occurred within the household. No sooner, for instance, has young Adèle quarrelled with her brother than her mother arranges that she should read *L'Histoire de Céphise,* the story of "une petite fille, bien douce, bien obéissante & qui n'avoit de sa vie contrarié son frère." Madame de Genlis reports the almost miraculous effect of this method: "Cette histoire fut lue avec avidité, & le soir même Adèle demanda pardon à Théodore, en l'assurant qu'elle ne seroit plus jamais contrariante." Encouraged by such results, Adèle's mother pursues her system: "Huit jours après, autre Colporteur, & nouvelle leçon." [37]

It was believed before Rousseau that vice *could* be corrected by means of good example; after *Emile* this theory was taken as far as supposing that a good example *must* necessarily reform those who have strayed from virtue. Madame de Genlis expresses this point of view in an extreme form when she writes: "Celui qui ne veut ni se corriger, ni s'instruire, lit ces Ouvrages pour s'amuser, & en les lisant, il se corrige, & s'instruit malgré lui." [38] Bouilly, the author of a short biography of Berquin, relates that the "Ami des enfants" also believed in what he called "l'attrait *irrésistible* d'une narration variée et attachante." [39] Berquin, like Madame de Genlis, set out to create for the child a framework of examples that would leave no choice but to conform; his ambition, in writing for children, is expressed as follows: "les porter naturellement à la vertu en ne l'offrant jamais à leurs yeux que sous les traits les plus aimables." [40] The program to be followed was clear; and the results to be gained were conceived by Madame de Genlis just as precisely. "Puissent tous les Enfans qui liront ces Pièces, être frappés des exemples qu'elles contiennent! Puissent-ils, par cette lecture, devenir meilleurs, plus sensibles, plus vrais, plus tendres pour leurs Parens, & tous les voeux de l'Auteur seront remplis!"[41]

It is this dynamic (or almost deterministic) conception of moral literature that I refer to in my title. Diderot, in his *Eloge de Richardson,* gives an early suggestion of this notion of the *inevitability* of fiction's moral lessons: "Richardson sème dans les coeurs des gens des vertus qui y restent d'abord oisifs et tranquilles: ils y sont secrètement jusqu'à ce qu'il ne se présente une occasion qui les remue et les fait éclore."[42] Other theorists, after Diderot—and not solely in the realm of pedagogy and didactic literature—were less patient, less ready to await the results of a good example: they postulated works of fiction which would forcibly impose a respect for virtue. If Berquin, in considering the reactions of his readers, expressed the desire that "l'instruction *pénètre* plus avant dans leurs âmes,"[43] the choice of this image was indication enough of his ambition to bring about aggressively a change in behavior patterns. Adult literature of the time provides similar examples. As early as 1767, in the preface to a novel, we can find an even more vigorous vocabulary, a blueprint for coercing the reader and, as it were, forcing him into submission. The work in question aims to "imprimer l'horreur du vice, inspirer des sentiments d'humanité; élever l'âme; faire naître le désir de devenir vertueux; consoler un infortuné . . . ; faire rougir un coupable; rappeler un coeur foible au bord de l'abîme . . . ; corriger d'un travers par le ridicule . . . ; réveiller une conscience assoupi . . .".[44] The "moral" novelist in the second half of the eighteenth century aimed at producing a measurable effect; and the search for methods to bring about the desired transformations of readers' personalities was carried out enthusiastically by children's authors in particular.

The notion of "dynamic" morality exerted an important influence not only on the subjects but also on the techniques of children's fiction. Writers wanted the "experience" provided by a story to produce upon the reader as striking an effect as possible, and they consciously sought the means to achieve this goal. Many of them (as was the case with Madame Leprince de Beaumont) claimed to have tried out their writings by giving them to children to read before publication. Madame de Genlis writes, for example, "avant de faire imprimer cet Ouvrage, j'ai desiré savoir positivement si mes *Lecteurs* pourroient comprendre sans effort, ce que j'ai voulu dire. J'ai rassemblé chez moi une société assez nombreuse; j'ai fait des *Lectures.*"[45] In a prospectus for the *Ami des enfants* Berquin maintains, "Il n'est aucun [de ces morceaux] dont on n'ait d'abord essayé l'effet sur des Enfans d'un âge & d'une intelligence plus ou moins avancés; & on a retranché tous les traits qui sembloient ne pas les intéresser assez vivement."[46] Here we find not merely the conventional desire to "please" the reader, but an attempt deliberately to construct works for a particular and clearly defined audience.

Having adopted this point of view, children's authors soon realized that they had to bring their subject matter as close as they could to the everyday reality their readers knew. If Ducray-Duminil, at the end of the century, still wrote fairy stories (for which he nevertheless coined the term "conte moral de féerie"!), these were only for the very youngest of children, whom he saw as needing fanciful stories if their imaginations were to be stimulated.[47] But for children of what he calls the "second âge," Ducray-Deminil promised rather that "ce sont des évènemens simples, des tableaux vraisemblables que nous allons avoir sous les yeux."[48] The program Berquin set out in the first prospectus of the *Ami des enfants* was even more precise: "Au lieu de ces fictions extravagantes & de ce merveilleux bizarre dans lesquels on a si long-tems égaré [l'] imagination [des enfants], on ne leur présente ici que des aventures dont ils peuvent être témoins chaque jour dans leur famille. Les sentimens qu'on cherche à leur inspirer ne sont point au-desses des forces de leur ame: on ne les met en scène qu'avec eux-mêmes, leurs parens, les compagnons de leurs jeux, les domestiques qui les entourent, les animaux dont la vue leur est familiere."[49] Berquin also took great pains to write in the "langage simple & naïf" of his readers and to make his characters speak in a natural manner.[50] If, from time to time, he was obliged to apologize for a delay in the publication of his periodicals, one of the reasons proposed was precisely the difficulty of maintaining a suitable style for children. [51]

Subjects were chosen then as a function of their close relationship with young readers' experience, but this criterion was far from being the only one applied. The moral lesson was absolutely basic, and the story had to be constructed in such a way that the message stood out unmistakably. To avoid any weakening of the moral effect, the children's author would remove any element in his work which might militate against the didactic aim. Madame de Genlis, in the preface of the *Veillées du château,* described her method of working: "Au lieu de *chercher & d'ajuster un résultat moral* à un joli sujet, j'ai arrangé & composé chaque sujet d'après une vérité morale." In discussing the general structure of the work, she wrote: "Je n'ai pas placé au hasard, à la suite les unes des autres, les Histoires qui forment ce Recueil. Avant de songer au plan *romanesque*, c'est-à-dire, aux situations, j'avois préparé le *plan des idées* . . . . Cette chaîne de raisonnement ainsi disposée, il ne me restoit plus qu'à faire une combinaison aussi facile qu'amusante; il s'agissoit de trouver les caractères, les petits incidents, & les situations qui pouvoient servir à démontrer de la maniere la plus frappante, les vérités que je voulois établir." [52] This procedure may well appear rather artificial, but it was at least indicative of a twofold aim: not only to construct a work whose thematic unity would be one of its principal features, but also to reveal the moral lesson through the story itself.

In spite of the confidence in the inevitable effect of moral examples that children's authors so loudly proclaimed in this period, they did not abandon narrative formulas that allowed a certain amount of commentary and overt explanation. Madame de Genlis gives the following explanation of her choice of a dialogue framework for the *Veillées*: "Des entretiens sans événements & sans *Histoires,* ont trop de sécheresse; des Histoires détachées, sans interruption, sans conversations, n'auroient point assez de clarté pour les Enfants."[53] Berquin, for his part, did not appear to share these hesitations, for the *Ami des enfants* and the *Ami des adolescents* are made up of independent items, where any commentary is given within a very simple narrative structure. Indeed, it is generally true that, apart from the problem of the dialogue frame, the narrative formulas of children's tales present few difficulties. Juvenile literature did not concern itself with that striving for realism through a "documentary text" (memoirs, letter-novel) that for too long preoccupied adult novelists and ended up by becoming a momentary obstacle to the further evolution of fiction. No doubt because of its close relationship with the long-standing conventions of the "conte," where the notion of verisimilitude had never been a vital element, and also because of its unsophisticated public, children's literature most often employed third-person narration, admitting, without any difficulty, the "omniscient narrator." One could perhaps add that there is nothing incongruous in seeing the authority of the tutor in front of his pupils being translated quite naturally into the context of children's fiction by means of a narrative voice that knows everything, describes everything, and comments on everything!

In the interest of greater clarity in my argument, I have concentrated, in this paper, on theoretical statements and have concerned myself more with outlining authors' intentions than with studying the way in which these intentions were actually put into practice. It must be said that late eighteenth-century children's texts are not always distinguished by the simplicity that was their overt goal; their "realism," their "unity," their narrative "freedom" too often remained unrealized. It is, however, no less true that those authors who were most successful as children's writers, the Madame de Genlis, the Berquins, were the ones who not only developed a very clear conception of their self-imposed task but who also succeeded in innovating, in renewing the genre; and their originality will be found quite as much in the area of the literary techniques they chose as in the range of subjects they made their special province.

The Techniques of Children's Stories and the General Development of Fiction

Throughout this study, we have met with examples of parallel developments in children's and in adult literature: in the origins and the popularity of the "moral tale," in the dynamic conception of literary moralizing. Do our conclusions about the originality and the success of certain children's authors have any significance for our approach to the general evolution of fiction during this period? The technical innovations that can be found in children's stories do show, as we have seen, that the notion of a dynamic moral influence was not a completely sterile doctrine. On the more general plane, likewise, it seems possible to argue that moralism was not solely the negative influence that historians of literature tend to consider it.

Within a short discussion, in which I have deliberately concerned myself with a minor portion of the fiction output of a given period, I cannot do more than draw from my conclusions some hypotheses that it is not possible to develop here. Nevertheless it does appear likely that the transformation of what had been largely a rhetorical flourish into a sincerely held doctrine meant that moralism did make three kinds of important contributions to subsequent fictional concepts:

1. The idea that fiction should represent a reality that the reader will recognize and identify with is developed and diversified. For a narrative to be morally effective, it must come as close as possible to the kinds of experience its readers will know, and at the same time the means by which verisimilitude is achieved must be as varied and subtle as possible.
2. The notion of the necessary unity of narrative becomes with time progressively more important. The didactic novel, the *roman à thèse* (in the widest sense of this latter term), must be rigorously constructed in a way that a less "serious" piece of fiction can more readily neglect.
3. The progressive abandonment of the eighteenth century's techniques for giving a would-be realistic text an almost

documentary status is in the line of future developments: the late eighteenth-century novel starts to return to the convention of the omniscient narrator, of third-person narration. The novelist who believes in his work's morality, on the one hand, feels less need to defend himself againat the accusation of mendacity so often directed against works of fiction; the moral novel, on the other hand, overtly seeks to impose a particular point of view, and belongs in a context where explanations and comment fall naturally from the pen of an author who is at once narrator and judge.

The process whereby, in the second half of the eighteenth century, the French novel adapted to the implications of accepting a moral stance is not summarized neatly in one or two masterpieces; for that we must go well beyond 1800. It is rather in a multitude of minor texts that we must study the evolution of the techniques of fiction at this period. At the very moment when Laclos summed up the lessons of the past in a monument that was also a technical impasse, other less-celebrated novelists (and among them our children's writers) were preparing the future of the genre. In their imperfect prototypes they prefigured the achievements of the nineteenth century, when moralism would become a less-overwhelming but nevertheless durable formative influence in the evolution of fiction.

NOTES

1 This text is an English adaptation of a paper originally entitled "De Marmontel à Berquin: La Notion de la 'moralité active' et les techniques de la littérature romanesque de la second moitié du XVIIIe siècle." For details of contemporary French theories of fiction and moral values in particular, see Georges May, *Le Dilemme du roman au XVIIIe siècle* (New Haven: Yale University Press, and Paris: Presses Universitaires de France, 1963), pp. 248ff.; Vivienne Mylne, *The Eighteenth-Century French Novel: Techniques of Illusion* (Manchester: Manchester University Press, 1965), pp. 4ff.; Henri Coulet, *Le Roman jusqu'à la Révolution* (Paris: Armand Colin, 1967), I, 318ff. Cf. the unflattering picture of the novel in

the second half of the century given in the classic study by Servais Etienne, *Le Genre romanesque en France depuis l'apparition de la "Nouvelle Héloïse" jusqu'aux approches de la Révolution* . . . (Paris: Armand Colin, 1922). A study closer to the point of view of the present article is Josephine Grieder, "The Novel as a Genre: Formal Literary Theory, 1760-1800," *French Review*, 46 (1972), 278-90.

2 Louis Charpentier, "A ma femme," in *Nouveaux Contes moraux* (Amsterdam and Liège, J. F. Bassompierre, and Brussels, J. Van den Berghen, 1767), 3 parts.

3 Séguier de Saint-Brisson, "Préface," in *Ariste ou les charmes de l'honnêteté* (Paris: Panckoucke, 1764).

4 May, *Dilemme*, p. 250.

5 Coulet, *Roman*, p. 418.

6 My observations are based on the following bibliographical survey: Angus Martin, Vivienne Mylne, Richard Frautschi, *Bibliographie du genre romanesque français* (London and Chicago: Mansell, in press). From a total of some 2,600 different titles published during this half-century (including translations and a certain number of marginal works), I have extracted for this study seventy works of fiction intended for youthful readers, together with a further nineteen pious works published for a somewhat wider public. (I have not included certain doubtful or insufficiently documented titles, or a dozen novels of education concerned principally with pedagogical theory.) Space precludes reproducing the detailed list of titles examined. In later notes, however, summary lists are provided of the authors of different categories of works consulted, and readers are referred to the bibliography just quoted for full references. Chronologically, our texts are distributed as follows (C = works for children; P = pious works): 1751: 1(P); 1754: 1(C); 1756: 1(C); 1757: 1(C); 1758: 1(C); 1759: 1(C), 1(P); 1760: 1(C); 1761: 1(P); 1762: 3(P); 1765: 2(P); 1766: 1(C), 2(P); 1767: 1(P); 1768: 1(P); 1770: 1(P); 1771: 1(P); 1772: 2(C), 1(P); 1774: 2(C); 1775: 1(C); 1776: 1(C); 1777: 1(C); 1778: 1(C); 1779: 2(C); 1781: 1(C), 2(P); 1782: 1(C), 1(P); 1783: 2(C); 1784: 2(C); 1786: 3(C), 1(P); 1787: 4(C); 1788: 4(C); 1789: 5(C); 1790: 1(C); 1791: 2(C); 1793: 1(C); 1795: 7(C); 1796: 1(C); 1797: 3(C); 1798: 2(C); 1799: 10(C); 1800: 4(C). These figures are certainly incomplete, as account must be taken of the "marginal" nature of many of these works in the context of a bibliography of fiction, of the ephemeral nature of children's publications, of the destructive use their public inflicted upon them, and of the slight literary value accorded them in conventional sources. The above statistics, nevertheless, appear to illustrate the growing popularity of "lay" children's function and the decline of works of piety.

7 *Le Magasin des enfants* (1756) by Madame Leprince de Beaumont, for

example, was republished some thirty times before 1800. *L'Ami des enfants* (1782) by Arnaud Berquin appeared, before the end of the century, in at least seventeen editions and was also included in a dozen versions of Berquin's works—figures that offer an interesting comparison with the twenty-eight editions over the same period of *Les Liaisons dangereuses,* which was also first published in 1782. The printed catalogues of the Bibliothèque nationale and the British Museum Library, together with the U.S. National Union Catalogue, under "Berquin" or "Genlis" for instance, give a first indication of the lasting popularity during the nineteenth century of the late eighteenth-century French children's authors.

8 For a list of studies of French children's literature, see my article "Notes sur *L'Ami des enfants* de Berquin et la littérature enfantine en France aux alentours de 1780," *Dix-huitième siècle,* no. 6 (1974), esp. pp. 307-8.

9 *L'Ami des enfans, par M. l'abbé de **** (Paris: Desaint et Saillant, 1765), p. xvi.

10 Ibid., p. xii.

11 From *Adélaïde de Witsbury ou la pieuse pensionnaire* (1744) to *Angélique ou la religieuse selon le coeur de Dieu* (1766). Other authors who exploited fiction for edifying purposes during our period were Baudrand, Compan, Champion de Nilon, Madame Leprince de Beaumont, Mademoiselle Loquet, Maydieu, and Molé.

12 See M. A. Reynaud, *Madame Le Prince de Beaumont: Vie et oeuvre d'une éducatrice,* 2 vols. (Lyon: the author, 1792).

13 I quote the "avertissement" from the following re-edition: Lyon: Jean-Baptiste Reguilliat, 1758, 4 parts, I, vi.

14 According to Ludwig Göhring, *Die Anfänge der deutschen Jugendliteratur im 18. Jahrhundert* (Nürnberg, 1904; rpt. Leipzig, 1967), the dialogue form was originally designed to present examples of model lessons to inexperienced tutors.

15 Leipzig: Siegfried Lebrecht Crusius, pp. 333–34.

16 Both works appeared in 2 volumes with the address "Lyon: chez Pierre Bruyset Ponthus."

17 The anecdote Marmontel tells in his memoirs about the almost accidental origins of the *contes moraux* has for too long been taken at face value. Research on the models offered by contemporary periodical literature, both French and foreign, has yet to be carried out.

18 On English moral periodicals (and their connection with fiction), consult Robert D. Mayo, *The English Novel in the Magazines, 1740-1815* (Evanston: Northwestern University Press, 1962), chs. I, II. Johnson's conception of the "picture of life" (p. 101) presents striking analogies with the moral tale in the manner of Marmontel. It appears that only

after the success of the *Contes moraux* did French publishers seek to exploit the narrative segments of the moral periodicals. For example, it is under the title *Contes . . .* , 2 parts (London and Paris: veuve Duchesne), that are published in 1774 extracts from Hawkesworth's *Adventurer.* Cf. *Contes, avantures et faits singuliers . . .*, 2 vols. (London and Paris: Duchesne, 1764), which are extracts from the abbé Prévost's *Pour et Contre.*

19 See Göhring, *Anfänge*, part I, section 2. On the moral periodical in Germany, consult Wolfgang Martens, *Die Botschaft der Tugend: die Aufklärung im Spiegel der deutschen moralischen Wochenschriften* (Stuttgart: Metzler, 1968). Is any importance to be attached to the fact that the term "moral tale" seems to have been used in Germany before the popularity of Marmontel's stories (first published in volume form in 1761) gave the expression its wide currency? In 1757 Pfeil, for example, published his *Versuch in moralischen Erzählungen* (Leipzig, 1757), where, according to the preface, "each individual piece has as its object the development of a particular moral precept" ("jedes einzelne Stück hat die Ausführung eines gewissen moralischen Satzes zum Gegenstande," p. iv).

20 For Berquin's borrowing from foreign children's literature see Martin, "Notes", quoted above, pp. 300-302, 306; and Renée Lelièvre, "Le Théâtre allemand en France (1750-1789)," *Revue de littérature comparée* (April-June 1974), 256-92 (esp. 261, 267, 269, 270, 273, 274, and 284). The journalistic activities of Madame Leprince de Beaumont in England are recalled in her *Œuvres mêlées . . . , extraites des journaux & feuilles périodiques qui ont paru en Angleterre pendant le séjour qu'elle y a fait . . .*, 6 vols. (Maestricht: Dufour et Roux, 1775). Berquin's familiarity with English periodicals is shown by the extracts from the *Idler,* the *Adventurer,* and the *Rambler* that he published under the title *Choix de tableaux tirés de diverses galeries anglaises . . .* (Amsterdam and Paris: veuve Duchesne, 1775).

21 On English children's literature and the career of Newbery in particular, see F. J. Harvey Darton, *Children's Books in England . . .* (1932; Cambridge: Cambridge University Press, 1966), chs. VII-XI; and M. F. Thwaite, *From Primer to Pleasure . . .* (London: The Library Association, 1963), ch. II. (In this latter work will also be found a brief discussion of the development of French juvenile literature and of Rousseau's influence in this area.)

22 Among the most popular examples was the abbé Barthélemy's *Voyage du jeune Anacharsis*, begun in 1788. Other exponents of the genre were Boiedieu, Jauffret, Lantier, Maréchal, Navarre. It is curious to note that Sade's *Aline et Valcour* appears to have links with this tradition.

23 Berquin offers his readers, for example, his translation of Thomas Day's *Sandford and Merton* in 1786 and, in 1787, *Le Petit Grandison* from the

Dutch of Madame Decambon van der Werken—works whose moralism is no doubt too insistent for modern tastes, but is nonetheless a long way from the heavy-handedness of earlier edifying biographies (for example, Marin's *Théodule ou l'enfant de la bénédiction,* 1762).

24 Twenty-seven of the seventy works surveyed are collections of tales with no frame. Twenty-two are conversations or letters, usually with stories that serve as illustrations. To this latter category may be added the four different versions of the German author Campe's *Robinson der Jüngere,* where dialogues serve as a framework to the adventures of Defoe's hero. Only ten short "novels" for children occur, to which may be added seven examples of the "voyage" in the style of *Télémaque* as discussed above. These total figures include eighteen avowed translations, most of which (fifteen) appeared after 1785. The following are the major children's authors represented in the survey but not included in summary lists given in previous notes: Aikin, Bérenger, Berquin, Blanchard, Campe, Couret de Villeneuve, Day, Decambon, Defoe, Didot, Duché de Vancy, Ducray-Duminil, Dulaurent, Epinay, Falques, Fréville, Genlis, Giraudeau, Godwin, Helme, Jauffret, Junker, Kühne, Lafite, Laus de Boissy, Leprince de Beaumont, Loquet, Los Rios, Maréchal, Maubert de Gouvest, Pilkington, Smith, Soave, Trimmer, Weisse, Wiesenhuetten.

25 Molé's *Légende dorée ou histoires morales* (Geneva and Paris: Dufour, 1768), for instance, presents lives of saints treated as moral tales.

26 And short "drames."

27 Ducray-Duminil, for example, in his *Soirées de la chaumière,* 4 vols. (Paris: Leprieur, l'an troisième de la République), imagines a rustic pedagogue seeking to give his charges, by means of moral tales, "une éducation naturelle, une éducation fondée sur l'exercice comme sur l'étude et même sur l'expérience."

28 See, in particular, Alice M. Laborde, *L'Œuvre de madame de Genlis* (Paris: Nizet, 1966).

29 Paris: imprimerie de Lambert et Boudouin, 1784, 3 vols.

30 Paris: Libraires associés, 2 vols.

31 Amsterdam and Paris: veuve Duchesne, 1776, and the same address, 1777, 2 vols.

32 *Almanach* . . . . (1776), p. vii.

33 For example, *Lectures pour les enfans ou choix de petits contes également propres à les amuser & leur faire aimer la vertu* (Paris: Delalain, 1775) (Baculard d'Arnaud, Marmontel, Voltaire, Gessner . . .), with a sequel in 1782. Or *Le Mentor vertueux moraliste et bienfaisant* . . . (Paris: Nyon l'aîné, 1788) (extracts from the same writers).

34 *Emile* (Paris: Garnier, 1957), pp. 121-27, 150-53, 186-88, 193-97, 204-9, among other examples. Cf. the notion of the *épreuve* in the Marmontel-

type story, typically brought about by the manipulation of the experience of the characters.

35 *Emile*, pp. 110-15, 210, 211, for instance.

36 Quotations are from the following edition: Paris: Libraires associés, 1782, 3 vols.

37 *Adèle*, p. 436. This devoted mother undertakes a curious form of press censorship when she surreptitiously replaces certain pages of the *Journal de Paris* with moral stories intended for her children. "Adèle & Théodore, dans la bonne-foi, lisoient toutes ces Feuilles avec un plaisir inexprimable . . ." (437).

38 *Veillées*, I, iv.

39 Biographical essay published in *L'Ami des enfants* (Paris: Masson et Yonet, 1829), I, ii.

40 Prospectus for *L'Ami des enfants,* January 1782, p. v.

41 *Théâtre à l'usage des jeunes personnes . . .* , 4 vols. (Paris: M. Lambert et F. J. Baudouin, 1780), I, 6. The specific reference here is to plays, on the acting of which great hopes are founded: "Après avoir joué un rôle rempli de bonté, de délicatesse, de générosité, [l'enfant] rougiroit d'être indocile ou insensible; enfin, il chériroit la vertu qu'il verroit aimable & applaudie" (*Adèle,* p. 204).

42 *Œuvres esthétiques* (Paris: Garnier, 1959), p. 31.

43 "Avis," in *L'Ami des enfants,* no. 12 (1783), p. 142.

44 Preface to Madame Benoist's *Lettres du colonel Talbert . . .* (Amsterdam and Paris, 1767), 4 parts. Cf. the notion of "pratique artificielle" discussed by J. Grieder, "Novel as a Genre," quoted above, pp. 286-88.

45 *Veillées,* I, ix.

46 January 1782, p. viii.

47 *Les Veillées de ma grand'mère . . .* , 2 vols. (Paris: Leprieur, an VII). See the "Discours préliminaire," I, v-xxi, and xix in particular.

48 *Contes moraux de ma grand'tante . . .* , 2 vols. (Paris: Le Prieur, 1807). See the "Prologue," I, 7. (The first edition of this work dates from 1800.)

49 January 1782, p. v.

50 Ibid., p. v.

51 Preface to *L'Introduction familière à la connoissance de la nature* (translated from Mrs. Trimmer's work by Berquin), 2 parts (Paris: au bureau de l'Ami des enfans, 1784), I, 9.

52 *Veillées,* pp. xi-xii.

53 Ibid., p. x. Berquin, among others, makes considerable use of dialogue within his stories, a technique that constitutes a further link with the "moral tale" as conceived by Marmontel.

The First-Person Narrator in the Abbé Prévost's Mémoires d'un homme de qualité

R. A. FRANCIS

One of the achievements of recent scholarship in the eighteenth-century novel has been to destroy any temptation to regard Prévost simply as a one-novel man. Several recent studies, of which that of Jean Sgard is the most important,[1] have directed attention to the scope and interest of the whole of his fictional output, and thus opened up a wide field for investigation in which much remains to be done. One particularly useful exercise would be a comparative study of Prévost's first-person narrators. Since Prévost's main narrative mode is first-person narration, this would be a good way of demonstrating his command of the technical skills of novel-writing, but above all such a study would take us to the heart of the often disturbingly ambiguous world of the Prévost hero. It is, of course, possible to make a general study of Prévost's heroes, extrapolating tendencies common to them all; Odile Kory has done that in her recent book, and it is a valid exercise. But it would underestimate Prévost's skill and range if we were to assume that all his heroes were the same, and I should like to make some tentative steps towards a study dwelling on the differences as well as the similarities. In the brief space available to me, I can attempt nothing more than a few brief illustrations of the kind of question such a study should ask, and therefore I shall discuss one novel only, the *Mémoires d'un homme de qualité*, and within it two narrators only, Renoncour, the *homme de qualité* himself who tells the central story, and Des Grieux, narrator of *Manon Lescaut*. This field, though narrow, will be sufficient to illustrate an approach which can be adopted on a broader front, and it may also help to situate *Manon Lescaut* in the context of the rest of Prévost's *oeuvre*, which is itself a useful exercise with a work so often studied in isolation.

First-person narration is necessarily a subjective way of telling a story, and the first thing we need to know about a narrator is whether he is the kind of person who is capable of telling his story reliably. The essential question here is whether he can give an adequate account of his own nature; is he capable of looking at himself and giving a lucid and honest representation of what he sees? Certainly one of the main problems with Des Grieux is to know how much credence we should give to his account of himself, and the case against it is too well known to need lengthy rehearsal here. He is a young man, writing shortly after the overwhelming events he describes and still too involved in them to view them with analytic detachment. He has done may wrongful deeds in his past, and though he appears to regret them and to want to lead a better life in future, he is reluctant to accept responsibility for his misdeeds and he still quotes all his old arguments justifying them. Above all, we know from his own admission that he is a skilled liar and hypocrite,[2] and we have no guarantee that the story he tells to Renoncour is any more honest than those he has told in the past to people he wants to influence. Scholars disagree in their assessment of his narratorial honesty; Sgard, relatively indulgent, thinks Des Grieux is at his "heure de la vérité," and is sincere at least in that he has convinced himself of the truth of his account, but Jeanne Monty, in her study of Prévost's novels, takes a harsher view of his rhetoric of deception and self-justification which is still too much in evidence.[3] The truth seems to lie between the two extremes. We are probably meant to accept his story as sincere, and indeed correct, in its essential facts; a careful study of prior occasions in the novel when he tells it reveals that he hides facts only when he has a precise reason for doing so, and now that Manon is dead, he has no such reason. Besides, if Prévost had wanted us positively to believe that Des Grieux's story was a pack of lies, he would surely have given some glimpse of what the real facts were, and this he nowhere does. Where we can much more readily doubt Des Grieux's word is in his self-estimation; he puts considerable casuistic and rhetorical ingenuity to the service of his biased and passionate nature, and we are by no means forced to agree with the resultant image of himself which he projects.

Renoncour in comparison seems much more reliable. He writes as an old man living in monastic retirement, detached from his past, and his moral character, though not impeccable, is respectable; he does not need to come to terms with his sins to quite the same extent as Des Grieux. Yet his life has not been totally blameless, and in his attitude to his past errors he shows signs of a smugness and self-approval which is in its way even more disturbing than Des Grieux's specious self-justification. His greatest sin was his defiance of religion by retiring to a living tomb for a year after his wife's death; he admits, looking back on this, that he has done wrong, but at the same time he manages to convey the idea that nevertheless his action was the sign of a forceful and resolute character, and he even hints at special providential protection during this time.[4] Force of character and loyalty to his dead wife are again evident in his resistance to the temptations of Mylady R——, the passionate widow whom he helps to escape from England. Though his resistance succeeds, Renoncour feels guilty that it should have been necessary at all, and when the lady dies in his house in violent circumstances, he blames himself acutely for having been too indulgent to her whims, at the same time casting doubts on the purity of his own motives. This is the only passage in the novel in which he indulges in serious and unresolved self-criticism. Normally, when his actions have turned out badly, he can justify them by saying, for instance, that he had done the best he could in the light of what he knew at the time and would no doubt do the same again. Now, however, a note of self-doubt creeps in which, in view of his habitual self-approval, is a humanizing and even endearing feature. Unfortunately he immediately spoils the effect. In one of the few narratorial interventions in this novel in which the hero as narrator takes a stance recognizably distinct from his stance as protagonist, he says that now, as an old man looking back on this moment of self-doubt, though he is still not sure whether it was justified or not, he is sure that he was right in principle to judge himself severely: "Ce qui me persuade aujourd'hui que je ne dois point me repentir de m'être jugé si sévèrement moi-même, c'est que plus je vois la mort de près, plus je suis satisfait de cette rigueur. Elle augmente la confiance que j'ai au souverain juge, et elle diminue la frayeur aux approches de l'éternité" (III, 86). His very doubts have thus become grounds for a confident belief that he has won his salvation; even here his self-approval triumphs in the end, albeit in an indirect way. His command of casuistic self-justification proves just as great as Des Grieux's, and when we ask which of the two men shows the sharpest awareness of the inadequacies of his past behavior, the answer is arguably Des Grieux. There are good reasons to doubt Des Grieux's word, but there are also good reasons not to accept Renoncour's smugness. Neither man presses his quest for self-discovery far enough to achieve a retrospective narratorial self-judgment substantially differing from the way he judged himself at the time of his actions, and both present images of themselves which the reader is free to examine critically.

Another question we need to ask about the reliability of each narrator is how good an account he can give of his surroundings, and in particular of the other people with whom he comes into contact. This is an area in which any first-person narrator must be able to break free of the essential subjectivity of his genre if his account is to be anything more than an introspective monologue, and Prévost normally gives his narrators some measure of psychological perspicuity. Both Renoncour and Des Grieux show shrewdness in divining the motives and feelings of others. Renoncour, an experienced man of the world, is an effective tutor to young Rosemont because he can read his ward's emotions like an open book, even to the extent of realizing that Rosemont is falling in love with the Spanish beauty Diana before Rosemont realizes it himself.[5] Des Grieux, a younger man, is slower to acquire experience, but he soon becomes a skilled actor who knows enough about the responses of his friends to be able to get what he wants from them with great ease. The perspicuity of both men is, however, limited in one important respect: it does not go far beyond people in the same noble élite as themselves. In this sense the word "noble" is deliberately used ambiguously, to mean both belonging to the aristocracy and being of generous spirit, because in Prévost's novels the two generally go together. Renoncour has the quality of being able to recognize and achieve instant communication with anyone he may chance to meet who is part of this noble élite; it enables him rapidly to achieve an ideally harmonious relationship with Sélima, their union being presented as one of soul mates who could have loved no one else if they had not met,[6] and the same quality draws him to men like Rosemont, Rosambert, and Des Grieux, to whom he serves as confidant; it is obviously a quality very useful in the central narrator of a novel like this which is full of interpolated tales. Des Grieux possesses the same faculty, though it is evident chiefly in the disturbing ability to use it for his own advantage; his calculated and self-interested act of winning M. de T——'s friendship looks little better than a parody of the genuinely disinterested sympathy which unites, say, Renoncour and Rosambert.[7] It begins to break down for both men, however, when they are confronted by baser characters. Renoncour, luckily for him, meets relatively few of them, but his ability to read even Rosemont's mind is severely diminished when Rosemont, constantly thwarted in his love for Nadine, departs from his noble values and sinks into crime.[8] For Des Grieux, living on the fringes of the Paris underworld, the problem is much more acute. There is enough genuine nobility in him to make him ill at ease in the company of swindlers, pimps, and corrupt financiers. He can outwit Tiberge or M. de T——, but he never gets the better of Lescaut or G. M.; they meet him on their own ground, and he is off his.[9] The crucial problem, however, is the one posed by Manon, herself a being of the underworld, whose concept of love is so obviously different from Des Grieux's that she can scarcely be regarded as his soul mate in the way that Sélima is Renoncour's. The degree of credence we are prepared to give to Des Grieux will clearly depend greatly on whether we feel that he has successfully understood Manon. This is of course a familiar problem. The main argument against him is that on numerous occasions he shows that even when he can predict her reactions, he has little penetration of the motives behind them.[10] The main argument for him is that if Manon's conversion to virtuous love on the way to America is genuine—and the case in favor of it is strong[11]—this does much to vindicate Des Grieux's belief that all along there has been something in Manon superior to the sum total of her acts. I do not claim to solve the problem in this paper; my purpose is simply to compare the reliability of Des Grieux's and Renoncour's assessment of other people and to conclude that their strengths and weaknesses are very much the same. If Des Grieux's judgments seem less reliable, it is mainly because of his youth and the company he keeps.

Sharper differences between the two men begin to emerge when we ask whether, over the course of the work, they remain consistent with themselves, and if they do not, whether the inconsistencies can be accounted for by a psychologically plausible evolution. From this point of view, Des Grieux is vastly superior to Renoncour as a literary creation. Renoncour's career falls into three distinct phases corresponding to different moments in the work's composition. First he is a passionate suffering youth, the main protagonist of the adventures he describes; next he is an elderly but indulgent tutor to Rosemont, reporting Rosemont's adventures rather than his own; finally he is the strict guardian of Nadine, protecting her honor against Rosemont's advances and again involved in his own passionate adventures. Some personality features are present in all three stages, and they help to hold the whole novel together, for instance his force of character in adhering to a decision once taken, his indulgent urbanity, and his contantly thwarted desire for a calm life of retirement. There are, however, considerable differences as well, particularly in his attitude to love. Despite the obvious analogies between his love for Sélima and Rosemont's for Diana and then Nadine, Renoncour never looks upon Rosemont's loves as the union of soul mates in the same way as he looks upon his own. When he discusses the effects of love in a noble soul, there is a difference between the optimistic views he expresses at the beginning of his tutorship of Rosemont and his pessimistic views at the end of it.[12] Such differences are not implausible; people do judge their own love affairs more indulgently than those of others, people do become less indulgent with age to lovers' aberrations, and above all Rosemont has given Renoncour ample grounds to doubt his earlier optimism. In Renoncour there are indeed the makings of an interesting psychological study of a passionate but well-intentioned youth gradually becoming world-weary and disillusioned through contact with harsh reality. This, however, is not really how Prévost develops the character. He is writing a sensational adventure story as much as a psychological novel, and the events he chooses to emphasize are those of intrinsic picturesque value or those which prepare a pathetic climax, not necessarily those with most psychological significance. Little is done to present a Renoncour in evolution, or to bridge the gaps between the different stages of his life. There is some evidence that in the interpolated tales added in 1756, Prévost was aware of this failing and was attempting to catch Renoncour at moments of transition; the story of the consul du Levant shows him moving towards his retirement from the world, and that of the comte his uncle prepares us for the change from indulgent tutor to strict guardian. But this is done at the cost of adding yet more episodes to an already over-episodic work. With Des Grieux, in a shorter space, Prévost achieves much more. The relative concentration of the *histoire* imposes an extra degree of formal discipline on him, a discipline which can be seen in the way he uses the repetitive nature of his plot. The story is basically a series of episodes in which rich men try to buy Manon away from Des Grieux, but the repetition of this pattern leads not to monotony but rather to an awareness of evolution in the characters. The response of Des Grieux to the threat, and of Manon to the temptation, is different on each occasion, and through these responses we can trace the slow and uneven progress of both characters from youthful inexperience, through corruption and depravity, to a more mature love based on selflessness and sacrifice. Patterns of evolution can similarly be traced in many minor aspects of Des Grieux's character. If we look at such things as his attempts to describe Manon, he attitude to borrowing money, his ability to control his emotions on receiving bad news, each of which recurs several times in the story, we will find clear evolutionary processes; his understanding of Manon grows, his scruples about borrowing fade, his self-control increases. It is in following through patterns such as these that we can appreciate the subtlety of Prévost's art at its best, and its presence in the portrayal of Des Grieux contributes in no small measure to the durability of *Manon Lescaut* as a work of art.

The final question inevitably raised about Prévost's narrators is the hardest to answer. This is what degree of moral approval we are prepared to give them; when they justify their actions, should we believe them? Prévost offers no clear cut answers to this question, and all I shall attempt to do is to suggest a way of analyzing the dilemmas raised which may at least help us to understand the problem. Prévost's heroes may conveniently be seen as oscillating between three overlapping but conflicting codes of behavior: first, the code of religion, demanding obedience to ecclesiastical authority, strict standards of virtue, and no sexual relationships outside marriage; second, the code of honor, more worldly and lax in moral standards but demanding conformity with accepted aristocratic patterns of behavior, esteeming loyalty and bravery and condemning the *mésalliance*; and finally what we may term the code of sensibility, by which a man capable of strong emotions, and in particular love, is a superior being worthy of esteem and sympathy even when his actions contravene the other two codes. If we examine Renoncour and Des Grieux in their position vis-à-vis these codes, we shall find considerable differences of emphasis. Renoncour is certainly tempted by the code of sensibility; his love for Sélima is strong, and though he is fortunate enough to be able to woo and win her without transgressing against virtue or honor, he does violate the religious code by living with her before they can be married, and again after her death, when he tries to perpetuate her memory by his quasi-suicidal living entombment. But the code of sensibility does not dominate his behavior; he constantly reiterates that worldly affairs should be governed by virtue and honor, and being a strong man, he can discipline himself to live according to their dictates. This explains why he eventually emerges from his living entombment and why in later years he opposes the love between Rosemont and Nadine despite his instinctive sympathy with the lovers. [13] Unfortunately, however, the codes of honor and religion do not always coincide, and they pull him in different ways. His dominant emotion is a desire to retire from the world, inspired partly by a genuine religious sense that the next world is more important than this, and partly by a wish to perpetuate his memories of Sélima; in this the codes of religion and sensibility work together. [14] But the code of honor obliges him to accept certain worldly responsibilities of which he would rather be free. This is why his attitude towards Rosemont and Nadine is so problematic, for their plan to marry, though perfectly acceptable under the codes of religion and sensibility, is not permitted by the code of honor, as it is a *mésalliance*, and Renoncour's responsibility to Rosemont's father makes it impossible for him to condone it. [15] Though he respects the code of honor, he would much prefer a religious retreat in which he could forget such disturbing matters.

Where Renoncour prefers religion to honor, Des Grieux seems to prefer honor to religion. Despite his bad behavior, he delays his rupture with his family to the last possible moment, and many of his reactions show the proud fiery spirit one expects of a young aristocrat. He is much less respectful towards religion. He should be seen as a blasphemer rather than a heretic, as he never actually denies that God exists or has authority over him even to punish, but he disagrees with orthodox notions of divine grace which Renoncour accepts,[16] and at times he speaks of his love for Manon in a blatantly disrespectful parody of religious language.[17] But it is not the clash between honor and religion which worries Des Grieux; it is the clash between both codes and the code of sensibility, for Des Grieux has done what Renoncour dared not do and allowed his behavior to be completely dominated by this third code. Whenever traditional values come into conflict with his love for Manon, he lucidly sacrifices the former to the latter at whatever cost to his scruples. He is also remarkably good at picking up Renoncour's timid statements in favor of the code of sensibility and exaggerating them. For Renoncour, "l'amour ne nous rend point criminels" (I, 8); for Des Grieux, "l'amour est une passion innocente" (*ML*, p. 72). For Renoncour, passion is permitted by Providence and can be controlled by reason and virtue; for Des Grieux, passion is imposed by a hostile fate and cannot be so controlled.[18] Renoncour seems to think in terms of a noble élite of refined sensitive souls, but it is Des Grieux who actually states that superior sensitivity is the sign of "les personnes d'un caractère plus noble" (*ML*, p. 81). It seems that Renoncour and Des Grieux face the same problems with similar instincts, but Des Grieux, by his own admission the weaker character, has surrendered to the indiscipline accompanying the code of sensibility far more than Renoncour could ever do.

In the light of this difference, we may perhaps look with fresh eyes at the much discussed "Avis de l'auteur" which precedes *Manon Lescaut*. I do not pretend to solve the problem of whether this text is a sincere and accurate expression of Prévost's purpose in writing *Manon Lescaut*, but it does make sense if it is taken not as a pronouncement of Prévost but as a pronouncement of Renoncour. Dr. Mylne, in her study of *Manon Lescaut*, plays down the value of this text by pointing out, perfectly rightly, that Renoncour's harsh judgment of Des Grieux in the "Avis" contradicts his indulgent treatment of him on their first meeting.[19] But surely this is typical of Renoncour, who is always wavering between indulgence towards passionate young men and harsh condemnation of their errors; he often accuses himself of being overindulgent, and his treatment of Rosemont certainly wavers between indulgence and harshness.[20] It would be characteristic of Renoncour to offer Des Grieux generous help and then, after listening to his story, be shocked and angry, not merely at Des Grieux's actions, but above all at his insidious perversion of Renoncour's own ideas, which makes him a much more dangerous threat than any ordinary wrongdoer to Renoncour's unstably smug equilibrium: The Avis is distinctly reminiscent of Renoncour's farewell oration to Rosemont; all he can produce in face of these two young men drifting uncontrollably into crime for love is impotent abstract moralizing.[21] In the context of the novel as a whole, Des Grieux's story has the effect of challenging and undermining the monastic complacency of the aged Renoncour, of showing that questions which he seemed to have solved, or rather to have opted out of, are in fact not solved at all.

This inevitably raises the problem of whether *Manon* is essentially an independent entity or merely a part of the *Mémoires*. My own view is that, though it would be a gross impoverishment of *Manon* to claim that everything about it could be explained by some role in the *Mémoires*, it does nevertheless fulfull a function in the overall structure, as indeed do many of the other interpolated tales. The problem is, however, too large to be more than hinted at in this essay, which, being a very brief foray into a huge field, has inevitably and deliberately raised more problems than it has solved. One general conclusion seems to impose itself, however, and that is that though there is a strong family resemblance between the two heroes discussed, there is enough difference between them to allow Prévost variety in his use of the techniques of first-person narration, and to allow scope to investigate a central moral dilemma from more than one angle. When the comparison is extended to the whole body of Prévost's narrators, it reveals a fictional world of great richness and psychological diversity.

NOTES

1 J. Sgard, *Prévost romancier* (Paris: Corti, 1968). Other worthwhile studies include J. R. Monty, *Les Romans de l'abbé Prévost*, Studies on Voltaire and the Eighteenth Century, no. 78 (Geneva: Institut et musée Voltaire, 1970); O. A. Kory, *Subjectivity and Sensitivity in the Novels of the Abbé Prévost*, (Paris: Didier, 1972); and V. Mylne, *Prévost: Manon Lescaut* (London: Arnold, 1972). There is useful discussion of Prévost in V. Mylne, *The Eighteenth-Century French Novel* (Manchester: Manchester University Press, 1965), and P. R. Stewart, *Imitation and Illusion in the French Memoir-Novel, 1700-1750* (New Haven: Yale University Press, 1969).

2 *Manon Lescaut*, ed. F. Deloffre and R. Picard (Paris: Garnier, 1965), p. 83. Future references to this edition will follow the quotation in brackets and be indicated by the abbreviation *ML*. References to the rest of the *Mémoires d'un homme de qualité* will be the appropriate volume number of the Slatkine Reprints edition of Prévost's *Oeuvres choisies* (Paris, 1810-16), vols. I-III. Spellings from this edition have been modernized.

3 See Sgard, *Prévost*, pp. 300, 305, and Monty, *Romans*, p. 51.

4 "C'est le ciel, sans doute, qui prit soin de me conserver la santé du corps, pour m'ouvrir un jour les yeux sur le danger de mon âme. . . . Chacun plaignit mon malheur, en même temps qu'on admirait ma résolution" (I, 282).

5 "Je craignis tout d'un coup, en le voyant, ce qui ne manqua pas d'arriver; c'est-à-dire qu'elle ne fît trop d'impression sur le coeur du marquis, et que, vif comme il était, une première passion, inspirée par une personne de ce mérite, ne lui fît oublier son devoir, et ne me préparât mille chagrins" (I, 419).

6 "Je ne saurais douter . . . qu'il n'y ait des coeurs formés les uns pour les autres, et qui n'aimeraient jamais rien s'ils n'étaient aussi heureux pour se rencontrer" (I, 196).

7 See *ML*, p. 100 and I, 56-59.

8 Renoncour knows at the beginning of Rosemont's love for Nadine that the affair will make him "plus difficile à conduire" (II, 263). Rosemont prevents Renoncour from forestalling his abduction of Nadine by lying to him "d'un air de sincérité dont je fus la dupe" (III, 97), and again succeeds in duping him when Renoncour shows him an edifying letter from Nadine from which Rosemont retains, not the sentiments, but merely the address at the head of the letter. Renoncour is powerless on these occasions against Rosemont's criminal scheming.

9 The only occasion on which Des Grieux fails in his favourite device of disarming his enemies by charm is when G. M. has arrested the lovers for kidnapping his son. G. M., a hard-headed *parvenu,* is immune to Des Grieux's aristocratic good manners, and has already found out facts about Des Grieux's plan to rob him which Des Grieux has hopefully assumed he does not know (*ML*, p. 156).

10 See, above all, his plea to prevent her from spending the night with young G. M. (*ML*, pp. 140-48); he correctly assumes that he will be able to stop her if he can reach her and plead with her, but he is so taken aback by her total absence of any sense of guilt that he completely loses the moral advantage in his debate with her.

11 It is true that Manon is a proven recidivist, that she dies before she is faced with any real temptation, and that it would obviously suit Des Grieux to be able to believe in her virtue; but there is nothing psychologically implausible about Manon's evolution, her actions seem to conform to her claim to be a reformed character, and above all Prévost has given no concrete evidence seriously contradicting Des Grieux's version.

12 Renoncour is not alarmed when he discovers that Rosemont's character is passionate, on the grounds that "la grandeur de l'âme suppose de grandes passions; l'importance est de les tourner à la vertu" (I, 352). He is convinced that the excesses of love can be rationally resisted (I, 362), and that the way to do so is by means of "des principes solides de vérité et de sagesse" (I, 389). But when he takes his leave of Rosemont at the end of his tutorship, he claims that though love can raise an "âme commune" above its "bassesse naturelle, . . . une grande âme se ravale et s'avilit par les passions amoureuses" (III, 80). Renoncour is perhaps overstating his case here in order to impress Rosemont, but on the face of it his opinions have diametrically reversed.

13 "J'étais attendri de leurs peines, et j'aurais souhaité de pouvoir les rendre heureux au prix de mon sang; mais c'était une chose absolument impossible" (III, 111).

14 During his first retirement, he tells us that "le soin de mon salut et le tendre souvenir de ma chère épouse faisaient mon unique occupation" (I, 341).

15 Renoncour predicts the reaction of Rosemont's father with complete accuracy; the Duc refuses Rosemont permission to marry on exactly the grounds anticipated by Renoncour. Compare III, 20 and III, 125.

16 Compare "S'il est vrai que les secours célestes sont à tous moment d'une force égale à celle des passions, qu'on m'explique donc par quel funeste ascendant on se trouve emporté tout d'un coup loin de son devoir, sans

se trouver capable de la moindre résistance, et sans ressentir le moindre remords" (*ML,* pp. 42-43), with "Le secours du Ciel n'est jamais refusé quand on le demande, et qu'il est toujours proportionné à nos peines et à nos besoins" (II, 70).

17 See *ML*, pp. 46, 91.

18 Compare "La Providence les permit [i.e., les passions] pour des fins qui ne nous sont pas toujours connus, mais qui sont toujours dignes d'elle" (I, 8) and "La sagesse veut . . . qu'on examine si la religion et l'honneur ne trouvent rien qui les blesse dans ces commencements d'affection. . . . Les passions qui ont une si belle source conservent ordinairement la noblesse et la pureté de leur origine" (I, 362), with "Je la lui représentai [i.e., ma passion] comme un de ces coups particuliers du destin qui s'attache à la ruine d'un misérable, et dont il est aussi impossible à la vertu de se défendre qu'il l'a été à la sagesse de les prévoir" (*ML*, p. 59).

19 V. Mylne, *Prévost: Manon Lescaut*, p. 17.

20 Note also Renoncour's tolerance in Rosemont's entourage of Brissant, like Des Grieux a youth of respectable origins down on his luck after a checkered career. He frequently condemns Brissant's role as Rosemont's *âme damnée* and threatens to dismiss the man, but never actually does so.

21 At the end of Renoncour's harangue to Rosemont, "le marquis écouta cette morale avec sa docilité ordinaire; mais, malgré mes déclamations contre l'amour, il me pria de lui apprendre, avant que de le quitter, ce que M. Le duc pensait de son inclination pour ma nièce. Cette question me fit juger que je devais attendre peu de fruit de mon discours" (III, 81). Renoncour's attempts to preach have clearly had no effect on the young man.

"Spectatress of the Mischief Which She Made": Tragic Woman Perceived and Perceiver

CYNTHIA S. MATLACK

Critics have repeatedly associated femininity with the pathetic in their efforts to describe and account for essential alterations in the tone and structure of tragedy that occurred in the last third of the seventeenth century. The argument is commonplace that as tragedy shifted away from the heroic or "masculine" during the Restoration it stressed increasingly the pathetic or "feminine,"[1] that as tragic grandeur and greatness diminished, pathetic elements merged and gradually supplanted the earlier tradition as artistic form responded to social and aesthetic evolution.[2] In historical dramas in which "feminine interests dominate,"[3] John Banks and other writers of "she-tragedies" focused on the plights of noble figures like Mary Queen of Scots, Anne Boleyn, Lady Jane Grey, and Queen Elizabeth, moving tragedy further in the direction of the pathetic.

The change in dramatic emphasis from "admiration" and tragic catharsis to pathos was accompanied by a new aesthetic tenor. Nicholas Rowe, a later playwright who "turned to the feminine view for tragic themes,"[4] wrote that the audience "should be struck with Terrour but always Conclude and go away with Pity, a sort of regret proceeding from good nature."[5] Like Rowe, Joseph Addison anticipated the increasingly intuitive responses of later critics like Hutcheson, Lillo, Home, and Burke when he wrote that "Terrour and Commiseration leave a pleasing Anguish in the Mind . . . much more lasting and delightful than any little transient Starts of Joy and Satisfaction."[6]

The relationship of "split-catharsis,"[7] or the aesthetic of pleasing pain, to dramatic structures becomes much clearer if we recognize that the principles which governed the action of pathetic tragedy were generated by certain assumptions about social organization that were held by both playwrights and audiences. A familiar premise was expressed by John Dennis when he wrote that "Passion is the Occasion of infinitely more Disorder in the world than Malice, . . . [and] Providence which governs the World should punish Men for indulging their Passion."[8] In pathetic tragedy, the passion which is to be most feared and exalted is explicitly sexual. Consummated love is always presented in the context of Dennis' prescript for "Disorder in the world," for in the plots, malice, ambition, and political intrigue are the disastrous aftermath of licentious dalliance and rape.

In pathetic tragedies most frequently performed during the eighteenth century in England, two persistent corollaries severely limited the playwrights' options for developing plot and character.[9] First, fathers (sometimes husbands) were totemic figures who transmitted absolute codes of public and private demeanor to wives and children. Second, because the social legitimacy of sexual expression was decreed by patresfamilias, female characters were polarized as virtuous and sensuous, or apostate and angelic. Accordingly, women in pathetic tragedy were not so much portraits drawn after a long and complex tradition as they were pencil sketches of two identifiable morphemes in the theatrical language of the period,[10] and their public sexual rhetoric reveals characteristics endemic to the age's ethos. Both dialogue and action reminded the audience of its communal possession of a feminine ideal and an inherited code of conduct. Inevitably, sexual excess (or even the threat of it) became the crucial symbolic action determining the development of the plot because it challenged the propriety of familial and contractual social obligations. Eroticism in Rowe's "she-tragedies" evinced the growing tendency to use sexual misconduct for didactic purposes in the theater.

The recurrent association of unlicensed love relationships with war and civil dissension, in pathetic tragedy, suggests the true psychological impetus for its didacticism. The political danger of women's erotic appeal can be seen in the extremely high incidence of metaphors describing the enslavement of the males by love. Because unrestrained "Passion" led to private and public "Disorder," at the level of ritual, females who were passion's vehicle were treated as the bringers of death, "desolation, horror, blood, and ruin" to the state.[11] The scenes in which these corrupted vessels compose themselves for death reveal them less as individuals than as transmitters of apocalyptic abstractions. Their destruction produces the allegorical tableaux of compulsive ritual, ultimately of iconographic performance. As scapegoats, female heteroclites were inevitably sacrificed to purge threatening symptoms of disease and pollution from society. No one seems to have noticed that their egregiously prolonged death scenes provide an erotic analogy to secular martyrdom which encourages conversion of the libidinous to the benevolent. Audiences enjoyed the spectacle of agony because it was presented for the purpose of eliciting "Pity," that "regret proceeding from good nature" for women who had been unfortunate enough to "swerve from virtue's rule, / . . . And in the softer paths of pleasure stray."[12]

The difference between Rowe's use of sensuality for didactic purposes and the sensational posturings of women by earlier Restoration playwrights is apparent in dialogue and stage directions. Often enough, in earlier tragedies, recently raped women had appeared on stage with "Hair dishevel'd, and mouth Bloody, as Ravish'd," "with torn Robes and hair," "swoln Eyes," or "Wounded in . . . Bosome, and Arms."[13] Rowe's greatly admired precursor, Otway, had both intensified and refined the techniques of lesser writers, but the appeal of Belvidera "titillating herself with thoughts of death"[14] was later identified as erotic by commentators as different as Jeremy Collier and Lord Byron, whose famous remark about "that maudlin bitch of chaste lewdness" was incisive.[15] On the other hand, in Rowe's work, passion and sensuality were personified and allegorized so that the salacious served to support the existing code of sexual conduct. Jane Shore laments:

> My form, alas! has long forgot to please.
> The scene of beauty and delight has changed:
> No roses bloom upon my fading cheek,
> Nor laughing graces wanton in my eyes;
> But haggard grief, lean-looking, sallow care,
> And pining discontent, a rueful train,
> Dwell on my brow, all hideous and forlorn.
> (I.ii.115-21.20)

Yet, even though Rowe's scenes present conventionalized treatment of the aftermath of sexual experience, his work at its best shows a new vitality, and in significant ways his artistic energy anticipates that of the romantic painter Benjamin Robert Haydon, who rejoiced when he found a miserable woman who had just witnessed her son being torn to shreds by a horse because it would enable him to make the mother's agony more vivid in his painting *Solomon.*[16] And as painters exult in unusual poses, the stylized posturing of Rowe's pathetic heroines in their moments of anguish tends to subordinate language to the pictorially salacious as its iconographic effectiveness increases.

Eugene Hnatko has argued that eighteenth-century tragedy "died because . . . it seems so admirably suited to what the age saw as the purpose of all writing–moral instruction–and the fulfilling of that purpose was inimical to the very nature of the genre in that it led to a simple poetic justice which allowed no room for tragic questioning or cosmic resolution."[17] In a somewhat similar vein, Wallace Jackson has emphasized what he calls the "straightened conception of allowable action" in tragedy beginning with *All for Love*, and asserted that the "conflicting claims of love and duty in these plays causes the agon to be less a debate than a revelation of the inevitable consequences" of error, that the "dramatic personae . . . do not generate value but merely signify it and act as its transmitting agents."[18] Both Hnatko's and Jackson's observations are substantially correct. Yet, an interesting development appears in Rowe's work in that his heroines and sometimes his villainesses cry out vigorously against the injustices of a social code that they feel victimizes them. Two remarkable speeches, the first Calista's and the second Jane Shore's, reveal that the restless discontent of George Lillo's Millwood, as she faces the scaffold, had been anticipated by Rowe:

> How hard is the condition of our sex,
> Through ev'ry state of life the slaves of man!
> In all the dear, delightful days of youth
> A rigid father dictates to our wills,
> And deals out pleasure with a scanty hand;
> To his, the tyrant husband's reign succeeds;
> Proud with opinion of superior reason,
> He holds domestic business and devotion
> All we are capable to know, and shuts us,
> Like cloistered idiots, from the world's acquaintance
> And all the joys of freedom; wherefore are we
> Born with high souls but to assert ourselves,
> Shake off this vile obedience they exact,
> And claim an equal empire o'er the world?
> (3.39–52.34)

Jane Shore shares Calista's exasperation with the repressive treatment of women, but her statement is more specifically directed against the double standard of sexual behavior:

> Mark by what partial justice we are judged;
> Such is the fate unhappy women find,
> And such the curse entailed upon our kind,
> That man, the lawless libertine, may rove

Free and unquestioned through the wilds of love;
While woman, sense and nature's easy fool,
If poor, weak woman swerve from virtue's rule,
If, strongly charmed, she leave the thorny way,
And in the softer paths of pleasure stray;
Ruin ensues, reproach and endless shame,
And one false step entirely damns her fame.
(1.2.180–90.22)

At such moments, Rowe's heroines achieve a worldly vitality that enables them to transcend mere existence as static one-dimensional figures sketched into an allegorical scene.[19] The presence of similar sentiments, however teasingly presented in Rowe's epilogues, indicates his sensitivity to undercurrents of social dissatisfaction.

It is significant, I think, that the most frequently performed pathetic tragedies in England in the eighteenth century include erotic scenes in which the doomed women embrace their imminent deaths by willingly presenting their bosoms to the phallic dagger of authority. At an elemental level of human semiotic exchange, this act of submission produces a transformation as the breasts which nourish progeny become the sign of domesticated eroticism. In *Venice Preserved*, Belvidera lovingly "leaps upon [Jaffeir's] neck and kisses him" while he menacingly brandishes a weapon over her,[20] and Imoinda lays her Hand on [Oronooko's], in order to give the death blow" to herself.[21] In *Tamerlane*, the importance of paternal inheritance and filial obligation is emphasized when Selima literally "embraces" the father who threatens to stab her:

Plunge the Poignard deep! [*She embraces him.*
The Life my Father gave shall hear his Summons,
And issue at the Wound–Start not, to feel
My Heart's warm Blood gush out upon your Hands,
Since from your Spring I drew the Purple Stream,
And I must pay it back, if you demand it.[22]

The wedding of eroticism to didacticism suggests an unrecognized cause for the prolonged popularity of pathetic tragedy and its appeal to both male and female members of the audience.[23] It also provides an explanation of its relationship to other dramatic structures and the subsequent development of melodrama and farce. If the moral values of tragedy and comedy in the period are sometimes at odds, the intensification of sexual action and imagery is central to both forms, and suggests that the desperate morality of the one mirrors the compacency of the other.

The evidence is overwhelming that violation of a father's authority through illegitimate sexual liaison is the major factor that determines the plot of pathetic tragedies.[24] The crucial characteristic is the response of the women to their predicament. At the extremity of their suffering, females who have transgressed sexually invariably beg forgiveness of the males whose honor they have discredited. Their language expresses flawed filial obligation by countering images of ripe sexuality (labor and birth) with those of rotten disease (contagion and death). In *The Fair Penitent*, at the conclusion of this agonized farewell, Calista kills herself:

> And dost thou bear me yet, thou patient earth?
> Dost thou not labor with my murd'rous weight? . . .
> For I am all contagion, death, and ruin,
> And nature sickens at me; rest, thou world,
> This parricide shall be thy plague no more;
> Thus, thus I set thee free. [*Stabs herself.*
> (V.i.228-34.68)

Sexually threatened virgins repeatedly call upon the shades of Roman paragons of virtue to give them the courage to commit suicide so that they may escape with honor intact: "*Lucrece* could bleed, and *Porcia* swallow fire" (*Tamerlane*, IV.i.89.76). Even a menace to sexual honor is often potent enough to make a woman's death inevitable.

In his discussion of drama as social history, John Loftis has reminded us that "Both comedy and tragedy turn on themes that represent judgments about contemporary life" and of the need to formulate the "social and political assumptions of the dramatists, collectively and individually, which conditioned their interpretation of what they saw about them."[25] It is not surprising, then, that the paternal monetary endowment accompanying virginity and chastity is irretrievably forfeited by the woman who rashly yields to passion. In *The Tragedy of Jane Shore*, Alicia refers to herself as "bankrupt" because she has "set at nought [her] noble birth" (II. 62.25). In that most popular of all pathetic tragedies, *The Orphan; or, The Unhappy Marriage*, Monimia throws herself on her knees when she is rudely pressed for sexual favors by the aroused Polydore. Her language evinces her understanding of the nexus between chastity and cash, for no woman evades the consequences of surrender in these plays:

> Here on my knees by heav'ns blest pow'r I swear, [*Kneels*.
> If you persist, I never henceforth will see you,
> But rather wander through the world a beggar,
> And live on sordid scraps at proud mens doors;
> For though to Fortune lost, I'll still inherit
> My Mothers Vertues, and my Fathers Honour.[26]

Sexual violation or misconduct leads to total loss. The threat of disinheritance is so overwhelming that Monimia, Belvidera, Alicia, Calista, and a host of others express their anxiety in images of barrenness, exile, desert, poverty, hardness, starvation, cold, death, and hellfire.

However, these women are rarely alone in their downfall. Civil dissension and war are frequent consequences of the bewitching power of their sexual charms. In *The Fair Penitent*, Sciolto blames Calista for dividing the senate and creating an "afflicted state . . . fierce factions . . . and anarchy." He points an accusing finger at his daughter:

> Amidst the general wreck, see where she stands,
> Like Helen in the night when Troy was sacked,
> Spectatress of the mischief which she made.
> (V.47-55.62)

In *Venice Preserved*, Pierre's motivation for joining a bloody plot to overthrow the senate results from his bitterness at Aquilina's infidelity with Antony, a rich, old, lecherous senator, and the Venetian state itself is repeatedly identified figuratively as "the Adriatic whore, / Dressed in her flames" (II.iii.96-97.31). Conversely, the chaste woman typically inspires patriotic activity, although, as Aboin tells Oronooko, there is danger if political allegiance does not take first priority in a man's choice of actions.[27]

The polarization of female roles seems to have been developed according to a set of criteria both ancient and persistent which limited the social function of middle-class women to pacifying the presumedly instinctive brutishness of males. Jaffeir's response to Belvidera is typical. In rapturous admiration, he exclaims "Oh Woman! lovely Woman! Nature made thee / To temper Man: we had been brutes without you" (*Venice Preserved*, I.i.336–37.18).

The utterly self-effacing, loyal wife, although somewhat less dramatically exciting, often appears for the purpose of offsetting the female protagonist's excesses. Lavinia cannot, it seems, even understand Calista's temptation:

> If women are such things,
> How was I formed so different from my sex?
> My little heart is satisfied with you;
> You take up all her room, as in a cottage . . .
> Where the good man, proud of his hospitality,
> Yields all his homely dwelling to his guest, . . .
> (*The Fair Penitent*, I.394-400.20)

Since the chaste woman is identified with virtue and patriotic activity and her power is gained through the conventional means of marriage, she is properly a comic protagonist, and in tragedy her sexual power is not emphasized.

The natural innocence of ladies usually is suggested by the language of romantic compliment drawn from a religious tradition which deified them as soothing vessels of moral perfection. Nicholas Rowe expressed the increasingly conventional idea that immoderate passion is foreign to virtuous women in his "Dedication" of *The Fair Penitent* to the Duchess of Ormonde: ". . . if I have in any way succeeded . . . it has been in describing those violent passions which have been always strangers to so happy a temper and so noble and so exalted a virtue as your Grace is mistress of" (p. 3). "Fair as the Fame of Vertue, and yet Chaste / As its cold Precepts" (*Tamerlane*, I.i.225-26.29), the social ideal of women reveals them as beatifically serene and above the emotional rants, possessiveness, and the "devil which undoes [the] sex," jealousy (*The Tragedy of Jane Shore*, II.83.25). Like the successful women in sentimental comedy, they control their "innocent" emotions. The special pathos and even poignancy of the "fallen" women in pathetic tragedies derives from their own agonized recognition that they have been cast out of the paradise of honorable family life.

Characters who deny the Edenic vision of ideal womankind are evil without exception. The villains, abductors, and seducers are not portrayed as "Men of Sense," but rather as men of passion who indulge themselves in mysogynistic rants against women's hypocrisies, inconstancies, wiles, painted outsides, and childish mentalities (e.g., Polydore, successful perpetrator of the bed trick, in *The Orphan*; Bajazet, defeated Emperor of the Turks, murderer and rapist, in *Tamerlane*; Richard, Duke of Gloster, and Lord Hastings, the one a usurper of a throne and murderer, the other a seducer and failed rapist, in *The Tragedy of Jane Shore*; and Lothario, the seducer of Calista, in *The Fair Penitent*).

Dramatists have always known that virginity and chastity as permanent conditions are theatrically less appealing to audiences than as preludial or postludial states. The writers of the dozen or so most frequently acted pathetic tragedies in the eighteenth century (Otway, Rowe, Southerne, Congreve, Philips, Dryden, Lillo, and Banks)[28] knew that even a virtuous woman can yield to "ecstacies" that are, alas, "too fierce to last forever" (*The Fair Penitent*, I.158-61.13). But to be worthy of the benevolent pity of spectators of her plight, the lady must be shown not to be responsible for her actions. (She is often the victim of a bed trick.)

The circumstances of her seduction are described for the audience's titillation in glowing erotic language, and although seduction or secret marriage makes these women only technically culpable, their tragic fate has been irrevocably determined by the betrayal of their paternal inheritance. By the end of the fifth act, even though they have been seduced and are therefore only guilty by default, their protests against the injustice of their moral condemnation have dwindled into absolute acceptance of the religious and social codes of allowable sexual expression, and they die in sensual agony, pleading to their fathers, husbands, and heaven for mercy.

NOTES

1 "[Otway and Banks] had reduced Elizabethan masculinity to a late seventeenth-century effeminacy." Donald B. Clark, "An Eighteenth-Century Adaptation of Massinger," *MLQ,* 13 (1952), 247. "Banks goes farther than Lee in downgrading honor, the more masculine of the perpetual antitheses. . . . In Banks' she-tragedies . . . women are the principals and the men are womanish." Eric Rothstein, *Restoration Tragedy: Form and the Process of Change* (Madison: University of Wisconsin Press, 1967), p. 97. "In Rowe . . . Dryden's manly thunder is frequently exchanged for a hysterical complaining: the whole tone is shriller and more feminine." J. R. Sutherland, ed., *Three Plays by Nicholas Rowe* (London: Scholartis Press, 1929), p. 21.

2 Eugene M. Waith analyzes the place of "tears" in seventeenth-century dramatic theory. He suggests that "it is a mistake to associate a tearful response exclusively with the unheroic . . . ." "Tears of Magnanimity in Otway and Racine," in *French and English Drama of the Seventeenth Century: Papers Read at a Clark Library Seminar March 13, 1971*, introduction by Henry Goodman (Los Angeles: Clark Memorial Library, 1972), p. 19. Cf. Rothstein, pp. 78-80.

3 See G. Wilson Knight, *The Golden Labyrinth: A Study of British Drama* (London: Phoenix House, 1962), p. 167.

4 The phrase is used by Malcolm Goldstein, "Pathos and Personality in the Tragedies of Nicholas Rowe," in *English Writers of the Eighteenth Century,* ed. John H. Middendorf (New York: Columbia University Press, 1971), p. 173.

5 Epistle Dedicatory to *The Ambitious Step-Mother*, 2nd ed. (London, 1702), p. [A4].

6 *The Spectator*, ed. Donald F. Bond, 5 vols. (Oxford: Clarendon Press, 1965), I, 169 (no. 40, April 16, 1711).

7 See *British Dramatists from Dryden to Sheridan,* ed. George H. Nettleton and Arthur E. Case, rev. George Winchester Stone, Jr. (New York: Houghton Mifflin Company, 1969), p. [501].

8 "To the Spectator, Upon his Paper on the 16th of April [1711]," in *The Critical Works*, ed. E. N. Hooker (Baltimore: Johns Hopkins University Press. 1939, 1941), II, 20.

9 I have drawn upon a list of the most frequently performed tragedies between 1702 and 1776 given by Emmett L. Avery, "The Popularity of *The Mourning Bride* in the London Theaters in the Eighteenth Century," *Research Studies of the State College of Washington*, 9 (1941), 115-16. In order of relative popularity the plays were Otway, *The Orphan* (1680), Rowe, *Tamerlane* (1701), Rowe, *The Tragedy of Jane Shore* (1714), Southerne, *Oronooko* (1695), Otway, *Venice Preserved* (1682), Rowe, *The Fair Penitent* (1703), Addison, *Cato* (1713), Congreve, *The Mourning Bride* (1697), Philips, *The Distrest Mother* (1712), Lillo, *The London Merchant* (1731), Banks, *The Unhappy Favorite* (1681), and Dryden, *All for Love* (1677). The acting histories of these plays can be traced in *The London Stage 1660-1800: A Calendar of Plays . . .* , 5 parts, ed. William Van Lennep, Emmett L. Avery, Arthur H. Scouten, George Winchester Stone, Jr., Charles Beecher Hogan (Carbondale: Southern Illinois University Press, 1960–68). The quantitative data now accessible through *The London Stage* Information Bank can improve the accuracy of Avery's list of numbers of performances. But although precise counts are desirable, my argument does not depend upon them any more than it does upon historical circumstances. However, the fact that *Tamerlane* and *Cato* were acted for political purposes or that *The London Merchant* was traditionally performed at Christmas and Easter may tend to strengthen it.

10 Certainly, the parameters of plot, language, and characterization as set by patriarchal precepts may have been abetted by the pairing of star performers like Boutell and Marshall, Barry and Bracegirdle, Porter and Oldfield. This is especially evident in the 1690s. Eric Rothstein observes that "leading actors were type-cast far less than leading actresses. Type-casting of Mrs. Bracegirdle and Mrs. Barry in particular shaped the various tragedies in which the two prima donnas appeared together" (p. 141). John Harold Wilson has commented on Boutell and Marshall, "goodness and chastity in opposition to . . . evil and lechery." *All the King's Ladies: Actresses of the Restoration* (Chicago: University of

Chicago Press, 1958), p. 97. The tremendous versatility of leading actresses, however, indicates that to the extent there was type-casting, it is at least as likely to have reflected the particular strengths of the players themselves. Actresses played both chaste and sensuous parts. For example, Barry's range of roles is given by Phillip H. Highfill, Jr., Kalman A. Burnim, and Edward A. Langhans in *A Biographical Dictionary of Actors, Actresses, Musicians, Dancers, Managers and Other Stage Personnel in London, 1660-1800* (Carbondale: Southern Illinois University Press, 1973), I, 313-25. Oldfield played Calista in *The Fair Penitent* but also the virtuous Marcia in *Cato*. Porter acted both Aspasia and Evadne in *The Maid's Tragedy*. Further evidence of the actresses' range is accessible in the indices of *The London Stage*.

11 Nicholas Rowe, *The Fair Penitent*, ed. Malcolm Goldstein (Lincoln: University of Nebraska Press, 1969), p. 65. Subsequent citations from all plays will be bracketed in the text and include act, scene, and line (if given), and page references.

12 Nicholas Rowe, *The Tragedy of Jane Shore*, ed. Harry William Pedicord (Lincoln: University of Nebraska Press, 1974), p. 22.

13 Wilson, p. 62. Cf. Rothstein, p. 155.

14 The phrase is Gordon Williams'. See "The Sex-Death Motive in Otway's *Venice Preserv'd*," *Trivium*, 2 (1967), 66.

15 See Aline Mackenzie Taylor, *Next to Shakespeare: Otway's "Venice Preserv'd" and "The Orphan" and Their History on the London Stage* (Durham: Duke University Press, 1950), for a survey of Otway's reputation.

16 See Geraldine Pelles, *Art, Artists and Society: Origins of a Modern Dilemma. Painting in England and France, 1750-1850* (Englewood Cliffs, N.J.: Prentice-Hall, 1963), pp. 140-41.

17 "The Failure of Eighteenth-Century Tragedy," *SEL*, 11 (1971), 459.

18 "Dryden's Emperor and Lillo's Merchant: The Relevant Bases of Action," *MLQ*, 26 (1965), 536, 541; cf. Moody E. Prior, *The Language of Tragedy* (New York: Columbia University Press, 1947), p. 4.

19 Cf. Clark, "An Eighteenth-Century Adaptation of Massinger," pp. 239–52.

20 *Venice Preserved*, ed. Malcolm Kelsall (Lincoln: University of Nebraska Press, 1969), p. 76. I have altered the customary italics of stage directions.

21 Thomas Southerne, *Oronooko; a Tragedy* (London, 1695), p. 83.

22 Nicholas Rowe, *Tamerlane, a Tragedy*, ed. Landon C. Burns, Jr. (Philadelphia: University of Pennsylvania Press, 1966), p. 103.

23 It has been argued often that middle-class females in the English audience were responsible for the popularity of pathetic tragedy. But John Lough has shown that love themes increase in French tragedy also, and has

pointed out "the obvious fact that the majority of male spectators seem to have shared women's taste." See his *Paris Theatre Audiences in the Seventeenth and Eighteenth Centuries* (London: Oxford University Press, 1957), p. 158.

24 With necessary qualifications, this point can apply to all tragic mythoi.

25 "The Limits of Historical Veracity in Neoclassical Drama," in *England in the Restoration and Eighteenth Century*, ed. H. T. Swedenberg, Jr. (Berkeley and Los Angeles: University of California Press, 1972), p. 30.

26 In *The Works of Thomas Otway: Plays, Poems, and Love-Letters*, ed. J. C. Ghosh, 2 vols. (Oxford: Clarendon Press, 1932), II, 18.

27 This is a major theme in Addison's neoclassical tragedy, *Cato*. Repeatedly, Cato and his daughter, Marcia, caution Juba to put off thoughts of love until military obligations have been met. She cools his ardor: "My father never, at a time like this, / Would lay out his great soul in words, and waste / Such precious moments." See *British Dramatists from Dryden to Sheridan*, p. 481.

28 The inclusion of Dryden, of course, is acceptable only if *All for Love* is classed as pathetic.

A Penchant for Perdita on the Eighteenth-Century English Stage

IRENE G. DASH

When *The Winter's Tale* finally gained acceptance on the eighteenth-century stage, it was not as Shakespeare's full-length play but in abbreviated versions derived from the last two acts. On March 25, 1754, John Rich presented a musical farce *The Sheep Shearing or Florizel and Perdita,* by MacNamara Morgan, as an afterpiece at Covent Garden.[1] Two years later, David Garrick presented his version of the play, also entitled *Florizel and Perdita,* at Drury Lane.[2] As their titles suggest, both versions center on the sheep-shearing, pastoral scenes of the last two acts. Garrick's, however, has far greater pretensions than does Morgan's. Presented as the mainpiece in a double bill with another work derived from Shakespeare, *Catherine and Petruchio,* it pledges to "lose no drop of that immortal man."[3] By eliminating the "gap of sixteen years," however, it amputates most of the first three acts—a contradiction that Garrick's critics were quick to observe. Nevertheless, the actor-manager had discovered the key to *The Winter's Tale*'s theatrical potential; his version remained popular to the close of the century.

Earlier attempts to revive the full-length play had had limited success. Giffard's famous "first-time-acted-in-a-hundred-years" production during the season of 1740-41 and Rich's the following season at Covent Garden survived nine and five performances respectively.[4] Nor was Hull's five-act version in 1771 applauded.[5] For even after audiences and critics no longer insisted on the unities, only the pastoral adaptations drew their support. Several factors explain this development: the cultural and intellectual atmosphere of the 1730s and '40s; the work of the early textual editors; but most of all, the character of the women themselves.

With the publication in 1739 of William Smith's first direct English translation of Longinus' *On the Sublime,* poets, playwrights, and painters began to reexamine their aims.[6] Smith's works prepared "the way for the ultimate rejection" of the neoclassical rules. Suddenly the outdoors—external nature and simple rural characters—provided new and vital sources of inspiration.[7] Seeking to evoke from their readers an emotional response approximating the sublime experience described by Longinus, poets indulged in vivid descriptions of nature's minutest changes. To compensate for the diminution of action and wit, they expanded their poems to include philosophical musings, discovering analogues to man's behavior in the constantly changing cycles of nature. Descriptions of natural phenomena were interspersed with contemplative passages on life and death and the transitoriness of man's existence. In Perdita's analogy of the flowers of the seasons to the ages of man, in the description of the storm at sea, and in the behavior of the natural rustic characters at the sheep shearing, *The Winter's Tale* fit the new mold. In 1747, it was therefore natural for Warburton, responding to the new intellectual climate, to commend for special reader attention most of the fourth and fifth acts of the play, thereby presaging the versions of the 1750s.[8] Before his work, Pope too had laid the groundwork for the pastoral adaptations when he subdivided the scenes in Shakespeare's plays into brief scenic units. Particularly in IV.iv where he created eight scenes, breaking down the long nine-hundred-line sheepshearing, Pope revealed a theatrical potential previously unrealized.[9]

On the whole, however, the first eighteenth-century editors indicated a progression of interest from the earlier to the later sections of the play: from the women of its potentially tragic first acts to Perdita who dances, strews flowers, and philosophizes at the sheepshearing. Rowe, for example, introduced excessive punctuation into the dramatically explosive sections. Because he himself was a writer of she-tragedies, one can only suspect that he hoped, through a plethora of dashes and exclamation points, to enhance the emotional intensity of Hermione and therefore of her appeal to contemporary audiences. Because he did not tamper with the text, however, she withstood his attempts, remaining aloof and self-contained.[10] Pope, too, revealed a bias for the early sections. Designating as memorable only two speeches, he chose Polixenes' reverie on the father-son relationship—"He's all my exercise, my mirth, my matter"—and Paulina's condemnation of Leontes—"A thousand knees,/Ten thousand years together . . . could not move the gods/To look that way thou wert." [11]

Flaws in Paulina's character and heightened sensitivity to some of the play's more sexually outspoken language marked the next step in textual responses to the play. Theobald challenged the propriety of Paulina's calling the king a fool (III.ii.184):

> It is certainly too gross and blunt in Paulina, tho' she might impeach the King of Fooleries in some of his past Actions and Conduct, to call him downright a Fool. And it is much more pardonable in her to arraign his Morals, and the Qualities of his Mind, than rudely to call him "Idiot" to his Face.[12]

Hanmer questioned the authenticity of the italicized sections of the following passage, labeling them "spurious," while Warburton deleted these lines from his text, attributing their authorship to "some profligate player": [13]

> It is a bawdy planet, that will strike
> Where 'tis predominant; *and 'tis powerful, think it,*
> *From east, west, north and south. Be it concluded,*
> *No barricado for a belly. Know't,*
> *It will let in and out the enemy,*

> *With Bag and baggage.* Many thousand on's
> Have the disease, and feel't not.
> (I.ii.201–7; italics mine)

Although this speech, with its inferences of sexuality and promiscuity, was the only one excised by editors, the mid-century revisers by discarding the first three acts accepted the implications of the precedent. But by removing the first half of the play, they cut out Leontes' passion-wracked passages, his intense spurts of jealousy, and his arrogance. Since characters in drama are defined by their interaction with other characters, the omission of the early scenes affected not only the portrait of Leontes but also those of Hermione and Paulina. Contrast, action, and reaction all help to project an image. Hermione's strength becomes unnecessary if there is no challenge, no contest, for her to face. And Paulina's role as the voice of conscience also loses its meaning. By revising, excising, and emending, both Morgan and Garrick substituted weak women for strong, and strong men for weak.

I believe that this is an important reason for the comparative popularity of the pastoral versions over those of the full-length productions of *The Winter's Tale.* However, it was not simply the strength of these women that was abrasive. For statistics on the popularity of Shakespeare's plays during the second half of the eighteenth century indicate that among repertory favorites were *Macbeth, The Merchant of Venice, As You Like It, Much Ado About Nothing,* and *Cymbeline.*[14] All have strong women. All save *Macbeth* have attractive, triumphant women, resembling those in *The Winter's Tale.* With the exception of Portia, however, none of the other women challenges the notion of the acquiescent wife. Imogen's dilemma results from her accepting too readily the message relayed through Iachimo. Rosalind and Beatrice, while they entertain us with their wit during the premarital and highly acceptable "chase," never hint at any prospect of irregular patterns of behavior after marriage. Just as their actions during the play, although brave and enchanting, conform to archetypal patterns of female coquetry, so their post-wedding ceremony demeanor may be expected to conform to acceptable stereotypes. In Hermione and Paulina, however, Shakespeare creates two married women who challenge male rule and reject male domination of female life experience.

The most outspoken of them, Paulina, exhibits a fearlessness and self-confidence that suggest her later role as the scourge of Leontes. It is she who charges the lords to the King to follow her—"be second" to her—in defying their sovereign. And it is she who, alternating between scorn and appeasement, promises first, "I have come to bring him sleep," then remonstrates:

> 'Tis such as you
> That creep like shadows by him, and do sigh
> At each his needless heavings—such as you
> Nourish the cause of his awaking.
> (II.iii.32-35)

Shakespeare also establishes her credentials earlier, at her first appearance in the jail scene. Through the jailer we hear of her virtue, "a worthy lady/And one whom much I honour" (II.ii.5–6). We also perceive that she is considered a threat, for the jailer has "express commandment" (8) to bar her entry. Her reputation precedes her. It is worth observing that although Hermione's scene with her women immediately precedes the jail scene, Paulina's first entrance is reserved for a scene of her own. Contrasted with the muted humble character of the jailer, her brilliance, wit, and sophistication sparkle. Thus introduced, not as a lady-in-waiting to the Queen nor as a member of Hermione's staff, Paulina functions as an independent, a woman with a staff of her own. "So please you, madam,/To put apart *these your attendants,* I/Shall bring Emilia forth" (II.ii.12–14, italics mine).

The characterization then moves from second person comments on her to positive examples of Paulina's strength when she convinces the jailer to relinquish the infant:

> This child was prisoner to the womb and is
> By law and process of great Nature thence
> Freed, and enfranchised; not a party to
> The anger of the King, nor guilty of,
> If any be, the trespass of the Queen.
> (II.ii.58-62)

Her ingenuity and mental acumen have defined the legal limits of the jail; her introduction is thus complete. The woman who strides into the King's chamber in the next scene is someone we know. Although the range of her capacities is still a mystery to us—and will remain so until the play's closing scene—we know that her challenge to the men to "be second" to her in courage and imaginative action is not empty ranting.

But this Paulina, the woman who cries out, even at her husband, "Unvenerable be thy hands, if thou/Tak'st up the Princess, by that forced baseness/Which he has put upon 't! " (II.iii.76-78), is not the Paulina of Garrick's version. In imposing a unity of place as well as time on *The Winter's Tale,* the eighteenth-century actor-dramatist brought Paulina to Bohemia there to accept the protection of Polixenes. In Garrick's text her function as the conscience of Leontes disappears. Ironically, her great speech, commended by Pope in 1725, is transferred to Leontes, who, weeping with self-pity, exclaims:

> *I can't* repent these things, for they are heavier
> Than all my woes can stir: *I must* betake me
> To nothing but despair—a thousand knees
> Ten thousand years together, naked, fasting,
> Upon a barren mountain, and still winter,
> In storms perpetual, could not move the gods
> To look *this* way *upon me.*
>
> (p. 11)[15]

With a few changes of pronouns from "thou" to "I," Garrick creates a repentant, sorrowful, and sorrowing male to be loved and forgiven. Paulina he transforms to a dependent, displaced person who has "fled with her effects, for safety of her life, to Bohemia" (p. 4). No longer is her great dramatic moment concentrated in the trial scene. Instead it has been shifted to the close of the play. No longer does her strength lie in intellectual power and righteous outrage. Instead the emphasis rests on Paulina as magician and Paulina the old woman who bemoans her single state: "I an old turtle, / Will wing me to some wither'd bough, and there / My mate, that's never to be found again, /Lament 'till I am lost" (p. 65). Although the lines are Shakespeare's, the characterization is Garrick's. For he has exorcized the scourge of Leontes and made the king his own man. If Garrick has also subverted the intention of the text, he has nevertheless enhanced its appeal to eighteenth-century audiences.

The second woman, Hermione, does not, on her first appearance, impress the reader or auditor as an independent, strong, self-confident person. She belongs to that race of human beings whose inner strength surfaces only during periods of trial. Thus, when we first meet her, she is happy, complacent, relaxed, and utterly womanly. In her physical being, large with child near the end of her pregnancy, she expresses visually as well as in her words a dependent, sexist role. Significantly, her first words are spoken in response to her husband's command: "Tongue-tied, our Queen? Speak you" (I.ii.27). Although in their bantering quality her words do not suggest a woman fearful of her husband, they do reinforce the first impression that this is a female who sees her primary role as wife to her husband, and hostess for his home and kingdom. Her wit and ingenuity are in the service of Leontes. Ironically, her success as wife and hostess proves her undoing. For, employing coquetry, charm, and the familiar skills expected of a woman, she convinces Polixenes to linger longer in Sicilia. Her mocking threats win Polixenes—but lose Leontes. The charm of her request and the warmth of her pursuit illuminate her womanliness. And it is this womanly loveliness that Leontes wants to possess wholly.

As the scene progresses, Shakespeare gives lines to Hermione that also suggest a sexuality and passion capable of arousing further the jealousy of her husband. Although the following passage is considered one of the cruxes of the play, defying absolute comprehension, it evokes images, although fleeting and temporary, that provide further insights into the character of Hermione. Persistently begging for a series of answers to her questions with, "What! Have I twice said well? When was 't before? " she admits delight in being praised, exclaiming:

> Our praises are our wages—you may ride's
> with one soft kiss a thousand furlongs, ere
> With spur we heat an acre.
> (I.ii.90,94-96)

The images are there: kiss, ride, spur, heat. And they suggest the sensuality of the speaker herself.

This concept of the womanly woman is reinforced in the following scene, that in the Queen's chamber. There we view the petulant, somewhat fatigued Hermione dismissing her son to the care of her women. Not until her life is challenged does Hermione reveal the core of strength that is to sustain her—first through the trial, then through sixteen years in seclusion. For exiting from her chamber in this scene, it is no longer the fatigued woman seeking rest whom we hear, but the regal Queen consoling her women:

> Do not weep, good fools;
> There is no cause; when you shall know your mistress
> Has deserved prison, then abound in tears,
> As I come out.
> (II.i.118-21)

She remains statuesque, calm, and reserved.

Hermione, then, is perceived first as a woman—the sexual bias of her role emphasized by the physical self that she carries through the first scenes. But Hermione develops emotionally during the play. When she comes to the court in the third act, she carries herself with remarkable restraint and calm, insisting on her own innocence at the trial. Did adversity kindle this inner strength? Or was it a quality belonging to the daughter of a king but submerged to help her conform to the female role she was physically destined to play? "The Emperor of Russia was my father" (III.ii.117), she asserts, implying that she should be respected and honored as an equal. Standing before a court of men and a hostile husband, however, she recognizes the impossibility of winning a just verdict.

Nevertheless, the queen persists: "My life stands in the level of your dreams, / Which I'll lay down" (III.ii.79–80)—but she never does. Instead, after fainting at the news of her son's death, she chooses to disappear, refusing to be a breeder of disposable children. That her reason for seclusion centers on the return of the infant, Perdita, is obvious in the single speech uttered during the play's closing moments:

> You gods look down,
> And from your sacred vials pour your graces
> Upon my daughter's head! Tell me, mine own,
> Where hast thou been preserved? Where lived? How found
> Thy father's court? For thou shalt hear that I,
> Knowing by Paulina that the oracle
> Gave hope thou wast in being, have preserved
> Myself to see the issue.
>
> (V.iii.121–28)

But Shakespeare's Hermione, like his Paulina, disappears from the versions usually performed during the second half of the eighteenth century. Not present at all in Morgan's version, she differs from Shakespeare's mature queen in Garrick's version. There she appears only in the last scene, and her single speech, quoted above, is divided into several parts. Adding new material as well, Garrick alters the dominant theme. Instead of a mother's joy at the restoration of a daughter, the scene revolves around a wife's ecstacy over reunion with a husband. First asking for blessings on both Florizel and Perdita, then insisting that all present pray "before this swelling flood o'er-bear our reason" (p. 64), Hermione finally exclaims: "This firstling *duty* paid, let transport loose, / My lord, my king,—there's distance in those names, / My husband! " (p. 65, my italics). There's no question of the source of Hermione's greatest joy. Garrick makes explicit what may or may not have been implicit in Hermione's embracing of Leontes in Shakespeare's drama. Moreover Hermione's words—the grouping together of "My lord, my king . . . / My husband"—suggest a subservience not indicated in the closing scene of *The Winter's Tale*. For Garrick revives the wifely Hermione of the early scenes and buries the more mature, self-reliant woman of the third and fifth acts. Furthermore, his technique illustrates Arthur Sherbo's thesis for the creation of a sentimental drama. [16] Sherbo argues that repetition and prolongation of certain elements account for a drama's fall into that "debased literary genre." By prolonging Hermione's effusive greeting to her daughter, extending the prayers to include Florizel, and inserting a multiplicity of references to husband, lord, and king, the eighteenth-century adaptor alters the tone and transforms an unusually reserved scene into one bathed in sentimentality.

Because Garrick "knew the temper of his audiences better than any other manager, possibly, that has ever lived," he was able to develop a successful formula for the statue scene. [17] Paradoxically, however, Hermione was not always retained in stage productions of *Florizel and Perdita*—probably because Garrick's work was a pastoral and as such was often abbreviated to conform to the requirements of time or personnel for a total evening's program. [18] But the success of this revision was not lost on subsequent producers and managers of *The Winter's Tale*. Even when, as in Kemble's case, a form of the full-length play was revived and the pastoral emphasis discarded in favor of the tragic, Garrick's transformation of the character of Hermione was adopted. [19]

Perdita, too, was slightly modified for eighteenth-century audiences. Fewer textual revisions were necessary in her lines, however, because in many ways Perdita's behavior resembles that of the idealized stereotypical woman. Despite the fact that she epitomizes the pastoral shepherdess of the "golden age," since she is endowed with beauty, wisdom, courage, and innocence and illustrates the ascendancy of "nature over nurture," she does defer with humility to the man she loves, a characteristic of the more human, and conventional, woman in love. Even in the contrasting of her private remonstrance to Florizel to return to his father with her public expansive declaration of love, she acts according to acceptable patterns. If Perdita is a little forward in her declaration

> O, these I lack
> To make you garlands of, and my sweet friend,
> To strew him o'er and o'er!
> . . . .
> . . . like a bank for Love to lie and play on,
> (IV.iv.127–30)

she is quick to retract, attributing her arrogance to the "robe" of queen which does "change [her] disposition" (135).

Perdita has some qualities, however, which link her to the two older women of the play. She exhibits self-confidence and individuality, particularly when confronting moral issues. Even if the issues seem somewhat removed from reality, as in the reference to bastard flowers—gillyvors—she insists:

> I'll not put
> The dibble in earth, to set one slip of them:
> No more than were I painted, I would wish
> This youth should say 'twere well, and only therefore
> Desire to breed by me.
> (IV.iv.99–103)

Although Polixenes is her guest, she refuses to play the perfect hostess. Again, when she cautions that the peddler "use no scurrilous words in's tunes" (215), she projects the portrait of the upright moral maiden. Finally, after Polixenes unmasks, her generalization about humanity—"The selfsame sun that shines upon his court / Hides not his visage from our cottage" (448-49)—indicates a view that all people are basically equal. Her comment courageously contrasts with Polixenes' damning outburst.

Nevertheless, Shakespeare's Perdita is not without moral imperfections. She has no scruples about leaving her father and brother in a rather dangerous predicament. Nor does she consider the possible "moral" consequences of travelling alone with Florizel. Although she retreats temporarily, "I'll queen it no inch farther, / But milk my ewes, and weep" (453-54), she is easily convinced by Florizel's "Lift up thy looks; / From my succession wipe me, father, I / Am heir to my affection" (483-85).

Because Perdita is the core figure of Garrick's and Morgan's versions, it is important to be aware of these particular responses of hers; the adaptors were. Conscious of her conformity as well as her nonconformity, they excised when she seemed too independent; they emended when she sounded too outspoken; and they invented when she seemed unaware of her moral obligations. Thus her debate with Polixenes over bastard flowers disappears from their texts. Reference to "maidenheads" becomes "maiden honours" and "Maiden blushes."[20] Finally, in a work that resembles a Harlequin entertainment more closely than it approximates Shakespeare's drama, Morgan imposes morality by bringing a priest to the sheepshearing. Garrick weights down Perdita with a sense of guilt for the division of father from son:

> Alas! I've shown too much
> A maiden's simpleness; I have betray'd,
> Unwittingly divorc'd a noble prince
> From a dear father's love.
>
> (p. 41)

From self-doubt to dependency is a short step. We note that Perdita leans "heavily on Florizel's bosom" during the closing scene. To the Prince's observation of her weakness, "My princely shepherdess! / This is too much for hearts of thy soft mold" (p. 63), Garrick adds her overly modest apology:

> I am all shame
> And ignorance itself, how to put on
> This novel garment of gentility.
>
> (p. 66)

Florizel, the strong male, supports her, promising to teach her the ways of the court.

Since some form of Garrick's or Morgan's version appeared for a total of ninety-six performances on an average of every two years during the second half of the eighteenth century, the persistence of these revivals indicates a penchant for Perdita and for the values she symbolized. For an attempt was made in 1771 to revive the full-length play. Inspired probably by the new attitude toward the neoclassical rules in the theater and by the support inherent in Samuel Johnson's "Preface" (1765), Thomas Hull revised the play, including the time span of sixteen years. The comments prefacing the text and the pseudo-literary footnotes explaining excisions, however, disclose the real estimate of the work and the continued rejection of the women whom Shakespeare created. After commending Garrick's version, the editor observes that "the present copy has been studiously prun'd and regulated by the ingenious Mr. Hull, . . . who has . . . made it much more bearable than the author left it." We are then told that it will never do well on the stage because it requires good actors "who find too small a scope for impressive, creditable exertion; save what belongs to Florizel, Perdita, and Autolicus."[21] This reference to the roles of Florizel, Perdita, and Autolicus prepares us for what we are to find in the text. For although the first three acts have been restored, they are skeletal. The main emphasis remains with the pastoral last two acts, those developed by Garrick and Morgan.

It is difficult for us today to understand this lack of interest in the psychologically challenging portraits of Leontes, Paulina, and Hermione as they debate Hermione's faithfulness or the infant's parentage. But Hull's version shows little sympathy for the play's older characters. Grouped together, Polixenes and Hermione are described as "watergruel character[s], equally distant from giving pleasure or disgust" (p. 154). The scene that sparks Leontes' jealousy—Hermione's successful invitation to Polixenes—"tho' curtailed, is still too long, quibbling and flat, conceived in terms, on the queen's side, rather childishly low, then maturely royal" (p. 156). The humanity of these first scenes with the imposition of family relationships on monarchy, as a foil for the later plot development, escapes the commentators. Preoccupied with the weakness of Hermione and probably conditioned by the more familiar stage characterizations of the time, they miss the implications of the scene. Rejecting also the bantering between

Mamillius and the Queen's women in the bedroom scene, as "one of the trifling excrescences which Shakespeare suffered to shoot from his luxuriant genius" (p. 164), the editor chooses to delete references to the physical and emotional weight of Hermione's pregnancy in a drama that is as much about children and infidelity as about pastoral innocence and beauty. Finally, when he excises lines of Leontes that show him to be "little better than a bedlamite" (pp. 156-57), the editor alters the "balance of power"—of inner power—between the men and the women.

Thus the penchant for Perdita in the eighteenth century took two forms: concentration on those sections of the play that revolved around the most conforming of the three women, Perdita, and rejection of those sections where the strength and conviction of Paulina and Hermione most clearly shine. Although the full-length play was returned to the stage in the nineteenth century, the eighteenth-century versions, particularly Garrick's, left a residue of influence on interpretations of the women. This was logical. For, in comparison with the short-lived productions of the whole work in the 1740s and in 1771, the versions of the fifties had prolonged theatrical exposure. In them, the images of the women who remained were altered to conform to acceptable female patterns. Bowing, therefore, to the power of the men who rewrote their roles and to the spectators who applauded their actions, the strong, self-reliant women of *The Winter's Tale* relinquished the stage.

NOTES

1 George Winchester Stone, Jr., *The London Stage,* part 4 (Carbondale: Southern Illinois University Press, 1962), I, 416. This work will hereafter be cited as *LS4.*

2 *LS4,* II, 521.

3 David Garrick, *Florizel and Perdita* (London: Tonson, 1758), prologue. Page numbers from this edition will subsequently be included in the text.

4 Charles Beecher Hogan, *Shakespeare in the Theatre, 1701-1800* (Oxford: Clarendon Press, 1952), I, 457-58.

5 Hogan, *Shakespeare,* II, 680-81.

6 Dionysius Longinus, *On the Sublime,* translated from the Greek, with "Notes and Observations" by William Smith, 2nd ed. corrected and revised (London, 1743), pp. 135-40, 151-55, 169.

7 John William Hey Atkins, *English Literary Criticism* (1951; rpt. London, University Paperbacks, 1966), pp. 186-224.

8 William Warburton, ed., *The Works of Shakespear in Eight Volumes* (London, 1747). Warburton enclosed in double commas all the speeches that he felt were memorable. For a more complete analysis see Irene Dash, "Changing Attitudes Toward Shakespeare as Reflected in Editions and Staged Adaptations of *The Winter's Tale* from 1703 to 1762," Diss. Columbia 1971, chapter 4.

9 Irene Dash, "The Touch of the Poet," *Modern Language Studies,* 4 (Fall 1974), 59-65.

10 Nicholas Rowe, ed., *The Works of Mr. William Shakespear* (London, 1709). For a fuller discussion of Rowe's exact changes, see my dissertation "Changing Attitudes," chapter 2.

11 All references will be to Shakespeare, *The Winter's Tale,* ed. Frank Kermode (New York: Signet Classics, 1964), I.ii.165–71; III.ii.205–12. Lineation from this edition will be included in the text.

12 Lewis Theobald, ed., *The Works of Shakespeare* (London, 1733), III, 105-6.

13 Sir Thomas Hanmer, ed., *The Works of Shakespear* (London, 1744), I, iii; Warburton edition, III, 287. Warburton's excision is of lines 203-6, "From East . . . baggage."

14 Hogan, *Shakespeare,* II, 716-19.

15 The italicized words are Garrick's alteration of Shakespeare's text: III.ii.206–12.

16 Arthur Sherbo, *English Sentimental Drama* (East Lansing: Michigan State University Press, 1957), pp. 48-49.

17 George Winchester Stone, Jr., "Garrick and an Unknown Operatic Version of *Love's Labour's Lost,*" *Review of English Studies*, 15 (July 1939), 328.

18 Because Hermione did not always appear in the staged versions, Stone in *LS4* and Hogan in *Shakespeare in the Theatre* do not always agree on whether to attribute a specific production to Morgan or Garrick. See Irene Dash, "Garrick or Colman? " *Notes and Queries,* 216 (April 1971), 154, for exact comparison of productions. Further evidence of the elimination of Hermione from Garrick's text appears in the copy of the play included in David Garrick, *Dramatic Works* (London, 1798), I, 242-75. There the entire last section, the statue scene, is omitted.

19 William Shakespeare, *The Winter's Tale,* adapted to the stage by J. P. Kemble (London, 1811). This is Folger Prompt *WT* 25.

20 Garrick's "maiden honours," p. 21; MacNamara Morgan's "Maiden blushes," "Florizel and Perdita" (1754), Larpent Manuscript Collection no. 110, Huntington Library, San Marino, California.

21 William Shakespeare, *The Winter's Tale* (London: printed for John Bell, 1773), introduction. This separate issue of the play, which was planned from the start, follows the same text and pagination as the Bell 1774 *Works.*

The Status of Women in Several of Lessing's Dramas

CHRISTINE O. SJOGREN

While numerous studies have been made of the main characters in Lessing's dramas, no one has yet adequately examined the position of women in the social milieu of these plays. In the three plays which bear a woman's name as title, *Miss Sara Sampson, Emilia Galotti*, and *Minna von Barnhelm*, the author deals primarily with the fate of women, notwithstanding his stated dislike for maidenly heroines.[1] The following examination of these plays is based on the assumption that they reflect the position of women in the Age of Enlightenment, and that the most illustrious German author of that period here expresses a criticism of his society's discrimination against women.

The two tragedies, *Miss Sara Sampson*, originally performed at Frankfurt in 1755, and *Emilia Galotti*, originally performed at Braunschweig in 1772, show striking parallels in the constellation of characters and their dynamic interaction. Presenting the dialectics of love versus lust, marriage versus liaison, virtue versus seduction, both plays are based ideologically on the configuration of a woman between two men: heroine between father and seducer. The abandoned mistress who also somewhat affects the action in each case, is mainly important as a personality and as a mirror image of the heroine. Whatever machinations trigger the catastrophe, the heroine's tragic fate is not caused by the other woman, but inevitably develops from her situation, which is indicated by a symbolic image early in the first act of each play. In *Miss Sara Sampson* a dream shows Sara following her lover "an dem schroffsten Theile des schrecklichsten Felsen" (*LM*, II, 274), while her father calls her back to himself and thereby causes her to lose her footing. In *Emilia Galotti* two paintings have been made of Emilia: one is in the hands of her father, the other is given into the hands of the prince.

Both plays show a young woman hard pressed by two opposing forces, that of a moralistic father and that of an egotistical lover. The father has instilled in the heroine an austere ideal of chastity; the seducer subjects her to unlicensed erotic emotions. In the struggle between the two opposing views inflicted upon her self—virtuous daughter or loving mistress—she loses her balance and develops neuroses which make her generally vulnerable. With her judgment impaired by the confusion of conflicting demands made upon her, she falls prey to evil forces around her. Victimized by the two men of greatest influence upon her, she must be regarded as the victim of a male-oriented society, which has denied her the development of a personal identity and the ability to make rational decisions based on self-interest. The fate of passive suffering is not unique to the women of Lessing's dramas; according to Otto Mann, it is typical for the women of this period.[2]

Though similar in structure, the plays differ in character portrayal: the early *Miss Sara Sampson* presents stereotypes and eclectic figures, while the later *Emilia Galotti* offers psychologically complex beings. Sara follows in the footsteps of the virtuous heroines in English sentimental novels and tearful comedies;[3] Emilia does not adopt the limited role of her Roman model Virginia as merely a political martyr, but remains an inscrutable personality. Among the secondary characters, Marwood (in *Miss*

Sara Sampson) represents the typical villainess of long tradition, but Orsina (in *Emilia Galotti*) is complex and enigmatic. Both plays, however, show women who are hampered in their human development and must suffer maltreatment by a male-directed society, as the following analysis will show.

The heroine of *Miss Sara Sampson*, seduced by the rake Mellefont, runs off with her lover, in defiance of her father Sir William. Instead of enjoying her liberation from parental authority, Sara spends her days and nights weeping, remorseful at having hurt her father's feelings, and frustrated at Mellefont's procrastination in regard to marriage. From the beginning of the play Sara is already lost, as F. Andrew Brown indicates, because there is no way out of her dilemma of "passion in conflict with principle."[4] Sara is so strongly impelled toward self-punishment that she rejects her father's forgiveness until she is made to realize the unnaturalness of her attitude. Even then she is more fearful than happy at the prospect of reunion with her father. Significantly, her own letter of reconciliation to Sir Willian is never finished. The stumbling block in the way of its completion is her conviction that she does not deserve reinstatement in his grace unless she be willing to renounce her sinful state and give up Mellefont, an act of penance which "she never for one moment contemplates," as Alison Scott has observed.[5]

In the revelation scene wherein the supposed friendly relative "Lady Solmes" exposes her true identity as Sara's rival and mortal enemy, Sara recognizes Marwood as the "mir ähnliche Person" (*LM*, II, 275) and the "mördrische Retterinn" (*LM*, II, 336) of her dream. Horrified at her own similarity to the image she detests,[6] and shocked at the disclosure of Marwood's valid claim on Mellefont as father of her (Marwood's) child, Sara loses composure and falls unconscious, thus delivering herself into Marwood's hands. Later as Sara lies dying of Marwood's poison, she is transfigured with the joy of deliverance from further temptation, to which her "weak virtue" might again succumb.[7]

Lessing's treatment of Marwood is ambiguous; while she has apparently been designed as a *Machtweib*, a villainess of tradition,[8] the author lets her off scot-free. As if sympathetic to her problem, Lessing makes her appear almost justified in fighting for Mellefont and for her child. The long duration of the liaison between Mellefont and Marwood and the existence of Arabella seem to give sanction to this union. Although Mellefont eventually chooses the tearful, virtuous Sara in preference to the evil enchantress who continues to beguile him with artful flattery, tenderness, passion, and deception, every dialogue between Marwood and Mellefont expresses a familiarity and affinity that mark them as the more suitable erotic partners. While Marwood's triumph at Sara's death still sounds the note of villainy, her plight as aging mistress deserted by a lover of long standing invites our compassion. Lessing evades the problem of providing a just punishment for Marwood's crime by simply removing her from the scene.

Though Marwood provides the poison for Sara, significantly, she does not administer it; the unsuspecting maid Betty innocently carries out this act. Perhaps this device of crime-transference is an indication that the technical killer is not necessarily the real criminal, that Marwood too, like Betty, is not ultimately guilty. It must be noted that Marwood cannot commit violence while in control of herself–she cannot kill by resolution, like Medea, for example. Only when she is beside herself, when possessed by vengeful rage, can she instigate the crime against Sara. She herself feels that this act was determined by her passions: "Rache und Wut haben mich zu einer Mörderinn gemacht" (*LM*, II, 349).

The onus of murder is clearly put on Mellefont, who confesses the crime and then commits suicide in contrition and repentance: "Und wer ist ihr Mörder? Bin ich es nicht mehr, als Marwood?" (*LM*, II, 350). Mellefont's egotism and inconstancy are the cause of the destructive passions aroused in Marwood, who herself is a victim of Mellefont, as Otto Mann points out: "Auch sie ist Opfer . . . sie hat zerstört, aber sie ist auch zerstört."[9] Mellefont made her his mistress and thereby damaged her formerly good name; he promised to marry her after the settlement of an estate, but never got around to it. Eventually tiring of Marwood, he began the relationship with young Sara, and the process appears to repeat itself.

Sara's father, though on the whole a sympathetic character, shares in the responsibility for the tragedy by having exposed Sara to Mellefont's charm and then refusing to accept the relationship which ensues, and stubbornly driving the couple away. Firm action against the seducer might yet have saved Sara, but, as Marwood points out, Sir William is too soft to strike out against the other man. [10] Sir William's main fault, however, lies in failing to prepare his motherless daughter for her inevitable encounter with love, or, in modern terms, to provide her with an adequate sex education. Sara, who has learned too late of the "inherently threatening ingredient" in erotic love, [11] tells her father to warn Arabella against the dangers of love: "Reden Sie dann und wann mit ihr von einer Freundin, aus deren Beyspiele sie gegen alle Liebe auf ihrer Hut zu seyn lerne" (*LM*, II, 350).

Emilia Galotti, a work which Goethe already found irritating, because he felt it to be rationally contrived ("Es ist alles nur gedacht") [12] actually offends not so much our sense of the aesthetic as our sense of justice, for "it closes on a shrill note of injustice, shame, and despair," [13] with events that seem deliberately provocative of our outrage.

The heroine Emilia is what the author said a young girl should be, pious and obedient. [14] Reared in the middle-class tradition of pride and principle by her highly respected bourgeois father Odoardo, she is not sentimental and argumentative like Sara; we never see her weep or hear her hold soliloquies. In fact, we hardly see her at all, because she seems to be perpetually in flight. At a ball, where she enchanted the prince of her region, [15] she was plunged into a turmoil of emotions ("Tumult in meiner Seele," (*LM*, II, 449), which even the strictest religious disciplines cannot subdue. On the very day of her wedding to the upright Count Appiani, she unexpectedly rushes alone to mass, because she feels desperately in need of Heaven's grace; but instead of finding peace of mind there, she again encounters the prince, whose presence distracts her from spiritual meditation. She is overwhelmed by his endearments and entreaties, which apparently put her into a state of shock and arouse a sense of guilt: "Stumm und niedergeschlagen und zitternd stand sie da; wie eine Verbrecherinn, die ihr Todesurtheil höret" (*LM*, II, 414). Later, after her bethrothed has been murdered in an ambush, and she herself has been abducted to the pleasure palace of the prince, she resigns herself to the thought, "dass alles verloren ist" (*LM*, II, 447), and demands that her father kill her to save her from the irresistable power of seduction in a house of joy.[16]

In order to fully understand Emilia's psychological state which causes her to will her own death,[17] we must examine her situation in regard to her betrothed, the prince, and her father.

Appiani, her betrothed, appears with Emilia in one brief scene, on the day they are to be married. When he enters the room, he is so lost in somber thoughts that he at first doesn't even notice his bride. The conversation between them deals with his melancholy, until Emilia finally reprimands him for having such a morbid imagination. She too, however, soon lapses into sadness as she relates a dream wherein all of the jewelry given her by Appiani turns into pearls, which, as she explains, "bedeuten Thränen" (*LM*, II, 404). The gloom of this nuptials day, while technically a foreshadowing device, also seems to indicate the absence of romantic passion between bride and bridegroom. Appiani's enthusiasm is aroused only once in this scene, namely when he speaks of his embrace with Odoardo, his admiration of Odoardo, and the honor of becoming Odoardo's son.[18] The notion of soon belonging to Emilia occurs to Appiani only as an afterthought, indicated in the text by a dash. Though willing to marry the pious and beautiful Emilia, Appiani is decidedly lacking in ardor. Emilia, on her part, has not objected to the marriage, because he is good and noble, her mother considers him a good match, and her father approves of him as "diesen würdigen jungen Mann" (*LM*, II, 396), with whom he has so much in common, notably the inclination to withdraw from society.

The impetuous prince, rather than the staid Appiani, awakens desires which excite and frighten her, as she shows by sudden flights and by the breathless remarks to her mother. Emilia's incomparable beauty, emphasized from the beginning as an important motif in the play, must be taken into account in understanding what the prince's proposition means to her.[19] Enrapturing both an artist (Conti) who appreciates aesthetic, perfect form with objectivity, and a royal libertine who knows and judges women's beauty subjectively, Emilia herself becomes aware of her extraordinary gift through the prince's adoration. The demands of her beauty become almost as compelling as the demands of her virtue. At the church she faces two images of herself: that of Odoardo's virtuous daughter, betrothed to a virtuous man who will lead her back into obscurity, and that of the prince's favorite at court, where her charms will be recognized, and a world of pleasure and celebration awaits her. In the symbolism of the two paintings of Emilia, the author leaves no doubt as to the outcome of her dilemma. The original painting remains in her father's hands; his standards have conditioned her, and she is not able to assume a new identity as courtesan.

Besieged by the prince at the pleasure palace, she hears of the calamitous events instigated by him, while she remembers the attraction she so recently felt for him and his society. Aware of being vulnerable to the prince's power as well as susceptible to the appeal of passion and pleasure, she doubts her own moral strength to maintain her integrity in this situation, which can only be thought of as excruciating. She realizes that she cannot expect assistance from the two men morally bound to protect her from harm: her father and her prince. Her father lacks the courage and the conviction to act on her behalf.[20] Vacillating between the urge to kill the villain prince and the bourgeois imperative of "Gelassenheit," Odoardo subdues his anger and is prepared to abandon his daughter. Placing more value on his own virtue than on her safety, he "controls" himself; placing more value on her virtue than her life, he is willing to kill her at request,[21] thereby, in the words of Robert B. Heitner, "[reducing] the principle of 'Gelassenheit' to an absurdity."[22] The prince has already shown that he is indifferent to the well-being of his subjects, whom he looks upon as tools or as objects of his possession,[23] while he pursues the gratification of his desires. Emilia senses herself alone and defenseless against inimical forces from the outside and from within herself. She reacts to the crisis in a manner typical of her—by flight. In her desperation she sees no way out except by fleeing from life. Even in this decision wherein she asserts her autonomy in regard to the prince, she cannot free herself from male domination; her suicide requires the action of her father and his implied approval.

Though the heroine here is spared a confrontation with the woman whose situation reflects Emilia's eventual fate as mistress of the prince, such a figure is introduced. The Countess Orsina, one of Lessing's most intriguing creations,[24] throws further light on the prince's character and his sexual exploitation of women. Her penetrating Medusa-eyes, which have always been a source of irritation to the prince, correctly size up the situation at the pleasure palace. With singular courage Orsina proclaims: "Der Prinz ist ein Mörder! " (*LM*, II, 432). Offended in her human dignity at being tossed aside like a worn-out toy, she rises above malevolence such as that exhibited by Marwood in the other play, and sympathizes with all the women seduced and betrayed by the prince. Marwood's complaint that men inevitably tire of a woman, no matter how diverse the entertainment she offers,[25] here is raised to an eloquent cry of outrage at the endless chain of the women deserted by the prince: [to Odoardo]"Ich bin Orsina; die betrogene, verlassene Orsina.—Zwar vielleicht nur um Ihre Tochter verlassen.—Doch was kann Ihre Tochter dafür? —Bald wird auch sie verlassen seyn.—Und dann wieder eine! —Und wieder eine! " (*LM*, II, 436).

A society which regards women as playthings does not favor their intellectual development. As the prince expresses uneasiness at Orsina's penetrating glance, so he and his chamberlain also disapprove of her interest in books, which, they claim, will destroy her mind altogether.[26] Orsina herself deplores her intellect, for she realizes that in a world where women exist only to amuse the Lords of Creation, a woman who thinks must seem unlovable, defiant, even loathsome: "Wie kann ein Mann ein Ding lieben, das, ihm zum Trotze, auch denken will? Ein Frauenzimmer, das denket, ist eben so ekel, als ein Mann, der sich schminket. Lachen soll es, nichts als lachen, um immerdar den gestrengen Herrn der Schöpfung bey guter Laune zu erhalten" (*LM*, II, 428).

While Lessing seems to favor his women characters by endowing them with loyalty, courage, and resolution, in contrast to the men, who are shown to be inconstant, pusillanimous, and egotistical, the women in these plays nevertheless give an alarming impression of psychological disturbance. With modern jargon one would say that Sara suffers from masochistic tendencies and guilt feelings, Marwood exhibits delusions of grandeur in her Medea complex, Orsina's behavior is manic-depressive, and Emilia is paranoid with suicidal tendencies. Violence is familiar to all of them: Marwood and Orsina carry a dagger and poison around with them; Sara is murdered by poison; Emilia is killed with a dagger.

The violence experienced and exercised by these women results from their desperate frustration in a society which applies a double standard of intellectual expression and sexual morality. Where man is elevated to the position of a god, and woman is reduced to the level of a thing, fathers are empowered to condemn or forgive their daughters according to whim, as the example of Sir William shows; fathers are also empowered to protect or kill, as we see with Odoardo; seducers have the license to use, enjoy, and then cast away women as mere objects of pleasure. Women, on the other hand, must accept subordinate position, please father and lover, and submit to men's standards and desires.

The oppression of women in a society thus oriented can only lead to outbreaks of irrationality, such as Marwood's diabolical attack on Sara, Sara's whining self-mortification, Emilia's grotesque suicide, and Orsina's impotent rage. The rebellious anger coursing through these plays has been noted, but has been interpreted politically, as the expression of middle-class resentment against the tyranny of the ruling class.[27] Lessing's depiction of the abuse of power and the consequences of such abuse encompasses a wider area than merely the political, however, as the tragic fate of the Countess Orsina alone shows. These plays express the author's outrage at society's injustice to its members whose sex relegates them to a position of weakness and inferiority.

In the period between these two plays, Lessing wrote the comedy *Minna von Barnhelm*, first performed at Hamburg in 1767. The basic motif here is not that of a woman in tension between the pressures of two men, but that of a man and a woman engaged as equal partners in the dialectics of ascertaining truth.[28] Minna is neither controlled by a father nor ensnared by a seducer, and she is indifferent to the prejudices of her society. Exercising an independent will, she struggles to reclaim her lover, with the same determination as that shown by Sara, Marwood, and Orsina. Her integrated personality, which combines intelligence with tenderness, sincerity with playfulness,[29] could develop because she was not subjected to oppression. Being herself free, she is able to liberate her lover from his false assessment of his worth. In contrast with Sara and Emilia, Minna is able to love without guilt, and to express virtue without self-sacrifice. She may be considered an exponent of the best in German Enlightenment.[30]

Lessing was pessimistic about society's readiness to grant women equality, however. His last play about a woman, *Emilia Galotti*, creates a darker impression even than the early *Miss Sara Sampson*. Emilia is granted no redeeming apotheosis; instead, attention is drawn to her mutilated and now ugly body with Odoardo's words to the prince: "Gefällt sie Ihnen noch? " (*LM*, II, 450). The prince does not repent like Mellefont, but passes the blame on to his chamberlain. No child remains to offer hope, as does Arabella, that women of the next generation will be accorded a better education and a better life. Lessing could hardly have chosen a more poignant image for the status of women in his society than the enchanting Emilia, who must die for a principle; nor could he have created more devastating images of social perverseness than the unscrupulous prince, whose skill at seduction arouses terror in his defenseless victim, and the father who kills his daughter to safeguard her chastity.

NOTES

1 See the letter to his brother Karl, Feb. 10, 1772, "Die jungfräulichen Heroinen und Philosophinnen sind gar nicht nach meinem Geschmacke," quoted from G. E. Lessing, *Sämtliche Schriften*, ed. Karl Lachmann, 3rd ed., rev. Franz Muncker (Stuttgart, Berlin, Leipzig, 1886-1924), XVIII, 18. All further quotations from Lessing's works are taken from this edition of 23 volumes, hereafter cited as *LM*. The above statement may be considered a defense against the possible accusation of his peers that he is excessively interested in the problems of women, a worry that Lessing voices in a letter to Gleim, March 22, 1772 (*LM*, XVIII, 28): "Meinen Sie nicht, dass ich der Mädchen endlich zu viel mache? Sara! Minna! Emilia! "

2 *Lessing: Sein und Leistung*, 2nd ed. (1949; rpt. Berlin: Walter de Gruyter, 1961), p. 201, "[Die Frauen] sind im Raum des bürgerlichen Lebens die für tragische Schicksale eigentlich Anfälligen, Opfer der Sittenordnung und sie bestimmender Zwänge. Das eigentlich tragische Schicksal des Erduldens und Leidens war in diesem Raum der Frau bestimmt."

3 For references to English literary sources and influences, see Curtis Vail, *Lessing's Relation to the English Language and Literature* (New York: AMS Press, 1966).

4 "*Sara Sampson*: The Dilemma of Love," *Lessing Yearbook* (hereafter cited as *LY*), 2 (Munich: Max Hueber, 1970), 146.

5 "The Rôle of Mellefont in Lessing's *Miss Sara Sampson*," *GQ*, 47 (1974), 396.

6 This interpretation follows that of Manfred Durzak, "Äussere und innere Handlung in *Miss Sara Sampson*," *DVLG*, 44 (1970), 60.

7 *LM*, II, 350.

8 For a study of this tradition, see Emil Staiger, "Rasende Weiber in der deutschen Tragödie des achtzehnten Jahrhunderts," *Stilwandel: Studien zur Vorgeschichte der Goethezeit* ([1961] Zurich: Atlantis, 1963), and Ursula Friess, *Buhlerin und Zauberin: Eine Untersuchung zur deutschen Literatur des achtzehnten Jahrhunderts* (Munich: Fink, 1970).

9 *Sein und Leistung*, p. 233.

10 Marwood would have acted more decisively, as she says: "Sir William ist ein zu guter alter Narr. . . . Ich hätte der Tochter vergeben, und ihrem Verführer hätt' ich—" (*LM*, II, 323).

11 F. Andrew Brown, "*Sara Sampson*: The Dilemma of Love," *LY*, 2, 145.

12 See the letter to Herder, July 1772 (*Der junge Goethe* [Leipzig: Hirzel, 1875], I,310). For a brilliant study of the affinities between Emilia and

Werther, see Ilse Appelbaum Graham, "Minds without Medium: Reflections on *Emilia Galotti* and *Werthers Leiden*," *Euph.*, 56 (1962), 3-24.

13 Robert Heitner, "*Emilia Galotti:* An Indictment of Bourgeois Passivity," *JEGP*, 52 (1953), 488.

14 See the letter to Karl, Feb. 10, 1772 (*LM*, XVIII, 18).

15 As Otto Mann, *Lessing: Sein und Leistung*, p. 256, states, "Der bezauberte Prinz hat bezaubert."

16 Alois Wierlacher, "Das Haus der Freude oder Warum stirbt Emilia Galotti? " *LY*, 5, 147-62, gives evidence that in Lessing's time "Haus der Freude" did not imply immorality or prostitution but instead denoted a place: "der Lebensfreude, der Lebenszugewandtheit, des Lebensgenusses" (148).

17 Hermann J. Weigand's answer in "Warum stirbt Emilia Galotti? " *JEGP*, 28 (1929), 479, "dem Gegner, der sie unterschätzt, mithin als Persönlichkeit verachtet, durch die drastische Tat zu zeigen, dass ihr Wille sich nicht zwingen lässt," is still valid today.

18 R. K. Angress, "The Generations in *Emilia Galotti*," *GR*, 43 (1968), 15-23, contending that the cause for the tragedy is "the search for and the failure of authority" (15), describes Appiani as "a young man in search of a father" (19).

19 Otto Mann, *Sein und Leistung*, p. 266, points out that Emilia's hamartia lies "in der Hybris ihrer Schönheit."

20 As F. J. Lamport notes in "Eine bürgerliche Virginia," *GLL*, 17 (1964), 308, there is evidence that Odoardo's inability to help her brings on a shock which "destroys the whole moral foundation of her life."

21 Gerd Hillen, "Die Halsstarrigkeit der Tugend: Bemerkungen zu Lessings Trauerspielen," *LY*, 2, 115-34, claims that this act is a consequence of the "Unmenschlichkeit" of Odoardo's extreme "virtue" (126).

22 "*Emilia Galotti*: An Indictment of Bourgeois Passivity," *JEGP*, 52 (1953), 489. Heitner considers Odoardo to be the main character of the play, as does Roy Cowen, "On the Dictates of Logic in Lessing's *Emilia Galotti*," *GQ*, 42 (1969), 11-20.

23 Manfred Durzak, "Das Gesellschaftsbild in Lessings *Emilia Galotti*," *LY*, 1 (1969), notes that even in his language the prince deforms persons into things (68). Frank Ryder, "*Emilia Galotti*," *GQ*, 45 (1972), contends that Emilia herself is "a victim par excellence of [this] crime of treating a human being as an object" (342).

24 Representative assessments of Orsina are the following: Benno von Wiese, "Die Entstehung der deutschen Tragödie im Zeitalter Lessings," *Die deutsche Tragödie von Lessing bis Hebbel*, 4th ed. (Hamburg, 1958), "mit moralischen Grundsätzen nicht mehr [zu] messen . . . jenseits von Gut und Böse" (40); Hans Mayer, "Lessings poetische Ausdrucksform,"

Lessing und die Zeit der Aufklärung, Veröffentlichung der Joachim Jungius-Gesellschaft der Wissenschaften Hamburg (Göttingen: Vandenhoeck und Ruprecht, 1968), "grossartigste Inkarnation einer Dialektik der deutschen Aufklärung" (142); Edward Dvoretzky, *The Enigma of* Emilia Galotti (The Hague: Nijhoff, 1963), "both manufactured and dispensable but without peer in German dramatic literature" (112).

25 "Bald sind es die schlüpfrigsten Reden, die buhlerhaftesten Scherze, die euch an uns gefallen; und bald entzücken wir euch, wenn wir nichts als Tugend reden, und alle sieben Weisen auf unserer Zunge zu haben scheinen. Das schlimmste aber ist, dass ihr das eine so wohl als das andre überdrüssig werdet" (*LM*, II, 286).

26 Marinelli: Sie hat zu den Büchern ihre Zuflucht genommen; und ich fürchte, die werden ihr den Rest geben.

Der Prinz: So wie sie ihrem armen Verstande auch den ersten Stoss gegeben.

(*LM*, II, 387)

27 Especially by Fritz Brüggemann, "Lessings Bürgerdramen und der Subjektivismus als Problem" (1926), *Gotthold Ephraim Lessing*, ed. Gerhard und Sibylle Bauer, Wege der Forschung, 211 (Darmstadt, 1968), pp. 83-126.

28 For an exposition of Lessing's dialectic technique, see Peter Heller, "Lessing: The Virtuoso of Dialectic," *Dialectics and Nihilism: Essays on Lessing, Nietzsche, Mann, and Kafka* (Amherst: University of Massachusetts Press, 1966), pp. 3-68.

29 A report on her play-acting ability is given by Fritz Martini, "Riccaut, die Sprache und das Spiel in Lessings Lustspiel *Minna von Barnhelm*" (1964), *Gotthold Ephraim Lessing*, 211, pp. 376-426.

30 As Georg Lukács observes in "Gotthold Ephraim Lessing" (1964), *Gotthold Ephraim Lessing,* 211, "In ihr ist das menschlich Beste der deutschen Aufklärung schlicht zur Gestalt geworden" (442). Hans Mayer, "Lessings poetische Ausdrucksform," points out that in the character of Minna the female principle is equated with Reason, while the male principle represented by Tellheim almost approaches "Unmenschlichkeit" (144).

The Matron of Ephesus in Eighteenth-Century France: The Lady and the Legend

ROSEANN RUNTE

The eighteenth-century tale of the Ephesian Matron was more than a legend steeped in mysogenic satire. It was a vehicle for the transmission of ideas, a symbol of the opposition between morality and perversity, between the laws of nature and those of society. Its almost universal appeal lay in its treatment of fundamental issues of a dramatic nature: death, love, and passion. The Matron of Ephesus presents an evolving portrait of a woman faced with the death of her spouse, faced with liberty, perhaps for the first time in her life.[1] It is notable that widowhood was frequently the state in which the character of the heroine was most fully developed.[2] It is more significant that eighteenth-century authors did not choose Dido as heroine, but preferred an anti-Dido, a woman who voted for life and its sensual pleasures and who freed herself from what Voltaire termed "un ancien abus."[3] Unlike the passive Virginie who died eyes raised to the heavens and one hand on her heart, this vivacious widow listened to the beating of that breast and actively refused either to die or to respect social mores.[4] The heroine in question represents a flesh and blood woman and not an ideal. A major distinguishing feature of eighteenth-century versions was the vindication rather than the condemnation of the woman for her frivolity and inconstancy. Voltaire said, "elle n'a qu'une faiblesse amusante et pardonnable."[5] Fréron pointed out that "toutes ces satires d'un sexe qui serait en droit d'en faire contre nous un plus grand nombre, et à plus juste titre, ne doivent être regardées que comme des plaisanteries."[6]

This lively widow arrived in eighteenth-century France on a well-traveled passport with a suitcase replete with disguises and under a number of aliases. A naturalized French citizen of Greek and Roman ancestry, she had sojourned in France since medieval times, making her appearance in such works as the *Roman des sept sages,*[7] the *fabliaux,* and Marie de France's "De la femme qui feseit duel de sun mari."[8] Sixteenth-century revivals include Marguerite de Navarre's "Seizième nouvelle de la deuxième journée."[9] The major intention of these versions is satire directed primarily against women and secondly against the frailty of all mankind.[10] The plot structure is similar in each case, with the presence of basic elements which did not vary. The widow inconsolably mourns her dead husband and is accosted by a soldier. She accepts his love and suggests they replace the stolen body he was supposed to guard with that of her deceased husband. Variants include the placement of the disappearance of the corpse before or after their encounter, the amount of description and emphasis on the widow's grief, the presence or absence of her family who unsuccessfully attempt to console her, and the inclusion or omission of her refusal to live by voluntarily starving and her eventual acceptance of food from the soldier.

While the medieval versions returned in the seventeenth century with Nevelet's "De Milite et Foemina,"[11] the Ephesian Matron also returned to her Latin sources with Saint-Evremond's translation of Petronius. La Fontaine's more innovative and graceful reworking of the translation led the way to a renewal of interest in the timeless legend and the ageless heroine. Both La Fontaine and

Saint-Evremond adapted the legend and the lady's dress to the sensitivities of the day. Saint-Evremond's changes were minimal but reflected a certain delicacy of interpretation. He substituted the word "body" for "cadaver" and had the Matron be taken at first for a phantom rather than a monster from the underworld. He had the servant be won over, not only by the bouquet of the wine, but by the soldier's discourse, and he had the Matron *have* the body drawn from the coffin rather than do it herself.[12] La Fontaine omitted the soldier's attraction to the widow's fortune as well as her beauty, her external signs of violent grief (scratches on her face, handfuls of hair torn out), and the voluptuous nights she spent with the soldier. The seventeenth-century *conteur* added the following elements: the replacement of the body is suggested by the servant, not the widow who merely consents, and the vague mention of a marriage. He has the god of love shoot the Matron and the soldier with his arrows (explaining an attraction beyond their forces), and to the reasons for which the Matron capitulates he added flattery and the question Would your husband have done the same for you?

Thus the Matron had already donned a more refined garb before the eighteenth century. She was no longer crude enough to directly offer her husband's body, and her marriage to the soldier is hinted at, thus giving a degree of respectability to her love. Neither of these circumstances alters her crime, but they place it in a different light and slightly attenuate her guilt.

This tradition of delicacy was continued throughout the eighteenth century, where she never suggested the replacement, never mutilated herself in her grief (indeed, she was rendered even more charming by her pallor and tears), and only once celebrated her passion in a free fashion—and then it was noted that love was the notary and priest.[13] On the other hand, marriage was specifically mentioned in less than eighteen percent of the versions. Since the responsibility for the actual conclusion was left to the reader's imagination, it is difficult to determine if this is not another case of what Barchilon terms "veiled eroticism."[14] Although the text is innocent and on the surface the Matron seems freed of a certain amount of culpability, the intent remains the same. For example, Fréron appears to have been oblivious to the superficially imposed morality of the story when he exclaimed: "Enfin (et c'est ici le point essential) les coupables désirs de la *Matrone d'Ephèse* sont satisfaits dans la tombe même, et presque sur le cercueil du mari."[15]

A second version of the tale featured the widow clad in a Chinese robe, holding a fan which she frantically waved over her husband's grave to hasten its drying. Her various names included Tien, Tian, the Matron of Soung or of Oung, and she voyaged to France in the vehicle of a translation by d'Entrecolles, a missionary.[16] The pretended death of her husband, a philosopher with supernatural powers, was conceived as a test of her fidelity. Unlike the Ephesian Matron who is guilty of giving in to the advances of the soldier with undue haste, the Oriental Matron is the temptress who corrupts one of her husband's young disciples. Upon the reappearance of her husband she hangs herself for shame. The French versions of this tale retained the plot but altered the details to suit the genre selected and the supposed location of the tale. Only Le Monnier, in his *La Matrone chinoise*, retained the magic powers of the husband. The other authors relied on a more natural explanation for his feigned death and sudden reappearance.

A third category of the tale is situated between the Petronius-La Fontaine group and the Oriental tales. It is characterized by the reappearance of the husband who was believed dead and who was prevented from returning to his wife by extraordinary circumstances (such as being sold into slavery).[17] Upon his return he discovered the infidelity of his wife. Of the five cases studied, in one he punished her by sending her to the convent, while in the remaining four the false widow repented and returned to her husband with renewed devotion.

The final major version of the tale was the reversal where the Matron was replaced by an equally unfaithful widower. Early examples of this reversal lacked bitterness. However, Steele's reversal, proposed as a counter-version of this tale, presented a merchant "coupable de l'ingratitude la plus affreuse."[18] Steele's version was based on a story reported by Raynal, who severely condemned this villain as a "monument infame d'avarice et de perfidie."[19] Examples which followed diverged from the trend of excusing the Matron by describing with greater delicacy her acts, using Cupid or a device as *deus ex machina* and as a more pardonable motivation instead. The widower had no saving graces, no hesitation in making immediate use of his freedom, and satisfied the purpose of this version as stated by Voltaire: "Il s'agit de prouver que les hommes ne sont pas plus constants que les femmes."[20]

This paper will be limited to the four versions already mentioned. Only works whose structure closely parallel the parent versions will be considered. This qualification is necessitated by the universal and compelling nature of the themes of death and passion in the legend.[21] The *Matron of Ephesus* is thus separated from the theme of widowhood. The chart in appendix A lists the texts following each version, and the chart in appendix B illustrates structural deviations from the parent version and classes the works generically.

Of the different parent versions, Petronius's tale was the most popular. This may be due in part to its greater reputation. The oriental version was not translated until 1732 and was thus not as well known. All poems and fables, as well as a majority of the plays (7 of 12), were taken from the Latin source. Although Fréron pointed out the dramatic nature of the oriental tale by underlining its unity, morality and satisfying conclusion (poetic justice), it was reproduced in only one play.[22] This may perhaps be related to the authors' intentions and the generic limitations. The oriental tale does offer a moral lesson, but the force of the lesson lies in the satire. The plays stressed the comic nature of the situation. The *deus ex machina* minimized the satiric thrust, and the device was used uniquely in the theatrical versions.[23] The fact that the poets also looked to Petronius for inspiration may be explained by the limitations of the genre. No characterization was necessary when referring to the Ephesian matron. Her name alone evoked a complete personality. The Latin tale was less complex than the oriental and was thus better suited to a brief poem. Finally, the moral was proverbial and could be insinuated without explanation in the fable. Although the moral of the oriental tale was the same, it was unfamiliar and would have required explanation. Thus, the *conte* favored versions in which satire was more important than humor, and the theater stressed humor over satire.

The theatrical genre differed from the short story not only in its comic intent but in its manner of presentation. In all of the plays, with the exception of *La Matrone ou le modelle des veuves*, the number of characters was doubled.[24] All of these doubled casts included a servant who not only performed the function of suggesting the replacement of the body but who acted as a second heroine, providing romantic interest, since she was generally paired with the soldier's valet or aide. The servant added comic highlights by her initial contrast to the widow. The former represented common sense and physical lust for life. The latter's tragic grief became more poignant by comparison.

Over the course of the century, the servant became more eloquent, and it was her argument which won over the widow. At the same time, the soldier became less well-depicted and more of a timid lover who had to be prompted by the servant. Not only did she assume the lead in verbal persuasion,[25] but the servant was responsible for the invention of numerous tricks, such as the touching up of a portrait of the deceased spouse to resemble the soldier and thus facilitate the transfer of the widow's affections.[26]

The servant's initial motivation in following the Matron was loyalty. This motivation became more refined. The servant either accompanied the Matron because she shared her grief (the deceased was like a husband to her; her husband was lost with the Matron's), or because she was confident she could change the widow's mind.[27] In the case of the latter circumstance, she had often schemed in advance to help the lover's cause. The servant increased in importance, evolving from a structural tool to a designer of structure, from a passive follower to an agent of action. In her role as a companion widow, she should have been the target of the mysogenic satire, for it was she who represented the carnal desires and moved first to satisfy them. The Matron posed the familiar objections and her hesitation reflected socially accepted opinions. The roles were nearly reversed. However, the Matron remained the fickle woman. Her faults, such as vanity, were highlighted by the servant's ruses and crafty manipulations. The Matron's social class and refinement gained in comparison to the lusty servant. The Matron's downfall remained the object of the play despite her weakness, or rather because of it.

The Matron herself changed. In Brinon's *L'Ephésienne,* she needed to fortify herself with a kiss before deciding to offer her husband's body: "Frontin, embrassez-moi, je sais bien un remède."[28] In the same play she accepted with little hestitation "d'un funeste tombeau faire un palais d'amour" (p. 36). In the eighteenth century this eroticism was veiled and among the arguments to which she lent her ear were philosophical statements. She was ennobled in her grief: ". . . sa douleur a je ne sais quoi de respectable, de touchant. . . ."[29] Her fall was thereby rendered all the more spectacular.

The eighteenth-century Matron was more conscious of public opinion than in preceding centuries. This led to two strong statements, the first of which was feminist in nature. Men would not do the same for their wives.[30] The second was that society was wrong in its mores. Le Gay clearly indicated that the Matron was only following nature.[31] In this sense, the works which emphasized this aspect were a form of social protest. The Goncourts' description of the strict requirements of mourning certainly justify their conclusion: "Dans cet étalage de la douleur et du regret, l'oubli, les idées de liberté, les projets d'avenir consolaient bien des femmes."[32] The Matron was still a bit quick in lifting her veil, but her act was justified when seen in the light of an escape from an unjust custom. She became not a victim of her own folly but a victim of society and a champion of nature. In each of the twelve plays considered, she was excused to some extent. Half of them attributed her vindication, at least in part, to social injustice.

The Matron's guilt was further extenuated by the image of her former marriage. Occasionally, the husband was characterized as old, jealous, and ill-humored. Her love for a young man was again partly the fault of a society which promoted ill-assorted marriages. It is only the suddenness of this love which shocks. However, it is this ability to change which causes her to be admired. In La Motte's version Lucas exclaimed: Alle [sic] va comme ça du blanc au noir? oh tatigué! qu'alle est femme cette femme-là!"[33] Saint-Marc Girardin's study, "L'Hamlet de Grammaticus Saxo," contains a revealing explanation: "Hamlet a eu ainsi dans ses deux femmes les deux types les plus célèbres de la femme, Griseldis [soumise, résignée, qui s'humilie sous la préférence de son mari pour une rivale], et la Matrone d'Ephèse [facile à promettre, lente à tenir, toujours prête à céder au plaisir, ardente dans ses nouveaux désirs, oubliant aisément le passé et ayant toujours les passions en haleine]. Quelle est celle qu'il aima le mieux? C'est la Matrone d'Ephèse, c'est Hermatrude, soyez-en sûr."[34] The Matron's glory lay in her flaw, and this was recognized in the eighteenth century and if not approved of was not condemned. The conclusions of these two plays illustrate the difference in attitude:

Houdar de La Motte, *La Matrone d'Ephèse* (1702): ". . . toutes les femmes sont désormais pour moi autant de monstres que j'abhorre! Ce n'est que légèreté, qu'inconstance, que perfidie, et tous les vice du monde ensemble! " (pp. 40-41);

Anonymous, *La Matrone d'Ephèse* (1756): "La veuve ne fait point la folle. . . . L'en blâmez-vous? moi, je n'en ai garde" (p. 20).

This admiration is also evident in other genres. For example, J.-B. Rousseau wrote: "De la célèbre Matrone / Que l'antiquité nous prône / N'imitez point de dégout; / Ou, pour l'honneur de Pétrone, / Imitez-la jusqu'au bout." He continues advising his widow to follow the Matron's example rather than that of Andromaque or Dido. He asks her to sacrifice herself to love, not to death.[35]

The eighteenth-century versions of the tale have a common difference with the source in the lack of detail. For example, in only two cases is the number of days without food mentioned, and in only two cases is reference made to the Matron's material wealth. The Matron is not physically described within the text, nor are the other characters. This vagueness is reinforced by the period. Just as the legend was timeless, so were the individual versions. The place is also nonspecific. It is generally a desolate spot, most often in the country near Ephesus. While the slight tinge of exoticism perhaps appealed to the eighteenth-century reader, it is never emphasized to the point of destroying the universality of the story.

The Ephesian Matron and her story doubtless owe their survival to their combined versatility. As the Matron was able to pass from tears to tender embraces, so was she able to move from condemnation to near vindication. Her story remained recognizable despite the addition of subplots, doubled conclusions, role reversals, and evolution of authors' intent. The authors' purposes can be generically categorized. Theatrical versions stressed humor, narrative versions satire, and verse versions both humor and morality. The three base versions of the tale were similarly classified. The oriental tale was primarily satiric as was the reversal. The Petronian version was most easily adapted to comic intent, although its original statement was satiric.

In the eighteenth century the Matron maintained her feminine frailty (her tragic flaw in this human comedy), but she used it as an arm against the injustice of abusive social mores. She rose from the depths of mysogenic satire, accused of cruel inconstancy and impudicity, to the heights of goodness (when Good is equated with Natural). Thus, while remaining a real woman and not an ideal, the Matron evolved from object to symbol and the legendary tale reached the proportions of a myth.

APPENDIX A

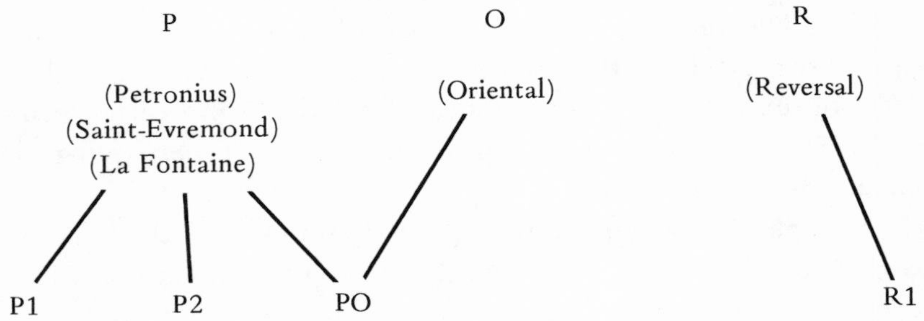

P

Houdar de La Motte, *La Matrone d'Ephèse* (1702)
Voltaire, "Le Bûcher," *Zadig* (1747)
Voltaire, "A une jeune veuve" [?]
Ganeau, *La Nouvelle Matrone d'Ephèse* (1765)
Anonymous, *La Veuve du Maldobar* (1770 and 1780)
Anonymous, "La Tourterelle, veuve du hibou" (1780)
Rétif de la Bretonne, *La Matrone de Paris* (1784)
Radet, *La Matrone d'Ephèse* (1792)
J.-B. Rousseau, "A une veuve," (1798)

O

D'Entrecolles, [translation], (1732 or 1735)
Voltaire, "Le Nez," *Zadig* (1747)
Fréron, "Tchoung-Tse et Tien, histoire chinoise," (1755)
Dutens, [translation], (1776)
Le Monnier, *La Matrone chinoise ou l'épreuve ridicule* (1764)

R

Le Sage, *Gil Blas*, vol. II, ch. XI (1735)
Raynal (1770)
Voltaire citing Steele (1776?)
Carmontelle, *Le Veuf* (1785)
Guichard, "Le Veuf qui perd la tête" (1802)

P1 (deus ex machina)

Fuzelier, *La Matrone d'Ephèse* (1714)
Anonymous, *La Matrone d'Ephèse ou le modelle des veuves* (1756)
Le Gay, *La Matrone d'Ephèse* (1788)

P2 (husband returns, but no test purposely involved)

Le Sage, *Gil Blas*, vol. I, ch. VII (1724)
D'Allainval, *Le Mari curieux* (1731)
Bielfeld, *Comédies nouvelles* (1753?)
Ganeau, "Le Pauvre Diable et sa femme" (1765)

PO

Wathelet, *Les Veuves ou la Matrone d'Ephèse* (1784)
(states origin as Petronius but contains test concept)

R1 (heroic version)

Le Guire de Richebourg, *La Veuve en puissance de mary* (1773)

Author	Title	Type	Genre	Differences
Ganeau	La Nouvelle Matrone d'Ephèse	P	conte	wife burns husband in effigy to cook lover's meal
Voltaire	Le Bûcher	P	conte	widow gives in to philosophical arguments but also considers marriage; antireligious satire
Ganeau	Le Pauvre Diable et sa femme	P2	conte	husband returns to find children—a gift of "le bon Dieu"
Le Sage	L'Histoire de Doña Mencia	P2	histoire dans un roman	longer period of mourning, widow gives in to family, husband returns, widow repents
Voltaire	Le Nez	O	conte	fan changed to shovel, brain changed to nose, suicide changed to banishment
Le Sage	Le Veuvage de Gil Blas	R	histoire	ends with consolation; no body
Guichard	Le Veuf qui perd la tête	R	conte en vers	widower can't restrain himself and starts caressing a lady friend even through his tears
Le Guire de Richebourg	La Veuve en puissance du mary	R1	nouvelle tragi-comique	husband reappears, widow rejects two lovers including one who saved her life
Voltaire	A une jeune veuve	P	épître	widow encouraged to follow Matron's example
anonymous	La Tourterelle	P	fable	widow encourages lover with eyes

J.-B. Rousseau	A une veuve	P	épître	widow encouraged to follow Matron's example
La Motte	La Matrone d'Ephèse	P	comedy	servants' intrigue and two lovers (father and son) added
anonymous	La Veuve de Maldobar	P	comedy	see Voltaire's "Le Bûcher"
Radet	La Matrone d'Ephèse	P	comedy	portrait episode, servants' intrigue, and letter episode added
Fuzelier	La Matrone d'Ephèse	P1	comedy	tripled plot; "ghost" of dead husband appears; Matron is married by a fairy on stage
anonymous	La Matrone ou le modelle des veuves	P1	Cantate burlesque	Matron dreams first of husband's death
Le Gay	La Matrone d'Ephèse	P1	comédie mêlée d'ariettes	soldier compared to husband; after widow consents to use body, the lost one is found
D'Allainval	Le Mari curieux	P2	comedy	husband returns, sends wife to convent, rewards his loyal daughter
Bielfeld	Comédies nouvelles	P2	comedy	husband reappears and wife capitulates
Le Monnier	La Matrone chinoise	O	comedy	husband turns himself into his own wife's lover
Carmontelle	Le Veuf	R	comedy	no body
Wathelet	Les Veuves ou La Matrone d'Ephèse	PO	comedy	double plot; servants' intrigue; husband's death is test, but he returns too late

NOTES

1 See Simone de Beauvoir, *Le Deuxième Sexe* (Paris: Gallimard, 1949), pp. pp. 175-76, who said that in the eighteenth century, liberty was an abstract concept for women.
2 For example, Dido, Jocasta, Phaedra, and Andromache.
3 François-Marie Arouet de Voltaire, "Zadig," *Romans et contes* (Paris: Garnier, 1960), p. 30.
4 Saint-March Girardin, *Souvenirs de voyages et d'études* (Paris: Amyot, [1851]), pp. 186-87.
5 Voltaire, *Dictionnaire philosophique*, vol. XVII of the *Oeuvres complètes* (Paris: Garnier, 1875-85), p. 196.
6 Elie Fréron, "Tchoung-tse et Tien, histoire chinoise," *Journal étranger* (Paris: Lambert, 1755), pp. 218-19.
7 Hans R. Runte, *Li Ystoire de la male marastre* (Tübingen: Max Niemeyer, 1974), pp. xlviii-lii; Runte, "The Matron of Ephesus: The Growth of the Story in the *Roman des sept sages de Rome*," unpublished paper, Kentucky Foreign Language Conference, 1974.
8 Marie de France, *Poésies* (Paris: Chasseriau, 1820), II, 172-73.
9 Marguerite de Navarre, *l'Heptaméron* (Paris: Flammarion, n.d.), I, 193-200.
10 Eduard Rudolf Grisebach, *Die Wanderung der Novelle von der treulosen Wittwe durch die Weltlitteratur* (Berlin: Lehman, 1889), p. 82.
11 Isaac Nicolas Nevelet, *Mythologia Aesopica* (Frankfort: Hoffmann, 1610), p. 521.
12 Charles de Morguetel de Saint-Denis de Saint-Evremond, *Oeuvres en prose* (Paris: Didier, 1962-65), II, 189-95. See note 3, p. 195, which indicates that this might not have been Saint-Evremond's innovation, but a fault in the manuscript he used.
13 Anon., *La Matrone d'Ephèse ou le modelle des veuves* (London: D. Barrow, 1756), p. 18.
14 Jacques Barchilon, "Uses of the Fairy Tale in the Eighteenth Century," *Studies on Voltaire and the Eighteenth Century*, 24 (1963), 116-17.
15 Fréron, p. 218.
16 Le Père François-Xavier d'Entrecolles, *Description historique de la Chine* (Paris, 1735), III, 324.
17 Alain-René Lesage, *Histoire de Gil Blas de Santillane* (Paris: Garnier, 1962), vol. I, ch. vii.
18 Voltaire, *Dictionnaire*, XVII, 196.
19 Raynal, *Histoire philosophique et politique des établissemens et du commerce des Européens dans les deux Indes* (Amsterdam, 1770), V, 197-98.

20 Voltaire, *Dictionnaire*, XVII, 196.

21 Elements of the tale may be found in many more works than herein indicated. For example, the story of the widow in *Les Illustres Françaises*, which in turn inspired Collé's *La Veuve* and Marivaux's *Les Fausses Confidences,* contained some elements of the legend. Other versions are yet to be found. For example, the lost manuscript of Laclos' *La Matrone*, a comic opera.

22 Fréron, pp. 217-18.

23 These devices included the relocating of the body, in Louis-Joseph Le Gay, "La Matrone d'Ephèse," *Mes souvenirs et autres opuscules poétiques* (Caen, Manoury and Paris: Belin, 1788).

24 Anon., *La Matrone d'Ephèse ou le modelle des veuves.*

25 See, for example, the difference between the servant Frosine in Antoine Houdar de la Motte, *La Matrone d'Ephèse* (Paris: Ribou, 1702), and Frosine in C. H. Wathelet, "Les Veuves ou la Matrone d'Ephèse," *Receuil de quelques ouvrages de M. Wathelet* (Paris: Prault, 1784).

26 See, for example, Jean-Baptiste Radet, *La Matrone d'Ephèse* (Paris, 1792).

27 La Motte: ". . . car je perds presque un époux moi, dans celui de Madame" (p. 4). The second case refers to Wathelet.

28 Pierre de Brinon, *L'Ephésienne* (Rouen: Osmont, 1614), p. 47. All further references will be noted in the text.

29 Radet, p. 19.

30 Wathelet: "Ma foi, nos deux époux / Jamais, au grand jamais ne seraient morts pour nous" (p. 223). See also Le Gay: "Votre époux n'est-il pas pleuré suffisamment? / Sa peine d'être veuf n'eût pas été si vive" (p. 29).

31 Le Gay: "Ne donnez point l'example à l'histoire, revenez sur terre, aimez un autre homme. / Ils n'y sont que pour nous et pour eux nous y sommes . . ." (pp. 8–9).

32 Edmond and Jules Goncourt, *La Femme au dix-huitième siècle* (Paris: Firmin-Didot, 1887), p. 185.

33 La Motte, p. 7.

34 Saint-Marc Girardin, pp. 186-87.

35 Jean-Baptiste Rousseau, "A Une Veuve," *Odes, cantates, épîtres et poésies diverses* (Paris: Didot l'aîné, 1798), I, 67.

Madame de Graffigny and Her Salon

ENGLISH SHOWALTER, Jr.

The salon, which, as every student of French literature learns, was the cradle of classicism and the home of good taste for two centuries, has disappeared not only from French society but apparently from the concerns of eighteenth-century scholars as well. The 1950 edition of the *Critical Bibliography of French Literature* required one hundred twenty-five entries, almost four per cent of the total for the eighteenth century, to cover the salons and the various salon hostesses; in the 1968 supplement, there are only twenty-three entries, less than one per cent. In recent years such bibliographies as *PMLA* are barren of titles mentioning the salon, and the recent directory of eighteenth-century scholars published by the Société française d'étude du dix-huitième siècle lists nobody who mentioned the salon as a current interest, except me. Even the famous hostesses, Mme. de Lambert, Mme. de Tencin, Mme. Du Maine, Mme. Du Deffand, Mlle. de Lespinasse, Mme. Geoffrin, Mme. Helvétius, appear infrequently and only as letter writers or in relation to someone else like Voltaire. This is all the more remarkable because there is an evident boom in studies on women: women writers, images of

Virtually all the material for this study comes from the unpublished Graffigny papers in the Beinecke Library of Yale University, by whose permission they are quoted.

women in literature, education of women, feminism, and the like.

The reasons for this neglect are, I think, complex and interesting. To simplify greatly, students of literature have tended more and more to favor purely textual analysis, while historians, although social history is enjoying a period of growth and innovation, have not yet moved into this particular void. The salon presents problems of documentation far more difficult than, say, the *Encyclopédie,* the provincial academies, or the periodical press, to cite three areas where quantitative methods and team research have produced excellent results; and previous histories of the salon, almost all anecdotal and imaginative, do not provide even the starting point for a reassessment. In the special section on "problèmes actuels de la recherche" in *Dix-huitième Siècle*, 5 (1973), several communications discuss the revolution in the social history of culture; and Eric Walter's article "Sur l'intelligentsia des Lumières" cites the salon among several similar topics remaining to be studied with the new methods. The analysis presented here is an attempt to use the voluminous documentation in Mme. de Graffigny's unpublished papers to provide the outline for a systematic study of the salon as a phenomenon of social history.

A basic definition of a salon states that it is a room, and by extension, a group of people who meet regularly in that room. The first and most obvious requirement for a hostess is then to possess a suitable space. The wealthy and aristocratic families began with an advantage in this respect; Mme. de Lambert, Mme. de Tencin, Mme. Geoffrin, Mme. Du Deffand, Mme. Helvétius, for example, surely never had much worry about where they would receive their guests. For Mme. Geoffrin, indeed, the rooms served as an additional pretext for patronizing her guests, since she decorated them with works of art. There is a second group, however, for whom the meeting place did represent an initial and even continuing problem. Julie de Lespinasse, living on the generosity of Mme. Du Deffand and receiving guests in her *chambre* before they went down to her protectress's salon, is a famous example.

Mme. de Graffigny risked a great deal in order to get a house, when the prospect of holding a salon was still very remote and had probably never occurred to her; but the house brought her a small measure of independence. When she first arrived in Paris, in the spring of 1739, she expected to live with the Duchesse de Richelieu as lady-in-waiting; but in August 1740 the Duchesse died, leaving Mme. de Graffigny without resources. For a while it seemed that Mme. de Graffigny would have to retire to a provincial convent, those in Paris being too costly. Ultimately, though, she became lady-in-waiting to the Princesse de Ligne, who had been involved in a scandal and sent by her husband to a convent, the Filles de Sainte Elisabeth. In 1741 the Princesse decided that she preferred to live in the country, and passed Mme. de Graffigny on to the Marquise de Coutances, a less congenial patroness; so Mme. de Graffigny took a room in another convent, the Filles du Précieux Sang, where she was admitted as the protégée of one of the Princesse's kin, Mme. de Lévis. That arrangement collapsed in September 1742, because Mme. de Graffigny had angered the nuns by making a match for a wealthy fellow pensioner, thus frustrating the community of a dowry. She had to move in with Mme. de Lévis, whom she found unbearably boring. It was more desperation than ambition that led her to sign a lease she could ill afford for a house on the rue Saint-Hyacinthe, near the site of the present Luxembourg station. This momentous move took place on November 27, 1742.

It was another two years before Mme. de Graffigny tried to entertain members of Parisian literary circles, and then they were a fringe group: Crébillon *fils,* Louis Cahusac, a minor playwright and librettist; La Bruère, sometime editor of the *Mercure*; Mlle. Fel, a celebrated singer at the Opera; Duclos, who was an Academician, but made a specialty of mingling in all societies. The dinner went reasonably well, but Mme. de Graffigny could not afford to repeat it for a long time. Both before and after this literary dinner, Mme. de Graffigny had frequent visits from a wide circle of friends, mostly natives of Lorraine. It was, in a sense, already a salon, and there must have been scores like it in Paris at that time. The rue Saint-Hyacinthe house thus met the minimum requirements; it was far from ideal, however, being too small, ill ventilated, hot in summer, chilly in winter, and old enough to frighten Mme. de Graffigny that it would collapse about her. Thus she began, with the first hints of prosperity and success, to look for a new house, and moved into it in July 1751. It was located on the rue d'Enfer, with a gate into the Luxembourg gardens; and it was there, during the next six years, that Mme. de Graffigny's salon made its deepest mark on the social and literary life of her age.

After the room itself, the second obvious necessity for a salon is a circle of friends. In a great many cases, the famous eighteenth-century hostesses took over a coterie that was already established. Mme. de Lambert's group, for example, went to Mme. de Tencin after the former died, and then on to Mme. Geoffrin after Mme. de Tencin's death. Mme. Geoffrin also acquired most of the artists who had been habitués of Mlle. Quinault's "Bout du banc" when the hostess quarreled with the Comte de Caylus. Mlle. de Lespinasse, of course, formed her salon by splitting off from the group at Mme. Du Deffand's. A hostess had to be acquainted with a wide range of well-known people, but that alone was not enough; she also had to have some call on their loyalty. That was the source of the conflict between Mlle. de Lespinasse and Mme. Du Deffand; the older woman would not be satisfied for her guests merely to keep appearing in her salon, if their primary loyalty had shifted to Julie.

Mme. de Graffigny knew an extraordinary number of people. When she first came to Paris, as a member of the Richelieu household, she mingled with the most prominent families: Brancas, Béthune, Aiguillon, Châtellerault, Courtenvaux, Crèvecoeur, Saint-Pierre, Croissy, etc. As a former resident of the court of Lorraine she knew the prominent noble families of that province: Guise, Pons, Lixin, Mirepoix, Beauvau, Boufflers, Ligniville, Haraucourt, Talmont, Stainville-Choiseul, as well as the ducal family and the ex-Duc's mother, the sister of the Duc d'Orléans. As a friend of Voltaire she made the acquaintance of numerous scholars and writers: Fontenelle, Buffon, Hénault, Mairan, Maupertuis, Clairaut, Gentil-Bernard, d'Argental, Pont-de-Veyle, Mouhy, Moussinot, Thieriot. And she met friends of their friends,

Dupin, La Popelinière, Bonnier, the Prince de Conti, the Princesse de Ligne and Mme. de Lévis. These friendships, all established by 1740, did not on the whole prove to be of much value to her. The nucleus of her salon emerged from an undistinguished circle of young writers, artists, administrators, and officers who had been in Lunéville or who had connections there. Before arriving in Paris in 1739, Mme. de Graffigny had developed close contacts with Chaumont de la Galaizière, chancellor of Lorraine. He had seventeen brothers and sisters, most of whom were prospering in some branch or other of government service, and Mme. de Graffigny knew several of them, the Abbé de La Galaizière, the Comte de Mareil, and the Comte de Lucé in particular. The chancelor himself, moreover, was married to a niece of the controller-general Orry, and Mme. de Graffigny thus knew his brother Fulvy and his chief clerk Masson. They constituted a network of friends, with considerable influence, even though their names are not well known. Mme. de Graffigny also had several people to look up on arriving in Paris: DuVigeon, a painter who had worked in Lunéville; Vennevault, a miniaturist who had also been in Lorraine; Mlle. Lubert, sister of an officer in Lunéville and author of fairy tales. Some of the young men who had flocked around the amiable Mme. de Graffigny in Lunéville came often enough to Paris to continue among her friends: Lubert, just mentioned; Desmarets, who was her lover until 1743; Adhémar, later a correspondent of Voltaire's; Saint-Lambert, destined for notoriety; Abbé Calabre Pérau, friend and agent of Henri de Saulx-Tavannes, black sheep of a distinguished Burgundian family, exiled in Lorraine for abducting the Marquis de Brun's daughter. By and large these people remained Mme. de Graffigny's friends throughout the 1740s, and in the 1750s, after the triumph of *Cénie,* they still made up the most loyal group, providing stability and continuity and a sort of critical mass, around which the salon formed.

Had they been the only regular habitués, it is doubtful that Mme. de Graffigny would be remembered today as a salon hostess. She owed her acceptance in Parisian literary circles to Mlle.

Quinault *la cadette.* Mme. de Graffigny met her in 1740; the two women apparently liked each other from the start, but at first Mme. Graffigny lacked the money and the freedom to pursue the relationship beyond an occasional meeting. In 1743, however, when she moved into her own house, she began to go regularly to Mlle. Quinault's dinners, which were then at their gayest. At the Bout du banc she met Maurepas, Saint-Florentin, Caylus, Coypel, Crébillon *fils,* Piron, Moncrif, Duclos, Gresset, La Chaussée, Cahusac, Voisenon, many of the actors of the Comédie française, and Helvétius. After the *Lettres d'une Péruvienne* became a great success in 1747, other writers and journalists began seeking her out, and the circle grew; but it already numbered enough lions, drawn from the Bout du banc, to have a reputation as a place to hear witty conversation and timely gossip, to keep abreast of fashions, and to meet interesting newcomers. The list of those who are known to have been there subsequently at one time or another is endless; it includes Voltaire and Rousseau, of course, although not together as legend would have it. Helvétius, Turgot, Malesherbes, and the Duc de Choiseul were assiduous visitors, as were several aspiring young writers, like Bret, Linant, and Palissot, who served as agents for Mme. de Graffigny in exchange for her using her influence on their behalf. As a group, they seem extremely eclectic, not to say ill-assorted. Mme. de Graffigny's works give somewhat the same impression, combining pell-mell most of the ideas and themes then in the air; and in both cases, the public response was favorable but the impact proved ephemeral.

The third and final element of the basic definition is regular meetings. Some of the salons convened with institutional regularity; Mme. Geoffrin, for example, had two "days," Mondays for artists, Wednesdays for men of letters. By temperament and social position Mme. Geoffrin could and did insist on strict organization. Mlle. Quinault also held her Bout du banc on the same day of each week. That appears to have been largely a matter of convenience, however; the guests varied greatly in number from week to week and often brought unexpected guests. The dinners were sometimes canceled at the last minute, to Mme. de Graffigny's disappointment.

For her part, Mme. de Graffigny held open house. Unlike her two rivals, she did not generally serve dinner, although anyone who appeared around dinnertime was commonly invited to share her commonplace meals; others who stayed late in the evening would be given supper. It was an unspoken and occasionally violated rule that such invitations were sought only by an inner circle of friends. They came to her house very often, some of them almost daily, and she never set a formal pattern. Although that may seem a trifling difference, it may be one of the major distinctions between Mme. de Graffigny and her better-known competitors. In fixing a regular day, the salon hostess came nearest to declaring that her activity was an institution. One can postulate a scale of sociability, beginning with the women who, though possessing the means and position, seldom if ever received guests, and ending with those who held frequent large receptions on regularly scheduled days. In between, although many factors governed the relative prestige of the salon, three fairly precise criteria seem to define status groups: first, the expansion of entertaining from infrequent special occasions to frequent receptions for large groups with no stated purpose; second, the creation of a select group through formal invitations to certain regular guests for special events; and third, the extension of the formal event from an occasional occurrence to a regular weekly meeting. More study may reveal important correlations between status and activities; but superficially, at least, Mme. de Graffigny's middle-status salon had much in common with higher-status ones. In trying to define its individual character, I will begin with these common aspects, and then look for subtle differences.

The hostess, who presumably conceived and organized the salon, gave her name to it, and in some sense embodied its spirit, had to be an exceptional woman. Even when social rank and inherited or married wealth furnished many external advantages, a powerful ambition, a talent for organization, and some kind of distinctive appeal were still required. Perhaps a strong constitution or at least some resiliency were even more important. One can easily belittle the achievements of Mme. Geoffrin by giving all the credit to her money; but there were other women in Paris with as much money and similar ambitions, and their names are forgotten today. Most of the famous hostesses learned their art as a guest of some other hostess: Mme. de Tencin learned from Mme. de Lambert, Mme. Geoffrin from Mme. de Tencin, Mlle. de Lespinasse from Mme. Du Deffand, and so forth. Mme. de Graffigny began by imitating Mlle. Quinault, and Mme. Helvétius served her apprenticeship in Mme. de Graffigny's salon.

The abilities and facilities needed by a successful hostess greatly advantaged mature women. Most of the prominent hostesses were over forty when they began holding their own salons. Their age provided the time necessary to acquire a wide range of acquaintances, as well as to learn the skills; and it also gave them a certain authority. Mme. de Graffigny had turned fifty before she attempted her first formal dinner. That age did not exempt her from the attentions of suitors and lovers both actual and would-be, nor were most of the other hostesses beyond the age of folly altogether. In all the salons, the guests were mainly men, and it is clear that the hostess's sexual appeal contributed to her success. Flirtation and banter were the stock in trade of polite conversation, and the hostess naturally played along. The consequences were usually slight, however; although some hostesses had engaged in promiscuous liaisons as younger women, in their later years they characteristically succumbed only to strong and durable passions. Mme. de Graffigny had been betrayed by her lover of fifteen years in 1743; she resolved shortly afterwards never to love again. In 1750 Bret very nearly succeeded in overcoming her resolution, but she resisted, and he remained a friend even after she had cooled his ardor. She had numerous other offers of marriage and numerous declarations of fleeting passion. If she is typical, most of this was pure badinage, a symbolic activity with just enough chance of turning real to give it spice.

The hostess usually had a young woman among her entourage who provided a complementary sort of sexual interest. Such was Julie de Lespinasse's role with Mme. Du Deffand, Mme. de Staal's with the Duchesse Du Maine, and Minette de Ligniville's with Mme. de Graffigny. The younger woman had to be vivacious and vulnerable, where the hostess was serene and in control. Relations between the two women were complex and often troubled; resentments built up on both sides over the tyranny of the older and the ingratitude of the younger. Mme. de Graffigny and Minette were no exception; Mme. de Graffigny wrote long complaints about Minette, calling her at various times "bête, capricieuse, entêtée, maussade, ingrate, odieuse." The younger women were usually forced into their role by some difficulty in their situation; they were poor, and had poor prospects for a suitable marriage. Almost the only alternative society had to offer was the convent. Mme. de Graffigny herself had spent years as a companion or lady-in-waiting, both at Lunéville and in Paris. Despite Mme. de Graffigny's outbursts, it is clear that many men found the charming Minette one of the attractions of her salon.

Within that broad pattern, the tastes and wishes of the hostess largely determined the distinctive qualities of the salon. Unlike the domineering Mme. de Tencin or Mme. Geoffrin, Mme. de Graffigny never enjoyed feeling herself an object of public attention and never tried to regulate any but the most trivial characteristics of her salon. Even in that her success was slight; she complained constantly that her time was being wasted by unwanted visitors, for example. To a degree, she was only following the lead of Mlle. Quinault, who encouraged the greatest freedom of speech and even behavior, within the limits of decency, among the guests at the Bout du banc. Mme. de Graffigny was usually amused there, as by Caylus and Maurepas drunkenly imitating tightrope walkers, by Voisenon singing bawdy songs, or by Crébillon *fils* reading a salacious pastiche of *Marianne*; but she was occasionally shocked, by a lewd dance, for example. Yet for all its freedom, the Bout du banc obeyed its hostess's orders—and its host's, for Caylus, who footed the bills, insisted on his pleasures first: he had Crébillon *fils* excluded for a while and never tolerated some of Mlle. Quinault's friends. Mlle. Quinault did fix regular days, the entertainments were often command performances, and she set tasks for the wits of her salon, such as the collection of parodies published in 1745 as the *Recueil de ces Messieurs*: she assigned subjects, received the manuscripts, made criticisms, demanded revisions, and served as editor.

Mme. de Graffigny never imposed such order on her guests. The only projects her salon undertook were efforts to have plays accepted and produced; for the most part this meant urging the more influential guests—the Prince de Clermont, d'Argental, the Prince de Beauvau, Malesherbes, and of course the actors—to use their influence. Some salons served as theaters where writers read their works before publication; the well-known painting of Mme. Geoffrin's salon, with Lekain reading Voltaire, although an imaginary composite scene, could have been real. Mme. de Graffigny attended many such events, but never organized one on such a scale; sometimes a friend read an act of a play or a poem, but she preferred working with the author in private. Conversation was almost the only activity of her salon. She aspired to make it the common meeting ground for the most diverse elements of polite society. As author she had hoped to appeal to readers of good will in all parties, Jansenists, Jesuits, philosophes, Parisians, provincials, aristocrats, servants, soldiers, and shopkeepers; and she thought at least that she had succeeded. Her salon reflected much the same ambition; rather than set a style or impose a fashion, she tried to find common interests among all who came her way. As a result, her salon welcomed a great range of famous people, but it lacked definition and visible impact. That is no doubt one of the reasons why it has remained so little known; but this widely respected effort to reconcile adversaries and foster tolerance is itself a significant social phenomenon.

Throughout her life and career, Mme. de Graffigny portrayed herself as self-effacing. Like the heroines in her works, she mutely bore her unjust burdens, dreaming of the dénouement when her very silence would force the recognition and admiration of her quondam oppressors. The salon, too, was a vehicle for self--effacement at the same time that it was a source of power and pleasure. In a real sense, the point of it for Mme. de Graffigny was the letter she would write later, that is, the expression of her secret thoughts about it and her smug sense of hidden resources.

Mme. de Graffigny's own views of her salon reveal persistent inner conflicts and paradoxes. In 1750, after *Cénie* and *Les Lettres d'une Péruvienne,* she had the reputation of an important writer; but the fame brought as many anxieties as satisfactions. One of the most striking images in her correspondence is her waiting at home for news of her play; she had sent her lackey with orders to return in the middle, to forewarn her. All the reports were good, of course, but not until the triumph was assured did she dare to go to the theater herself. In the days that followed, the critical praise was welcome, to be sure; but it could not counterbalance the rumor of a hostile epigram by the insignificant poet Roy, which produced a crisis. She perfectly illustrates Mme. de Staël's statement, "L'aspect de la malveillance fait trembler les femmes, quelque distinguées qu'elles soient." Ultimately, Mme. de Graffigny converted her public celebrity into more private channels; instead of continuing to write for publication, she turned out a steady stream of playlets for the edification of the Emperor's children in Vienna. The salon brought similarly ambiguous rewards, and Mme. de Graffigny tried to make it conform to her personal tastes in similar fashion.

Most of the famous salons are known in part because the group collaborated occasionally in some major enterprise, political or literary. Even though Mme. de Graffigny tried to wield her influence more discreetly, she relied on the same basic sources of power as other hostesses: she could speak directly to men who controlled the government, the theater, finances, and the like. Mme. de Graffigny spent much of her time and energy trying to have herself put on pension lists or included in lucrative deals. Failures were numerous, successes rare, but just profitable enough for her to survive. She got something from the King for Minette via the tax farmer Du Vaucel. She got a pension from Vienna. She earned a fee for her part in having Du Boys de Riaucourt named to the Parlement of Nancy. She arranged the marriage of Helvétius and Minette, and got gifts from him. She was also paid for her writing, and success increased her market value dramatically. In 1747 the widow Pissot had bought the manuscript of *Les Lettres d'une Péruvienne* for three hundred livres; in 1752 Prault paid three thousand for a revised edition, but Malesherbes's protection also counted for something. Yet all of it combined never amounted to an adequate income. The salon cost more than it brought in, for Mme. de Graffigny had to provide the house, dress properly, hire servants, furnish some food. Perhaps a more conscientious bookkeeper could have managed better and perhaps a more single-minded person could have succeeded more often in winning the pension or the contract. It still seems unlikely that anyone could have made a living solely on incidental favors from her guests; but given even marginal outside resources like Mme. de Graffigny's, the salon offered enough access to income to keep hope alive, a little money coming in, and credit good.

Mme. de Graffigny tried also to help her young writer friends. In fact, in 1739 she brought with her to Paris plays by Devaux and Saint-Lambert with the intention of having them put on by the Comédie française. Saint-Lambert wisely gave up on his, but Mme. de Graffigny persisted with Devaux's for twelve years and finally got it staged in 1752. Naturally it flopped. Mme. de Graffigny had worked equally hard on behalf of Palissot, to get his *Zarès* produced, and she did the same thing for Bret and Guimond de La Touche. She was able to obtain a discreet opinion on the Abbé Gautier's *Réfutation du Celse moderne,* a naively well-intentioned defense of Christianity, which everyone agreed made the other side look better; but she got the manuscript back from the censor, and Gautier published it in Lorraine. Such activities made up a great deal of Mme. de Graffigny's life; she would no doubt have enjoyed being a literary agent, had such a profession existed then. With more luck, she might have gained real celebrity in this way, but the most brilliant of her protégés—Turgot, Saint-Lambert, Helvétius, even Palissot—did not publish their major works until later, when Mme. de Graffigy had died or they had ceased frequenting her salon. Those who were active in her prime were inferior—Bret, La Touche, Galli de Bibiena, Linant, La Bruère, La Rougère, Devaux.

Mme. de Graffigny thus shows the ways in which a salon served its hostess: it could produce prestige, power, and money. Because of her uncertain social position, Mme. de Graffigny shied away from the prestige, and this no doubt hampered her efforts in the other fields. In addition, her lack of wealth and some bad luck prevented her from scoring any great successes. Once again, this relative failure is a reason why so little has been said of her salon until now; but her case may be more instructive about the patterns of social life and the structures of its institutions than are the famous salons whose very triumphs and reputations diverted them from the typical course.

Neither the works published by Mme. de Graffigny during her lifetime nor the unpublished works among her papers would lead us to suppose that posterity lost a great author because Mme. de Graffigny abandoned writing to devote her energies to her salon. Her contemporaries judged her writing differently, however, and the question remains to be answered whether the change was a deliberate choice or the passive response to social pressures. It is well established that women writers found their lives difficult in eighteenth-century France; Mme. Roland, who evaded the problem by collaborating with her husband, summed it up succinctly: "Jamais je n'eus la plus légère tentation de devenir auteur un jour; je vis de très bonne heure qu'une femme qui gagnait ce titre, perdait beaucoup plus qu'elle n'avait acquis." Mme. de Graffigny clearly had more than a slight desire to become an author, but a sample of success proved unsettling. The etiquette of female authorship was rigid, and required *Cénie* to be in prose rather than verse, for example. Prudish relatives condemned her, and a few satirists like Roy mocked her. Typically, when her works were popular, they were attributed to a man, the Abbé Pérau, whereas in fact she had helped him with his works more than he had done for her.

Despite all the disadvantages and vexations of authorship, Mme. de Graffigny might have persisted; under a pseudonym she did actually submit another play in 1751, but it had been written earlier. In reality she never had the chance to go on. From the day of *Cénie*'s triumph until her prestige began to wane, Mme. de Graffigny's time was the property of her public. At all hours of the day they came asking to be fed, entertained, advised. She thus lost all her hard-won freedom. Some of her male admirers took up almost permanent residence in her house at critical times—Duclos when his mistress died, Turgot when his mother died, Bret when he fell in love, Palissot when he wanted his play produced, Helvétius when he was courting Minette. Mme. de Graffigny never felt that she could close her door to them, unless she was ill; perhaps that feeling betrays some weakness of resolve or some unconscious choice, but it is simultaneously the direct expression of a fundamental social dynamics, which Mme. de Staël described in *De la littérature*: "Ce que vous êtes forcé de faire par votre état, par votre position, trouve mille approbateurs; ce que vous inventez sans nécessité, sans obligation, est d'avance jugé sévèrement." Society urged on a talented woman the role of hostess, and provided compensations for the difficulties; on the other hand, it made the role of author as painful and unrewarding as possible. Nobody came offering to insure her peace and quiet while she wrote her next work, as various patrons did for the great male writers; she did have offers of a place as lady-in-waiting, to the Marquise Du Châtel among others, but it meant a return to the companion's place she had found so onerous when she first came to Paris. Publishers did not come forward with contracts, despite the popularity of *Les Lettres d'une Péruvienne*; the actors did not solicit a new play, despite the success of *Cénie*. The best offer was the Emperor's request for children's plays, and Mme. de Graffigny accepted, although her time was so short by then that she had to beg her friends to write these playlets for her. More often the friends came with their own manuscripts, to seek Mme. de Graffigny's advice and patronage.

Like most such decisions, Mme. de Graffigny's was neither wholly deliberate nor wholly unwilling. She was of her society as we are not. She shared most of the prejudices that drove her away from literature and toward sociability. This was an age when ambitious young men found ways to make a career of writing, which had formerly been an aristocratic avocation. Women, even when they wrote from pressing practical motives, found it difficult to concentrate on their work; it was more profitable to divert their success into social channels. There were in fact no professional careers open to women, unless we count convents. Mme. de Graffigny wrote to earn a living, but she could not earn her whole living with her pen, and the struggles were painful. Instead of pursuing that career, she made her prestige as a writer one of her assets as a hostess; her books served her as youth, beauty, charm, or wealth might serve another. The ultimate goal was some form of self-fulfillment and achievement; the means were very limited. Mme. de Graffigny was not forced to become a salon hostess, even as opposed to being a writer; but she soon grasped the fact that the salon afforded the optimal means for realizing the potential of her resources, including her talents as an author. Although for her rivals the salon may have been at best only a substitute for a career, for Mme. de Graffigny it combined all the elements of an authentic career.

Attitudes toward Women in Two Eighteenth-Century French Periodicals

KAY WILKINS

Research dealing specifically with the study of women in eighteenth-century France (whether from an historical, sociological, or literary viewpoint) is of relatively recent vintage.[1] In the past an occasional female scholar would turn her attention to a woman author—Emily Crosby's *Une Romancière oubliée: Madame Riccoboni* (1924) is a case in point. But with the growth of women's studies, a fresh enthusiasm and realization of the paucity of our knowledge about this area has led to such works as Pierre Fauchéry's monumental study of literary portrayals of women in the eighteenth-century European novel, *La Destinée féminine dans le roman européen du XVIIIe siècle: Essai de gynécomythie romanesque, 1713-1807* (1972), to the four-volume *Histoire mondiale de la femme* (1965–66), to Bardèche's two-volume *Histoire des femmes* (1968), and to such related studies as Philip Stewart's *Le Masque et la parole: Le Langage de l'amour au XVIIIe siècle* (1973). Two recent American Ph. D. dissertations have dealt with Diderot and women, another with Voltaire and women, and three more with a reappraisal of the fortunate Madame Riccoboni.[2] My own attempt is limited in scope but nevertheless yields some interesting conclusions. I have examined two runs of different periodicals, the *Mercure de France* (1720-25) and the *Journal encyclopédique* (1780-83), and have analyzed the depiction of women in them. Although I am aware that the periodicals are of different types and that any conclusions represent only a small insight into a vast area of study, it is apparent that attitudes changed to some degree in the sixty-year period separating the two series I examined.

The *Mercure de France* was a highly successful periodical which made sufficient profit to be able to provide substantial pensions to men of letters. It aimed at a sophisticated audience interested in court affairs, social and foreign events, and the latest cultural activities in Paris. A typical number (Jan. 1720) included an article analyzing the attribution of the title "très chrétien" to the king, a letter about America, a harangue to the king by a missionary to the Algonquins, a list of royal edicts and laws, some very mediocre verse, a short story, reviews of the latest French and English theater presentations, an historical account of the Compagnie des Indes de France, some enigmas and songs, details of notable births, marriages, and deaths, foreign news, the Paris journal, and some advertizements, such as news of a powder which causes a nursing mother to lose her milk within forty-eight hours (a product that will not be advertized in the post-Rousseau climate of the *Journal encyclopédique*).

The qualities of the ideal woman for the editors and contributors to the *Mercure de France* seem to be summed up in the funeral eulogy of a royal princess: "Epouse, elle fut fidèle; mère, elle fut tendre; Princesse, elle sacrifia tout aux intérêts de l'Etat; veuve, elle ne songea plus à plaire; chrétienne, elle remplit les devoirs de la Religion" (Jan. 1723, p. 97). Constancy and strength in the face of adversity are also desirable qualities—in a rare moment of praise for the female sex, the editors include a letter from the French envoy to Algeria relating the courage of one Miss Bourk (of Irish family) who coped bravely with capture and imprisonment by barbarians (March 1720, pp. 84-92). Above all, however, woman is valued for her reproductive and nourishing faculties; the Jan. 1722 *Mercure* includes a letter praising the king's nurse for her fine body and good health, which have ensured Louis' well-being. The many poems and speeches celebrating the king's marriage remark on the queen's virtue which should be rewarded by "la douce humanité,/La sainte piété, la modeste prudence,/Et l'heureuse fécondité" (Oct. 1725, pp. 2356-57). Women are admired for their devotion to religion—one Mademoiselle de la Baronie was posthumously praised for spending whole winters without a fire so as to meditate and study religion without any possible distraction (Dec. 1723, pp. 1256-58). Female intelligence is not attacked. The essay competitions advertized in the *Mercure* are open to both sexes, and there are several contributions by women writers.[3] But debates about educated women do not figure in the pages of the *Mercure*. Perhaps the *Portrait d'une dame de Rennes* (Dec. 1722, pp. 56-59) aptly sums up the ideal intellectual woman as opposed to the virtuous princess I mentioned before. Emilie is beautiful, modest, "sage, spirituelle, l'esprit bien tourné," and, the supreme compliment, "Emilie est une très-aimable femme, qui a toutes les qualitez d'un honnête homme."

What male contributors to the *Mercure de France* seem principally to fear is female inconstancy and infidelity. Friendship is safer than love, "ce petit Dieu volage,/Convient mieux au sexe léger" (May 1722, pp. 129-30). Female flirtatiousness threatened a man's sole possession rights. Many third-rate pastoral idylls bewail the pains of unrequited love and the cold inhumanity of women. It is better for a man to take the initiative and be fickle himself; an ode to one Monsieur G— on the inconstancy of his mistress advises, "il faut tromper une belle,/Même avant que l'infidelle/Medite d'en faire autant" (Aug. 1723, p. 216). Love is often associated with suffering in the verses of the *Mercure,* and the escape route for a man seems to be to "conquer" the pride of a beauty, using violence if necessary.[4] Love is seen as weakening in a typical poem, *La Sagesse, victorieuse de l'amour*; it is "lâche" and "odieux" (March 1725, p. 423). Such misogyny appears frequently, as in a poem on marriage by Vergier: "Chiens & Chats ne s'accordent gueres,/Maris & femmes encore moins./Le parti qu'il nous faudroit prendre,/Ce serait de nous dégager/De ce lien fatal" (May 1725, p. 938). The "sexe trompeur, qui rompt tous les liens" is almost inevitably the female sex, despite the protestations to the contrary of Mademoiselle L'Heritier, a well-known poet and a lone voice (at least in these five years of the *Mercure*) to criticize the insincerity of men: "Et l'amour empressé que nous montrent les hommes,/N'a rien qui nous dût frapper" (June 1725, p. 1273). But by sheer weight of lines of verse men win out. The last word in misogyny surely belongs to Vergier, a very mediocre poet, commenting on a marriage between a Frenchman and a German woman who does not know French at all: "Qu'un mariage est plein d'appas,/Quand la nuit un époux peut contenter sa flamme,/ Et que le jour il n'entend pas,/Les sottises que dit sa femme" (Dec. 1725, p. 3049).

Misogyny apart, the emphasis upon the theme of fidelity is worthy of serious consideration. The short stories serialized in the *Mercure* often have as a central theme a test of male and female virtue. Even when at fault, men usually emerge unscathed. One tale, *La Méprise concertée* (Jan. 1720, pp. 72-86; Feb., pp. 42-59) relates a stratagem used by the lively but virtuous heroine Lucinde to test the fidelity of her lover. To her dismay, he is proved unfaithful. She lives to regret her hasty action in rejecting him for this minor fault, particularly as her refusal of an arranged marriage with a rich man results in her confinement in a convent. All's well that ends well, however—the rich man loses his money and Lucinde is reunited with her albeit faithless lover. The *Histoire d'Abulmer* set in Egypt (July 1722, pp. 30-77) focuses on a young man who embarks on an affair with a mysterious and beautiful woman who demands of him fidelity as proof of his love. Abulmer resists temptation to his utmost, but is finally unfaithful with a beautiful princess whom he has rescued from a wicked genie. To his consternation, the princess in front of his eyes takes on the form of his loved one. But Abulmer is pardoned—his love explains that she is a sylph and will excuse human infidelity. The moral seems to be that only sylphs, not men and women, are constant. Another long and involved story, *Les Apparences trompeuses* (Aug. 1723, pp. 257-73; Sept., pp. 440-56) concerns the marriage of two close women friends to men of rival families who are enemies, with the ensuing complication that each man falls in love with the other's wife. The women's friendship stands this test and, by complex ruse and intrigue, the situation is righted—the men realize the error of their respective infatuations, and the constancy of the women's feelings is justified. It is revealing to note that in these tales men are allowed weaknesses and are welcomed back generously by their wives and lovers.

Women, on the contrary, are often harshly treated. The heroine of Madame de Lafayette's short story *La Comtesse de Tende* (June 1724, pp. 1267-91) pays dearly for her infidelity. In effect abandoned by her husband who has tired of her, she tries to suppress her passion for the chevalier de Navarre by encouraging him to make a financially advantageous marriage. Their liaison continues, however, complicated by the fact that the Comte de Tende has once again fallen passionately in love with his wife "comme si elle n'eût point été sa femme." She becomes pregnant by Navarre and, on hearing news of his death, informs her husband by letter of her infidelity and decides to die. Her son is still-born at six months, and she dies several days later. The Comte de Tende is relieved by this outcome and never remarries. A woman who transgresses society's laws and commits adultery is cruelly punished; her honesty places her in an untenable position, and she chooses death as a self-affirmation. In a less tragic vein, Vergier explored the theme of involuntary infidelity in a *Nouvelle Portugaise* (Jan. 1725, pp. 46-64; Feb., pp. 214-34). Two young lovers, Don Juan and Isabelle, are separated because of the disparity of their fortunes. Don Juan is reported killed in Brazil and Isabelle reluctantly agrees to marry Don Gusman, the brother of her best friend, who is deeply in love with her. The unexpected return of Juan and Isabelle's sense of guilt lead to a plan on the part of the lovers to flee together, forestalled only by the kidnapping of

Isabelle by pirates. Juan sets out on an epic journey to rescue her, only to find her on the point of death, having swallowed poison rather than be dishonored. Vergier subconsciously sees to it that women suffer before attaining happiness. Juan is in time to administer an antidote, and on their return to Portugal, Don Gusman yields his claims to Isabelle in the face of such an enduring passion. In this tale, Isabelle is portrayed as a passive being, constantly acted on by others, who has to expiate her fault. Women, then, generally have little control over situations and can rarely exert their will unless it be through death or ruse. The *Mercure* of the early 1720s reflected male desire for a virtuous, faithful, and beautiful woman who would yield gracefully and remain constant. Very often the depiction of human relationships is taken from seventeenth-century writers such as Vergier and Madame de Lafayette reflecting a negative view of women and a consciousness of their powerlessness except in matters of deceit.

The *Journal encyclopédique* of the early 1780s presents a somewhat different view of women. It was a serious publication echoing the views and preoccupations of the philosophes and dealt particularly with reviews of works in the natural sciences, history, economics, etc., affording less space to literary concerns. A typical number (Jan. 1, 1780) contained review articles of works on commerce, the proceedings of the Académie de Berlin, the treatment of rabies, a work of world history, the first two volumes of the *Bibliothèque des romans,* a volume of the *Annales poétiques,* a translation of Shakespeare, accounts of charitable works, unusual events (for example, a case of Siamese twins), new inventions, and literary, political, and court news. Within this diverse range of material, female characteristics are often discussed.

A certain degree of distrust of women is still apparent. A Comte de M— in his *Réflexions sur l'amour* (1780.iv.500–54) believes that contact with women, presumably sexual, leads to "l'abattement, la perte des forces, les maladies de langueur, une vieillesse prématurée" (p. 503). Not only do women weaken man, they are also gluttons who will take the food out of his mouth. A short poem, *La Perdrix,* in the December 1780 issue of the *Journal,* relates the greed of a woman who, having eaten her husband's and the priest's supper, contrives to set them against each other and escape reprisals herself. Even the beauty of the female body is put in question on one occasion. Winckelmann's opinion that women are physically inferior to men is quoted; he had stated that the breast was intended primarily to nourish and that its beauty does not last long (1782.iv.72-87). The editors of the *Journal* are more conciliatory and claim that ideas differ, many still believing the female breast to be an object of beauty. In some ways women compare unfavorably with animals. Béranger's poem *Les Deux Chiennes* (1782.ii.479-81) praises two bitches—Sultane, an expensive lapdog, and Diane, a kitchen mutt—who suckle their own pups. When Sultane's milk runs dry, she brings her pup with great difficulty to Diane to suckle and then provides the other bitch with food. The episode is held up as a moral lesson to women, who may or may not have resented being compared unfavorably with bitches.

In the period examined there were reviews of several novels and plays with a tragic ending or presenting a narrowly averted tragedy. Loaisel de Tréogate's *La Comtesse d'Alibre ou le cri du sentiment* (1780.ii.285-90) relates the sad tale of a girl who, out of daughterly duty, marries a man she does not love. In despair at being the cause of her unhappiness, her father dies of grief. She has a baby by her lover, is imprisoned by her jealous husband to die of starvation, is saved too late for survival, and is shortly followed to the grave by her grief-stricken lover. Alexandrine, the heroine of Mademoiselle de Saint-Léger's *Alexandrine ou l'amour est une vertu* (1782.vii.458-63)[5] had been raped and had a child by the age of thirteen. She fell in love with a noble young man but abandoned him to marry a rich man. She died of chagrin as a result, realizing that she had foregone the joys of family life. Loaisel de Tréogate's philosophic novel *Dolbreuse ou l'homme du siècle ramené à la vertu par le sentiment et par la raison* (1783.vii.279-86) deals with the gradual lessening of Dolbreuse's love for his wife Ermance as business takes him more and more frequently away from home. He is unfaithful to her and leads a dissolute life. Imprisoned for debt, he is rescued by the faithful Ermance, who settles his obligations. The reconciliation turns to tragedy when Ermance dies during pregnancy. Dolbreuse has her body cremated and takes the ashes away to a solitary retreat to meditate on his sins and his loss. The feminist reader continues to wish for a somewhat more positive reward for female virtue! The message becomes clearer. True love should win out over all obstacles and those who oppose it are at fault. The pathos of a situation such as that of the Comtesse d'Alibre or of Dolbreuse is well calculated to move the sentimental eighteenth-century audience. Stress is put upon the unhappiness caused by the failure to recognize or by the prevention of fulfillment of true love. Money, position, and birth should be inconsequential factors in the choice of a marriage partner.

A 1780 review of Baculard's *Les Epoux malheureux* exemplifies ideal happiness. A father opposes the marriage of his son to a woman of lower social rank and even succeeds in obtaining an annulment of the marriage. But he finally repents and allows the couple to be reunited, not before a conniving countess, who is in love with the hero and has fed the father's anger, commits suicide. A sequel, the *Suite des époux malheureux* (1783.v.284-89), presents the united family, grandparents, parents and children, all revelling in the joys of the hearth. Marriage then should be the natural outcome of love, unsullied by thoughts of commercial gain or prestigious alliances.

Rarely is love presented as a dangerous passion. The tone of a review of a comic opera *Aristote amoureux, ou le philosophe bridé* is light and humorous. Even a sober philosopher can lose his reason and become a slave to a pretty woman. Only once in the period did I find female fickleness sharply attacked. In a poem *La Galerie des femmes du siècle* (1783.iv.298-306), the author, Beaumarchais, comments ironically that the women of his time are so delicate in sentiment that they balk at taking more than four lovers at one time! The message is misogynistic: "Toute femme vaut un hommage,/ Bien peu sont dignes d'un regret" (pp. 305-6). But essentially the middle-class ideal of monogamous marriage dominates the pages of the *Journal.* It is not surprising to find an energetic refutation of a work advocating polygamy. The nobility even encouraged marriage and childbirth. In 1780 the Vicomte de Ségur is praised for financing the marriage of a poor couple. A poem is quoted praising the virtuous action of a girl who got an advance on her dowry from her father to give to a widow with eight children (1782.iv.470-73). A freemasons' lodge in Paris enthroned a mother of eighteen children (1783.iii.131-2), who was further honored by having the Baronne de Champlot act as godmother to number nineteen. And the supreme example of female virtue is that of a woman who takes in her husband's illegitimate child to nurse and raise (1780.vii.149-50). Married love is seen as a rational passion, and the value of having a husband as friend as well as lover realized. Self-sacrifice for one's family and children is preached. One short story favorably resumed concerns a noble village girl sacrificing her virtue to the lord of the manor to save her brother. Like Mademoiselle de Saint-Yves in Voltaire's *L'Ingénu,* her noble action puts all to shame, but, unlike Voltaire's heroine, she is rewarded by a happy marriage to an honest village boy. In the 1780s one is allowed to be dishonored if it is with good motives. The same collection of stories (Imbert's *Lecture du matin, ou nouvelles historiettes en prose* (1782.vi.457-68) includes the tale of a flirt, Constance, who has a daughter out of wedlock. She conceals her identity from the girl, becomes her servant, and inspires her with virtue, revealing her true identity only on her death bed.

How to produce such a gentle, self-abnegating creature? Many works in the *Journal encyclopédique* are concerned with education. Madame de Genlis' *Théâtre à l'usage des jeunes personnes* reviewed in April 1780 includes plays encouraging "bienfaisance," virtue, and piety, and exhorts mothers to busy themselves with their daughters' education. She also produced an *Annales de la vertu, ou cours d'histoire à l'usage des jeunes personnes* (1781.iii. 41-52), highly praised by the reviewer. Women are forever advised to be charitable and virtuous. The review of Madame d'Epinay's *Conversations d'Emilie* (1781.iii.390-98) highlights a banal conversation between Emilie and her mother on the joys of charity. And we read in the *Nouvelles littéraires* of 1781 (viii) of a new publication by Mademoiselle Loquet, the *Entretiens d'Angélique pour exciter les jeunes personnes du sexe à l'amour & la pratique de la vertu*! Another work reviewed, Madame de Genlis' *Adèle et Théodore, ou lettres sur l'éducation* (1782.iii.191.211; 417-40), deals with the decision of a noble couple to bring up their two children in the country, far from the corrupting influence of Paris. The reviewer singles out for criticism two female traits— flirtatiousness and frivolity. Adèle's weakness lies in spending her monthly allowance on frivolities and she is encouraged to be serious and considerate of others. And of course the editors of the *Journal* frown on sexual promiscuity—a review of Rousseau's *Confessions* reveals the contributor's angry disapproval of Rousseau's acceptance of madame de Warens' conduct. The ideal submissive woman would be the result of the education preached in an English work, *Letters Addressed to Two Young Married Ladies* (reviewed 1783.iii,406-14). While cultivation of the intellectual faculties in women is encouraged, they should above all be trained in modesty and in keeping their husbands happy even if the men behave badly. A wife should always be "douce, prévenante & honnête." A work such as Wandelaincourt's *Cours d'éducation* (1782.v.352-6; vii.55-66) offers women an enlarged course of studies, but argues that less time should be spent on their education than on that of men, as they are less capable of sustained thought and application. They need practical knowledge to apply to the running of a household. One feels that this spurt of interest in education for women has the interests of male comfort and security at heart. Even the academy of sciences of Châlons-sur-Marne offered a prize for the answer to the question "Quels seraient les moyens de perfectionner l'education des femmes en France? " But the only possible rôle for women that is preached at this period in the *Journal* is that of wife and mother.

It is no doubt because of this that male doctors felt a moral responsibility for dealing with female complaints. There is serious concern about puerperal fever.[6] One writer in fact asserted that men have a moral obligation to come to the aid of the mother of the species. References in the *Journal* indicate the active encouragement of breast-feeding. The academy of Bordeaux even offered a prize for suggestions of how to supply mother's milk to foundlings. And one Monsieur de Lacroix went so far as to suggest that the state establish places where women would be free to go and suckle their own babies (were their husbands to object to this practice at home) and even suckle others whose mothers have no milk (*Réflexions philosophiques sur la civilisation,* reviewed 1783.iv.32-7). One feels that the invention mentioned in the 1783 *Journal* (vii.535) of a pump designed to release milk from swollen breasts might have been a solution acceptable to the Bordeaux academy. Even the stigma of illegitimacy is attacked. A review of a German work argues that the state should try to make life easier for unmarried mothers and not moralize to them (*Quels sont les meilleurs moyens praticables d'empêcher l'infanticide,* 1782.vi. 33-9). The life of the child has become valuable and the same Monsieur de Lacroix is concerned to prevent unmarried women from being shamed and mocked, which might cause them in desperation to kill their offspring. From one angle, these arguments are positive; from another, negative, in that they continue solely to see women as childbearers and perpetuators of the race.

Searching for traces of feminism in the *Journal encyclopédique* is not a rewarding task, although it is more fruitful than searching in the *Mercure.* In the period studied, reviews of works specifically about women were rare and the interest evinced mainly historical, in studies of famous women of the past.[7] A few brave attempts were made to stand up for women's rights. One Madame D—, writing from Caen (1780.v.144-6), complains of the inequality of the law, that it is always the woman who is arrested in cases of seduction and prostitution. She argues that men are equally guilty and should also be punished. Another contributor writes in to tell of the physical courage of a female boatman who maneuvered her boat to save a drowning man while the male boatmen did nothing (1780.vii.523-25). Women are as brave as men, argues the contributor. Her example perhaps encouraged the editors to print an account of Lady Harriet Ackland, who performed prodigies of valor while on campaign with her husband in North America, crossing enemy lines in an advanced state of pregnancy to join her wounded husband (1781.i.335-38). Another unusual essay (1782.vii.124-33) deals with the compensation for time lost of individuals unjustly imprisoned. The contributor argues that single women should receive as much as men on a scale according to their position, and that married women should receive two-thirds compensation. Although few and far between, these examples point to an embryonic realization of the unjust social system and its preconceived ideas about women.

It is now apparent how much views about women changed during the eighteenth century. The *Mercure de France* in the 1720s primarily reflects male fears about the deceit, frivolity, and fickleness of women. Love is conceived of as a dangerous passion. It is perhaps revealing that it is in fiction that faithful women are portrayed, women who would die rather than betray their lover. Gradually the ethic of virtuous behavior passes from the fictional realm to treatises on morality. Interestingly, the Marquise de Lambert, writing advice to her daughter in 1728, insists, in much the same terms as the moralists of the late eighteenth century, on the need for a sound education for women, subordinate only to an education in morality and virtue, which is a safeguard for women in an unjust world. The emergence of what has been defined as a bourgeois ideal of marriage and ethics strongly influences the choice of works reviewed in the *Journal encyclopédique*. Woman has been metamorphosed from sinner to saint, and by instilling in her from youth moral precepts praising her role as dutiful wife and mother, men hope perhaps to preserve for themselves great liberty of conduct while being assured of a serene home with a loving wife. Writers who believe women's intellectual capacity to equal that of men are extremely rare. Even Diderot, who tends towards this view, shares the opinion of a theorist such as Thomas, who argues that women, because of their physical make-up, are more sensitive and imaginative than men and excel in different areas.[8] The areas suggested in the *Journal encyclopédique* are rather constricted. It is interesting to speculate why so many women enthusiastically adopted virtuous behavior and selfless devotion to husband and family as a model. Is it instinctive or is it a form of self-protection? The law discriminated against the wife in matters of adultery, as she could bring *false* heirs into the family, but punished the husband only if he brought another woman to the married home. If you make yourself impregnably virtuous, as Madame de Lambert argues, you can never be criticized and you are in control. We might agree when we see the tragic results of the Présidente de Tourvel's departure from virtue in the *Liaisons dangereuses,* which may be interpreted variously as a reinforcement of the moral lessons on fidelity or as an ironic comment on the impossibility of expecting women to be totally absolute and constant in their emotional lives. The tensions caused by the dual image of women portrayed in the *Mercure de France* and the *Journal encyclopédique* are still with us today.

NOTES

1 There are notable exceptions; see, for example, L. Abensour, *La Femme et le féminisme avant la révolution* (Paris: Leroux, 1923), and E. and J. de Goncourt, *La Femme au XVIIIe siècle* (Paris: Didot, 1862).

2 S. Sherman, "A Portrait of Woman Through the Eyes of Denis Diderot," *Dissertation Abstracts International (DAI),* 32, 400A; S. Markiewicz, "The Question of Feminine Liberty in the Writings of Denis Diderot," *DAI,* 33, 6921A; P. De Gain, "Voltaire et les femmes," *DAI,* 34, 1900A-1A; O. B. Cragg, "The Novels of Madame Riccoboni," *DAI,* 31, 6598A; J. Stewart, "The Novels of Madame Riccoboni," *DAI,* 32, 456A-57A; P. Rose, "Introduction to the Life and Works of Madame Riccoboni," *DAI* 34, 2651A.

3 Female contributors are mainly poets of stylized and platitudinous verse. I also noted an article on the plague in Arles by a woman (Feb. 1722, pp. 62-74).

4 See, for example, *Borée & Orythie* (Dec. 1724, pp. 2503-6).

5 The reviewer comments that the author is producing her second novel within a year, a prodigy for a sex "voué à la dissipation."

6 Reviews of *Mémoire sur la maladie qui a attaqué en différents temps les femmes en couche à l'Hôtel-Dieu de Paris* (1783.iii.244-8); *Recherches sur la nature et le traitement de la fièvre puerpérale* (1783.viii.215-27).

7 See, for example, a life of Renée, Duchess of Ferrara, a scholar and Lutheran (1781.iv.pt.iii), and a translation, from the English, *Exemples remarquables de l'influence des femmes et du rôle important qu'elles jouent en Asie* (1781.vi.503-11).

8 See A.-L. Thomas, *Essai sur le caractère, les moeurs et l'esprit des femmes dans les différents siècles* (Paris: Moutard, 1772), p. 151.

Toward a Definition of Utopia

OSCAR A. HAAC

In order to arrive at a creative definition, one enabling us to trace the basic literary theme, admittedly in a philosophical and political context, we do not aim to encompass all possible uses of the term but nonetheless one broad enough to allow for the diverse approaches in the writings we shall discuss.[1] In so doing we postulate no specific attitudes, optimism or a belief in progress, for instance, nor shall we limit ourselves to a given literary form such as the novel. In many ways, our diverse concerns parallel those gathered by Frank Manuel, in *Utopias and Utopian Thought.*[2] Our objective here is to discover a common ground.

The spirit of utopia was movingly defined by Martin Buber; we reproduce his poetic passage in condensed form:

> Utopias . . . are . . . "fantasy" . . . [but fantasy] not driven . . . by the winds of caprice, . . . something primary . . . which it is [man's] destiny to build. . . . In the history of the human spirit, the image-creating wish [for utopia] . . is the longing for the *rightness* which, in religion or philosophical vision, is experienced as revelation or idea, and which by its very nature cannot be realized in the individual, but only in human community. . . . All suffering under a social order that is senseless, prepares the soul for vision, and what the soul receives in this vision, strengthens and deepens its insight into perversity. . . . The longing for the realization of "the seen" fashions this picture.[3]

Buber sees utopian vision arising in the social context, primarily from injustice and the need for reform. For him, utopia is no escape, and the dream of a better world is ever present as a significant hope.

In accord with Buber's implications, we shall therefore exclude from our consideration not only individual adventure, as in *Robinson Crusoe,* but also nostalgic religious evocations of paradise, and, indeed, theories concerning the origins of mankind, for these lack the future dimension of utopia even when they involve a critique of man's present state. On the other hand, we shall not judge utopias by their implementation. The dream in literature concerns us here, not its realization. We are, therefore, far from agreeing with the rigid Marxist views of Raymond Ruyer,[4] who felt that the typical utopian author had lost touch with reality; Ruyer rejected eighteenth-century writers much as Marx castigated utopian socialists. Buber's definition is most helpful here, for it related the dream, the vision of what is not—and utopia is not, by definition—to justice and the necessity for change.

The debate concerning utopia has been clouded not only by the antagonism between Marxists and utopian socialists, without which Mannheim's fundamental contrast between ideology and utopia[5] would be hard to explain, but also by the attempt to identify a complex structure of archetypes. The most striking example here is Roger Mucchielli,[6] who studies forms of revolt, types of visions of freedom, leading to utopian communities or to revolution. In Mucchielli, utopia appears like a hidden god, revealed by the phenomenology of the ideal city. For him, utopia is a vision, a Promethean protest against the human condition, but since it is not the actual reform movement or revolution in history, it cannot be comprehended by the sociologist, especially since all reformers seek power and are likely to establish rigid systems, petrified utopias which no longer are ideal cities. Nor is it a subject matter for the psychologist, for the personal problems that impel the utopian leader cannot explain the motivation of thousands of followers; the individual dream is not the group's vision of reform; the personal needs of an author (for example, Rousseau's search for a refuge) cannot explain his plan for social organization (as in the *Contrat social*). Thus Mucchielli wants to safeguard the philosopher's prerogatives in defining utopia, but it is doubtful whether his categories clarify the vision. We prefer to reduce the archetypes to two, refuge and reform, as suggested by Giulio Bruni Roccia in his superb study of Campanella,[7] but modifying his point of view. While he considers refuge and reform as mutually exclusive alternatives (enlisting Campanella in the ranks of the fighters for reform), we propose to use them as the opposite poles of a scale against which we can measure individual proposals.

Let us illustrate this first by recalling the problem of Candide's garden. Is it a refuge or a base for action? It is partly refuge, for Candide could scarcely mediate while running the gauntlet of Bulgar swords, but in the garden he can exchange his "candid" views with brother Martin's pessimism and the optimism of Pangloss. On the other hand, the garden is as much a base for action as Ferney, where Voltaire hardly lived as a hermit. Candide chose to stay not in remote Eldorado, prosperous but meaningless to the world, but where philosophizing could produce plans for reform.

A second example of the interplay between the search for refuge and the call for reform is provided by Rousseau. When editing the *Projet de paix perpétuelle* by the abbé de Saint-Pierre, he shows his respect for the "noble" dream but feels that a second coming of Henri IV is not an eventuality: the powers of Europe will hardly acquiesce and abide by a rational ideal. Still, Rousseau sees merit in his enterprise:

> Je vais voir, au moins en idée, les hommes s'unir et s'aimer; je vais penser à une douce et paisible société de frères, vivant dans une concorde éternelle, tous conduits par les mêmes maximes, tous heureux de bonheur commun, et réalisant en soi-même un tableau si touchant; l'image d'une félicité qui n'est point m'en fera goûter quelques instants une véritable.[8]

Such happiness is a refuge and a vision of what ought to be. Rousseau is realistic. He admits that the *Projet* is impractical[9] and that the belief in the rule of reason is naïve:

> L'homme n'est qu'un être sensible qui consulte uniquement ses passions pour agir et à qui la raison ne sert qu'à pallier les sottises qu'elles lui font faire.[10]

But then he is also the author of *La Nouvelle Héloïse*, where Julie calls Saint-Preux to Clarens in order to harness his passions and where, after her initial surrender, "la faute," Julie rises to saintliness. Such progress may be "literature," the *littérature* he condemned in the *Confessions,* but everywhere Rousseau assumes that obstacles do not invalidate the ideal. Man's inalienable rights are, for example, not suspended but only temporarily vitiated when one is threatened by a brigand's pistol (*Contrat* I, 3). War may be a reality, inevitable as Voltaire calls it in the *Dictionnaire philosophique* ("Guerre"), but it is not justice. When writing constitutions for Poland and Corsica, Rousseau pictures Poland surrounded by threatening neighbors[11] and Corsica ruled by foreign interests, adding: "Quiconque dépend d'autrui et n'a pas les ressources en lui-même, ne saurait être libre."[12] And yet, he writes the constitutions! The utopian ideal remains a plan for action.

Rousseau emphasizes the need for reform a great deal more than Hobbes, but even Hobbes gravitates between the poles of surrender and of resistance. Hobbes is apt to justify the power of the sovereign, but he also states that the subject is no longer bound by the compact when his sovereign fails to defend and protect him.[13] Rousseau extends the natural right of self-defense to the civil right of recall, of replacing magistrates who have proved unsatisfactory. Compared to Hobbes, Rousseau has increased the part of action and moved on the scale from the idea of utopia as a refuge toward the conception of utopia as a call for reform.

It would seem desirable that any literary definition which encompasses this myth be applicable to the essential writings of the century from the abbé de Saint-Pierre to Voltaire, Rousseau, and Diderot, to the *Supplément au voyage de Bougainville* as much as to Morelly's *Basiliade* and *Code de la nature.* We will, therefore, not limit our definition to as circumscribed a genre as the imaginary voyage and the utopian novels that created the genre: *L'Histoire des Sévarambes* (1675) by Denis Vairasse, a rational image of government not unrelated to the principles of Locke; *Les Aventures de Jacques Sadeur ou La Terre australe connue* (1676) by Gabriel de Foigny, a deistic view of society and religion with a parody of sexual mores in the description of hermaphrodite Australians; *Les Voyages de Jacques Massé* (1710) by Tyssot de Patot, a philosophe who shed every vestige of orthodoxy. These novels, with others in a more realistic vein, led to a vast literature part of which is gathered in the startling collection of Charles Garnier, *Voyages imaginaires, songes,* and related writings.[14]

While proposing our broader definition centered between refuge and reform, one fitting the contributions to our present program, we are ready to admit that the utopian novel deserves a history of its own such as has just been provided by Raymond Trousson,[15] who would like to reserve the term *utopia* for this genre:

> La réalisation de l'utopie requiert l'utilisation du roman. . . . On pourra donc parler d'utopie lorsque, dans un cadre narratif (ce qui exclut les traités politiques comme le *Contrat social* ou les critiques pures de l'ordre existant, comme le *Testament* de Meslier) se voit animée une collectivité (ce qui exclut la robinsonnade).[16]

Our less restrictive definition aims to illustrate the dream, the concept rather than a literary form. Here the *traité* seems as significant as the novel, evocations of reformed societies as important as lands of fantasy. We must add that these elements are frequently intertwined, as in *Cleveland,* where utopian societies in Africa and America are pictured along with the progression toward natural religion. Indeed, the bibliographies furnished by Trousson far transcend the limits he sets in his literary definition.

What attracts us to utopia is the myth, the creative vision, the normative ideal which calls for social change, the view of a better world into which the author projects himself. He may, of course, be doing so without adequate regard for contemporary realities: Rousseau's *Discours sur l'inégalité,* for instance, assumes the model of a republican Geneva in which citizens of Geneva could not recognize themselves.[17] Still, this does not diminish the pertinence of the *Discours.* Mercier, who prided himself on having predicted the reforms of the French Revolution in *L'Année 2440,* is not, for all that, more perspicacious; his book seems less than brilliant, his idea of book-burning repulsive, his concept of history more static than dynamic, his work further removed from reality than that of Rousseau. It should be clear, however, that our appreciation of Rousseau and strictures of Mercier derives from the quality of their contributions; they are independent of the question of whether or not their reforms became reality. The adequacy of utopian vision does not lie in the realization of social change; the author need not be borne out by future developments. The Daedalus conference was unable to discover a relationship between utopia and future experience except to agree that the future is unknown. Utopia is "Noch-nicht-Erfahrung," to use the term coined by Ernst Bloch.[18] The future cannot be the measure of utopian vision, even if it is shaped by it.

The history of these visions remains to be written and described in its multiple manifestations during the eighteenth century. This could be accomplished in the way Robert Mauzi traced *L'Idée du bonheur au dix-huitième siècle,*[19] but it will be no easy task for a century rarely given to withdrawing into aesthetics. On the other hand, it becomes more feasible now that we have gained distance from the unrestrained ideas of progress and plans for utopian communities found in the nineteenth century. Indeed, interest has greatly increased. After the Daedalus conference (1964-65) there have been others, including the Colloque international des lumières at Lille (1973) with an important section devoted to utopia.[20] Many of its participants also contributed to a special issue of the *Revue des Sciences humaines* with a lead article by Raymond Trousson, an invaluable commentary on recent publications.[21]

This activity cannot obscure deep differences in interpretation; in fact, they keep the issue alive. The recent dialogue can be said to have begun with Karl Mannheim and continued in the debate between Raymond Ruyer, an orthodox communist, and George Duveau's "serious attempt at a rehabilitation of the 'realistic' eighteenth- and nineteenth-century utopias as worthy guides for the world of tomorrow, in preference to Hegelian-Marxist determinism."[22] George Kateb, in *Utopia and Its Enemies,*[23] opposes Duveau from another point of view; he harbors sharp animosities not only against optimistic and rationalistic theories of progress but against what he considers abuses, like "conditioned" virtue in B. F. Skinner's *Walden Two.* To Kateb, this is no virtue but part of technocracy and dystopia, the nightmare first described in Aldous Huxley's *Brave New World* (1932). A pertinent parody of egalitarian democracy is "Harrison Bergeron" (1961) by Kurt Vonnegut,[24] where government makes sure that genius cannot manifest itself. Such perspectives of infinite power make what Edward Bellamy envisioned as a cure for private greed, the industrial army proposed in *Looking Backward* (1888), seem like an ominous anticipation of the horrors of state control. Gunther Stent, in *The Coming of the Golden Age,*[25] even suggests that the society of plenty and technological control is at hand without having brought utopia one inch closer. The problem is that we cannot look at the past, at utopia in the eighteenth century, without the dubious benefit of our historical experience, from the French Revolution to the faith in progress of Fouriéristes and Icarians, two world wars, and recent views of dystopia. They will intrude in our most objective evaluations, in our attempt to analyze eighteenth-century utopia as an essential myth and a driving force.

The essays which follow involve our broad definition of utopia as a creative vision and normative ideal. Happiness in the abbé Prévost is one topic, the theme of hope set against unsurmountable obstacles, the key to an utopian vision. Others develop plans for reform in France or Spain, plans which often led to nothing but remain essential aspects of the eighteenth-century world view. Some schemes for organizing the Revolution involve a paradoxical structure, restrictive laws promising freedom. The problem is the one faced by Rousseau when he postulated that, to maximize freedom, the individual must heed the general will and, should he resist, must be "forced to be free."[26] Bertrand Russell concluded that Rousseau was the precursor of Hitler,[27] but this interpretation seems patently unjust. An author should not be judged because someone later misused his ideas; a dream of reform can be valid even if poorly realized, and such a dream, systematized into a form of government, is no longer a utopian vision.

Eighteenth-century utopias are far more often a driving force for reform than a refuge; they propose no paradise, no pastoral idyl, in an age which mobilized even the good savage to criticize contemporary society. At times, utopias may appear as illusions, but more frequently they are a creative force, a vision like that which guided Antoine Adam, who wrote:

> En un temps où toutes sortes de sollicitudes invitent les Français à chercher un refuge dans l'irrationnel et l'inhumain, à tenir pour non avenue la tradition de l'humanisme . . . il est nécessaire d'entretenir . . . le culte d'une littérature où s'affirment de façon prestigieuse le refus de l'imposture, l'exigence de la lucidité, la foi dans la raison, un sentiment héroïque de la liberté.[28]

The rational ideal here expressed seems central to eighteenth-century utopia.

NOTES

1 This essay is conceived as an introduction to those which follow, all part of the round table concerning utopia, part of the Fourth International Congress on Enlightenment held at Yale University, July 13-20, 1975.

2 Boston: Beacon Press, 1967; a remarkable collection of contributions to the Daedalus conference. It includes an introduction (pp. vii-xxiv) referring to previous work and conferences and analyzing present perspectives, as well as the article "Toward a Psychological History of Utopias" (pp. 69-98), both by Frank Manuel. He is the co-editor, with

Fritzie P. Manuel, of *French Utopias* (New York: Free Press, 1966), and the author of studies on H. de Saint-Simon and other utopians.

3 *Paths in Utopia* (Boston: Beacon Press, 1958), pp. 7-8.

4 *L'Utopie et les utopies* (Paris: Presses Universitaires de France, 1950).

5 *Ideology and Utopia* (London: Kegan Paul, 1936), where "ideology" is generally linked to the conservative-intellectual outlook, while "Utopia" expresses all revolutionary protest.

6 *Le Mythe de la cité idéale* (Paris: Presses Universitaires de France, 1960).

7 "L'Utopia del Campanelle e gli architipi della società politica," in Academia nazionale dei lincei, *Problemi attuali di scienza e di cultura,* vol. 126: *Atti del convegno internazionale sul tema: Campanella e Vico* (Rome, 1969), pp. 181-219. Roccia argues that *La Città del sole* is pertinent today because it was a plan for reform, not for refuge.

8 Rousseau, *Oeuvres complètes* (Paris: Gallimard, 1964), III, 563-64.

9 Ibid., p. cxxxiii, note of May 6, 1759.

10 Ibid., p. 554; *Fragments politiques,* XVI, "Des moeurs." Cf. pp. cxxix-cxxx. Mably agreed with Rousseau.

11 Ibid., p. 959.

12 Ibid., p. 903.

13 *Leviathan* II, 31. Cf. II, 17-18 on the social compact.

14 Amsterdam, 1787-89, 39 vols., analyzed by Philip Gove, *The Imaginary Voyage in Prose Fiction* (New York: Columbia University Press, 1941), pp. 31-63. He concludes: "No final and exclusive definition of the imaginary voyage is possible."

15 *Voyages aux pays de nulle part: Histoire littéraire de la pensée utopique* (Brussels: Editions de l'Université de Bruxelles, 1975).

16 "Utopie et roman utopique," *Revue des sciences humaines,* fasc. 155 (1972-74), pp. 367-78, esp. pp. 372-73.

17 Franco Venturi, *Utopia and Reform in the Enlightenment* (Cambridge: Cambridge University Press, 1971), p. 77.

18 Manuel, *Utopias and Utopian Thought,* pp. xi, xiv, *n*2.

19 Paris: Armand Colin, 1960.

20 Three vols. of proceedings are to appear.

21 "Utopie et roman utopique" (see *n*16 above).

22 *Utopias and Utopian Thought,* p. xi, where Manuel evaluates the posthumous work by Georges Duveau, *Sociologie de l'utopie*, ed. A. Canivaz (Paris: Presses Universitaires de France, 1961). In "Résurrection de l'utopie," a chapter published in 1958, Duveau explains the renewed interest in utopia: "Il est bien entendu que l'univers dans lequel nous vivons aujourd'hui, un univers labouré, ensemencé par l'utopie, permet de mieux comprendre dans quelles conditions l'*Aufklärer* et le dialecticien hégélien ou marxiste se sont affrontés" (p. 40).

23 New York: Schocken Books, 1972.
24 In *Welcome to the Monkey House* (New York: Dell, 1973).
25 New York: Museum of Natural History, 1969.
26 *Contrat social,* I, 7.
27 *A History of Western Philosophy* (London: Allen and Unwin, 1946), p. 711.
28 *Histoire de la littérature française au XVII*[e] *siècle* (Paris: Del Duca, 1964), V, 6.

L'Utopie: Tentative de réintégration universelle

E. ROGER CLARK

> Dans toute révolte se découvrent l'exigence métaphysique de l'unité, l'impossibilité de s'en saisir, et la fabrication d'un univers de remplacement. La révolte de ce point de vue, est fabricatrice d'univers. Ceci définit l'art aussi.
>
> Albert Camus, *L'Homme révolté*

> . . . a serious vision of society as a single intellectual pattern, in other words a Utopia.
>
> Northrop Frye, *Anatomy of Criticism*

Le privilège du texte utopique est de participer à la fois au rêve (création de l'imagination individuelle ou collective) et à la réalité (par son reflet d'un état actuel et immédiat). Cette double fonction, insérée dans un cadre littéraire, nous permet d'identifier un genre particulier qui a créé sa propre tradition en se renouvelant à différents moments de l'histoire et dans différents pays. Nous examinerons trois façons par lesquelles l'utopie littéraire en France au dix-huitième siècle cherche à être non seulement le point de rencontre du rêve et de la réalité, mais aussi le lieu de réintégration de ces deux modes.

La fonction réintégrante de l'oeuvre utopique serait ainsi la résolution d'une confrontation (ou d'un écart) de valeurs qui par leur nature même se trouvent en opposition fondamentale. L'article "Songe" de l'*Encyclopédie* décrit la manière par laquelle l'imagination créatrice et consciente arrive à rétablir un équilibre essentiel: "L'imagination de la veille est une république policée, où la voix du magistrat remet tout en ordre; l'imagination des *songes* est la même république dans l'état d'anarchie."

Par son analyse et son remaniement des phénomènes de l'inconscient collectif le créateur d'utopie joue un rôle important dans le maintien d'une stabilité sociale, d'où l'aspect conservateur de grand nombre d'utopies. Mais l'utopie pousse également au prolongement de ces mêmes rêves de l'inconscient et devient par là oeuvre de rupture et éventuellement de révolution. Dans les deux cas cependant, assimilation de l'inconscient au conscient analytique et passage de l'état rêvé à un idéal platonique, il semble que l'utopie tend à une réintégration fondamentale ou à un dépassement de la dualité angoissante de la condition humaine. La République de l'Homme est ainsi remise en ordre et par là elle se rattache à la perfection même. Par ce double jeu, l'utopie, tout en soulignant l'incongruité de la réalité immédiate, devient la *révélation* et la *réalisation* du potentiel de l'homme socio-politique et de l'homme philosophe. Il est sans doute difficile, sinon impossible, de mesurer l'apport précis du texte utopique à l'acte révolutionnaire, quoique le lien entre les deux soit évident. Il est cependant utile de souligner en passant la fréquence avec laquelle des idées dites révolutionnaires trouvent leur première expression dans le texte utopique.

Sans nous laisser séduire par les attraits de l'exercice des définitions, nous tenterons ici de présenter trois aspects d'un phénomène qui nous semble appartenir à toute utopie: celui d'une tentative de réintégration universelle. En nous référant à des textes utopiques, nous présenterons trois dimensions de ce phénomène: Celle d'une *mythologie*, celle d'une *idéologie*, et celle d'une *ontologie*, afin de suggérer la fonction précise de cette aventure de l'esprit humain qu'est l'utopie. Pour le faire, il nous semble plus important de considérer la mentalité utopique en soi, que de réduire cette tradition à un catalogue limité et par là seule définissable.

Comme mythologie, l'utopie participe au rêve non seulement d'un âge d'or perdu mais en même temps d'un avenir magique. Elle représente ainsi l'étape centrale du passage d'une nostalgie collective tournée vers le passé à un espoir de réalisation dans l'immédiat. *Et in Arcadia ego*, triste devise des bergers de Poussin et d'un dix-septième siècle classique qui deviendra lui-même un des mythes du siècle suivant,[1] restera longtemps encore l'inspiration d'une théorie de renouveau socio-politique. La vision d'un jardin d'Eden transposé au plan laïque et redonné à l'homme *ut operaretur eum* n'est point étrangère au siècle des lumières, et de la Bétique qui "semble avoir conservé les délices de l'âge d'or" (*Télémaque*) à l'élaboration d'une doctrine physiocratique à base agricole il n'y a qu'un pas—pas qui traverse la propriété de Ferney, qu'on imagine comme la métairie de Candide ou comme Salente, "cultivée comme un jardin" (*Télémaque*).

Le jardin (*παράδεωος*) redevient pour le dix-huitième siècle le symbole de la restauration, à travers l'art, de la pureté et de l'innocence perdues. L'*Elisée* de Julie dans *La Nouvelle Héloïse* est avant tout la réalisation d'une oeuvre civilisatrice et la transposition du paradis terrestre à une réalité pratique. Le *Dictionnaire académique* de 1789 l'indique clairement par sa définition du mot "Elysée": "Terme de mythologie. Séjour où il n'y a d'admis que les héros et les hommes vertueux." C'est la définition même du pays utopique dont l'inaccessibilité ne fait que renforcer l'écart qui la sépare de la réalité sociale d'où elle est sortie. Il importe de ne pas perdre de vue ces liens essentiels à tout texte utopique et qui relient la réalité présente à cette autre réalité du passé qu'est le mythe.

Mais si l'utopie mythique s'efforce à éliminer la dimension historique, conséquence fatale d'une Chute primordiale, elle retrouve le Temps pour se projeter vers un avenir à réaliser et une postérité dont elle pressent déjà les qualités, car elles sont essentiellement les mêmes que celles des habitants du Paradis perdu. Le temps et l'espace imaginaires de la mythologie utopique restent en contact permanent avec l'évolution "réelle"[2] de la société dont elle est le produit, et forment la base d'un ensemble de croyances religieuses et mythiques qui servent de guides à l'homme social. Cette fonction directrice de l'utopie est à l'origine de sa raison d'être: exemple et enseignement qui permettront au groupe social de monter vers un état supérieur (du point de vue social et politique autant que moral).

L'existence de cet état idéal est l'élément principal du jeu utopique et est parfois tout simplement laissée au royaume de l'hypothèse—autant d'ailleurs que celui qu'on a "perdu": "état qui n'existe plus, qui n'a peut-être point existé, qui probablement n'existera jamais" (J.-J. Rousseau, *Discours sur l'origine de l'inégalité*). Cette perfection fabuleuse et irréalisable de l'utopie est reconnue comme telle par les auteurs de ces textes et renforce le caractère mythique du genre. A la conclusion de son *Utopie* Thomas Morus rend claire la distinction qu'il fait entre le "possible" et le "probable": ". . . fasse le Ciel que ce Monde puisse *s'Utopianiser!* C'est ce que je souhaite du fond de l'Ame, comme bon Individu de notre Espèce; & c'est ce que je n'espère point du tout."[3] Même le roi Stanislas avec son optimisme parfois naïf admet au début de son histoire du royaume de Dumocala l'impossibilité de son idéal: "Qu'il est triste que le bonheur du genre humain ne se rencontre qu'en des Pays inconnus, & qui nous sont inaccessibles!"[4] Enfin, le marquis de Sade lui aussi regrette "que ce ne soit que dans le pays des chimères que se trouve seulement le juste et le bon."[5]

Par son jeu permanent entre la réalité de l'immédiat et l'irréalisable d'un avenir fondé sur un passé mythique, l'utopie se crée une tension et une énergie vitales qui sont essentielles à sa fonction littéraire. Ces mondes, reflets de nos désirs, sont moins le produit d'une fuite de la réalité, que les formes authentiques que les hommes essaient d'imiter et d'atteindre, et qui deviennent en même temps des générateurs d'un dynamisme social remarquablement efficace.

Le parallèle entre utopisme et millénarisme a souvent été proposé et il semble que ce soit le même mouvement cyclique qui embrasse la mythologie utopique que celui qui domine la vision chiliastique. C'est ainsi que l'auteur du *Nouveau Cynée*, concluant son projet de paix universelle en 1623, proclame son désir de "ramener ce beau siècle que les anciens Théologiens promettent après la révolution de six mille ans. Car ils disent qu'alors le monde vivra heureusement & en repos."[6] Cet usage du mot "révolution" est un panneau indicateur de la direction que prendra la littérature utopique au courant des deux siècles qui vont suivre et à travers lesquels la recherche du paradis perdu trouvera sa motivation principale. Plus qu'une tradition, l'utopie est une manifestation du moment où la contemplation hésite avant de passer à l'acte. Sans elle l'acte perd son sens profond, par elle le mythe de la perfection collective est perpétué et garanti.[7]

Le mythe de la perfection collective devient idéologie lorsqu'on en tire un programme d'action politique, et il est certain qu'utopie et idéologie se côtoient dans leur analyse et leur critique implicite (ou explicite) de la réalité sociale, même si l'utopie se définit et se distingue par son aspect non pratique, que ce soit dans le temps ou dans l'espace.[8] C'est aussi ce que remarque Jean Le Clerc dans ses commentaires sur l'*Utopie* de Morus, traduit par Gueudeville en 1715: "En bâtissant une République dans le Nouveau Monde, que personne n'avoit vue & ne verroit jamais; il reprend obliquement les défauts que l'on remarque dans l'Ancien."[9] Il serait inutile d'insister sur cet aspect critique qui appartient à toute oeuvre utopique et qui se manifeste à des niveaux très divers, allant de la naïveté des pays de cocagne à la complexité des projets constitutionnels comme ceux de Stanislas ou de Morelly. Pourtant, c'est à partir de cette confrontation dialectique entre rêve et réalité politiques qu'on voit s'élaborer un ensemble de structures qui font partie de l'essentiel de la doctrine socialiste: transformation de la société par un retour au principe fondamental de la communauté unique (et fermée) avec tout ce que cela implique d'égalité réelle ou hypothétique.

Le rêve communautaire tel que l'utopie nous le livre n'est point étranger à cette mythologie dont nous venons de faire l'analyse. Si les variations sur ce rêve sont illimitées, le thème principal reste le même et est sans cesse repris par les textes utopiques. Une doctrine générale, même si elle est interprétée à travers des plans politiques très précis, laisse une place généreuse à une critique étendue de la réalité immédiate, mais on revient continuellement à la question de la propriété et de l'inégalité sociale qui en est la conséquence principale. De Thomas Morus

("Je suis donc entièrement persuadé . . . qu'il faudrait nécessairement abolir le Droit de propriété"[10]) jusqu'à la vision communiste de Morelly (". . . là où il n'existerait aucune propriété, il ne peut exister aucune de ses pernicieuses conséquences"[11]) l'analyse profonde de la réalité sociale reste en grande partie la même.

Cette idéologie retrouve le mythe par son rêve d'un nouveau système ou d'un nouvel ordre social basé sur ce que chacun interprète comme son propre "code de la nature," code universel dont la seule découverte suffit pour expliquer la structure génétique du corps social. Dans le miroir de l'utopie les nouveaux Prométhées promènent leurs flambeaux régénérateurs, mécanismes infaillibles qui feront que la société des hommes rejoindra la perfection de l'univers. Combien de sages législateurs ne trouve-t-on pas à l'origine des communautés idéales, législateurs qui par leur génie permettront aux citoyens de connaître les desseins du Grand Architecte: "Pour découvrir les meilleures règles de société qui conviennent aux nations, il faudrait une intelligence supérieure qui vît toutes les passions des hommes, et qui n'en éprouvât aucune; qui n'eût aucun rapport avec notre nature, et qui la connût à fond; dont le bonheur fût indépendant de nous, et qui pourtant voulût bien s'occuper du nôtre; enfain, qui, dans le progrès des temps se ménageant une gloire éloignée, pût travailler dans un siècle et jouir dans un autre. Il faudrait des dieux pour donner des lois aux hommes."[12] C'est ainsi qu'un ensemble de préceptes pourra devenir la clef du bonheur social et promettre un monde "où l'on est gouverné par les lois plutôt que par les hommes."[13]

On ne s'étonne donc pas de découvrir cette série d'utopies d'inspiration maçonnique au dix-huitième siècle qui, sous les formules d'une initiation mystique, renouvellent tous les rêves d'un avenir à réaliser: "C'est ainsi que le siècle de fer succéda au siècle d'or: Il durera dix mille ans; pendant ce temps Saturne se cache dans une retraite inaccessible; mais à la fin il reprendra les rênes de son empire, et rétablira l'univers dans son premier éclat: Alors toutes les âmes seront réunies à leur Principe."[14] L'apport de la littérature et de la pensée maçonniques à la doctrine révolutionnaire est également difficule à saisir, mais par sa cristallisation d'une réflexion politique ayant pour base la loi naturelle du Divin Architecte, la franc-maçonnerie participe à une idéologie utopique largement répandue au dix-huitième siècle. Quoi de moins surprenant que Montesquieu, législateur par excellence de son siècle, soit aussi un des premiers franc-maçons français (initié en Angleterre vers 1730). Lorsqu'une partie importante de la société trouve un ensemble de signes autour desquels se formulent des aspirations politiques pressantes on n'est pas loin de cette rupture qui s'appelle parfois révolution. Cet ensemble de signes trouve sa meilleure expression dans les textes utopiques du dix-huitième siècle: tradition idéologique qui existe pour encourager la réalisation du rêve dans la réalité sociale et pratique.

Pourtant l'utopie reste le plus souvent oeuvre de création littéraire et produit d'une pensée unique et abstraite. C'est au niveau d'une vision philosophique individuelle que nous constatons le plus clairement la tentative de réintégration inhérente au texte utopique. Partant de l'analyse d'une réalité absurde l'utopiste nous propose un état rêvé d'où sont disparues les incohérences de notre monde. L'avantage de ce jeu utopique, c'est qu'en créant ses propres règles il assure en même temps son unité intérieure. Tout tient ensemble, que ce soit dans le pays des merveilles enfantines de l'abbé Coyer (tigres dont les griffes et les dents "n'étaient qu'un cartilage flexible," arbres "sans solidité" et animaux "n'ayant que le volume sans avoir le poids proportionnel"[15]) ou dans les mondes fermés du marquis de Sade.

Au-delà de tout commentaire d'ordre moral, l'utopie se maintient par un dynamisme qui lui est propre et qui, par sa définition même, est le garant de la perfection. L'univers clos de l'utopie peut devenir la tentation de ceux pour qui la réalité imparfaite du monde est insupportable et qui retrouvent dans le rêve une autre réalité, celle de l'homme révolté, étranger à sa condition humaine. Aux abords de ce que l'on nomme folie ou génie, l'utopie atteint son apogée: celui où elle forme un système uni et unique, indépendant de toute position socio-politique particulière. L'unité du monde utopique exige sa loi, mais cette loi existe avant tout comme agent catalyseur: "Il faut donc créer de toutes pièces un monde qui soit à la mesure exact de la nouvelle loi. L'exigence d'unité, déçue par la Création, se satisfait à toute force dans un microcosme."[16] Par là l'homme échappe "à la dispersion et au hasard"[17] et dans la coïncidence utopique de la loi et la vie on voit renaître le rêve idéal sans cesse poursuivi par des individus en révolte contre leur réalité.

Par sa dimension ontologique l'utopie recrée au plan social la même vision d'unité parfaite qui traverse le monde individuel et pourtant profondément humain de Rousseau, "état simple et permanent" qui touche au mysticisme: "Délivré de toutes les passions terrestres qu'engendre le tumulte de la vie sociale, mon âme s'élancerait fréquemment au-dessus de cette atmosphère, et commercerait d'avance avec les intelligences célestes. . . ."[18] L'utopie permet ainsi la réintégration de l'individu, pris par l'absurdité d'un monde dualiste inacceptable, à un univers parfaitement coordonné dont il fera désormais partie. "Que voulez-vous donc dire avec vos individus? Il n'y en a point, non, il n'y en a point. . . . Il n'y a qu'un seul grand individu, c'est le tout."[19] Ces paroles du "philosophe qui rêve," rattachées à une interprétation matérialiste de l'être et de l'univers, mettent en relief la signification utopique du *Contrat social*: "Celui qui ose entreprendre d'instituer un peuple doit se sentir en état de changer pour ainsi dire la nature humaine, de transformer chaque individu, qui par lui-même est un tout parfait et solitaire, en partie d'un plus grand tout dont cet individu reçoive en quelque sorte sa vie et son être."[20]

L'utopie est une vaste métaphore (plutôt qu'une allégorie) par laquelle les réalités de la volonté (mode idéologique), de la réflexion (mode ontologique), et de la contemplation (mode mythologique), se trouvent transportées au-delà du plan historique pour prendre une place centrale parmi les rêves de l'humanité: rêves qui tendent tous vers cette réintégration ultime où l'être rejoint l'essence, la réalité rejoint le rêve, et l'on atteint l'unité totale et universelle. L'utopie doit être nécessairement oeuvre *centripète* plutôt que *centrifuge*: son relief et sa structure géographique en sont le reflet fidèle. L'isolement et les défenses naturelles de l'utopie soulignent sa concentration spirituelle, retrouvée dans ses formes concentriques dont le modèle de la République de Platon nous fournit l'image idéale.

Bien que l'utopie se définisse par sa contradiction initiale,[21] elle trouve sa force principale dans cette impulsion universelle qui tend à l'unité plutôt qu'à la désintégration, qui cherche l'ordre plutôt que le désordre, le simple plutôt que le complexe, et une évolution organique plutôt qu'une entropie générale. La mystique de l'Un est une force absolue enracinée dans la mentalité collective des hommes. Il nous semble qu'elle trouve son expression la plus frappante et la plus généreuse dans l'oeuvre utopique et dans l'utopie littéraire avant tout.

NOTES

1 Voltaire parlera de l'âge classique comme "le siècle le plus éclairé qui fût jamais" (*Le Siècle de Louis XIV*). Dans certains textes de la Restauration (notamment l'*Ami du roi* du 31 mars 1818) on peut trouver des descriptions tout à fait utopiques de l'époque d'avant la Révolution considérée comme un âge d'or.

2 L'usage des termes "réel" et "réalité" peut suggérer une ambiguïté ou une dualité qui au fond n'est qu'apparente. "La pensée logique établit une distinction trop tranchante entre l'imaginaire et le réel" (Alexandre Cioranescu, *L'Avenir du passé* [Paris: Gallimard, 1972] , p. 12).

3 Thomas Morus, *Idée d'une république heureuse: ou l'Utopie* (Amsterdam, 1730), p. 348. ". . . there are many Things in the Common-wealth of *Utopia*, that I rather wish than hope to see followed in our Governments" (édition anglaise de 1737, p. 140). Le verbe "s'utopianiser" est une invention du traducteur Nicolas Gueudeville, comme aussi "s'utopier" ("Préface," édition française, p. xiii).

4 Stanislas Lesczinski, *Entretien d'un Européen avec un Insulaire du royaume de Dumocala* (s.l., 1752), Avis de l'éditeur.

5 Sade, *Aline et Valcour ou Le Roman philosophique* (Paris: Editions 10/18, 1971), p. 19.

6 Eméric Crucé, *Le Nouveau Cynée* (Paris, 1623), p. 222.

7 "Le mythe permet de saisir d'un coup d'oeil certains types de relations constantes, et de les dégager du fouillis des apparences quotidiennes" (Denis de Rougemont, *L'Amour et l'Occident*, cité dans Pierre Albouy,

Mythes et mythologies dans la littérature française [Paris: Armand Colin, 1969], p. 10).

8 Voir Louis Marin, *Utopiques: Jeux d'espaces* (Paris: Minuit, 1973). "L'histoire ne peut involuer. Telle est la rude réalité du temps après celle de l'espace. L'utopie ne s'accomplit pas: elle est toujours déjà accomplie comme un ensemble équilibré et harmonieux" (p. 348).

9 Jean Le Clerc, *Bibliothèque ancienne et moderne* (Amsterdam, 1717), VII, 212.

10 *Utopie* (édition de 1730), p. 86.

11 Morelly, *Code de la Nature* (Paris: Editions Sociales, 1953), p. 47.

12 Jean-Jacques Rousseau, *Du contrat social*, Livre II, ch. vii.

13 Marquis de Lassay, *Relation du royaume des Féliciens* (1727), dans *Recueil de différentes choses* (Lausanne, 1756), IV, 347.

14 André-Michel de Ramsay, *Les Voyages de Cyrus* (Paris, 1727), II, 14-15.

15 Gabriel-François Coyer (abbé), *Découverte de l'isle Frivole* (La Haye, 1751).

16 Albert Camus, *L'Homme révolté* (Paris: Gallimard, 1951), p. 61.

17 Ibid.

18 Jean-Jacques Rousseau, *Les Rêveries du promeneur solitaire* (Paris: Garnier, 1960), p. 74.

19 Denis Diderot, *Le Rêve de D'Alembert* (Paris: Garnier-Flammarion, 1965), p. 94.

20 *Du contrat social*, Livre II, ch. vii.

21 "Toute construction utopique suppose une dissociation de l'idéal et du réel, et c'est précisément la conscience de cette dissociation qui fait l'unité de l'écriture et de la lecture" (Claude-Gilbert Dubois, "Une Architexture fixionnelle," dans la *Revue des sciences humaines* [Numéro spécial consacré à "L'Utopie"], no. 155 [1974], p. 461).

Utopian Dream as Psychic Reality

ISABEL F. KNIGHT

The title of my essay contains a claim that at a certain level of analysis there is no opposition between dream and reality, that for the psyche "reality" is not confined to that which has or will be given objective existence. In a dream—or a fantasy—there is no distinction between remembered events and imagined events, between what is plausible and what is impossible, between the perceived and the projected; all are equally manifestations of psychic reality. But all are not equally transparent. The expression of repressed wishes and anxieties, which lie at the deeper levels of the psyche, is necessarily (in order to safeguard the repression) obscured. The illumination of these dark places of the soul has been the work of three generations of psychoanalytic theory and practice.

In their recent book *The Wish to be Free,* Fred Weinstein and Gerald Platt used the Freudian framework to analyze the psychic sources of fundamental value change.[1] Their work is stimulating and suggestive in the connections it makes between individual and collective psyche, between psychic reality and idea systems, and between idea systems and social change. I intend to take up certain of their suggestions and apply them to this exploration of the utopian imagination.

Underlying my venture is a set of interlocking historical and psychological assumptions. It is assumed that the stability and coherence of any society rest upon individual internalization of the most fundamental values, behavior patterns, and authority relations of that society. The internalization of norms means that they are perceived as inevitable and universal, that they are not available for rational criticism, and that wishes which would violate them tend to be repressed. Significant changes in the normative structure of society require that such repressed wishes come to the surface and that hitherto untouchable values and authority relations become available for criticism; in short, that there be a breakdown in internalization. Furthermore, this breakdown must become general; idiosyncratic dissonance is not sufficient to bring about social change. But the breakdown of internalization is a traumatic experience, both individually and socially. The withdrawal of emotional commitment from one institution or value structure tends to threaten the commitment to adjacent institutions or values which the psyche is not yet ready to abandon. The coming to the surface of some formerly repressed wishes tends to open an avenue for still other wishes which the individual or collective ego cannot yet bear to confront. In order to cope with the intense anxiety generated by this breakdown, compensatory mechanisms are needed. So, for example, if one authority relation is denied, another will be clung to still more tightly than before, or a new one will be set up which is at least as rigid as the one it replaces. If overt expression is given to a formerly repressed wish, then the lid must be clamped down tightly on other wishes lest they too spring forth to claim satisfaction.

The Enlightenment is the intellectual expression of a breakdown of internalization. Emotional commitment was systematically withdrawn from the institutions and values of the Ancien Régime, which then could become subject to rational criticism. One side of this eighteenth-century withdrawal is contained in its vast literature of attack; another side is manifest in its utopias. A utopia is an alternative society; implicit in it is a complete normative statement about the universe. Utopian writers may differ in the practicality of their intentions; some mean to predict the future, even to provide a blueprint for building it; others are mainly concerned with criticizing the present; and still others are merely escaping into wish-fulfillment fantasies. But all are free of the constraints imposed by the here and now, for the place they are describing is *nowhere*—nowhere, that is, except the kingdom of the psyche, which is real and not a dream, though it reveals itself in dreaming. I wish, then, to map those features of the utopian terrain which the collapse of internalization has thrown up, and I shall look for them in the structure of authority and repression which even in utopia, indeed especially in utopia, seems necessary to keep at bay the chaos which the wayward drives and impulses of humanity forever threaten to bring on. The interest here is not in establishing the *fact* of utopian repressiveness—for that has often been pointed out—but in exploring its variable patterns.

I have located three types of utopia in the eighteenth century: utopias of reason and order, where happiness is a function of rational organization and symmetry; utopias of virtue and sentiment, in which harmony springs from the community feeling and fundamental goodness of the citizens; and utopias of sexual liberation and instinctual release, in which erotic gratification is the cornerstone of the good life. Each of these utopias has its characteristic structure of authority and repression; each has a list of forbidden attitudes and acts, and a set of sanctions to impose against those who commit them. But in the eyes of each utopian writer, what he is proposing is *not* repressive, because he perceives the behavior he forbids as so monstrous that only a mentally or morally deformed person would be tempted to indulge in it. It is characteristic of utopias to regard those who violate the community's norms as having defined themselves out of the community (which is, by definition, perfect), and they are therefore treated as pariahs, rather than as merely erring citizens who must pay a penalty but are citizens nonetheless. And this, of course, is the point: repression in utopia, however different from repression in the real world, is absolute—for the behavior which is prohibited springs from wishes which the utopian legislator deeply fears and whose very existence must therefore be repudiated.

An example of a rationally ordered utopia is the constitution appended by Morelly to his *Code de la Nature* (1755).[2] Morelly attributes the tyranny of his own time, with all its repressive prohibitions and punishments, to the false assumption that men are evil by nature, or at least that they must inevitably be made so by society. It is Morelly's contention that men need not be wicked, that if society conformed to Nature and Reason they would indeed find wickedness virtually impossible and so repression would no longer be needed.[3] This natural, rational society is collectivist and patriarchal: all government is in the hands of male heads of household over fifty; all goods are held in common and distributed uniformly and without charge; all work is planned and directed through a strict occupational chain of command.[4] The laws of Morelly's utopia scarcely touch on what are usually considered crimes in the real world. This is what he means by the lifting of repression—one need not have a law against theft when there is no private property to steal. Instead, his laws regulate such things as town-planning, building function and design, family life, dress, choice and organization of work, child-rearing, story-telling, and philosophical speculation. The force of these regulations is to impose uniformity of behavior, appearance, and opinion upon all citizens. Virtue and social harmony, it seems, require the absolute repression of individual differences. Therefore, all towns are to be identically geometrical in plan; all citizens will wear uniforms until they are thirty, and are forbidden vain adornment or distinctive dress at any age.[5] Marriage is compulsory at the age of fifteen, with one divorce, whose timing and conditions are precisely stipulated, allowed.[6] Children move from the parental hearth to the children's barracks at five, to their place of apprenticeship at ten; they marry and return to the husband's paternal home at fifteen, go on to the agricultural barracks at twenty, and finally establish their own households at twenty-five.[7] Occupational choice is severely restricted. Fiction, fantasy, and metaphysical or moral speculation are all proscribed.[8] Infractions are punished by isolation and imprisonment. The worst crime of all is the advocacy of private property, which is defined as a malignant insanity and is punished by "civil death"—that is, the criminal's name is stricken from the roll of citizens and his family dispersed; he himself is shut up for life in a cell in the town cemetery, where food is brought to him, but where he is otherwise isolated from all human contact.[9]

The forms of repression in Morelly's putatively nonrepressive utopia are psychologically coherent. They are designed as rigorous defenses against the threat of unregulated ego-demands, whose partial and dangerous expression has already been permitted by Morelly's attack on traditional authority. Thus his argument stems from an inability to acknowledge the claims of the ego as legitimate. For Morelly, it is the assertion of the ego which threatens the social order (in its utopian form, the projection of his own need for order): where the ego is given free play, vicious, disruptive, acquisitive, and criminal behavior follow. This has been the source of evil in society from the beginning of time, and has required what Morelly calls "tyranny" to keep the anarchy of the ego in check. Morelly's solution is to tighten the screws of repression—and call it reason. The laws of his utopia would stifle the ego at a lower level, at the level of awareness of self as different from others and the expression of that awareness in personal style and choice and ownership. He does not perceive this as repression, however, because the conformity it imposes on individuals with one another is defined as conformity to Nature herself. And to compel someone to be "natural"—like forcing him to be free—cannot be repressive.

Louis Sébastien Mercier projects a different vision of happiness in his dream of the future: *L'an deux mille quatre cent quarante,* published in 1770.[10] France in the twenty-fifth century, under the rule of a wise, humane, paternal king, is still a monarchy, but with a representative assembly for expressing the general will. This, and other massive reforms, had come about three hundred years earlier when a philosopher-king had voluntarily renounced his arbitrary power and initiated a revolution from the top. [11] The king still rules, however, but as much by moral presence as by legal authority. He lives in Paris (Versailles having been abandoned to ruin) where he moves freely among his people, who respond to him with deferential love. The words or even the though "what if the King should pass" are enough to stop any citizen from committing a shameful or disorderly act. [12] The key to social harmony in Mercier's utopia is neither organizational nor economic. It is rather based on a new internalization of community values symbolized by the relationship of the citizens to the kind, and reinforced by a universal solemnity of speech and conduct, to which wit and raillery are alien and a deep affront. [13] But the internalized values of 2440, unlike those of 1770, are based on nature, and therefore submission to them requires no distortion of the human mind or character. Hence, no real repression is implied in the laws and customs which safeguard this society from threats to its peace or integrity. Those threats are principally two: licentious minds and shameless women.

In order to protect his society from the licentious minds of the past, the revolutionary king of the twenty-second century had conducted a ceremonial public book-burning, "an expiatory sacrifice offered to truth, common sense, and good taste." [14] A large part of the literary and philosophical treasures of Western civilization went up in smoke on the altar of these principles: Herodotus, Lucretius, and Ovid, Malebranche, Pascal, and Bossuet are among those whose words are erased from memory. Much of Voltaire goes, too, for he is regarded as shallow, but Rousseau is preserved entire, as are Plato, Vergil, and Descartes, as well as a whole host of English writers from Shakespeare to Richardson. Some of the surviving works are restricted in use: poetry may be read only by men past the turmoil of adolescence, and history only by those who are resolute enough not to be discouraged or corrupted by the long story of triumphant vice. [15]

In the official ideology of 2440, however, censorship and

suppression of opinion are denounced (for it is only the "useless lumber of the past" that has been wiped out), and a free press is celebrated as the measure of a free community.[16] Indeed, government-imposed censorship is clearly superfluous, for this society has so internalized its truths that it can be counted on not to provide a hospitable home to dissent, that is, to licentiousness. The spontaneous public response to unwelcome ideas takes the form of public shame, systematic brainwashing, and ceremonial rehabilitation for the penitent. If the dissenter has put his thoughts into print, he is required to wear a mask in public as a badge of disgrace and isolation. Members of the community visit him daily to point out his errors and urge him to retract. If he does so, it is a great occasion and he will be warmly welcomed back into the community. If he persists in his error, and if his error is extreme (atheism, for example), then he is declared insane and the community is forced, in profound grief and much against its will, to banish him.[17]

Licentiousness of mind is most dangerous, and most distressing to Mercier, when it appears in women, whose disposition to irresponsibility and downright debauchery must be vigorously checked at all times. This, too, is not repression, for it serves not only to protect society, but to help woman resist her own corruption and conform to her true nature, on which she evidently has but a tenuous hold. Clearly Mercier is in the grip of a profound ambivalence toward the character of women. On the one hand, the true woman is one who knows her place and keeps it; she will be innocent, blushing, and virtuous; she will be submissive to her husband, and indeed deferential to all males, gracefully acknowledging their moral and intellectual superiority. On the other hand, it appears that women will only conform to this ideal if they are made to by all the force of civil and conjugal authority; they must be made, in Mercier's words, to wear a bridle and bit; the male must be master and absolute judge of his wife, with the power to expel her from his house and to deprive her of her children without having to show cause and without appeal. Only the fear of this fate will protect her from herself, and protect society from her power. For if woman is let loose, all society becomes debauched and corrupt.[18]

The inconsistencies in Mercier's logic reveal his psychic dilemma. His fantasied community of warmth, and nurture, and innocent solidarity depends upon the efficacy of internalized values. But he has seen in his own time—in the wit of Voltaire and in the light-minded skepticism of the Parisian intellectuals—the collapse of internalization. Indeed, in his criticism of the institutions and practices of the Ancien Régime, he has shared in it. The violence of his repression of both mental and moral licentiousness, as well as his obvious projection of his fear of arrogance and sensuality onto women, reflects the intense anxiety aroused by the breakdown of internal restraints and his wish that those restraints be restored—not in the name of the Régime but in the name of Nature herself.

Where Mercier identifies nature with sentiment, and Morelly with rational order, Restif de la Bretonne couples nature with passion. The range and voluminousness of Restif's writings, shot through with utopian themes, preclude a simple statement of his utopian vision.[19] His schemes for improving society, ranging from the sketchy to the elaborate, are full of contradictory proposals. Nevertheless, there is a dominant theme in Restif, a theme which is a key to both the liberating and the repressive elements in his many utopias. For Restif, the passions are central to human life and happiness, their expression and release the only possible ground of a tolerable life.[20] Civilization as it exists is evil and unnatural because it simultaneously represses and exploits the passions. It exploits them by offering constant titillation in ballroom and salon, on the stage and in the streets, thus stimulating erotic desire far beyond the possibility of gratification.[21] The resulting frustration perverts feelings from their natural tenderness into corrupt and violent lust. At the same time that the vicious habits of civilization inflame the passions, its moral code insists on their repression by surrounding sexuality with notions of condemnation and guilt, so that what should be, in Restif's eyes, a holy act is regarded as full of shame and sin.[22]

Restif's treatment echoes the very ambivalence he denounces. For although he celebrates the ecstasies of erotic love and dreams of a social regeneration based upon its recognition, he also deeply fears its anarchic power, fears that if passion is not tightly controlled, endless debauchery will result. This fear operates with varying intensity throughout his work. In *La Découverte australe,* he is able to envision a society based on freely chosen, frequently changing unions, with only a cautionary reference to the counter-productive effects of overindulgence.[23] In *Le Pornographe,* he provides for erotic gratification by elevating prostitution to the status of a highly regarded profession for which careful training is necessary. But in other works, like *L'Andrographe* and *Les Gynographes,* he shrinks from so much sexual freedom and devises elaborate regulatory codes which he nevertheless distinguishes from the repressions of civilization on the grounds that his code would simply contain passion within its natural channels while contemporary morality both swells and dams up passion, thus forcing it over its banks or perverting it into unnatural courses.[24]

In Restif's utopia, marriage is to be governed by a merit system, in which the most virtuous youths are given their choice of the most beautiful maidens. To prevent the married couple from dissipating their erotic energies through excessive indulgence, as well as to keep desire fresh, the wife remains in her parents' house for the first fifteen years of marriage, where her husband must devise ingenious means to visit her undetected. Not only is infidelity, or rather the mere suspicion of infidelity, severely punished, but all provocative behavior, such as indecent laughter, is prohibited.[25] Work is made compulsory for all, for reasons which are rather moral than economic. Work is sublimation, not because of the pleasure gained from performing one's chosen task or from realizing oneself in one's calling, for Restif does not leave room for vocational self-direction, but simply because work consumes energy which would otherwise be available for erotic purposes, and fills with useful activity time which, if given over to idleness, would certainly be libidinously employed.[26] Restif, it appears, is afraid of the very passion he most wishes to liberate, and so, after arguing powerfully that human happiness depends upon instinctual release, he flees from his own fantasies into a new repression which will protect society, and himself, from the full impact of that release.[27]

Our three utopias reveal a pattern of repression which, though substantively diverse, displays a common structure in which the liberating impulse generates its own repressive mechanism. Morelly wishes to liberate reason by reorganizing society on rational principles, but his plan requires that the ego, which is the source and instrument of rationality, be repressed almost at its first expression. Morelly's rational society would create unthinking robots. Mercier wishes to liberate community feelings of solidarity and love by restoring the paternal functions of nurture and moral exemplification to the king and sentiments of trust and reverence to the citizens. But sentiment is so vulnerable to the assault of licentiousness—whether of dissent or sensuality—that family life must rest on patriarchal tyranny and the whole moral order on internalized intellectual conformity. Finally, Restif wishes to liberate passion, but passion so threatens the psychic and physical energies which are its base that it must be moderated and channeled by an elaborate code of work and marriage. The dream of liberation, projected upon the screen of utopian fantasy, carries with it fundamental anxieties which are superimposed upon the same screen, and thus turns every utopia into its own distopia.

NOTES

1 Fred Weinstein and Gerald Platt, *The Wish to Be Free: Society, Psyche, and Value Change* (Berkeley and Los Angeles: University of California Press, 1969).

2 Morelly, *Code de la Nature, ou le véritable esprit de ses lois,* ed. Gilbert Chinard (Paris: Raymond Clavreuil, 1950). Morelly is a shadowy figure in the Enlightenment; not even his first name is known.

3 Ibid., pp. 159–60.

4 Ibid., pp. 302-3; 286-91; 297-98.

5 Ibid., pp. 293-96; 301-2.

6 Ibid., pp. 310-12.

7 Ibid., pp. 314-18.

8 Ibid., pp. 318, 320-22.

9 Ibid., p. 323.

10 Louis Sébastien Mercier, *L'an deux mille quatre cent quarante: Rêve s'il en fut jamais,* 2nd ed., 3 vols. (Paris, 1786). The first edition, of which this is an expanded version, was published in Amsterdam in 1770.

11 Ibid., II, 109–10.

12 Ibid., I, 36.

13 Ibid., II, 150-76, 224-26.

14 Ibid., I, 327-28.

15 Ibid., I, 320-67. One of the longest chapters in the work is devoted to cataloguing the ravaged and restricted library.

16 Ibid., I, 67-68.

17 Ibid., I, 65-70, 180-82.

18 Ibid., II, 150-66, 230; III, 19-25.

19 See Mark Poster, *The Utopian Thought of Restif de la Bretonne* (New York: New York University Press, 1971). Poster's study of Restif's utopian writings has been extremely useful to me. He also performs the great service (pp. 9-13) of locating the utopias and utopian themes in Restif's staggering output of over two hundred volumes. The edition of Restif available to me was *L'Oeuvre de Restif de la Bretonne,* ed. Henry Bachlin, 9 vols. (Paris: Editions du Trianon, 1930-32). For material not contained in the Bachlin edition, I have relied on Poster's summaries and quotations, and on excerpts in *French Utopias: An Anthology of Ideal Societies,* ed. Frank E. Manuel and Fritzie P. Manuel (New York: Schocken Books, 1966).

20 Poster, p. 34.

21 *Les Nuits de Paris*, vol. 1 of *L'Oeuvre de Restif de la Bretonne*, ed. Bachlin, is an exhaustive account of all imaginable provocative and corrupting scenes witnessed by Restif in endless nocturnal strolls through the city.

22 Poster, pp. 45-47 (references to *Monsieur Nicolas, L'Andrographe,* and *Le Pornographe*). Since Restif's works have appeared in so many editions, and since there is no one generally available edition (of either a single

work or several), I have resorted to this rather unscholarly mode of reference. Poster refers in his notes to various editions (even of a single work) and it seemed an uneconomical use of space to reproduce his scholarly apparatus here.

23 *French Utopias,* p. 173 (*La Découverte australe*).

24 Poster, p. 45 (references to *Les Gynographes* and *Le Pornographe*).

25 Poster, pp. 42-43 (references to *L'Andrographe, Le Nouvel Abeilard, Les Gynographes, Le Thesmographe, Monsieur Nicolas*). *French Utopias,* pp. 175-82 (*L'Andrographe*).

26 Poster, pp. 52-56 (references to *L'Andrographe, Les Gynographes, La Découverte australe, Monsieur Nicolas,* and *Le Thesmographe*).

27 For insight into other eighteenth-century attitudes toward excessive indulgence, see the fascinating article by Angus McLaren, "Some Secular Attitudes toward Sexual Behavior in France, 1760-1860," *French Historical Studies,* 8 (1974), 604-25. McLaren deals with medical texts and pamphlets which detail the gruesome consequences of various forms of sexual intemperance. His findings reinforce my fundamental thesis. It seems to me that what he is describing is a widespread attempt to relieve the anxiety aroused by the breakdown of previously internalized religious prohibitions by reconstructing and reinternalizing those same prohibitions on scientific grounds.

L'Abbé Prévost et l'Utopie

JEAN GARAGNON

Dans l'*Histoire d'une Grecque moderne*, la belle esclave grecque Zara, favorite du sérail et comblée de richesses, soupire pourtant: "Ce qui occupait mon âme," dit-elle, "était *le désir d'un bien dont je n'avais pas l'idée*" (p. 39).* Dans *Manon Lescaut*, le jeune chevalier Des Grieux, enivré par la rencontre de Manon, s'émerveille: "Mon coeur s'ouvrit à *mille sentiments de plaisir, dont je n'avais jamais eu l'idée*" (p. 21). Nostalgie du bonheur, ou éblouissement devant le bonheur; le bonheur est bien le thème fondamental de Prévost.

Mais qu'une oeuvre soit vouée à la recherche du bonheur n'implique absolument pas qu'elle soit aussi à la recherche d'une utopie. L'utopie en effet, si elle inclut bien le bonheur, ne s'y résume pas. Elle le dépasse par les trois dimensions suivantes:

1. Plutôt que le bonheur, l'utopie décrit les *conditions* du bonheur: conditions nécessaires, et aussi suffisantes, c'est-à-dire que leur réalisation rendra nécessairement heureux les hommes qui

*Je cite d'après les éditions suivantes: *Manon Lescaut*, édition F. Deloffre et R. Picard (Paris: Garnier, 1965); *Histoire d'une Grecque moderne*, édition R. Mauzi (Paris: Union Générale d'éditions, Bibliothèque 10/18, 1965). Pour les autres oeuvres, édition d'Amsterdam, 1783–1785. C'est moi qui souligne.

auront su les recréer. Plus qu'une description l'utopie est une méthode (et une méthode infaillible) de bonheur. L'utopie est rationnelle: elle est, non le bonheur, mais un système pour être heureux.

2. L'utopie est *collective*: elle veut faire le bonheur, non d'un individu, mais de l'humanité. L'utopie s'incarne spontanément en cité idéale, en république platonicienne, en pays d'Eldorado, en peuple des Troglodytes, en contrat social, etc. Un bonheur individuel ne relèvera de l'utopie que s'il se présente comme *exemplaire*.
3. Enfin l'utopie est *éternelle*: elle vise à instaurer un bonheur stable, définitif, situé en dehors du temps et de l'histoire; l'utopie est immobile, son seul temps est celui de la répétition.

Par tous ces traits, donc, l'utopie dépasse le simple bonheur. On ne peut alors guère s'attendre à la trouver chez Prévost, qui s'intéresse avant tout, semble-t-il, au bonheur individuel, et au bonheur précaire. Il semble au fond que la structure romanesque elle-même exclue l'utopie: le roman suppose des personnages nettement *individualisés* (et même, à la limite, non seulement distincts des autres, mais en opposition avec eux: Des Grieux et Manon sont des victimes de la société; Cleveland est un proscrit); et le roman suppose une alternance de revers et de triomphes, un temps, une *précarité*, qui excluent la peinture d'un état stable. Les peuples heureux n'ont pas d'histoire: il n'auront donc pas non plus de roman. Le roman du bonheur (individuel et menacé) ne peut, semble-t-il, se dépasser en roman de l'utopie.

C'est pourtant l'intérêt de Prévost qu'il ait tenté ce dépassement. Sans qu'il parle directement de l'utopie, c'est pourtant l'idée utopique qui hante son oeuvre: cet homme que poursuit l'obsession la plus *intime* qui soit (le regret de son enfance et du paradis perdu), et qui l'exprime à travers les aventures *singulières* de ses héros, à travers des quêtes individuelles du bonheur, ne cesse pourtant de s'interroger sur le bonheur de l'homme en général. Par-delà sa quête personnelle et les personnages de fiction en qui elle s'incarne, il poursuit un rêve universel: celui d'une humanité réconciliée et heureuse. Une fois même, il évoque directement une société utopique: c'est dans l'épisode de la colonie insulaire de *Cleveland*, sur lequel on reviendra. Sa quête est bien celle d'une utopie—même si elle aboutit, en définitive, à un échec.

On retracera cette quête (et son échec) en évoquant tour à tour les trois grand problèmes que toute construction utopique rencontre, et que Prévost a parfaitement posés:

1. La définition d'une société idéale
2. Le pouvoir de l'éducation, par laquelle l'individu est intégré à la société
3. Le bonheur individuel

Nous nous attarderons plus longuement sur le premier point, en effet fondamental: la définition d'une société idéale.

Existe-t-il une société idéale? C'est la première démarche des utopistes: trouver un modèle (existant ou à créer) d'organisation sociale. Cette quête est souvent symbolisée par le *voyage*: Candide découvre l'Eldorado en Amérique du Sud; Diderot place la société idéale à Tahiti, Montesquieu chez les Troglodytes d'Arabie, Cyrano dans la lune, et Voltaire, plus prosaïquement, chez les Anglais. C'est aussi la démarche de Prévost: il fait voyager ses personnages, et peut donc passer en revue différents types de sociétés—réelles ou imaginaires. Mais il ne s'arrêtera, lui, à aucune.

Le voyage suppose d'abord que l'on condamne sa propre société—la société française en l'occurrence—dont on cherche à s'éloigner. C'est le cas chez Prévost (dont la vie fut d'ailleurs souvent celle d'un fugitif, d'un exilé, ou d'un voyageur traqué). Nulle part cette condamnation n'est aussi claire que dans *Manon Lescaut*: Manon et Des Grieux sont victimes de la société française à la fois en ce qu'elle a de corrompu (vénalité générale, financiers qui savent que tout s'achète, valets fripons), et dans ce qu'elle essaie de préserver de respectabilité de façade (la police qui réprime le libertinage, les prêtres ou le père, témoins d'un âge révolu, qui croient encore à une vertu étroite et répressive). Ces deux aspects qui paraissent contradictoires s'allient en réalité fort bien, et collaborent pour écraser le seul sentiment vrai, l'amour. Lorsque le vieux débauché G... M... veut se venger de Des Grieux, il va très vertueusement le dénoncer à la police et à son père comme libertin: et "les pères" (l'un débauché, l'autre vertueux) font déporter Manon. Alliance paradoxale, où le vice sait utiliser jusqu'à la vertu pour mieux triompher.

Lorsque Des Grieux vogue vers l'Amérique, il résume parfaitement ces deux traits de la société européenne: "les fureurs de l'avarice" et les "idèes fantastiques de l'honneur" (p. 180). Par le vice, comme par la vertu abstraite, la société française exerce une oppression égale sur l'individu. Aussi Des Grieux conclut-il: "Je ne regrettais point l'Europe" (p. 184).

Est-ce alors l'Amérique qui offrira le modèle de société? On le croit un instant, et Des Grieux le croit aussi: "Plus nous avancions vers l'Amérique, plus je sentais mon coeur s'élargir et devenir tranquille" (p. 184). Plus exactement, l'Amérique offre à la pensée du dix-huitième siècle non pas une, mais deux images de sociétés idéales, qui toutes deux deviendront des clichés: les bons sauvages, antithèse d'une Europe trop civilisée, et les libres colons, parias chassés d'une Europe oppressive, qui ont fondé, dans un pays neuf, une société plus juste. Des Grieux donne un instant dans ces deux idylles exotiques: il imagine des sauvages pacifiques, qui vivent "avec simplicité" et qui "suivent les lois de la nature" (pp. 180-81). Quant à la société blanche, il y vit dans la plus parfaite "félicité," il y trouve un "petit emploi," y assure sa "petite fortune," engage une servante pour Manon et un valet pour lui, il est "réglé dans [sa] conduite," et il jouit paisiblement de l'amour de Manon et de "la confiance et l'affection de toute la colonie" (p. 189). C'est le bonheur de Candide établi en Turquie, c'est la "petite société idéale, c'est l'utopie réalisée."

Mais très vite le rêve se dissipe. Le cliché du "bon sauvage" est dénoncé comme tel, lorsque Des Grieux passe sans transition au cliché opposé: le pays, dit-il, est "habité par des bêtes féroces, et par des sauvages aussi barbares qu'elles" (p. 193). Ces clichés se détruisent l'un l'autre. Et quand il évoque enfin calmement la réalité, les sauvages reprennent leur vraie figure: des primitifs qui peuvent être dangereux, mais que l'on peut aussi "apprivoiser," et qu'on peut à l'occasion utiliser comme guides. Bref, une réalité banale, des contacts superficiels et purement utilitaires: on est bien loin de l'utopie.

La désillusion est la même avec la société coloniale de La Nouvelle-Orléans. Après l'installation paisible (mais sur laquelle Prévost avait habilement projeté l'ombre menaçante de la maison du gouverneur), le malheur renaît, et exactement *sous les mêmes traits qu'en Europe*: un rival puissant qui sait jouer de ses relations, un gouverneur tyrannique, un aumônier qui prêche la soumission, une loi absurde et injuste. L'Amérique n'est pas l'antithèse de l'Europe: elle en est plutôt l'enfer, la caricature où tous les traits sont accentués et durcis. Le Nouveau Monde n'est pas si "nouveau": il est né du Vieux Monde, il le prolonge outre-mer, et il reproduit, en plus brutal et en plus inhumain, tous ses vices et ses injustices.

Ce n'est donc ni l'Amérique des sauvages, ni celle des colons qui permettront à l'utopie de s'incarner. Prévost ne croit pas à l'idylle coloniale. Mais il existait, dans la pensée du dix-huitième siècle, une autre antithèse à l'Europe: l'Orient. Or la seule oeuvre de Prévost qui se déroule dans un cadre oriental, l'*Histoire d'une Grecque moderne*, réfute ce mythe.

La plus grande partie du roman se déroule à Constantinople, où l'ambassadeur de France a racheté, pour la libérer, une jeune esclave grecque. Tout est fait pour organiser la confrontation des deux civilisations: l'ambassadeur de France représente l'Occident (il loue les moeurs non seulement de la France, mais plus généralement des "pays chrétiens"). Constantinople représente l'Orient, les principes des deux civilisations sont systématiquement comparés et opposés (tyrannie d'un côté, liberté de l'autre), et, plus même qu'une confrontation, on va jusqu'à la rivalité ouverte, dont l'enjeu sera la jeune Grecque. Femme, donc plus proche de la nature, elle doit montrer naïvement quel système l'emporte.

Or l'expérience tourne à la confusion simultanée des deux systèmes. Le système occidental tout d'abord, que l'ambassadeur veut faire triompher, échoue, et par les mêmes défauts que l'on a pu voir dans *Manon*. Mais l'expérience—et c'est ce qui nous intéresse—n'est pas davantage favorable à l'Orient. La civilisation orientale est fondée sur un principe simple: la soumission, dont la forme la plus évidente (mais non la seule) est l'esclavage. C'est assurément un système très efficace par l'ordre qu'il assure: de nombreuses scènes montrent la parfaite soumission des femmes aux hommes (dans des sérails où règne l'ordonnance la plus exacte), des esclaves et des serviteurs à leurs maîtres, et de ceux-ci au sultan. Le moindre écart est aussitôt sanctionné, et d'ailleurs le système est si sûr de lui qu'il est le plus souvent fort doux: les esclaves sont bien traités, les femmes des sérails sont entourées d'attentions. Mais cette construction parfaite (et apparemment harmonieuse) est fondée, sinon toujours sur la crainte, du moins sur la *domination*: c'est-à-dire qu'elle est fondamentalement injuste (alors même qu'elle paraît bien acceptée), et par là même fragile. Même bien traitées, les femmes du sérail s'ennuient et soupirent (sans en prendre clairement conscience) après la liberté. Il suffit que l'ambassadeur parle à Zara de la liberté dont les femmes jouissent en France, pour qu'aussitôt son imagination s'enflamme; ce discours de la liberté, c'est celui qu'elle attendait inconsciemment: "Il ne vous échappa rien [dit-elle plus tard à M. de Ferriol] dont je ne trouvasse aussitôt le témoignage *au fond de mon coeur*" (p. 40). La liberté est une aspiration de la nature. La soumission, même acceptée en apparence, demeure contraire à la nature humaine: elle est rejetée tôt ou tard. Zara libérée par M. de Ferriol, s'exclame: "Je dois ma liberté au plus généreux de tous les hommes" (p. 46). Et M. de Ferriol raconte: "Son premier mouvement fut de se jeter à mes genoux, qu'elle embrassa avec un ruisseau de pleurs . . . . Elle m'adressa mille fois les noms de son Libérateur, de son Père et de son Dieu" (pp. 21-22). Si tel est le bonheur de Zara d'échapper à une domination qu'elle avait pourtant acceptée (et même recherchée), on devine celui des esclaves ou des serviteurs d'échapper à une domination subie. L'Orient de Prévost est plein de ces scènes de saturnales, où la disparition du maître crée aussitôt le désordre: tout le monde va et vient, ne pense plus qu'à soi, pille, vole; une folie soudaine s'empare de tous. L'ordre s'est effondré en un instant, ce qui montre à nouveau son caractère artificiel et précaire. Plus généralement, et sans aller jusqu'à ces scènes où la domination se dissout d'un coup, on devine que chacun *mine sourdement* l'ordre auquel il est soumis. Les serviteurs sont faux, les femmes du sérail intriguent en secret. Les maîtres sont obéis en apparence, mais tout leur échappe, ils peuvent être trahis à chaque instant, tout se fait double et fuyant autour d'eux. D'où cette impression, que Prévost a bien rendue, de se mouvoir parmi un peuple de muets, de fantômes insaisissables: Constantinople est peuplée d'ombres. L'ordre simple et lumineux se fait d'un coup opaque et inquiétant: cette atmosphère constante de trahison, c'est l'expression d'une liberté irrépressible, qui regimbe contre l'ordre, et ne peut s'exprimer que sous cette forme dégradée. Quand la révolte est interdite, la duplicité et la dissimulation sont la seule liberté des esclaves. Monde de la fourberie et de la cruauté, l'Orient que nous montre Prévost est un univers malade et instable. L'ordre fondé sur la domination reste extérieur à l'individu: il heurte trop l'instinct premier de la liberté, et ne peut créer une société harmonieuse. On est loin de la colonie utopique que Candide et sa "petite société" fonderont près de Constantinople, on est loin du paisible jardin de Candide et des pâtisseries de Cunégonde, loin du sage Turc et de ses sorbets.

Prévost a rejeté l'Europe. Il n'a pour autant trouvé la société parfaite ni dans l'idylle coloniale, ni dans le mirage oriental. Puisque aucune société existante ne répond à ses voeux, il ne lui reste plus qu'à imaginer cette société idéale, à *créer sa propre utopie*: c'est ce qu'il fait au livre III de *Cleveland*, dans le remarquable épisode de la colonie insulaire près de Sainte-Hélène.

Prévost a essayé de recréer dans l'île toutes les conditions d'une société heureuse. Il y a rassemblé les traits les plus caractéristiques de l'utopie. D'abord la colonie est isolée, protégée du monde extérieur: elle est dans une île bordée de montagnes, en sorte que la colonie, installée dans les vallées du centre, est invisible de la mer. L'île est d'ailleurs si éloignée des routes de navigation que personne ne s'aventure dans ses parages.

La colonie est peu nombreuse. Et de plus les citoyens qui la composent sont choisis: ce sont des proscrits, qui étaient partis pour L'Amérique avec le ferme dessein d'y créer une société libre et heureuse, et ont fait naufrage à Sainte-Hélène. Petite communauté donc, soudée par un malheur commun et une entreprise commune.

L'utopie se manifeste par bien d'autres traits. Le culte établi est la religion naturelle. L'organisation géographique de la cité est parfaitement géométrique. On a instauré la communauté des biens. On a aboli le règne de l'argent, et donc le règne de l'ambition et de "l'avarice." L'égalité est parfaite, ou du moins les seules distinctions sont fondées sur l'autorité morale: les pères de famille sont supérieurs aux domestiques "comme la tête l'est à l'égard des membres." Les habitants ont enfin renoncé aux politesses formelles, "aux civilités gênantes et aux vains compliments": ils ont retrouvé entre eux ces rapports naturels et transparents dont la nostalgie habite toutes les utopies.

Telle est donc cette île heureuse: le royaume de l'ordre, de la raison, et de la nature. Elle est si harmonieuse que Bridge, en y débarquant, l'appelle un "nouveau monde" (comme une Amérique idéale), un "jardin enchanté." C'est l'Eden, le paradis retrouvé.

Or le désordre va éclater dans l'île, lorsque Bridge (le demi-frère de Cleveland), Gelin et leurs compagnons y débarquent. On retrouve d'ailleurs là, en apparence, un nouveau trait de l'utopie: le mal ne peut venir que du dehors, la société parfaite n'est menacée que par une corruption venue du monde extérieur. Mais ici l'arrivée des voyageurs a une autre signification: loin d'introduire le désordre dans le système, ils ne font en réalité que révéler le désordre latent qui existait *à l'intérieur même* de ce système. Les voyageurs en sont non pas la cause, mais l'occasion: ils font éclater une contradiction interne de l'utopie.

Quelle est cette contradiction? C'est celle, pour schématiser, du bonheur collectif et du bonheur individuel. Les nouveaux arrivants, à demande des habitants de l'île, vont s'installer dans le pays et y prendre femme. Chacun a son élue, et tout devrait aller pour le mieux: Prévost se place dans les conditions idéales, aussi bien du point de vue de la société que du point de vue de l'amour (il n'y a aucun tragique amoureux, contairement à d'autres oeuvres de Prévost, aucun amour ne se heurte à la fuite ou à l'indifférence de l'être aimé). Nous avons donc des amour parfaites dans une société parfaite. Or c'est justement entre l'amour (c'est-à-dire la passion individuelle) et la société que la contradiction éclate.

Les nouveaux venus ne sont en effet que six, et il y a dans l'île cent jeunes filles à marier. Les autorités décident alors que les mariages se feront par tirage au sort, car la liberté de choix serait humiliante pour les jeunes filles qui auraient été dédaignées, et "blesserait la loi de l'égalité naturelle." Deux aspects de la nature sont ainsi mis en contradiction: son aspect social, "l'égalité naturelle" (pour qui il est en effet injuste que certains soient préférés à d'autres, et pour qui les seules dinstinctions doivent être introduites par la loi égalitaire du tirage au sort), et son aspect individuel, la liberté naturelle, dont l'expression la plus fondamentale est la spontanéité de la passion, du choix amoureux.

C'est en effet au nom de la nature et de la liberté que les nouveaux arrivants se rebellent. Au nom de la nature: "Des hommes ne sauraient renoncer aux sentiments de la *Nature*" (IV, 393). Au nom de la liberté: "On nous traite ici comme des *esclaves*" (IV, 324). "Nous sommes nés *libres*. . . . Des Anglais et des Français ne souffrent qu'on *tyrannise leur coeur*" (IV, 368).

Ils s'insurgent donc contre le gouvernement de l'île, qu'ils découvrent être un gouvernement de "cruauté" et de "superstition." Ils enlèvent leurs amantes, qu'ils épousent selon le "mariage naturel," c'est-à-dire selon le "coeur" et selon le "Ciel," provoquent une révolution, assassinent le "ministre" et instaurent un régime à leur convenance. Ils croient, ce faisant, agir au nom de la nature, qu'ils libèrent contre l'oppression: mais plus exactement (et c'est là qu'est le problème), ils agissent au nom d'*un aspect* de la nature (la liberté individuelle) contre *un autre*, tout aussi respectable, à savoir la paix sociale, l'ordre et l'égalité. Les habitants le leur font bien voir: au lieu de remercier leurs libérateurs, ils leur font les plus amers reproches: "Nous vivions paisiblement dans cette île avant que de vous y avoir reçus. Vous y avez mis le trouble en séduisant nos filles, en massacrant notre ministre et en voulant nous imposer des lois à force armée. Enfin, vous nous avez apporté toute la corruption de l'Europe dont nous

nous étions crus à couvert ici pour toujours" (IV, 474-75). On croirait entendre les malédictions du vieillard de Tahiti contre Bougainville. Mais notons là encore qu'un même mouvement lyrique recouvre deux réalités bien différentes: ce qui est vrai pour Tahiti (pays heureux où la corruption a été introduite du dehors), l'est moins pour la colonie protestante: les voyageurs n'ont pas vraiment "apporté toute la corruption de l'Europe," ils ont fait éclater une contradiction interne de l'utopie.

Chacun dit parler au nom de la nature: les nouveaux arrivants défendent le droit naturel au bonheur contre un ordre qui leur paraît arbitraire; les habitants de l'île défendent leur paix et leur innocence naturelles contre la "corruption de l'Europe." Ils ont tous raison, et tort en même temps: c'est bien la nature qu'ils défendent, mais contre un autre aspect de la nature elle-même. La nature veut à la fois le bonheur collectif et le bonheur individuel, l'ordre et le désordre, la raison et la passion. Elle n'est pas une: elle est contradictoire. L'épisode de Sainte-Hélène contient en fait non pas une, mais deux utopies, dont chacune dénonce l'autre: l'utopie collective repose sur une mutilation de l'individu, qui doit refouler la passion (est-ce un hasard si l'île du refoulement est peuplée de protestants puritains?); l'utopie individuelle de l'amour partagé, en ce qu'elle suppose de préférence individuelle et irrationnelle, est incompatible avec l'égalité et avec la raison. Le conflit—indépassable—est dans la nature elle-même.

Dans ce même tome de *Cleveland*, Prévost avait imaginé qu'entre le sauvage primitif et l'Européen trop civilisé, il existait quelque part un "point" idéal de civilisation: ce "point" idéal restait concevable, même si aucune société existante ne réussissait à l'atteindre. Même si aucun groupe humain existant ne s'y conformait, la "condition naturelle" de l' "humanité" demeurait comme une norme, provisoirement vide, mais toujours valable. Or, ce que l'épisode de Sainte-Hélène révèle, c'est que cet idéal lui-même n'est plus soutenable. Au-delà des échecs historiques des sociétés réelles, Prévost découvre l'échec plus essentiel de la société idéale, sa radicale impossibilité. Seule une nature simple pouvait fonder la société sans conflits de l'utopie: dès que la nature se révèle contradictoire, l'utopie n'est plus concevable.

Le second problème qu'aborde la réflexion utopique est celui de l'éducation. Après tout, il n'a peut-être manqué aux voyageurs de Sainte-Hélène que d'avoir été élevés dans l'île: ils auraient alors accepté aussi bien que les habitants une contrainte qui leur a paru "cruelle." La nature peut se modifier, et c'est l'éducation qui permet d'assurer cet effort sur la nature.

Prévost croit-il au pouvoir de l'éducation? L'un de ses romans est tout entier consacré à ce problème: c'est l'*Histoire d'une Grecque moderne*. Si nous laissons de côté les conséquences psychologiques du rapport éducatif (l'amour du vieux maître pour sa jeune élève), c'est ce rapport éducatif même qui est au centre du livre. Ce roman est une expérience à l'état pur, une expérience de laboratoire: sur un être jeune et malléable, deux éducations s'exercent tour à tour, l'orientale et l'occidentale, aussi opposées qu'il est possible. On a déjà dit que toutes deux échouaient, et que l'expérience permettait de dénoncer les deux systèmes de valeurs. Mais par delà ces deux *contenus* éducatifs, c'est l'*idée même d'éducation* que Prévost remet en cause: même un système harmonieux de valeurs ne pourrait s'enseigner durablement. Il est un ordre, et il vient du dehors: c'en est assez pour que tôt ou tard la liberté (c'est-à-dire l'imprévisible et l'individuel) regimbe contre lui. Zara échappe aux deux systèmes non parce qu'ils sont mauvais (un seul l'est) mais parce qu'ils sont systèmes.

Pourtant, le début de l'*Histoire d'une Grecque moderne* semble affirmer la toute-puissance de l'éducation. Zara se soumet avec une docilité parfaite aux deux formations qu'elle reçoit. Formation turque d'abord, dont elle a parfaitement assimilé les principes: "[Je me mis] à réfléchir sur mes premières années, pour chercher quelque *règle* qui pût servir à ma *conduite* . . . . Je ne trouvai que deux *principes* sur lesquel on avait fait rouler mon *éducation*; l'un, qui m'avait fait regarder les hommes comme l'unique source de la fortune et du bonheur des femmes; l'autre qui m'avait appris que par nos complaisances, notre soumission, nos caresses, nous pouvions acquérir sur eux une espèce d'empire" (p. 31). Elle dit encore: "Une femme [n'a] point d'autre bonheur à espérer que celui de plaire à son maître" (p. 9). A ces principes que son père lui a inculqués, elle se soumet entièrement. Et sa sincérité n'est pas feinte, puisque c'est après la mort de son père qu'elle est entrée au sérail: elle a fait d'elle-même ce à quoi il la destinait, et qu'il n'est plus là pour lui faire faire; elle pourrait être libre, mais n'y songe pas un instant. Le maître du sérail, Chériber, s'étonne lui-même de sa facilité: "Avec l'étendue et la vivacité de génie que je lui connais, j'admire quelquefois qu'elle ait pu s'assujettir sitôt à nos usages, et je n'en puis trouver d'autre raison que *la force de l'exemple et de l'habitude*" (p. 8).

La docilité de Zara est la même lorsque M. de Ferriol la rachète et veut faire d'elle une Européenne parfaite. Il lui trace un "plan" de vie: étude du français, lecture d'une "infinité d'excellents livres," peinture et portrait (que l'Islam lui interdisait), et tous "les arts et les exercices de l'Europe." C'est l'éducation éclairée, par opposition à la soumission turque. Et Zara, rebaptisée Théophé pour mieux marquer son changement de vie, entre avec ardeur dans ce plan. Son esprit s'ouvre d'un coup: "Elle me fit mille questions nouvelles, comme si elle n'eût pensé qu'à se préparer des sujets de méditation pour la nuit suivante. Etait-elle frappée de quelque usage de ma nation, ou de quelque principe qu'elle entendait pour le première fois, je la voyais un moment recueillie pour le graver dans sa mémoire; et quelquefois elle me priait de le répéter, dans la crainte de n'avoir pas saisi tout le sens de mes expressions, ou dans celle de l'oublier" (p. 56). Une élève fort docile donc, et qui fait de rapides progrès.

Et pourtant, cette toute-puissance de l'éducation est illusoire. L'être humain n'est past infiniment malléable. Antérieurement à toute éducation, il existe dans la nature humaine un instinct de liberté:* si l'éducation brime cet instinct, il finit tôt ou tard par la rejeter; si l'éducation le favorise, il tire profit d'elle, mais pour ses fins propres, à son propre avantage, et non selon une finalité sociale pour s'intégrer à une civilisation. C'est ce que montre l'échec successif des deux éducations de Zara.

*Instinct que symbolise, dans le cas de Zara, sa naissance princière: elle est héréditairement rebelle à tout joug. Cette nature sociale symbolise évidemment une nature plus profonde.

L'échec de l'éducation turque est le plus évident, et il est d'ailleurs largement dû au contenu de cette éducation: elle enseigne la soumission, et la soumission ne peut durablement étouffer la nature. Malgré la "force de l'exemple et de l'habitude," et malgré la sincérité avec laquelle Zara croit accepter cette soumission, elle s'ennuie vite dans sa cage dorée: elle passe son temps dans la "rêverie," dans l' "indifférence," dans la "mélancolie," elle se dit "dégoûtée." "Je me demandais encore ... pourquoi je n'étais pas heureuse avec tout ce que j'avais désiré pour l'être. Je m'informais quelquefois si dans un lieu où je croyais toute la fortune et tous les biens réunis, il n'y avait pas quelque plaisir que je n'eusse point encore goûté, quelque changement qui pût dissiper l'inquiétude continuelle où j'étais" (p. 139). D'où sa joie lorsqu'elle est libérée. Cette première éducation n'a visiblement pas été très efficace.

Plus intéressant encore est l'échec de l'éducation européenne. Car elle se fonde, elle, sur la liberté. M. de Ferriol assure solonnellement: "Je ne l'ai achetée que pour la rendre libre" (p. 18). Et l'éducation qu'il lui fait donner est très précisément une éducation libérale. A ses yeux d'ailleurs, ce n'est même pas une éducation: il lui permet simplement d'être enfin elle-même, et de renouer avec sa vraie nature par-delà l'épisode turc; Zara ne fait que retrouver l' "heureux penchant" qu'elle "ne [doit] qu'à [elle-] même," et que l' "éducation" et l' "habitude" du sérail ont "tenu jusqu'à présent comme lié." Cette éducation coïncide donc parfaitement avec la nature même de Zara: or elle échoue, et cela est révélateur.

C'est que cette liberté qu'on enseigne à Zara reste une liberté sociale: valeur authentique par elle-même, mais faussée par l'usage social et éducatif qui en est fait. Elle épanouit l'individu, certes, mais ce n'est pas pour lui-même: c'est pour qu'il puisse plaire, pour qu'il soit de contact plus facile et plus agréable. Les arts d'agréments, les langues, tout cela fait partie d'une éducation mondaine. La vertu même, les livres de morale, doivent contribuer à former ce personnage d' "honnête femme" dont rêve M. de Ferriol: la vertu est une charme de plus, elle est une autre façon de s'intégrer harmonieusement dans une société heureuse. La liberté, c'est la liberté d'allure, l'aisance sociale.

Or Zara prend au mot ce qu'on lui enseigne: elle va pratiquer ces valeurs pour elles-mêmes (et pour elle-même), et non pour le bonheur social auquel elles lui donnent accès. Sa liberté, ce sera de se refuser à son bienfaiteur, de le fuir, et de fuir toute la bonne société pour errer sur le port et dans Constantinople, en des escapades d'apparence douteuse; être libre, c'est pouvoir refuser d'être de moeurs libres, contrairement à l'attente intéressée d'autrui. Sa vertu, ce ne sera pas une vertu mondaine et traitable; ce sera une vertu un peu folle, une honte de ce qu'elle a été, une frénésie d'expiation qui la pousse à fuir tous ceux qui savent d'où elle sort, donc à fuir celui-là même grâce à qui elle en est sortie. Elle se rend peut-être malheureuse ce faisant: mais c'est la vertu telle qu'elle la voit et la vit. Zara reprend les valeurs qu'on lui enseigne, mais pour les tourner à ses fins propres, pour les mettre au service de son *authenticité*: et par là elle se retourne contre celui qui lui a enseigné ces valeurs, et contre la société qui les pratique. Son éloignement final et sa mort marquent bien cette opposition: même lorsque les valeurs enseignées sont intrinsèquement bonnes, le simple fait qu'elles soient enseignées, le simple fait qu'elles visent à assurer une intégration sociale, une identification à un modèle (aussi parfait que soit celui-ci), tend à les rendre inauthentiques. L'individu peut se reconquérir grâce à elles, mais contre celui qui les lui enseigne, contre le rapport d'éducation.

Le plus remarquable est que Zara se reproche parfois de ne pas répondre exactement à ce qu'on attendait d'elle; elle s'accuse d'ingratitude. C'est qu'il y a en elle toute une part raisonnable qui la pousse à être reconnaissante à M. de Ferriol, et à s'intégrer dans la société. Mais toute une autre part d'elle-même, irrationnelle, impulsive, sait qu'elle ne se trouvera que par la rupture. D'où le rythme du roman, tout en fuites soudaines et en retour coupables. L'être est partagé entre l'usage social des valeurs, et leur usage à ses fins propres; entre une liberté harmonieuse dans la société et une liberté sauvage, imprévisible, donc antisociale; entre son être social et son être intime, incommunicable. Zara, comme Albertine, est un "être de fuite" (aux deux sens du mot: qui échappe à la compréhension, et qui s'échappe par des fugues). La manifestation la plus claire de cet être intime, c'est la *passion*: aussi est-ce dans ses fugues amoureuses (ou supposées telles) que Zara est à la fois le plus mystérieuse, et le plus elle-même.

L'éducation turque interdisait à Zara de se trouver: aussi cette éducation était-elle précaire, et a-t-elle disparu sans laisser de traces. L'éducation européenne lui a permis de se trouver ... c'est-à-dire de fuir ses éducateurs. Le "plan" de vie bien réglé et bien raisonnable, qui devait former la femme parfaite, conduit aux fugues irrationnelles, à un être qui échappe et que M. de Ferriol renonce à comprendre. Education réussie, si l'on veut, par la naissance d'un être à lui-même; mais éducation manquée par rapport aux fins sociales qu'elle s'était fixées. Zara est perdue pour la société heureuse, et cela par l'éducation même qui devait l'y faire accéder. La raison a conduit à l'irrationnel, les entretiens philosophiques et l'étude des langues ont conduit à l'incommunicable et au silence, la sociabilité a conduit à la fuite imprévisible d'une sauvageonne.

On pourrait dire que l'éducation turque a échoué parce qu'elle était mauvaise, et que l'éducation européenne a échoué, elle, parce qu'elle était bonne. Le plan de vie de Zara semblait tiré de la plus charmante des utopies: philosophie, arts, liberté et vertu. S'il échoue, c'est que l'éducation utopique est impossible.

L'homme est le plus authentiquement lui-même dans ses impulsions irrationnelles, imprévisibles: il ne se trouvera donc que contre la rationalité—fût-ce contre la plus belle des rationalités, c'est-à-dire contre l'utopie. L'utopie est *système* (fût-il système du bonheur), l'homme est un "être de fuite": on ne peut éduquer l'un en vue de l'autre.

Ne pourrait-on alors envisager une autre forme de l'utopie, une utopie plus limitée: celle du *bonheur individuel*? Si (comme le montre l'épisode de Sainte-Hélène) le conflit est toujours possible entre le bonheur collectif et le bonheur individuel, même dans une société parfaite, et si (comme le montre l'*Histoire d'une Grecque moderne*) l'éducation ne parvient pas à réduire ce conflit, à intégrer définitivement l'individu, on peut alors penser que c'est dans l'individu lui-même qu'il faut chercher la source du bonheur: que chacun soit libre de créer son propre bonheur, et, chacun coïncidant parfaitement avec soi, une forme de perfection terrestre aura été créée. Prévost a exploré aussi cette voie.

Constamment en effet ses personnages, sans doute hantés par le paradis perdu de l'enfance, cherchent à se créer un univers clos, protégé, où leur bonheur sera immuable. Ils rêvent d'une vie simple et sage, innocente, et éternellement pareille à elle-même. Ils parlent sans cesse de "plans," d' "arrangements," de "systèmes de vie," qui doivent "établir" et "assurer" leur bonheur; ils se créent des règles, prévoient rigoureusement leur avenir, ils se font un bonheur durable et protégé.

Cette vie réglée peut d'ailleurs s'incarner dans des images aux tonalités variées. Tantôt ce sera un *bonheur studieux*: ainsi Des Grieux, ramené chez son père après sa première aventure avec Manon, retrouve-t-il la paix grâce à ses livres (par eux, il renoue avec son enfance de bon élève). Tantôt c'est l'image d'un *bonheur rustique* que Prévost évoque: ainsi la retraite champêtre dont rêve Des Grieux, "la maison écartée avec un petit bois et un ruisseau d'eau douce au bout du jardin" (pp. 40-41). Tantôt ce plan de sagesse inclut *un être aimé*, et inclut même des *plaisirs mondains*, pourvu qu'ils restent modérés et réglés, et par là même durables:

> Mon bonheur me parut d'abord établi d'une manière inébranlable. . . . Voici le plan que je me proposai: soixante mille francs . . . peuvent nous soutenir pendant dix ans. Deux mille ècus nous suffiront chaque année, si nous continuons de vivre à Chaillot. Nous y mènerons une vie honnête, mais simple. Notre unique dépense sera pour l'entretien d'un carrosse, et pour les spectacles. Nous nous règlerons. Vous aimez l'Opéra: nous irons deux fois la semaine. Pour le jeu, vous nous bornerons tellement que nos pertes ne passeront jamais deux pistoles. (Pp. 49-50)

Tantôt enfin c'est l'*amour* tout seul, pourvu qu'il paraisse assuré et sans nuages, qui fonde le bonheur: on retrouve l'image de la chaumière et des deux coeurs, dans l'épisode de la Louisiane, par exemple.

On voit que le contenu du bonheur peut varier: tantôt studieux, tantôt amoureux, tantôt amoureux et mondain, etc. Mais ce qui est constant, c'est l'aspect *réglé* de ce bonheur, sa *constance*, l'*éternité* qu'il promet.

Or ce bonheur si bien établi n'est jamais durable. Le sage élève d'Amiens, ou le séminariste studieux de Saint-Sulpice, sont d'un coup "transportés," "emportés" par la seule vue de Manon. Les sages résolutions prise ensuite avec Manon sont aussitôt emportées par la "passion du plaisir" et de la dépense. Le bonheur retrouvé avec Manon est aussitôt compromis par les bons tours que, dans une impulsion irréfléchie, les jeunes gens veulent jouer au vieux financier G... M... ou à son fils. Et chaque fois, cet entraînement soudain conduit à la catastrophe.

Ne disons pas que Prévost veut par là nous mettre en garde contre l'amour, passion destructrice; car s'il est vrai que parfois l'amour est cet entraînement irréfléchi qui détruit le bonheur, d'autres fois c'est lui qui constitue le bonheur, et qui est détruit par l'entraînement irréfléchi. Le conflit ne tient pas au *contenu* du bonheur: il tient à sa modalité. C'est chaque fois un bonheur réglé, stable (quel qu'en soit le contenu) qui est détruit par un vertige, une impulsion imprévisible.

C'est qu'il existe pour Prévost deux modalités du bonheur: à côté de l'utopie sage et bien réglée dont rêvent ses personnages, il existe le bonheur plus intense et dangereux de la passion. Deux bonheurs inconciliables, et entre lesquels l'homme est partagé, car ils sont tous deux dans sa nature. Ils s'opposent terme à terme: d'une part un plan de sagesse où tout est prévu, de l'autre un entraînement imprévisible; d'un côté un bonheur modéré ("nous nous règlerons . . . nous nous bornerons"), de l'autre un bonheur intense, un "transport" qui "enflamme"; un bonheur transparent, dont les éléments sont soigneusement répertoriés et énumérés, et un vertige trouble, obscur; un bonheur fait pour durer, et l'entraînement d'un instant; un bonheur volontaire, construit de façon délibérée (Des Grieux parle de "résolutions"), et un entraînement subi, par lequel l'être "se trouve emporté tout d'un coup . . . sans se trouver capable de la moindre résistance" pp. 42–43); un bonheur immobile (Des Grieux parle de "situation tranquille") et une agitation violente, des "mouvements tumultueux." C'est l'opposition de la raison et de la passion.

Là encore, ne lions pas ces deux modalités du bonheur à des contenus particuliers. On n'est pas dans le domaine de la moralité banale, où la raison consiste à s'abstenir d'actes immoraux (l'amour, le jeu, le vol, etc.), auxquels la passion au contraire nous entraîne. Toute acte (moral ou immoral, peu importe) peut être vécu sur l'un ou l'autre mode: l'amour le plus illégitime peut assurer un bonheur stable, les plaisirs du monde peuvent être goûtés avec modération, l'escroquerie au jeu peut constituer une ressource régulière et donc faire partie d'un plan de sagesse, et même ce goût du danger qui perd souvent Manon peut être une mystification innocente, tel l'épisode du prince italien, qui ne fait que renforcer le bonheur tranquille des deux jeunes gens. Le partage entre les deux formes du bonheur n'est ni d'ordre moral (ce qui est bon et ce qui est mal), ni d'ordre social (ce qui est permis et ce qui est interdit): c'est le partage entre deux façons d'être, entre une vie réglée, et l'abandon à l'imprévisible. L'homme aspire à l'éternel, et vit dans l'instant.

L'homme n'est pas transparent à lui-même. Il y a en lui toute une part trouble, irrationnelle. On le voit par les changements soudains de Des Grieux: il passe d'un monde à l'autre, il ne se reconnaît pas, il ne trouve pas de mots pour décrire ses sentiments nouveaux, il s'effraie de sa propre dualité: "J'en étais épouvanté. Je frémissais, comme il arrive lorsqu'on se trouve la nuit dans une campagne écartée: on se croit transporté dans un nouvel ordre de choses; on y est saisi d'une horreur secrète" (p. 45). Il y a dans l'homme un être imprévisible et irrationnel, un être qu'il s'effraie de découvrir et qui est pourtant lui-même. Par l'utopie du bonheur individuel, l'homme voulait au fond se défendre contre cet être, il voulait s'en tenir à la part claire de lui-même: il reproduisait à l'intérieur de lui-même le refoulement qu'il accusait la société utopique de pratiquer. L'utopie n'est donc pas stable: l'être irrationnel peut ressurgir à tout moment et exiger son bonheur à lui, un bonheur sauvage, à la fois intense et destructeur. Le partage est indépassable, car il est dans le coeur même de l'homme.

On ne peut pas dire, en somme, que Prévost ne croie pas au bonheur. Ce à quoi il ne croit pas, c'est au bonheur *durable*: il ne croit pas à l'utopie. Sociale, l'utopie entre tôt ou tard en conflit avec l'individu; individuelle, elle entre tôt ou tard en conflit avec la partie irrationnelle et impulsive de l'individu lui-même. Prévost ne croit qu'au bonheur précaire: le bonheur sage est détruit en un instant par le bonheur fou, et ce dernier se détruit à son tour lui-même. Bonheur menacé et voué au malheur: la vision de Prévost—sans grandiloquence, mais profondément—est tragique.

C'est en cela peut-être que réside son originalité par rapport aux Lumières; originalité d'ailleurs double: face aux utopistes, mais aussi face à leurs critiques. Face aux utopistes, il maintient que l'homme est plus complexe qu'on ne le croit, que sa nature est contradictoire, et que l'utopie est impossible. Face aux critiques de l'utopie (qui étaient souvent, comme l'a remarqué Werner Krauss, des bourgeois libéraux: ils trouvaient qu'elle faisait la part trop belle à l'Etat, et donnait dans un dirigisme excessif), Prévost maintient que ce n'est pas telle ou telle institution de l'utopie qu'il faut critiquer, mais que c'est l'utopie elle-même qui est impossible: sa critique est d'emblée métaphysique, fondée sur la nature divisée de l'homme. Là est son originalité; là est peut-être aussi sa grandeur: en restant lucide dans une époque parfois naïvement optimiste, en ne donnant à l'homme qu'un bonheur éphémère et d'autant plus émouvant, en faisant enfin de cette vocation au malheur le signe d'une élection, et de cette fragilité une sorte d'aristocratie de la souffrance, il a su créer, sur les ruines du bonheur utopique, une autre morale, et peut-être un autre bonheur. L'homme est irrémédiablement divisé; mais il peut du moins aller jusqu'au bout de son malheur, il peut être lui-même et s'assumer: par-delà l'utopie, s'esquisse une autre forme de plénitude, peut-être plus émouvante, celle de la *fierté tragique.*

Dreams of Reality: Enlightened Hopes for an Unattainable Spain

IRIS M. ZAVALA

For skill is known to all
To be of greater worth than raw material.
Tomás de Iriarte

In 1651, Baltasar Gracián published in partial anonymity one of the finest examples of the allegorical utopian novel in Spanish letters, *El Criticón.* Critilo (The Critic) finds a primitive man in an uninhabited island after a shipwreck. Some time later, this primitive creature is given a name—Andrenio (Adam)—and both the civilized man and the primitive share doubts, experiences, conflicts, and problems. To make a long novel short, another shipwreck allows them to leave the island, and they start a lengthy journey through the world in quest of Felisinda (Happiness). Neither Critilo nor Andrenio ever solves the essential mystery of "utopia." The ideal world is not to be found, regardless of what men can do to change society. Man, in a sense, has been doomed to evil by God. The only possibility for the realization of the utopian dream—if any—is in the afterworld, effected by virtue alone. As baroque works of art, few novels have surpassed *El Criticón*, which was translated into English in 1681; it inspired many imitations and was also acclaimed by Voltaire, apparently influencing *Candide.*[1]

Imaginary voyages to lands of utopian perfection were common in European literature of the eighteenth century. Political or social fantasies about distant kingdoms and travels to unreal perfect states abounded. Spain, however, was somewhat of an exception to this trend, although some works of fiction did make use of the imaginary voyage to criticize Spanish society. In this essay, I am particularly concerned with political treatises, and how the most progressive of them manifested a utopian dream. Reasons for the emergence of this socioeconomic literature are manifold, the most striking being social and economic decline, as well as pressing political problems which left little space for speculation and fantasy. Economic literature had flourished since the sixteenth century and was later ridiculously called *arbitrismo* by the *Siglo de Oro* writers.[2] My point is that the determining policies which the Spanish *reformadores* tried to implement were not theories simply borrowed from the *philosophes.* Since the reign of Philip II (1556-98), if not before, lengthy *memoriales* or *discursos* were sent to the king or to his counsellors.[3] Topics would vary from agrarian to industrial problems, but the best were minute analyses of specific social and economic conditions. The influx of gold and silver or the price revolution—so well studied by E. J. Hamilton[4]—and the ultimate ruinous extension of credit had opened a great chasm between rich and poor. Vagabondage, prostitution, banditry, and riots were the signs of the bitter despair in which commoners, decimated by famine and disease, lived in preindustrial societies. No wonder that in 1600, after a great plague, a *letrado* of Valladolid, Martín González de Cellorigo, sent one of the most lucid critiques of Spanish society to the king. In a highly persuasive fashion Cellorigo summarized, in his *Memorial de la política necesaria y útil restauración a la república de España*, the basic features of economic decline, and stated in conclusion: "Spain is poor because it is rich." He used the dialectical method in a masterly way, arguing that in Spain there was no middle class and the commoners lived in subhuman conditions. This kind of ideology would be given a more theoretical form by the writers of the Enlightenment.

Analyses such as this are the common ground, the substratum of the eighteenth-century *reformismo*, so much so that some of the *arbitristas* were then either reedited or published for the first time.[5] The most important reformers, such as Gerónimo de Uztáriz, Pedro Rodríguez de Campomanes, and Pablo de Olavide, repeated most of the theses of the "primitive economists," as Pierre Vilar so rightly calls them.[6] Obviously the problems persisted, the topics remained relevant, since there had been little change in economic and social conditions. There was still a lack of industry and commerce, a surplus of *hidalgos*, *latifundia*, and many unemployed poor. The *arbitristas* and their heirs are describing an essentially rural society which had remained stagnant and had greatly deteriorated as a result of lack of markets, cost of civil and foreign wars, and inflation. The *Siglo de Oro* of Emperor Charles V turned into the impoverished nation of the Philips and Charles II, "the Bewitched." By then, the wealth of Spain was composed of the spoils claimed by the other nations of Europe. The utopian program of Erasmian philosophy, interpreted as a *philosophia Cristi* or *evangelium aeternum*, was no longer possible.[7] As the French envoy, the Marquis de Villars, wrote in 1668, "It would be difficult to describe to the full extent the disorder of the government of Spain."[8] When the "bewitched" king died in 1700, the armies of other nations ravaged the peninsula.

As the seventeenth century ended, moral and intellectual bankruptcy were rampant. When the first Bourbon king, Philip V, entered the Peninsula, the War of Succession started. It was finally ended by the Treaty of Utrecht in 1715.[9] At that point the concept of utopia, for the *novadores*, suggested a government capable of promoting the national interest and solving the pressing social and economic problems. This led to the formation of an alliance between the state and the lesser nobility and to the creation of a bureaucratic administration capable of implementing the reforms. Philip and his various efficient ministers and advisors cleared the way and reorganized the state by introducing institutional changes in government and administration; he also took significant political measures. Similar policies would be carried out by Ferdinand VI and particularly by Charles III.

Shifts in perception and style thus accompany, in temper and tempo, a profound transformation during the Enlightenment. The works of the economists Pierre Vilar and Gonzalo Anes provide perceptive insights and explore the nature of aspirations and economic forms during this period.[10] Changes in social mentality are more difficult to assess, however, as they transcend literary texts and tastes. The *reformismo borbónico* emerged as the reorientation of productive forces already active in the last decades of the previous century. There is a close link between economic factors and enlightened ideas; the demographic explosion, the rise of agricultural prices and of the price of land, favoring the aristocracy and the clergy, brought these groups closer to the urban bourgeoisie. Literature was used as a tool for change, as were other cultural endeavors. Academies were created, as were libraries, journals, museums, and roads, factories, and schools. Once again Spaniards were sent to foreign countries to study new disciplines (one must remember that in 1559 Philip II, afraid of the epidemic of "lutheranism," had recalled all students to Spain).[11] A certain spirit of tolerance permeated the country, and although the traditional enemies of progress, the Church and the Inquisition, were still present, some battles, however ephemeral, were won. Poets, scientists, and politicians labored to tear down the rotten building and replace it with a grander structure. Utopia was the *topos* for this process: a reformed Spain free from superstition, intellectual lethargy, and rigid orthodoxy, as well as modern in its techniques. Intellectuals took on the task of encouraging this process.[12]

In the first half of the century the Benedictine monk Fray Benito Jerónimo Feijoo gave voice to the new hopes.[13] His were no imaginary voyages; the voyage Feijoo took was into Spain itself. Far from drifting into fantasies, he vividly depicted Spanish life. His *Teatro crítico universal* (8 vols., 1726-39) was a stage where the author represented the ills of society. The same could be said for his *Cartas eruditas* (3 vols., 1742–50). There are two topics which recur throughout the eleven volumes: "new science" and tolerance. Both are woven and interwoven into an intricate relationship. Feijoo advocated that the clear light of reason be used to dispel the shadows of superstition, fanaticism, and ignorance. He also reacted strongly against national insularity and was a superb disseminator of ideas, many of which had been expressed by others but which he simplified and rejuvenated. Far from remaining in an abstract or conceptual realm, Feijoo's observations were firmly rooted in the everyday experience of small-town society. He attacked the superstitions he knew and which were common in his homeland. No wonder that one of his most perceptive essays was "Honra y provecho de la agricultura" ("Honor and Benefit of Agriculture"), where the monk described the pitiful life of the impoverished peasants of Galicia, León, and Asturias. He writes, "El descuido de España lloro, porque el descuido de España me duele" ("I weep for the ruin of Spain, because the ruin of Spain pains me"). Using the terms of the Pauline *corpus mysticum*, he expressed this more concretely: "Spain has gout," he tells us, because the peasant, the feet of the *corpus*, lives in perpetual misery and is brutalized by poverty. Rather than an archaic vision of a traditional agrarian community, Feijoo affirmed the necessity for change, there and then, with little room left for the idealization of the past. Virtue does not mean living according to the laws of nature, but rather working and changing the social order. Incidentally, he criticized in his "Fábulas de las Batuecas y países imaginarios" fictitious imaginary voyages as common errors.

With the reign of Charles III (1759-88), solutions to practical questions were sought with even greater urgency. This was particularly true under the ministry of Campomanes, who from 1760 to 1780 focused his attention on the needs of modernizing the country, urging Spaniards to imitate the technology of Britain, France, and Holland. The emergence of what has been called a bourgeois mentality appears in most literary texts of the period. The agrarian question is perceptively analyzed by Pablo de Olavide, a Peruvian who arrived in Seville in 1765 with a large private library.[14] A progressive thinker, Olavide soon became the mentor and friend of all the *reformadores*. For him, as for the rest, better education and social welfare went hand in hand. Within a short time, Olavide entered into contact with the agricultural reformers who were promoting new techniques; he was responsible for the creation of model agrarian communities in Andalusia.[15] He supported and urged the colonization of Sierra Morena, as well as the social and cultural transformation of Seville. His *Informe al consejo sobre la ley agraria* (1768) is as important as his *Plan de estudios* (1766), recently unearthed by Francisco Aguila Piñal.[16] In both works Olavide threatened vital Church interests, and intended to reform clerical abuses and tighten royal authority over the clergy. But he was not allowed to continue much further; he was imprisoned and condemned by the Inquisition in 1778 as a warning to other audacious *reformadores*.

The agrarian situation was analyzed by Gaspar Melchor de Jovellanos, also, in his famous *Informe en el expediente de la ley agraria* (1795). It is so devastating an account of the Spanish agrarian scene that the author suffered an inquisitorial trial and was exiled for several years.[17] Once again, Jovellanos was not projecting an ideal state, but rather specific social changes which would help modernize the country and develop its productive forces. For instance, when he advocated the transformation of social agrarian structures, his was not a dream of a society of abundance but rather a call for national revival in all spheres of life. He saw his own role as that of encouraging the efforts of others. Nevertheless, Jovellanos did touch on the fundamentals of society, since his economic and pedagogical reforms favored the "middle class" at the expense of the aristocracy. Spain was never to implement his *Ley agraria*, though he was able to create model schools, the first of which was inaugurated in 1794. "The well-being of this country devours me," he wrote to his friend Posada in 1793.[18] Political reform, moral amelioration, and economic development were his ends; the keystone was education. Through it, he once wrote, there will be a confederation of societies and nations, a universal society, worthy of the high destinies which the Creator designed.[19] Utopia? Hardly. Jovellanos dealt with urgent practical matters, and although there might have been occasional dreams of a near-perfect society or nation, history, contemporary history, law, and reform were the shapers of the future. Through them men were to attain virtue and material welfare.

The three authors just mentioned are not exceptions; rather, they are the rule. The hope for economic progress was their dominant theme. Their concern was not for speculative political questions, and they were not searching, like Sir Thomas More, for the best possible government, for that "nowhere land" where the general law recognized a national system of education and freedom of thought and religion. Poetry, the theater, the novel, and the essay in eighteenth-century Spain depicted the pressing problems of an immense rural population. The reformers hoped to make the peasantry patriotic and virtuous through work. At times this matter-of-fact analysis had a dream-like aura, as when Jovellanos hoped for the tenant to live on his plot, free from the clash of passions which agitate other men. The old familiar topic of the *Beatus ille* seemed to reappear. In their own towns, the tenants would be removed from corruption and luxury. Fraternal love would reign, and so would peace, charity, and hospitality.[20] Everybody would live happily ever after. But such indulgences were the exception, not the rule. The plans of the *reformadores* were not futuristic; rather, they encompassed explicit criticism and urged reform in the present, not idealization of the past, and this reform was to succeed through the methods of deduction as derived from experimental science. Criticism and reform were supported by the careful observations of reality, that is, through an analysis of the social classes and of their concrete modes of existence. Both Olavide and Jovellanos hoped for the emergence of a "middle class" in a country in which there was still an *imperium monachorum*. Cultural changes were part of a general program for imposing social and political change. They were economic reformers; they sought to increase the trade of the country, build up its industry, release the natural wealth which lay unexploited at hand. "Land, men, and money lie neglected," wrote Bernardo Ward in 1762.[21] The reformers denounced the slave trade (not through utopian literature, but through nonfictional treatises) and the oppression of the American Indian. They protested the persecution of the gypsies and opposed social inequalities, including the privileges of the nobility, the subjection of women, and the inequity of the law. They demanded the reduction of monasteries, the abolition of superfluous schools, the lifting of taboos against trade. Some of these aims were realized. The historian Antonio Domínguez Ortiz has pointed out that Spanish society during this period evolved towards a modern, contractual system of substantial agricultural exploitation. This fact has also been stressed recently by Gonzalo Anes.[22]

The voyages these men took were into their own internal reality. One notable exception in this antiutopian trend were the *Cartas marruecas* (1771-74) of Colonel José Cadalso. In this work, a Moor and a Spaniard debate what an ideal country or state should be. However, there is no voyage to an imaginary place, nor is there an Orwellian country projected into the future, but there is a voyage to Spain itself. In mordant epistles, the Moor and the Spaniard discuss Spanish mores and social conditions, giving an almost exact account of everyday life at Court.

Tomás de Iriarte, the fable writer, pointed out very clearly the program of change encouraged by the *reformadores*:

> The good patriot will not be the one who declaims, but who works; the one who writes one of the tremendous number of books we need. . . . With respect to industry and commerce, when the shirt we put on will be ours, when such precious raw materials like the wool will not leave the country, when, etc., then we shall be able to boast.[23]

Despite the realistic purposes of the reformers, the *topos* remained that of a utopian dream. Here lies, to my understanding, the fundamental contradiction of the *reformismo borbónico* in Spain. The enlightened climate of thought never brought about an attenuation of the power of the Church and its defense of tradition and economic privilege. As a result, these concrete analyses failed to be thoroughly implemented because of the frequent opposition of both clerics and laymen. The clergy and the conservative allies of the ruling classes finally defeated the reforms. The Inquisition tightened its grasp at the end of the reign of Charles III and even earlier; for instance, such a modest satire as *Fray Gerundio de Campazas* (Part I,1758; Part II,1770), Isla's novel, though a best seller, was prohibited. So were many other books, both autochthonous and foreign, even though they could hardly be accused of spreading agnosticism or revolution. One by one the audacious *novadores* found themselves in difficulties with the Inquisition, which greatly feared the invasion of French philosophy, whose influence was increasingly widespread as 1789 approached.[24]

These kingdoms of reason failed, perhaps because they went beyond the limits imposed upon them by their epoch. The reformers were defeated by their own society. The absence of a well-defined middle class plus the natural strength of the old institutions finally overpowered them. After Charles IV and the French Revolution, crucial moral questions predominated and sentimentality became the major style in Spanish letters. The intellectual lost confidence in his own capacity and took refuge in emotions and sentiment.[25]

To conclude, we may ask whether these plans for specific reform can be called utopia. As a hypothetical answer I suggest what was admirably synthesized by William Wordsworth in *The Prelude* (1799-1805):

> Not in Utopia,–subterranean fields,–
> Or some secreted island, Heaven knows where!
> But in the very world, which is the world
> Of all of us,–the place where, in the end,
> We find our happiness, or not at all![26]

Yes, an "acre in Middlesex is better than a principality in Utopia," Thomas Macauley wrote some years later to Lord Bacon (July 1837), vividly implying that utopia meant the rise of the bourgeoisie. Perhaps that tangible acre somewhere in Spain is what our eighteenth-century authors had in mind.[27]

NOTES

1 See Dorothy M. McGhee, "Voltaire and Gracián's *El Criticón*," *PMLA*, 52 (1937), 778–84. It should be remembered that Defoe's *Robinson Crusoe* dates from 1719.

2 In a very perceptive book, Jean Vilar has proved that the term *arbitrismo* is a derogatory word coined by Cervantes; its first use in this sense occurs in the *Coloquio de los perros* (1613). See *Literatura y economía: La figura satírica del arbitrista en el Siglo de Oro* (Madrid: Revista de Occidente, 1973), particularly pp. 23-57. Not only Cervantes but Lope, Quevedo, and Gracián, among many others, caricaturized the *arbitrista* as a concoctor of lies and dreams.

3 Until recently the first *memorial* was thought to have been written by Luis Ortiz, a mercantilist, in 1558. However, Joseph Pérez has unearthed one by Rodrigo Luján, sent to Cardinal Cisneros in 1516. See *L'Espagne du XVIe siècle* (Paris: Armand Colin, 1973), pp. 164-68.

4 See *American Treasure and the Price Revolution in Spain, 1501-1650* (Cambridge: Harvard University Press, 1934), and *War and Prices in Spain, 1650-1800* (Cambridge: Harvard University Press, 1947). His conclusions have been rectified by Pierre Vilar, "Histoire des prix, histoire générale: Un nouveau livre de E. J. Hamilton," and "Remarques sur l'histoire des prix," both in a Spanish version in *Crecimiento y desarrollo: economía e historia, reflexiones sobre el caso español* (Barcelona: Ariel, 1964).

5 Campomanes himself reedited some *memoriales* and *discursos* as an appendix to his *Discurso sobre la educación popular de los artesanos y su fomento* (Madrid, 1775).

6 See *La Catalogne dans l'Espagne moderne* (Paris: S.E.V.P.E.N., 1962), particularly vol. I, and *Crecimiento y desarrollo*.

7 See Marcel Bataillon, *Erasmo y España* (México: Fondo de Cultura Económica, 1967), for a minute analysis of how Erasmus was interpreted in Spain.

8 J. H. Elliott quotes this letter in his *Imperial Spain, 1469-1716* (New York: Saint Martin's Press, 1963), pp. 361-62. Elliott gives a very good account of the economic collapse. See also John Lynch, *Spain under the Hapsburgs* (Oxford: Basil Blackwell, 1964), and more recently, Antonio Domínguez Ortis, *El Antiguo Régimen: Los Reyes Católicos y los Austrias* (Madrid: Alfaguara, 1973).

9 The most-detailed study of this war is that of Henry Kamen, *The War of Succession in Spain, 1700-1715* (London, 1969).

10 Vilar, *La Catalogne*, vol. III, and Gonzalo Anes, *Las Crisis agrarias de la España moderna* (Madrid: Taurus, 1970).

11 Bataillon, *Erasmo y España, passim.*

12 See my "Jovellanos y la poesía burguesa," *NRFH*, 1-2 (1969), 47-64, where I show that the various topics and themes of literary creation are closely related to the emergence of a bourgeois mentality. In this sense, Jovellanos was the mentor of the younger generation.

13 See my "Tradition et réforme dans la pensée de Feijoo," in *Jean-Jacques Rousseau et son temps*, ed. Michel Launay (Paris: Nizet, 1969), pp. 52-71, for a detailed study of Feijoo's topics. In English, a good synthesis is I. L. McClelland, *Benito Jerónimo Feijoo* (New York: Twayne, 1969).

14 The best study on Olavide is Marcelin Défourneaux, *Pablo Olavide ou l'afrancesado, 1725-1823* (Paris: Presses Universitaires de France, 1959); see also Jean Sarrailh, *L'Espagne éclairée de la second moitié du XVIIIe siècle* (Paris: Imprimerie Nationale, 1954).

15 Défourneaux, *Pablo Olavide*, 129-45.

16 *La Sevilla de Olavide (1767-1778)* (Seville, 1966) and *La Real Academia Sevillana de Buenas Letras en el siglo XVIII* (Madrid: Consejo Superior de Investigaciones Científicas, 1966).

17 Gonzalo Anes has studied this *Informe* in the light of mounting tensions between landowners and peasants; see *Economía e "ilustración" en la España del siglo XVIII* (Barcelona: Ariel, 1969). The close relationship between this *Informe* and the inquisitorial trial was given attention by Edith Hellman, "Some Consequences of the Publication of the *Informe de ley agraria* by Jovellanos," in *Estudios históricos: Homenaje a Archer M. Huntington* (Wellesley, Mass., 1952). See also J. H. R. Polt, *Jovellanos and His English Sources: Economic, Philosophical, and Political Writings*, Transactions of the American Philosophical Society, new series, vol. 54, part 7 (Philadelphia: The American Philosophical Society, 1964).

18 Quoted by Sarrailh, *L'Espagne éclairée*, p. 180.

19 See J. H. R. Polt, *Gaspar Melchor de Jovellanos* (New York: Twayne, 1971), pp. 137-38, for an English version.

20 See Ibid., p. 95, for some translations of the *Informe*.

21 *Proyecto económico en que se proponen varias providencias dirigidas a promover los intereses de España con los fondos y medios necesarios para su planificación, escrito en el año de 1762 por . . . del Consejo de S. M. y su ministro de la Real Junta de Comercio y Moneda.* Obra póstuma (Madrid, 1779).

22 Ortiz, *La Sociedad española en el siglo XVIII* (Madrid: Consejo Superior de Investigaciones científicas, 1955), and Anes, *Las crisis, passim.*

23 English version by R. Merrit Cox, *Tomás de Iriarte* (New York: Twayne, 1972), p. 52. I have used this translation as the basis for my own.

24 Richard Herr, *The Eighteenth-Century Revolution in Spain* (Princeton: Princeton University Press, 1958), gives a good account of these years.

See also my "Picornell y la revolución de San Blas: 1795," in *Economía y sociedad en los siglos XVIII y XIX. Historia Ibérica*, I (Madrid-New York: Anaya-Las Americas, 1973), pp. 35–58, where I study an intended republican revolution in Spain headed by the schoolteacher Picornell. Marcelin Défourneaux has given a very good description of French books prohibited by the Inquisition in his *L'Inquisition espagnole et les livres français au XVIIIe siècle* (Paris: Presses Universitaires de France, 1963). I deal at length with this problem in my forthcoming book, *Clandestinidad y libertinaje erudito en los albores del XVIII* (Barcelona: Ariel, in press).

25 This trend has generally been called Romanticism. See Russell P. Sebold, "Enlightenment Philosophy and the Emergence of Spanish Romanticism," in *The Ibero-American Enlightenment*, ed. A. O. Aldridge (Urbana: University of Illinois Press, 1971), pp. 111–40. For another point of view on Romanticism, closely related to historical and political problems, see my "Características generales del siglo XIX: Burguesía y literatura," in *Historia de la literatura española (ss. XIX y XX)*, ed. J. M. Díez Borque (Madrid: Guadiana, 1974), pp. 11-57.

26 William Wordsworth, *The Complete Poetical Works* (Boston and New York: Houghton Mifflin Co., 1925), III, 264-65.

27 As this paper was being prepared for publication, Monroe Z. Hafter published "Toward a History of Spanish Imaginary Voyages," *Eighteenth-Century Studies*, 83 (1975), 265-82, an article which provides new insights and information on the subject of this essay.

Executive Board, 1976–77

President: GWIN J. KOLB, Professor of English, University of Chicago

Past Presidents: GEORGES MAY, Sterling Professor of French, Yale University

VICTOR LANGE, John N. Woodhull Professor of German, Princeton University

First Vice-President: J. G. A. POCOCK, Professor of History, The Johns Hopkins University

Second Vice-President: PHILLIP HARTH, Professor of English, University of Wisconsin, Madison

Executive Secretary: PAUL J. KORSHIN, Associate Professor of English, University of Pennsylvania

Treasurer: JEAN A. PERKINS, Susan Lippincott Professor of French Literature, Swarthmore College

SHIRLEY A. BILL (1978), Professor of History, University of Illinois, Chicago Circle

WALTER GROSSMANN (1979), Professor of History and Director of Libraries, University of Massachusetts, Boston

ROBERT HALSBAND (1978), Professor of English, University of Illinois, Urbana

JEANNE R. MONTY (1979), Professor of French, Tulane University

LEONARD G. RATNER (1977), Professor of Music, Stanford University

MADELEINE B. THERRIEN (1977), Professor of French, Emory University

Institutional Members

of the American Society

for Eighteenth-Century Studies

Bryn Mawr College
University of Calgary
University of California, Berkeley
University of California, Davis
University of California, Irvine
University of California, Los Angeles/William Andrews Clark Memorial Library
University of California, Riverside
University of California, San Diego
Case Western Reserve University
Catholic University of America
University of Cincinnati
City College, CUNY
Claremont Graduate School
Cleveland State University
Colonial Williamsburg
University of Colorado, Denver Center
University of Connecticut
Dalhousie University
University of Delaware
Delta State University
University of Denver
Detroit Institute of Arts, Founders' Society
Emory University
Fordham University
University of Georgia
Georgia Institute of Technology
Georgia State University
University of Illinois, Chicago Circle
University of Illinois, Urbana
The Johns Hopkins University
University of Kentucky
Lehigh University
Lehman College, CUNY
The Lewis Walpole Library
University of Maryland
University of Massachusetts, Boston
McMaster University/Association for 18th Century Studies
The Metropolitan Museum of Art
University of Michigan, Ann Arbor
Michigan State University
Middle Tennessee State University
The Minneapolis Institute of Fine Arts
University of Minnesota
Université de Montréal
Mississippi State University
Mount Saint Vincent University
University of New Brunswick
State University of New York, Binghamton
State University of New York, Fredonia
State University of New York, Oswego
Noel Foundation Library, Shreveport, La.
University of North Carolina, Chapel Hill
North Georgia College
Northern Illinois University
Northwestern University
Ohio State University
University of Pennsylvania
University of Pittsburgh
Princeton University
Purdue University
Rice University
Rockford College
Rollins College
Smith College
University of South Carolina

University of Southern California
Southern Illinois University
University of Southern Mississippi
Stanford University
Swarthmore College
Sweet Briar College
University of Tennessee
Texas Tech University
Tulane University
University of Tulsa
University of Utrecht, Institute for Comparative and General Literature
University of Victoria
University of Virginia
Virginia Commonwealth University
Washington University
Washington and Lee University
Washington State University
Wayne State University
West Chester State College, Pennsylvania
West Virginia University
University of Western Ontario
The Henry Francis du Pont Winterthur Museum
University of Wisconsin, Madison
University of Wisconsin, Milwaukee
The Yale Center for British Art and British Studies
Yale University

Index